Office Building Management

Editorial Consultants
David G. Domres, CPM®
Charles S. Lowen, CPM®
O. Gene Powell, CPM®
Donald R. Tait, CPM®

Bruce T. Holmes
Director, Education

Caroline Scoulas
Senior Editor

Daniel Lohmann
Graphic Designer

Office Building Management

IREM® Institute of Real Estate Management
CHICAGO

Library of Congress Cataloging-in-Publication Data

Office building management.
p. cm.
Includes index.
ISBN 1-57203-081-X
1. Office buildings--Management. 2. Real estate management. 3. Office leases.
Institute of Real Estate Management.
HD1393.55 .O35 2002
647'.9623'068--dc21

2002068662

Printed in the United States of America

1 2 3 4 5 6 7 8 9 10 Printing / Year 11 10 09 08 07 06 05 04 03 02

Publisher's Preface

The skyscraper as a concept and a reality has been around for little more than one hundred years. However, office-type uses go back to ancient times. While tall buildings have long been concentrated in the central business districts of cities, more and more office buildings are being built outside of the cities, in park-like suburban campuses and even further out. A more recent addition is the single-story, no-frills structure designed to accommodate light manufacturing and warehouse-shipping operations in addition to office activities. A tenant may be seeking space for one or another of these uses or for all three. Regardless of size or configuration, office buildings that are professionally managed can be expected to be more desirable to tenants and therefore easier to lease. Building operations will likely be more efficient so that the property owner will receive the desired return on the investment. This book provides an overview of office building management and the role of the office building manager.

The text begins with an Introduction to Office Buildings and Their Management. In addition to historical background information, this chapter describes the ways real estate can be owned and how different ownership objectives guide the management of the office building. It also catalogs some of the challenges office building managers are already facing and are likely to encounter in the future. Chapter 2 covers Office Building Assessment. It explores the criteria tenants, in particular, evaluate in determining where to lease office space. It also describes different types of office buildings.

Chapter 3, Business Solicitation and the Management Agreement, focuses on strategies for acquiring management business and the contract that documents the management arrangement. Chapter 4, Management Take-Over and Fiscal Responsibilities, outlines the take-over process and describes the various accounting, budgeting, and reporting activities that are required of office building managers.

Chapter 5, Management Planning and Standardization of Operations, provides an overview of the contents of a property operations manual and discusses how policies and procedures are related to the management plan for the property. Chapter 6, Staffing and Team Management, addresses the entire spectrum of human resources management—recruiting, hiring, training, and motivating employees as well as termination of employment—and includes a discussion of different alternatives for providing the staff needed to manage an office building.

Chapter 7, Market Analysis and Rental Schedule, describes the market area (region, neighborhood) of an office building and explores issues of supply and demand, absorption rates, and positioning the property to attract tenants. It then looks at the use of comparison grid analysis to develop a rental schedule and provides a brief overview of leasing parameters. The goal is to develop a marketing plan. Chapter 8, Marketing and Leasing Office Space, covers advertising media, public relations, and other promotional tools. It also outlines specific leasing strategies and describes the contents of a lease for office space.

Chapter 9, Space Planning and Construction Management, describes building standards, tenant improvement allowances, and space planning as a process. It also addresses construction of improvements for tenants in different circumstances and concludes with discussions of construction management and the construction contract. Chapter 10, Lease Administration and Tenant Retention, covers moving tenants in, rent collection policies, tenant retention strategies, and move-out procedures.

Chapter 11, Maintenance Management, is an overview of this aspect of office building management. It reviews building inspection, describes the various types of maintenance work that are performed in office buildings, and discusses bidding of service contracts and computerization. Workplace safety, environmental concerns, and other regulatory issues are also addressed along with energy conservation. Chapter 12, Risk Management, Security, and Emergency Preparedness, outlines types of risks and how to identify them and discusses various types of insurance coverages available to office building owners. Various tools and strategies for providing security in the building are also described. The chapter concludes with a discussion of the need for and role of an emergency response team.

The book concludes with a closer look at some of the components of a management plan. Chapter 13, Maximizing Value—Analysis of Alternatives, emphasizes the financial aspects of a management plan, including the property owner's goals, identification of problems that need to be addressed, exploration of alternative approaches to overcoming those problems, and weighing costs versus benefits to determine which of the proposed alternatives best meet the owner's goals.

Readers will learn about the principles of real estate management as they apply specifically to the management of office buildings.

ACKNOWLEDGMENTS

The Institute acknowledges with deep appreciation the professional experience and shared insights contributed by the following individuals.

David G. Domres, CPM®, is Senior Vice President of Corporate Real Estate for U.S. Bank in Milwaukee, Wisconsin, where he is responsible for a portfolio of approximately 35,000,000 square feet of space. In his 20-year career, he has also worked in property management for full-service real estate firms covering commercial, industrial, and other types of properties, including troubled assets.

Locally, Mr. Domres is active in the IREM Milwaukee Chapter where he has held numerous offices, including Chapter President, and received the chapter's CPM of the year award in 1995 and 2001. He has also been actively involved in IREM education at the national level and is a member of the IREM National Faculty.

Mr. Domres also holds the Certified Commercial Investment Member designation from the CCIM Institute and is a member of the Building Owners and Managers Association (BOMA). He is an adjunct faculty member and Chair of the Advisory Committee for the Property Management Degree Program at Waukesha County Technical College.

Charles S. Lowen, CPM®, is Executive Vice President and Partner of Coldwell Banker Commercial American Spectrum based in Denver, Colorado. He oversees 7,000,000 square feet of space under contract for third-party property management, including office, retail, and industrial/warehouse space as well as residential properties. He has more than 30 years' experience in commercial and residential property and asset management, construction management, and real estate brokerage. His previous experience includes responsibility for managing more than 11,400,000 square feet of office and retail space in eleven states for a national real estate development company.

Mr. Lowen is a Past President of the IREM Northern Colorado Chapter, where he received the CPM of the Year Award in 1989. He is also active in IREM at the national level, where he has served on various committees, both as a member and in leadership roles, including a two-year term as a Regional Vice President. In addition, he is a member of the IREM National Faculty.

O. Gene Powell, CPM®, is President of Gene Powell & Associates in Hamilton, Virginia, which manages property in the Washington, D.C. area, and on the West Coast. He has more than 30 years' experience managing office space, shopping centers, industrial parks, and other types of properties. Before starting his company, Mr. Powell held corporate leadership positions with several major U.S. real estate and real estate management companies, where his responsibilities included acquisition, construction, and real estate development.

Mr. Powell has served on national committees for the Institute of Real Estate Management and is a member of the IREM National Faculty. He has also taught at various colleges, presented seminars at colleges and universities, and served as guest lecturer at conventions of major real estate professional associations. He has written numerous articles for magazines addressed to real estate and real estate management professions. Mr. Powell also holds the Certified Shopping Center Manager (CSM) designation from the International Council of Shopping Centers.

Donald R. Tait, CPM®, is Senior Property Manager for T. Stacy & Associates, Inc., in Austin, Texas, where his responsibilities include property management of a four-building portfolio comprising 412,000 square feet of office space, managing the renovation of a 100,000-square-foot building, overseeing construction, leasing, and operations for a brand-new office building, and all the attendant administrative activities. His nearly 30 years of experience include management of medical office buildings in addition to multitenant office buildings, retail centers, and industrial properties.

Mr. Tait is a Past President of the IREM Austin Chapter and a member of the IREM National Faculty. He is also a Certified National Instructor for the BOMI Institute (Building Owners and Managers Institute), where he was awarded the Real Property Administrator (RPA) and Facilities Management Administrator (FMA) designations. He is active in the Building Owners and Managers Association (BOMA) International and has held various leadership positions in BOMA Austin, Texas BOMA, and BOMA International.

Additional information and insights were provided by **Anthony R. Diana, CPM® Emeritus,** President of Diana Management, Inc., in Bel Air, Maryland; and **Howard K. Lundeen, CPM®**, Senior Property Manager with CMD Realty Investors, L.P., headquartered in Chicago—Mr. Lundeen is based in Dallas, Texas.

About the Institute of Real Estate Management

The Institute of Real Estate Management (IREM) was founded in 1933 with the goals of establishing a Code of Ethics and standards of practice in real estate management as well as fostering knowledge, integrity, and efficiency among its practitioners. The Institute confers the CERTIFIED PROPERTY MANAGER® (CPM®) designation on individuals who meet specified criteria of education and experience in real estate management and subscribe to an established Code of Ethics. Individuals who meet specified educational and experience requirements in residential site management and subscribe to an established Code of Ethics are granted the ACCREDITED RESIDENTIAL MANAGER® (ARM®) certification. Real estate management firms that meet specific organizational and professional criteria and subscribe to Minimum Standards and a Code of Professional Ethics are granted the ACCREDITED MANAGEMENT ORGANIZATION® (AMO®) accreditation.

The Institute's membership includes more than 8,800 CPM® members, nearly 3,800 ARM® members, and 550 AMO® firms. Among CPM members in the United States, nearly 46.7% manage conventionally financed multifamily rental housing properties, 16.4% manage federally assisted housing, and 17.6% manage condominium and cooperative ownership properties; approximately 47.6% manage office buildings, more than 33.8% manage shopping center and retail strip stores, and roughly 24.2% manage industrial parks and warehouses.

Since 1933, IREM has been enhancing the prestige of property management through its activities and publications. The Institute offers a wide selection of courses, seminars, periodicals, books, and other materials about real estate management and related topics. To receive current information about IREM programs, write to the Institute of Real Estate Management, 430 North Michigan Avenue, P.O. Box 109025, Chicago, Illinois 60610-9025, or telephone 1-800-837-0706. Also visit our web site at www.irem.org.

Contents

1

Introduction to Office Buildings and Their Management

The modern office building is a product in transition. As computers and other new business technologies evolve, office tenants will want to lease space in buildings that have been built—or can be retrofitted—to accommodate technological innovations. As new construction materials and methods enhance building safety and usability, these will be used in developing new office space. The office building of the future may be very different. However, the need for professional management of the building and its operations is not likely to change. No matter what the future brings, real estate managers will still have to conduct regular inspections of the building and the property, schedule custodial and preventive maintenance to preserve the structure and tenant spaces, and develop programs to market and lease space in the building. There will still be a need for analysis of the office building within its marketplace, assessment of current and future financing needs, and comprehensive reports to the owner about the property's physical and fiscal status. The principles of real estate management as they apply to office buildings will be discussed throughout the remainder of this book. As a starting point, however, it is appropriate to review how the modern office building came to be what it is.

Historical Background

Space dedicated to office-type activities goes back to ancient times. After the invention of writing, scribes were employed to maintain agricultural and trade records, working in rooms set aside for this purpose in the kings' palaces and at royal outposts. In later times, feudal kings and wealthy landowners, merchants, and traders had similar arrangements because few people other than scribes knew how to read and write.

The Renaissance in Europe brought changes to the business world as well as the arts and literature. Among them were the concepts of double-entry bookkeeping (balancing debits against credits), discount banking (the time value of money), and capitalism (private ownership of the means of production). More and more business activities were being conducted in cities during this period as European capitals became banking and trading centers.

By the mid-eighteenth century, specific technological changes began to reshape commerce. Invention of the steam engine led to changes in manufacturing and transportation. Many goods that were previously manufactured by hand could now be manufactured by machines. The ability to produce more goods in less time meant finished products could be sold for lower prices. Railroads and steamships made it possible to move goods and people long distances more quickly. The landscape changed as manufacturers and merchants located their businesses along rail lines and near rail transfer points in cities. Railways and new means of communication such as the telegraph stimulated business activity and growth, and people moved from rural areas to cities in search of jobs in the new manufacturing industries.

As more businesses and more people became concentrated in the city centers, land became scarce and land prices escalated. Multistory buildings were already being built to house business activities in the early nineteenth century. As congestion increased, living conditions in the cities declined. People sought refuge from the noise, dirt, and danger of the congested city by moving to the suburbs and commuting to jobs in the city. This relocation was facilitated as rail lines were extended and electric-powered streetcars were introduced. In the city centers, vacated housing was cleared away and the land redeveloped for more intensive commercial use. At the same time, manufacturers and other businesses that could not afford the high land prices and rents relocated to the edge of downtown or outside of it. This cleared the way for other types of businesses that could afford to pay high rents and taxes to move closer to the city centers where they would have access to the wholesalers, sources of financing, transportation facilities, and governmental agencies that had not moved away. The new types of businesses included department stores, publishing enterprises (books and magazines as well as newspapers), hotels, real estate firms, insurance companies, and professional and other services, all of which could be located in multistory buildings.

Evolution of the Office Building. The earliest office buildings were only four or five stories tall. They often had storefronts at street level with a single entrance between them. Office spaces were on the upper floors, and workers and visitors climbed stairs to get to them. Lighting was provided by gas or oil lamps. Fireplaces and stoves were used for heating. Sanitary facilities consisted of chamber pots, and fire protection was buckets of water. Before the twentieth century began, gas lamps were being replaced with electric lamps. New means of communication—the telephone and wireless telegraphy among them—and new tools such as the typewriter were also changing the way office work was performed.

Technological developments made it possible to build taller buildings. Among these were the skeletal frame and steel-reinforced concrete. Initially, building height was limited by practical considerations: Taller buildings meant the exterior walls had to be thicker and thicker at the base to support each added floor. The steel frame overcame the issue of weight versus height by supporting lightweight curtain walls from the inside and allowing for larger windows and more interior space. Invention of the elevator allowed large numbers of people to be moved to the upper floors of a building quickly and safely.

Building mechanical systems were developed and improved over time. The flush toilet eliminated problems disposing of sanitary wastes. Heat was provided by radiators filled with hot water and, later, with steam. Simple air inlets behind radiators were replaced by ductwork and air conditioning. Terra cotta, a ceramic material often used for decorative exterior facings as well as interior wall and floor tiles, was replaced by lathe and plaster in building interiors.

Developers continue to build high-rise office buildings using refinements of these techniques and materials. Modern buildings have combined heating, ventilating, and air conditioning (HVAC) systems that are electric-powered and windows that cannot be opened. Most light fixtures are ceiling-mounted with fluorescent lamps. Individual work spaces for managers and executives may still be fixed-in-place offices arranged around the exterior walls so they include windows, but support staff often have workstations configured from standard components that can be rearranged and relocated. Many interior finish materials are treated to resist fire, and complex smoke and fire alarm systems alert occupants to vacate the premises in the event of fire. Electrical and communications wires and cables are built into the walls and floors, and workstation panels include outlets for connecting telephones and computers and their adjunct components. While such infrastructure is expected in new construction, many older buildings have been successfully retrofitted to accommodate the new ways of working and extend their useful lives.

Office buildings in urban centers continue to include store spaces. In smaller buildings, the retail tenants may be chosen to provide a service to other tenants' employees—a newsstand that also sells magazines and candies, a fast food outlet. Larger buildings may be designed with an arcade of shops in the lobby or on a mezzanine level. New high-rise structures often include a plaza on part of the property, incorporating trees and other plantings to create a green oasis amid all the concrete and provide a pleasant place where building workers and passersby can sit.

While office space in suburbs was initially configured as low-rise structures (one to three stories) in a park-like setting, some suburban office complexes include much taller buildings. More recently, there has been movement toward construction of one-story buildings, called *flex space,* which can be configured to accommodate both office and light manufacturing uses and easily reconfigured as tenants and their space needs change. As office uses change, office buildings will continue to change with them.

Managing the Office Building. Early office buildings were managed directly by their owners who leased space to tenants, collected rents, and made needed repairs to the building and equipment. Management of office buildings by someone other than the owner is a fairly recent phenomenon and has only been recognized as a specialized activity since the founding of the National Association of Building Owners and Managers in 1907. (The organization is known today as the Building Owners and Managers Association International or BOMA). The management role was expanded beyond office buildings to rental apartments and other commercial properties when the National Association of Real Estate Boards (NAREB), also founded in 1907, organized its Property Management Division in 1923.

Real estate management evolved into a profession during the early years of the Great Depression. Business owners who survived the stock market crash in 1929 were increasingly concerned that their real estate holdings would lose value unless they could be managed profitably. At the same time, members of the Property Management Division of NAREB recognized a need for standard management practices and a means of accrediting those who managed real estate for others. In 1933, the NAREB Property Management Division was reorganized into a separate professional organization, the Institute of Real Estate Management (IREM). Initially, its membership comprised management firms that agreed to certain specific practices:

1. Set up separate accounts for the firm's funds and those of its clients.
2. Carry a fidelity bond on all applicable employees.
3. Disclose to and obtain permission from the client before making any arrangement by which the firm would benefit financially from a client's funds.

In 1938, the Institute's founders agreed that accrediting individual real estate managers was more important because a firm's standards can change as its staff changes while an individual's standards usually remain the same over his or her life. Subsequently, the Institute was reorganized as an association

Income Tax Law and Real Estate Investment

Changes in income tax laws can specifically encourage or discourage investment in income-producing real estate. For example, the Tax Reform Act of 1980 created a variety of tax shelters that made real estate investment attractive. A property might generate little or no income, but the owner could still make a profit because losses from real estate investments could be used to offset income from wages and other sources. However, the Tax Reform Act of 1986 reduced many of the earlier Act's investment incentives. Among other changes, this new law defined rental income from real property as *passive activity income* when the investor does not materially participate in earning those funds. Likewise, losses from such passive activities could no longer be deducted from *active income* (i.e., wages). The law also changed the deductions for depreciation (calculation methods and cost recovery periods) of real property and capital improvements.

of individuals, and the *CERTIFIED PROPERTY MANAGER® (CPM®)* designation was inaugurated. To achieve the CPM designation, individuals must have successfully completed a series of relevant courses, worked in the profession for a prescribed number of years, and managed a required size portfolio; they must also subscribe to a Code of Professional Ethics.

Ownership Forms

Ownership of real property may be held in one of several business forms. Each has implications for the property and its management as well as for the investor-owner. For individual owners, the business form determines how profits from income-generating real estate are distributed to them and reported to the U.S. government as taxable income. It also determines the extent of their personal liability.

Sole Proprietorship. This form is uncommon among owners of properties valued in millions of dollars. It is used most often by individuals who invest in small buildings—a house to rent, a small multifamily dwelling, a storefront usable as office space, a small strip shopping center. A sole proprietor receives all of the profits from the investment and is responsible for all of its financial losses. Such losses may be deductible from taxable income, subject to IRS passive loss limitations.

Partnership. Two or more investors may form a *general partnership* to invest in real estate. The extent to which individual partners share in the financial rewards and obligations of ownership will be stated in a partnership agreement, and the partnership holds title to the property. In a general partnership, each partner's personal liability for the debts of the partnership is unlimited—the partners are responsible individually and collectively for debts owed by the partnership *(joint and several liability)*. Profits and losses are apportioned among the partners according to the partnership agreement, and each partner is responsible for paying taxes on that income; the partnership itself does not pay income taxes.

A *limited partnership (LP),* as the name implies, has at least one and sometimes more than one general partner who is responsible for supervising the investment along with a number of limited partners whose participation is determined by the amount of their financial investment. In this form of ownership, the general partners' liability is unlimited while limited partners' liability does not extend beyond their equity stake in the property. (Note: Additional protection from liability may be afforded to general partners in either type of partnership by organizing it as a limited liability general—or limited—partnership.) Profits from the investment are distributed to all partners as taxable personal income according to their participation. Limited partners have no say in the management of the investment property, but they do have a say in selling and financing it.

The number of participants determines whether a limited partnership is regulated by the Securities and Exchange Commission (SEC). A *private limited partnership* having thirty-five or fewer participants usually does not have to register with the SEC but may have to file a certificate with state authorities. A *public limited partnership,* which may have an unlimited number of participants, is required to register with the SEC when the number of partners and the value of its assets reach certain levels.

A real estate *syndicate* is a special type of partnership. An individual, a corporation or group of corporations, a general or limited partnership, an unincorporated association, or a joint venture may invest in a syndicate. A syndicate may be formed to purchase a specific property or rely on an experienced syndicator to acquire potentially profitable properties. Additional partnership interests may be sold if more capital is needed. (The Tax Reform Act of 1986 significantly diminished the role of real estate syndication as an investment strategy.)

Corporation. A corporation is an independent legal entity; it is chartered by a state and considered to have a legal life of its own. It is obligated to pay local, state, and federal income taxes, and its tax deductions cannot be passed through to its shareholders. The liability of corporate owners (stockholders) is limited to the amount of their investment. Two types of corporations are recognized under U.S. income tax law. The *C corporation* pays federal income taxes, and there are no restrictions on the types of stock it issues or how many shareholders it has. Despite double taxation—corporate income may be taxed to the corporation and again when dividends are distributed to individual shareholders—the limited liability for all participants (directors as well as shareholders) makes this an attractive form of real estate ownership. The *S corporation,* on the other hand, combines the ownership features of a partnership with those of a corporation. It does not pay federal income tax (no double taxation), and its profits and losses are passed directly to its shareholders. Because owners are shareholders, not partners, individuals' liability is limited to the value of the stock they own.

Limited Liability Company. Another way multiple owners can invest in real estate is by forming a limited liability company (LLC). An LLC is chartered by state statute. (Most states have adopted LLC laws, but the rules and fiduciary responsibilities vary.) Like a corporation, an LLC may have different classes of ownership, all of which enjoy limited liability. However, if structured properly (i.e., profits and losses are passed through to participants), it will be taxed like a partnership. Investors are called *members,* and the managing entity may be a participating investor *(manager member)* or a nonparticipant appointed by the members.

Condominium. An office building may be subdivided into separate parcels of real estate that are sold to different owners. The purchaser owns the space enclosed within the perimeter walls, ceilings, and floors of the demised premises plus an undivided interest in the land and the common elements of the building—roof, structural walls, corridors, lobbies, and mechanical systems that serve the building as a whole. The individual owners' *common interest* is expressed as the percentage of the total space in the building represented by the condominium owner's space. This percentage defines the occupant's pro rata share of the building operating expenses. Real estate taxes are assessed separately on each "unit," which is also separately mortgaged. Each owner is a member of a condominium association from which membership a board of directors is elected to conduct the business of the association, including contracting for professional management for the building. State condominium laws determine the structure of the condominium and set limitations on the way it is operated. Usually the association is required to incorporate itself as a nonprofit entity, and there may be specific requirements regarding establishment of reserve funds and accounting for them.

Condominium ownership of office buildings is not common. It works best for businesses that have fixed space needs and no plans for long-term growth. A medical office building where physicians and other health care professionals can set up private practices is just one example.

Cooperative. Another form of multiple ownership of an office building is through a cooperative, which incorporates itself to purchase or build an office building. The cooperative issues shares in the corporation to represent the proportion of ownership of the entire property, and shareholders receive a *proprietary lease* that entitles them to occupy a defined space in the office building. There is a single mortgage on the property, and real estate taxes are assessed against the property as a whole. Decisions for the cooperative are made by a board of directors comprised of shareholders in the corporation. The board is responsible for paying the mortgage, real estate taxes, and other costs of operating the property. Shareholders are assessed a proportionate share of those payments based on the number of shares they own. Individual owners' shares in the corporation can be sold to others, but the sales may be subject to approval by the board.

Cooperative ownership of office buildings is not common. However, where common ownership forms are employed, it is sometimes preferred over condominium ownership because ownership by a single entity facilitates arrangements for financing and construction of improvements.

Real Estate Investment Trust. Individuals with limited capital may invest in large real estate ventures via a real estate investment trust (REIT). This type of entity can invest in real estate by direct purchase (equity trust) or by providing mortgage financing (mortgage trust) or both. To raise capital, the REIT issues *shares of beneficial interest* that can be publicly traded. It must distribute ninety-five percent of its taxable income to shareholders to avoid double taxation as a corporation, and other requirements must be met to ensure that most of its income is derived from real estate. Investors' liability is limited to the amount of their investment (shares purchased).

Joint Venture. A joint venture offers a way for different types of investment entities (sole proprietorships, partnerships, etc.) to share in the risks and rewards of owning real estate. The business form selected for the joint venture will determine its investment advantages and disadvantages and the tax obligations of the participants. The relationship between an institutional investor (insurance company, pension fund) and a developer is a common example. The institution provides the capital or the land or both while the knowledge and expertise contributed by the developer form the basis for the project's success. Foreign capital is often invested in U.S. real estate via joint ventures.

Ownership Objectives

People invest in office buildings for a variety of reasons. Some investors are interested primarily in having a regular income (periodic return) while others are motivated by tax considerations (income tax advantages). Still others invest for the long-term with the expectation of selling the property for a higher price at a future date (capital appreciation). A corporation or other business entity may own an office building, not as a real estate investment, but to provide the space needed to conduct its business (use by owner).

Exhibit 1.1

The Cash Flow Chart

	Gross Potential Rental Income
minus	Vacancy and Collection Loss
plus	Miscellaneous Income
equals	Effective Gross Income
minus	Operating Expenses
equals	Net Operating Income (NOI)
minus	Debt Service (Interest and Principal)
minus	Reserves for Replacement and Capital Expenditures
equals	Pre-Tax Cash Flow
minus	Income Tax
equals	After-Tax Cash Flow

In office building management, where leases require tenants to reimburse operating expenses of the property as a separate pass-through charge in addition to base rent, such revenues may be itemized below gross potential rental income in a separate category called expense pass-throughs, additional rent, or other scheduled income. (This issue is discussed in more detail in regard to budgeting and establishing a chart of accounts in Chapter 4.)

Also a consideration is *pride of ownership*. To an individual, owning real estate may symbolize power, wealth, or financial security. Many trophy buildings that were built as company headquarters are identified by or have the owner's name emblazoned on them even long after the property has been sold to others. The Chrysler Building in New York and the Wrigley Building in Chicago are just two examples. Owners who take pride in their investments and maintain them well also enjoy financial rewards: Maintaining and improving the building makes it a desirable location for tenants who will pay higher rents and increases the value of the property when it is sold at a later date.

The manager of the office building must understand the owner's objectives for the investment and manage the property to achieve them.

Periodic Return. Periodic return is the *cash flow* generated by a real estate investment. It is what remains after operating expenses and debt service have been deducted from the gross receipts (office rents and other revenue) as shown in Exhibit 1.1. The rate of return on the investment in real estate is determined from the cash flow in relation to the owner's equity in the property (cash flow ÷ equity = rate of return).

The real estate manager can enhance the periodic return by maximizing occupancy at the highest rents possible while also controlling operating costs. However, a property's revenue stream is subject to prevailing market conditions which affect rents and occupancy. New construction, absorption of new and existing space, and the general business climate in the area will pose specific challenges to management.

Income Tax Advantages. Investment in income-producing real estate affords certain income tax advantages. Regular operating expenses are itemized as deductions from net operating income. Deductions may also be taken for mortgage interest paid on a loan used to purchase the real estate and for depreciation (cost recovery) of the property over time. The latter is a non-cash deduction from property income. Under U.S. income tax law, it is assumed that a building has a useful life over which it produces income, and the investor is allowed to recover the cost of the investment over that useful life. The depreciation period varies by property type. Owners of commercial properties such as office buildings recover their costs over thirty-nine years (the current prescribed period). The deduction applies to the value of the building and other improvements to the land but not to the value of the land itself. Cost recovery deductions also apply to capital improvements that increase the value or productivity of the property or extend its useful life. These are investments in alterations or equipment that have a useful life of more than one year (e.g., a new roof, an improved HVAC system). Certain types of equipment purchased for use in operating the investment (e.g., passenger automobiles and computer systems) are also assumed to have a finite useful life over which the owner must recover the investment cost; they cannot be deducted as ordinary operating expenses of the property.

Capital Appreciation. Assets such as real estate typically increase in value over time, a process called capital appreciation. This is realized by the owner when a property is sold at a higher price than was paid for it originally or when the property is refinanced to reduce mortgage payments or provide cash to the owner. Capital appreciation is more often a long-term goal of real estate investors although it may be a consideration for short-term holdings as well.

Within this context, investors also view real estate as a means of *capital preservation*. They see safety in such a long-term investment and seek out properties that are low risk based on their having a prime location, solid construction, an established tenancy, ability to generate sufficient income to pay operating expenses and debt service, an absence of liens and other encumbrances, and the potential to increase in value over time. Like precious metals, land is considered to have intrinsic value—i.e., it is inherently useful. For those seeking capital preservation, the intrinsic value of a property should approximate the purchase price and increase (appreciate) at a rate at least equal to inflation.

Managers of office buildings can increase the value of a property by positioning it to achieve its *highest and best use*—i.e., to generate as much revenue as possible by controlling operating expenses to the extent possible and preserving, maintaining, and improving the building and its systems. A property will be more desirable and sell for a higher price if its income is increased beyond any increases in operating expenses. Other factors also play a role. Rehabilitation of a property adds value, as does a change in use. The market also influences value when the local economy improves and when demand for the type of property is increased. (These considerations are discussed in more detail in Chapter 13.)

Use by Owner. A business entity may build or buy a building in order to have all of its operations under one roof. Banks and insurance companies were among the first businesses to own their own buildings. Major corporations, including real estate developers and holding companies, often own buildings in several cities where they do business. Sometimes these buildings include more space than the owners need, especially after changes in a firm's operations, and leasing the extra space to other tenants makes sense as a way to provide additional revenue to the company. On the other hand, a property may have been developed intentionally to include additional tenant space as a source of income.

While such a building needs to be managed as a real estate investment, the individual who manages the building is often called a *facility manager*. Facility managers coordinate the physical work place with the people and the work of an organization. Their primary function is to plan, establish, and maintain a work environment that effectively supports the goals and objectives of the business organization. They may also be responsible for managing the real estate by leasing space to other businesses, providing maintenance services to those tenants, and performing the record keeping and reporting on the company-owned real estate. In addition to real estate owned by private entities such as corporations, properties owned by public entities (government, military) and nonprofit institutions (colleges, universities) are also usually managed by facility managers.

Management Challenges

Working for different types of owners presents many challenges. Sole proprietors often take a more active role in the management of their investments, which can place excessive demands on an office building manager's time. Because general partners may not always agree on how their property is to be managed, it may be desirable to centralize management control under one individual. If a limited partner has direct influence on management of the property, he or she may be reclassified as a general partner and lose the liability protection of limited partner status. More importantly, the Internal Revenue Service (IRS) may reclassify the limited partnership so that it is

Challenges Facing Office Building Managers Today and Tomorrow

- Accommodating space needs of tenants who grow via mergers and buy-outs.
- Retaining tenants who downsize their work forces or encourage their staff members to work at home.
- Retrofitting existing buildings for tenants' computer requirements (wiring, cabling, high-speed Internet access).
- Negotiating effective agreements for access to the building by telecommunications service providers.
- Embracing and using technology in order to remain competitive.
- Using the Internet effectively to market the office building and space available for lease.
- Protecting the physical asset and the people who work in the building while also maintaining reasonable access for tenants' customers and clients and the general public.
- Ensuring compliance with increasingly complex federal, state, and local laws, codes, and regulations.
- Finding acceptable ways to escalate rents in an era when the Consumer Price Index (CPI) is a less-reliable indicator of inflation.
- Finding creative ways to structure leases for technology and e-commerce businesses.
- Dealing with tenants who declare bankruptcy and the implications of their actions for the property's income stream.

taxable as a corporation. The administrative aspect of working for corporate owners is often complicated. Corporations must report to the government as well as their directors and shareholders, and such reports may have to conform to the accounting standards of the corporation. The manager employed by a condominium association reports directly to the board of directors. To avoid conflicting instructions and ensure efficient operations, one board member (usually the president) should be the manager's direct contact person. Since there is no rental income as such, the management fee is a flat monthly amount that is prorated as an operating expense across all of the units. Typically, the management agreement will include an hourly rate for adjunct activities assigned to the manager, such as attending more than a set number of board and/or association meetings. The manager will have to work with the owners, both directly and through the management agreement, to clarify ownership's role in managing the property and ensure that extra services requested or required by the owners are compensated appropriately. An office building owned by a cooperative corporation will pose similar management challenges.

Office building managers are also being challenged as technological developments raise tenants' expectations of what they receive in return for the rent they pay. Tenants want office buildings to have the infrastructure to support their computer and telecommunications needs. New buildings incorporate such infrastructure by design; older buildings will have to be retrofitted in order to compete effectively. Tenants are also concerned about their bottom lines, and they are constantly looking for ways to operate more efficiently and cost-effectively. Occupancy costs (rent and other charges) will be scrutinized as a growing component of tenants' annual budgets. Managers will have to monitor building systems closely to control operating costs that are passed through to tenants. Businesses grow—and sometimes shrink—as a result of mergers and buyouts. Their space needs also change as new technologies change the way they do business. More and more companies are allowing employees to work at locations other than their employers' offices. These workers may connect to their employer's office directly via telephone lines (a strategy called *telecommuting*), or they may use home computers, telephones, facsimile (fax) machines, and the Internet (e-mail) to connect with the main office *(home-officing)*. Consequently, lease terms may have to be structured differently to accommodate tenants' changing space needs. Managers will also be challenged to fulfill tenants' expectations regarding service quality and response times as part of an effective tenant retention program.

2

Office Building Assessment

Skyscrapers may dominate a city's skyline, but they are not the only buildings that need professional management. There are far more opportunities and challenges among the more-numerous office buildings that are smaller in size. In fact, the so-called trophy properties such as Sears Tower and the Empire State Building represent only a fraction of the office buildings that require full-time management.

The office building is a complex mix of tangible and intangible characteristics that will be evaluated by prospective tenants seeking space for lease. In addition to rentable space, the building includes public areas and mechanical systems. A high-rise will have elevators and, perhaps, escalators. Maintenance and other services provided by management will be factored in, as will the features of the neighborhood—nearby restaurants and shops, availability and cost of parking, and accessibility via public transportation—and its reputation. Each building component plays a role in the prospect's decision to lease office space in a particular building. It is also a factor in office building classification.

Building Classification

Before it can be managed, the office building must be evaluated to determine how it is perceived by current tenants, prospects, and others in the market. The first step in this process is to classify the building. While there is no definitive standard, people and publications in the real estate profession commonly classify office buildings in the following way:

- *Class A* buildings command the highest rents because they are the most prestigious in their location, tenancy, and overall desirability. They include new structures with the most up-to-date features, finishes, and amenities as well as fully renovated older buildings in prime locations. Generally they have a complete service staff on site that includes full-time maintenance and security personnel.
- *Class B* office buildings may not differ structurally from Class A buildings, but they cannot command the same high rents because they are in less-desirable locations, offer lower-quality finishes, and provide fewer amenities and services, or they cannot accommodate tenants' infrastructure needs.
- *Class C* buildings are usually older (formerly Class B or even Class A) and often located on what is now the perimeter of the central business district (CBD). While still reasonably well maintained, they are below current market standards for quality of finishes, systems, and amenities. As a result they command less rent and appeal to tenants who are extremely sensitive to price.

Two prevailing issues in building classification are age and obsolescence. An older building may be notable and potentially appealing, but it must also be able to accommodate current business needs. If a building cannot be retrofitted for advanced office systems or the space in it cannot be configured for efficient use by current standards, the class of the building will decline and so will its economic potential.

While classification of office buildings is subjective at best, it offers a useful means of conveying the desirability of a particular building in comparison to others. A number of factors contribute to a building's classification, including its tenancy, its overall appearance and condition, its systems and equipment, and the reputations of its ownership and management. Building amenities and interior finishes may also play a role. The importance of different attributes will vary from market to market and with changes in the economy. A primary factor in determining the desirability of a particular office building is, of course, its location.

Location. A building's proximity to other business facilities is a major consideration in determining its desirability. As one part of a city increases in popularity, the desirability of particular buildings will change. This is evident in most large cities. The CBD develops initially at the intersection of a city's two main streets, and most of the buildings there will be Class A. Property values and prestige diminish as you move away from the main intersection although the buildings may still be considered Class B. As the area of the CBD is increased, locations on the perimeter become less desirable because of where they are in relation to the "heart" of the CBD—expansion of the

Office Building Classification Factors

- Location (street address, neighborhood)
- Accessibility (transportation, parking)
- Prestige (image, reputation)
- Tenant mix
- Building management
- Tenant services
- Building exterior (curb appeal)
- Lobby
- Elevators
- Corridors
- Mechanical systems
- Rest rooms
- Office interiors (finish materials)
- Floor configuration

CBD may be in the opposite direction, changing a building's classification from A to B or B to C based on its location alone. On the other hand, growth of the CBD or changes in use or both can reverse such decline. Over time, areas adjacent to the CBD will become popular again. The land becomes relatively inexpensive, offering opportunities for potential new development. At the same time, obsolete buildings in the area may be candidates for rehabilitation or demolition. As the land is redeveloped or buildings are rehabilitated, occupancy rates will increase, leading to an increase in rental income and a better property classification.

There are also Class A office buildings outside the CBD. Lower land prices and rents in outlying areas attract businesses that want to reduce their occupancy costs. Demand for office space in the suburbs results in development of discrete business centers near major highways and airports. At the same time, population growth in the area provides a large pool of workers.

It should be pointed out, however, that desirability based on location is influenced by several factors, not least of which is the appearance of neighboring properties. (A well-constructed, well-maintained office building may be rated Class A only if its surroundings are also attractive and clean.) In addition to the attraction of a particular location, desirability is heavily influenced by such factors as accessibility and prestige.

Accessibility. Office workers must be able to travel to and from their work places rapidly. Locations that are served by several modes of transportation (buses, elevated and subway rapid transit lines, commuter trains, highways) are generally more desirable because employers benefit from the availability of a large pool of labor. Parking is also a consideration. In the suburbs, parking is usually abundant and free while the amount of parking in CBDs is usually limited, and downtown parking fees are often high. On the other hand, buildings in large urban centers may require less parking than do those in suburban locations because of the availability of public transportation.

Prestige. Because image and reputation are important factors in business, locating in a building with a prestigious address and reputation will enhance a firm's prestige. Building size also contributes significantly to prestige. A building that is prominent in the city's skyline may command higher rent, and a large building can include more extensive amenities, which will further enhance the prestige of the site. Although much of a building's prestige may be attributable to location alone, the tenant mix, management standards, and services offered to tenants of the building can enhance its status.

Tenant Mix. Prospective tenants want to lease where the other tenants in the building will enhance their reputation. They also look for other tenants that serve their industry. A building whose major tenant is a bank will be attractive to other entities that provide financial services (brokerage firms, mortgage bankers). A book publisher will attract businesses that provide editorial, illustration, and graphics services. Office building managers should be wary of prospects whose businesses might have a negative effect on other tenants' businesses and reputations. These include certain medical uses and nonprofit entities and governmental agencies that are controversial and likely to become targets of protesters as well as businesses characterized by high employee density (e.g., telemarketing firms) and those whose employees' unprofessional behavior can impact the appearance and condition of the building. Such tenants can also diminish the property's image and reputation and reduce its income.

Building Management. Management has a dual role. While its primary responsibility is to the building owner, management also has an obligation to the tenants. Effective managers are responsive to tenant requests and understanding of tenants' problems. The quality of the management enhances the value of the space in the building and contributes to the reputations of the firms that occupy it.

Tenant Services. The type and quality of services included in the rent or available separately will be an important consideration for prospective tenants. They will want to know how janitorial or custodial services, HVAC maintenance, and security are provided, how after-hours access to the building is provided and controlled, and how quickly on-site maintenance personnel can be expected to respond to service requests. They will also want to know about arrangements for after-hours HVAC and the charges that will apply. Some office buildings include special amenities such as conference rooms that can be rented by tenants. A conference room equipped with audiovisual or teleconferencing equipment is a benefit to tenants who are unlikely to invest in such facilities themselves. Concierge service may be provided by the building management while a day-care facility might be a tenant in its own right.

Building Components

Prospective tenants wishing to lease office space evaluate the components of a building individually. Beginning as their representatives approach the building and then as they walk through it and, finally, view the specific space being offered to them, the physical elements that comprise the building should make a favorable impression. The following sections outline some of the details that need attention so each component will be presented in the best light.

Building Exterior. One's first impressions of a building are the result of architectural design and the manner in which the exterior is maintained. Building signage and lights need to be cleaned regularly, and exterior surface finishes may need occasional repairs. Glass curtain walls and some applied finishes (e.g., terra cotta) require frequent inspection to ensure their stability and detect cracks or other damage. Glass in doors and windows at street level needs frequent cleaning to look its best.

The Lobby. From lighting and decor to cleanliness and overall appearance, the lobby establishes a building's character. It also creates an impression on visitors to the building as part of the setting in which tenants' business is conducted. An up-to-date directory of tenants and easy access to elevators are essential. Any ground-floor retail establishments should be enhancements to the lobby and add to the array of building amenities. Retail tenants in the lobby are often selected to provide specific services to tenants' employees.

Elevators. Rapid, efficient vertical transportation is critical in multistory buildings. People who work in the building will form opinions about elevator service based on a number of factors. These include location, appearance, and speed.

Location of elevator banks is very important. In newer buildings, elevators are usually visible when people walk in the door. Buildings with several banks of elevators that serve different groups of floors should have each bank clearly marked with the floors they serve—e.g., floors 1–12, floors 12–20). Typically, there will be an overlap of one or two floors (transfer floors) so that people can travel between floors within the building without coming all the way down to the lobby. In older buildings where elevators may be less easily accessible, their location should be clearly marked, and signs should direct people to them. The desirability of space in a building will be

The Americans with Disabilities Act

As people with disabilities enter the work force in increasing numbers, it is likely that prospective tenants will also want to locate in a building that is compliant with the Americans with Disabilities Act (ADA). A major thrust of the ADA is removal of barriers. While new construction and renovation of existing office buildings must include accommodations for people with disabilities, areas in existing buildings that comprise so-called *public accommodations* also have to be made compliant. Restaurants, service establishments such as barber shops and lawyers' offices, day-care centers, and lobbies are just a few examples of public accommodations.

The law requires changes for accessibility only where such changes are readily achievable. Among the features of an office building that are affected by these requirements are parking facilities, paths of travel, entrances, elevators, and rest rooms. Most buildings now include one or more automatic doors that allow easy access by people in wheelchairs, and almost all parking areas include designated handicapped spaces.

To ensure wheelchair accessibility, elevator cabs and entrances must comply with specified minimum dimensions as required under the ADA. The ADA also requires operating panels in elevators to be positioned so they can be operated from a wheelchair, and control buttons inside elevators and call buttons on all floors must include raised markings. Furthermore, changes in floors have to be indicated by audible as well as visible signals. Elevator cabs and entrances in many existing buildings are of a size that meets the ADA dimensional requirements. Repositioning of elevator controls may be all that is needed to make them compliant. For some buildings, ADA compliance may have to be part of a major renovation that is intended to increase the overall desirability of the building as a place to lease office space.

The ADA also requires rest room facilities to be wheelchair accessible—the law spells out specific dimensions for doorways, toilet stalls, and lavatories. Compliance depends on building size and existing rest room facilities as well as how much of the building is considered a public accommodation. In many buildings, accessibility may be limited to rest rooms that serve the general public as well as building occupants, rather than modifying every rest room in the building. However, tenants whose employees include people in wheelchairs may want the rest rooms on their floor or within their leased space to be wheelchair accessible.

Note: The information presented here is not intended to be a comprehensive discussion of the ADA or its requirements. Managers of buildings that are not yet in compliance with the ADA should consult appropriate professionals regarding what changes are needed and how to achieve them effectively and economically.

lessened if people have to walk a long distance from the entrance to the elevators and again from the elevators to their destinations on the occupied floors.

The appearance of elevator car entrances and interiors is another aspect that can affect people's perceptions of the building as a whole. Anything that can create negative impressions about the elevators might also raise questions of safety in the minds of elevator passengers. Elevators are expected to have adequate lighting, good ventilation, easily understood controls, and well-maintained wall and floor coverings. Mirrors or other reflective surfaces can be used to make the interior space appear larger; such surfaces will also require frequent cleaning.

Speed is the measure of elevator efficiency. For passengers, elevator speed includes more than travel time in feet per minute. They measure travel time from the moment they press the call button to the moment they reach their destination floor, which includes time they spend waiting for the elevator to arrive. Most elevator systems are computer controlled and can be reprogrammed if crowds are not being moved quickly enough during rush periods (morning arrivals, lunch time, evening departures).

A variety of factors affect elevator speed. These include the number of floors in the building, the numbers of elevators and elevator banks, the number of people (tenants' employees) on each floor and the total population of the building, how many people visit the building each day, and how often and how well the elevators are maintained (usually this is a contracted service). Yet another factor is how tenants operate their businesses. Tenants occupying multiple floors may have employees traveling between floors frequently. Those whose employees work in shifts may need extended hours or round-the-clock elevator service.

Freight elevators and their efficiency are also a consideration. In addition to their use for move-in and move-out of tenants' furniture and equipment, freight elevators are vital for transporting goods delivered to the building as well as tools and personnel involved in maintenance and tenant improvement construction. In the absence of a freight elevator, passenger elevators may have to be monopolized by tenants who are moving in or out. Passenger elevators usually are not designed to accommodate freight. Even with wall pads and a protective covering on the floor, finishes in the elevator cab can be damaged. Elevator efficiency is also reduced. On the other hand, requiring tenants to move during off-hours incurs overtime costs for the move, which can be a hardship for a small business.

Corridors. The public corridors in a building also create an impression on those who visit or work there. Whenever possible, they should appear to be an extension of the tenants' offices. Good lighting and neutral colors may be complemented with artwork. Signage should be up-to-date, discrete, and uniform throughout the building. All these elements should reflect the visual appeal of the building as a whole and be maintained in immaculate condition.

Mechanical Systems. As technological advances create new tools for performing office work, office tenants demand more from a building's electrical and HVAC systems. Building standards should spell out the numbers and placement of light fixtures in tenants' spaces. Existing ductwork may dictate where HVAC vents are positioned in the ceiling. Photocopying machines and other special-use equipment may require heavy-duty wiring or dedicated circuits. Large mainframe computers place heavy demands on electrical and HVAC systems. They may operate around the clock and have to be maintained within fixed ranges of temperature and humidity, which may require installation in a separate room and dedicated HVAC equipment. The newest telephone systems are computer controlled, and large systems may also need a separate room for equipment.

New construction includes state-of-the-art mechanical systems that meet tenants' needs efficiently and economically. Computer controls monitor and regulate electricity and HVAC usage throughout the building, including after-hours lighting and HVAC usage. Existing buildings may lack some or all of the facilities to accommodate tenants' needs for additional wiring and cabling for computers and other high-technology equipment. In some situations, retrofitting may be the answer. However, the cost to do the work may be prohibitive, or it may be difficult or impossible to retrofit a particular building for efficient, cost-effective operation because of unalterable design factors. This is one reason Class A buildings may be downgraded to Class B or Class C despite having good locations and being maintained to high standards.

Rest Rooms. Above all, rest rooms must be kept clean. Soap, towel, and other dispensers should be checked and refilled as needed throughout the day. The rooms should be well lighted, and well ventilated. Walls and other surfaces (e.g., countertops, partitions) should be kept clean and in good repair. Rest room security is an important issue, especially on multitenant floors where the facilities are shared. Push buttons or keypads may be used as well as locks and keys.

Office Interiors. Previously occupied office space usually is reconfigured to conform to a new tenant's business needs and aesthetic preferences. In this case, desirability depends on alternative floor plans rather than the existing layout and decor. Depth of the space from corridor to outside wall, width of the space between supporting columns, ceiling height, existing lighting, and acoustics, as well as the number, size, and relative locations of windows and the view from them can limit the possibilities for making changes. A prospect will try to determine whether and how well the space can accommodate its particular needs based on staff size (e.g, how many people must have private offices), amount and variety of office equipment, and technological infrastructure requirements. A reception area, coat closets, a conference room, and storage space are other considerations. Prospects will also want to know specifics about building standard finishes and tenant improvement allowances (discussed in Chapter 9).

Floor Configuration. The shape of the floors in an office building will determine how easily they can be adapted to accommodate individual tenants' requirements. Rectangular shapes are more efficient than curved or irregular shapes. Also critical are the usable space available for tenant occupancies and how much space is taken up by building core elements (elevators, stairways, rest rooms, distribution and equipment rooms, and mechanical, electrical, and telecommunications risers). On multitenant floors, the core area includes the corridors from which tenants' suites are accessed. (The corridors are included in the demised premises on single-tenant floors.) Ideally, the space available for tenant use will be column-free to allow maximum freedom in positioning interior walls and workstation furniture systems.

Building Types and Uses

Real estate professionals also differentiate office buildings based on type of structure and use. The following sections describe some of the different types of office buildings that are professionally managed.

High-Rise. Within the real estate industry, there is no standard definition of high-rise or, for that matter, of low-rise or mid-rise as they apply to office buildings. (Note: Municipal building codes define high-rise specifically as it relates to fire and life safety issues; however, these definitions vary from one locale to another.) *Where there are concentrations of skyscrapers in major cities,* the following guidelines apply:

Low-rise—up to twenty stories

Mid-rise—twenty to forty stories

High-rise—forty stories or more

In a small city where most other buildings range between five and ten stories, the tallest building at fifteen or twenty stories would be considered a high-rise. In most suburban markets, low-rise would apply to buildings up to eight stories tall, mid-rise to those with eight to twelve stories, and high-rise to anything taller. However, as suburbs attract more density of office uses, the definitions of low-, mid-, and high-rise can be expected to expand upward.

Rental rates will vary with building height and location. Class A space in a high-rise building in the CBD commands the highest rates per square foot. Class C space in an older building on the edge of the CBD may have the lowest rates per square foot. Desirability of space in a particular building may be related to other factors.

Garden Office Buildings. The so-called garden office building is usually a low-rise structure located in a suburban area rather than a large city. Typically they are one or two stories tall with no elevators. Second floor space in such a walk-up building can be difficult to lease. Upper level space in buildings with multiple floors is more desirable when there are elevators.

Garden office buildings are often clustered together in *office parks*. Located near major highways, such parks offer abundant parking. Some may also be served by bus lines. Office parks may be located so they are convenient to amenities for tenants and their employees. In outlying areas, the amenities may be built into the office park itself. It is important to have access to restaurants, shopping, and various services and to be accessible from highways and major thoroughfares. While tenants may be able to attract employees from among suburban residents, in many metropolitan areas, suburban office locations may encourage reverse commuting—workers coming from the city to the suburbs—especially if public transportation is available.

Suburban rental rates are generally lower than those in the CBD, and businesses looking to economize may locate in the suburbs initially or relocate to the suburbs to save on occupancy costs. Major corporations that once required a CBD address for their identity have moved some of their administrative and support functions to the suburbs, maintaining a presence in the CBD within a much smaller space. Others have opted to move their entire operations, including corporate headquarters, to suburban locations. One example is Sears, Roebuck and Company, which moved its headquarters out of Sears Tower in downtown Chicago to a sprawling site in Hoffman Estates. Often the suburban sites are closer to where some or all of a company's employees live. A challenge of such relocation is how employees who commute downtown on public transportation will get to work if they do not drive.

Flex Space. Designed to facilitate different configurations to accommodate both large and small space users, flex space is built as single-story structures and often located in so-called business parks. The buildings have no lobbies and are devoid of fancy fixtures. There are no add-on charges or load factors to consider. Likely tenants include telecommunications, Internet, and e-commerce companies that need large blocks of inexpensive space to set up data centers or customer service call centers and businesses that need to combine office and warehouse or light manufacturing uses at one location. Flex space may also be set up as *incubator space* for start-up businesses.

Mixed-Use Developments. Sometimes the highest and best use of a piece of land is a mixed-use development (MXD). These structures or complexes combine at least three different revenue-generating uses in a single structure or group of structures. Trump Tower in New York City has 13 stories of office space, 36 stories of condominium residences, and an upscale shopping center. Water Tower Place in Chicago includes 100,000 square feet of office space, an eight-story vertical shopping mall, a 431-room hotel, 40 stories of condominium residences, and multilevel paid parking below ground. Suburban MXDs often cover more than 100 acres. Usually they include several buildings of varying heights. There may be small low-rise office or retail buildings or large high-rise office or residential towers. One of the earliest suburban MXDs was the Galleria outside of Houston, which includes one million square feet of high-rise office space, a super-regional mall, and a 405-room luxury hotel tower.

3

Business Solicitation and the Management Agreement

Real estate managers may be employed to supervise the operations of an office building in several ways. A real estate management firm may be contracted by a property owner to manage a single office building or a portfolio of buildings. Under such an arrangement, a real estate manager employed by the management firm will be assigned responsibility for managing the building. Similarly, an individual may contract directly with a building owner. Both of these situations create an *agency* relationship under which the management firm or the individual manager is authorized to act on behalf of the owner and is compensated by a management fee. Real estate managers may also be employed directly by investors, financial institutions, and other entities whose real estate holdings warrant an in-house management function. Governmental agencies, educational institutions, and corporations that own their own buildings are likely to employ real estate management personnel as facilities managers. In this book, the emphasis will be on fee management and the agency relationship, and it is assumed that the office building manager is an employee of a real estate management firm.

Acquiring Management Business

Major investors seeking real estate management services will usually issue a *request for proposal (RFP)* that identifies the property or properties and describes the type and extent of the services being sought. As part of a management firm's business development activities, one of the executives

Management Company Self-Assessment: Business Considerations

Other questions to ask and answer in preparing a response to a request for a management proposal include the following:

- Do we have experience managing the specific type of office building for which the management proposal is being sought?
- Do we have managers on staff with sufficient experience and expertise to manage the particular property?
- Do we have time available to handle an additional property or client?
- Will it be necessary to obtain additional, specialized insurance coverages if our management proposal is accepted?
- Can we provide the needed services in a manner that is cost-effective for the property owner and profitable for us?

should be actively seeking opportunities to respond to such RFPs. A management firm or an individual manager may also solicit business directly, either from existing clients or from new owners coming into the marketplace. While existing clients who are well served will already know the capabilities of professionals they have worked with previously, soliciting business from new clients will pose special challenges. In either case, the property should be carefully evaluated, and a comprehensive proposal for its management should be prepared.

Assessing One's Strengths. Before an individual or a management firm can offer services to an office building owner, a great deal of information is needed and a number of decisions will have to be made. Experienced managers know how long it takes to perform different management tasks. Based on a building's size and tenancy, they can estimate the amount and extent of the work and the size of the staff that is needed to maintain it on a daily, weekly, monthly, and annual basis. They will have established forms and procedures for performing and documenting property operations and financial data. They can differentiate the role of the building manager from the duties and responsibilities of other personnel who will work on site.

In addition to such management details, those seeking to manage office buildings for others must know their strengths and their weaknesses. An assessment of a firm's capabilities can be made by answering a series of questions:

- Do we offer all of the services being sought by the owner of the building? If not, can we add staff or subcontract effectively with other entities to meet the prospective client's needs?
- Do we have in place the software required to generate the financial information requested? If not, can we obtain the software and quickly

train our accounting personnel to use it? (Will our management personnel need special training to read and interpret the information?)

- Do we have sufficient maintenance staff or contracted maintenance services to undertake additional assignments? If not, can we add staff or extend our contractual arrangements so that we can do the needed work?
- Do we have the skills or the outside contacts to effect cost savings for the prospective client?
- Do we offer any unique services or programs that would benefit the property and enhance its revenue picture?

These are not the only questions, of course. The owner of an older building might not have thought about retrofitting its systems or upgrading its standard finishes as strategies for retaining existing tenants and attracting new ones. A management firm with experienced staff and relationships with sources of construction materials could incorporate these strategies in a management proposal. Analysis of the building may have revealed an environmental problem, and the firm may have a contract with an environmental professional who can expedite a cost-effective restoration of compliance. There may be items of deferred maintenance that, if given immediate attention, could markedly improve the building's curb appeal. Looking beyond the day-to-day management of a building, it should be possible to identify one or more strategies that can give the management firm an edge in the bidding.

Developing a Management Proposal. A management proposal should not only respond to a specific RFP, but also sell the management firm and its services. The typical proposal will include general information about the company and its services followed by an analysis of the property, a proposed plan for its management, and an outline of proposed terms for a management agreement.

Company Information. Information about the company should provide an overview description of the firm, its personnel, and its management portfolio:

- A brief history of the organization and its founding.
- A general description of its portfolio, highlighting properties that are similar to the subject of the proposal and listing the firm's achievements in meeting any special challenges in their management.
- A list of key personnel with biographical information about the individuals who would be directly involved in managing the property.
- A statement of the company's goals and commitment to its clients—its *mission statement.*

Contents of a Management Agreement

- Parties to the agreement (owner, agent)
- Description of the property (building name, address, other details)
- Term (duration) of the agreement
- Manager's authority, duties, and responsibilities
  —Bank accounts
  —Collections
  —Payments
  —Financial and other reports
  —Leasing
  —Maintenance
  —Employees
- Owner's obligations
  —Contingency reserve funds
  —Property insurance
  —Indemnification of management
- Management compensation
- Other provisions
  —Force majeure
  —Termination

It is also appropriate to include a list of clients for whom the firm provides management services.

Services Offered. The services offered usually include property management, maintenance, and accounting, budgeting, and reporting. For each type of service, the firm's standard practices and procedures should be outlined, with emphasis on the way they would be applied to the client's property. If marketing and leasing are also desired, the firm's capabilities in this area should be described as well. A copy of the firm's standard operating procedures manual may be included as a way to provide specifics. Other services may be described as appropriate. For example, if the proposal recommends renovation of the building, the firm's construction supervision services should be outlined.

The Management Agreement

The arrangement under which a real estate manager undertakes the responsibility of operating a property or properties for an owner should be documented in a written management agreement. This ensures that all parties to the arrangement understand their respective roles and responsibilities. It also provides a basis for clarifying the intentions of the owner and the manager if it becomes necessary to go to court to settle a dispute.

A management agreement, when signed, is a legal contract. As such, it must include the following basics:

- Identification of the parties to the agreement
- Identification and description of the property to be managed
- The duration of the arrangement
- The duties and responsibilities of the manager
- The responsibilities and obligations of the property owner
- The manager's compensation

To ensure that the management agreement will stand up in a court of law, the final negotiated arrangement should be reviewed by both parties' attorneys before it is signed.

The management agreement establishes the authority of the manager and sets forth any limitations on his or her actions or authority to act. Most management firms will have a basic management agreement form that they can tailor to the arrangement with an individual owner for management of a specific property. This will include many provisions that are considered standard or boilerplate, and it is usually written from the perspective and for the protection of the manager. However, it is common practice to modify provisions as necessary to ensure that the property owner's requirements and any unique aspects of managing the property will be properly documented. Some property owners, especially institutional owners of large portfolios of properties, will have and prefer to use their own agreement form. While either party's form is negotiable, the party whose form is used usually has an advantage in the negotiations: All of its issues are already spelled out in an acceptable format, and the other party must take care to understand all the provisions that are in place and negotiate any changes and additions to them.

The Parties. The agreement form should identify the property owner and the real estate manager as the parties to the arrangement. When either party is a business entity (partnership, corporation), it is important to establish the authority of the individual who will sign the agreement as its representative. The agreement should also spell out the relationship between the parties. It should state that the manager or the management firm is appointed as the *agent* of the owner and that the management arrangement does not create any other kind of business relationship between the parties (partnership, joint venture, employer-employee).

As the agent of the owner, the office building manager assumes a *fiduciary* obligation to exercise a standard of care in managing both property and money. The manager must be loyal to the owner's interests and not benefit from the agency role in any way that has not been previously disclosed to and approved by the owner.

When the managing agent is a management firm, the agreement may identify the individual who will manage the property and authorize all employees of the management firm to act as the owner's agent.

Note: Fee management is not always performed under an agency arrangement. Some owners, especially institutions, prefer the manager to be an *independent contractor* as a way to limit the manager's authority and lessen ownership's liability. However, the status and liability of an independent contractor differ substantially from those of an agent, and advice of an attorney should be sought before a manager agrees to accept such an arrangement.

The Property. The agreement should identify the property to be managed, including a building name if applicable, street address, and a brief description. If what is to be managed is part of a larger complex (a single building in a multibuilding grouping or the office component of a mixed-use building), additional details regarding its location may be necessary for accurate identification. It may be appropriate to append a full legal description of the property to the agreement as well.

The Term. A management agreement can be established for any period of time. Usually there is an initial term of one or more years, with stated beginning and ending dates and provision for automatic renewal on an annual basis thereafter, subject to either party notifying the other of a desire to terminate the arrangement. (Termination is discussed later in this chapter.) An agreement for management of an office building should be of sufficient duration for the manager to accomplish the owner's goals and realize a fair profit for services provided.

Management Responsibilities. The manager is authorized to establish bank accounts for the owner's funds, collect rents and other revenues, and pay the operating expenses of the property. The manager may also be authorized to make regular debt service payments on the owner's behalf. The various financial activities must be reported to the owner on a regular schedule. If the building has a stable occupancy, the manager may be responsible for renewing leases and finding new tenants when spaces are vacated. In most situations, however, office leasing is a separately contracted function, and the leasing agent is supervised by the real estate manager. The manager is also authorized to maintain the building and its equipment and to hire personnel in order to do that.

Bank Accounts. The agreement should state the name under which the property bank accounts are to be established. This may be the owner's name or the building name. If building leases call for security deposits, it may be desirable to have separate accounts for operating funds and security deposits. However, unless such separation is requested by the owner or required by law, security deposits can be held in the operating account. Usual practice is for the manager to select the bank or other depository.

Good management practice includes development of a capital reserve fund to pay for equipment upgrades and replacements or building renovation. Such funds should be deposited in a separate interest-bearing account.

As a protection for both parties, the agreement should require the manager to obtain *fidelity bonds* in an agreed-upon dollar amount for all personnel who will handle the owner's funds. The manager may also be required to obtain crime insurance. The costs of such guarantees are usually considered a property operating expense.

Collections. The manager is authorized to collect rents, security deposits, and other property revenues and deposit them in the operating account. This includes pass-through operating expenses as well as reimbursements for tenant improvements and any fees for special services.

Payments. The manager is given authority to pay the expenses of the property, including the management fee, from the operating account. A requirement that the manager pay debt service may also be included, in which case the contingency reserve should be reviewed and adjusted to ensure availability of funds for this regular payment. The agreement may set a dollar limit for a single expenditure beyond which the owner's approval must be sought. It usually also provides that prior approval is not required for expenditures to address emergency situations.

The managing agent may be obligated to make payments of the net proceeds (cash flow) to the owner each month. This is the owner's periodic return on the investment after operating expenses and debt service have been paid and funds have been set aside for capital reserves. While a check drawn against the operating account may accompany the manager's report each month, sophisticated investors will often arrange for an electronic sweep of their property accounts, removing the excess funds any time the balance exceeds a prescribed amount.

Financial and Other Reports. The manager is required to provide periodic reports to the owner, documenting monies received and paid out as well as other management activities. Among the items to be reported are tenants, occupancy and vacancy rates, current payments from tenants and monies owed, marketing and leasing activity, and variances from budgeted income and expenses. (Specific components of the monthly report are described in detail in Chapter 4.) Such reporting is usually done on a monthly basis. When the number of specific reports is large, a list may be attached to the agreement as an addendum rather than incorporate all of them in the agreement text.

Preparation of an annual operating budget that estimates the income and expenses of the property is also the manager's responsibility. The agreement will indicate when the budget is to be submitted (calendar versus non-calendar fiscal year) and how long the owner has to approve or amend it (usually at least thirty days). Other budgeting requirements (e.g., capital expenditures, marketing and leasing) may be included in the agreement as well. Usually there is also provision for the property accounts to be audited on a set schedule at the owner's expense.

Leasing. As noted before, the leasing of office space may be contracted separately. An agent or broker who does leasing exclusively is often in a better position than the building manager to identify prospective tenants for an office building. Lease-up of a new building and excessive vacancies under soft market conditions certainly deserve full-time attention of a leasing specialist. However, the manager is the person who will sign the lease as the owner's agent and administer the lease terms once the tenant is in place. The manager also determines the rental rates and other parameters within which the agent will negotiate individual leases so that the owner's investment goals can be achieved. Therefore, the management agreement should be specific as to the manager's role in leasing and lease renewal activities. (Chapter 7 provides more information about the rental schedule, and Chapter 8 addresses the manager's leasing role.)

Maintenance. The manager is authorized to make necessary repairs and replacements to maintain the present condition and operating efficiency of the building. This includes authority to contract for improvements to tenants' leased spaces. The agreement will usually set a dollar limit on a single maintenance expenditure that has not been previously authorized by the owner with an exception for work that must be done in an emergency situation to preserve the integrity of the structure or ensure the safety of the tenants' employees.

Personnel. When an office building requires an on-site management team, the manager is given authority to hire, supervise, compensate, and discharge such employees as are needed for the management, maintenance, and operation of the property. This includes authority to make payroll deductions and file employer information and tax returns. Such employees' wages are an operating expense of the property.

While on-site staff should be considered employees of the property owner, the owner may want them to be employees of the managing agent. Whoever is to be the *employer of record* should be stated in the agreement. Note, however, that local jurisdictions vary in their interpretation of this type of situation, often declaring the agent to be the employer regardless. To ensure compliance with applicable laws, the manager should consult an attorney for accurate, up-to-date information on the question of who is the employer.

Management Compensation. Real estate management is typically compensated by a fee that is a percentage of the gross receipts of the managed property. To ensure adequate compensation for services rendered, a minimum fee should also be stated. This would apply in any period when the percentage fee based on gross receipts falls below the minimum amount. The income sources to be included in gross receipts for purposes of establishing the management fee should be agreed to by both parties and stated in the management agreement. This varies from market to market and within markets and may specifically include or exclude expense pass-throughs or other property income in addition to base rents.

Care must be taken in setting the management fee. The manager's goal should be to recover the costs of managing the property and realize a profit. Careful evaluation of the owner's requirements is a good place to start along with an analysis of the property. The following are some of the factors to be considered.

- *The owner's goals*—Is the owner planning to hold the property for several years and use the periodic income to fund other business activities? Are major renovation and re-leasing required so the property can be sold at a profit in 18–24 months? Each of these goals requires a different approach to a management fee. The first requires basic management directed at maintaining and enhancing the income stream under a long-term arrangement. The second offers only a short management term with little or no possibility that the manager would continue to manage the property after it is sold. However, it also suggests an opportunity for additional or separate fees for construction supervision and intensive leasing activity on a short-term basis as well as for assistance with due diligence and preparation of information needed to facilitate the sale.
- *Level of service*—Will the manager work on site and supervise a staff of maintenance and administrative employees? Will the manager provide only periodic oversight of janitorial services and preventive maintenance provided under contracts with outside vendors? Is the management reporting requirement different from the manager's usual practice? A high level of service (daily hands-on supervision of property operations, more frequent or more complex reporting) requires more of the manager's time than does a moderate or low level of service (managing from a distance, basic monthly reports).
- *Complexity*—Does the building have mechanical problems because of deferred maintenance? Is a major retrofit needed to provide adequate wiring for current and future tenants' business equipment? Do on-site personnel need special training or re-training? A building that poses these kinds of challenges will take more of the manager's time than one that has few or no such problems.
- *Cost of management*—What are the actual costs of providing the requisite management services, compiling financial data, and preparing

the monthly reports to the owner? Most real estate managers and management firms know how much time will be spent performing different management activities and will develop a list of costs and charges to facilitate calculation of the cost of managing a particular property.

Note: The management fee may be stated as a "gross" fee that covers all services provided directly by the management firm exclusive of building operating expenses paid out of property funds. However, some agreements state the compensation as a "net" fee and allow the management firm to bill some main office expenses back to the property. The particular charges and basis for such billing would be specified.

Real estate managers may be compensated separately for services provided in addition to property management. If the manager is to perform leasing, construction supervision (renovation, disaster restoration, tenant improvements), real estate tax appeals, or other such non-management services, an appropriate additional fee should be negotiated for each such activity and stated in the management agreement. Leasing fees are often a commission, which may be based on the total dollar value and term of the lease or a flat rate per square foot leased. Compensation for construction supervision may be a sliding scale of fees based on the cost of the project—for example, less than $5,000, $5,001–$10,000, $10,001–$20,000, etc.—and stated either as a dollar amount or a percentage rate. (The construction supervision fee may also be stated in individual leases as appropriate, indicating whether this expense is to be borne by the building owner or the tenant.) Compensation for other activities may be a flat fee or a percentage of the cost of the work. It is also advisable to include an hourly fee to cover other non-management services that may be needed from time to time, such as attending zoning meetings or preparing special reports. The agreement may also provide for interest to be paid when any monies due the manager are not paid within a set time after they are due.

Note: It is often desirable to include in a management agreement a provision that establishes the managing agent as the sales agent in the event the property is sold. However, the agent's role in and compensation for selling the property should be stated in a *separate* sales agreement. Even if the managing agent is not appointed as the sales agent, the manager will be involved in due diligence efforts and preparation of information prior to the sale, and these activities should be compensated appropriately.

Owner's Obligations. The owner is required to provide funds so that the manager can pay operating expenses from the moment of take-over. A specific dollar amount is usually stated, and this initial deposit to the property operating account should reflect anticipated expenses for the first month. The owner is also required to maintain a minimum balance in the operating account (contingency reserve) and to deposit additional funds if the account balance falls below an agreed-upon amount. It may be advisable to provide a mechanism for effecting such deposits, as by a line of credit or electronic transfer of funds.

Insuring the property is also the owner's responsibility. This should include coverage for financial losses due to damage to the property itself and for liability resulting from injuries to people or damage to others' property arising out of incidents that occur on the property. In most situations, the manager consults an insurance agent who evaluates the property and recommends the types and amounts of coverages to be obtained. Then, with the owner's approval, the manager pays the premiums. While the policies are issued in the owner's name, the managing agent should be identified as an additional named insured party.

Since an owner's insurance policies do not cover tenants' property within their leased premises, office tenants should be required to maintain adequate casualty and liability insurance coverage for their employees, their business activities, and their leased premises (including leasehold improvements and personal property). Specifics would be spelled out in the individual leases, including a requirement to provide proof of such coverage (i.e., certificates of insurance) to the manager. The management agreement may or may not address this issue in a provision requiring the manager to collect and maintain an up-to-date file of proofs of tenants' insurance coverage.

The owner should also indemnify and hold the manager harmless in regard to any financial losses or liability for bodily injury or property damage occurring on the property (except in the event of willful misconduct or gross negligence on the part of the manager). Any expenses incurred by the manager in connection with any claims or lawsuits filed against the property or the owner or the managing agent based on violation of any federal, state, or local laws that apply to employment practices, accessibility requirements, or the like should be paid by the owner, including fees for legal advice regarding compliance with such laws.

The owner is responsible for compliance with building codes and regulations that apply to the structure and its mechanical systems and equipment. However, the manager is obligated to inform the owner promptly upon receiving any notices of noncompliance.

Other Provisions. Management agreements typically include the following additional provisions:

- Contracts—Limitations on the manager's authority to contract in the owner's name for utilities and other services (e.g., maintenance) may be set at a maximum dollar amount, above which the owner's approval must be sought. There may also be a requirement to obtain a minimum number of competitive bids (usually three) for certain types of services.

- Liability—Usually there is a declaration that the manager assumes no liability for any acts or omissions of the owner of the property (or its previous ownership or management) regarding previously unknown violations of any laws or regulations that become known during the term of the agreement.
- Source of funds—The owner is required to provide funds to make up any shortfall in the operating account. The manager is not required to advance funds to pay expenses of the property; however, any funds the manager may advance to make payments on the owner's behalf are to be considered a loan to be repaid with interest at a rate stated in the agreement.
- Management office—When on-site management is required, the agreement should provide for the manager or the management company to have office space in the building rent free and for the cost of operating that office to be an operating expense of the property. This may be included in the operating expenses that are passed through to the tenants. However, expenses pertaining to the management firm and not the property should be borne by the management firm.
- Force majeure—The manager is excused from performing his or her obligations as the owner's agent in the event of any natural disaster or other disruption of property operations by a cause that is beyond the manager's control.
- Termination—The agreement may be terminated if either party fails to cure a breach of the agreement within a prescribed period or in the event excessive damage makes it impossible to operate the building. Other causes for termination may also be stated. As with any contractual arrangement, the parties may discover early that they cannot work together effectively. It is therefore appropriate to provide for compensation to the manager in the event the agreement is terminated before the end of the initial term. This may be stated as a percentage of the management fee for a set number of months or for the remainder of the term. The intent is to reimburse the manager's costs of taking over the account, which would normally be included in the monthly management fee over the initial term.

There is no standard management agreement form that can be used for all property types. Office buildings differ from other commercial properties and from residential properties in significant ways, and each office building will have unique features and issues that need to be considered in documenting the management arrangement. Likewise, if the management role includes marketing and leasing, the agreement must include specific provisions defining this role and its compensation.

As with any written contract that is in force for an extended period, it may be necessary or desirable to modify some of the terms of a management agreement to keep it current. This can be done by negotiating the change or changes and creating a written amendment or addendum that is signed by both parties after approval by their attorneys.

Note: The Institute of Real Estate Management publishes a general Management Agreement form and Explanation whose boilerplate language can serve as a starting point in addressing most of the issues related to managing office buildings.

4

Management Take-Over and Fiscal Responsibilities

The manager's actions once an agreement is in place will set the tone for the entire management term. The process of taking over a management account provides an opportunity to get acquainted with the tenants while also conducting a thorough evaluation of the property and its operations. Attention to details is very important. The information gathered during take-over will form the basis of the manager's operating strategy and record-keeping system.

A management firm will have a standard take-over checklist of actions to be taken and items to be collected, with space for assigning tasks to specific personnel and noting when each has been completed. (Exhibit 4.1 shows a portion of a take-over checklist.) Usually there are blank spaces to add items, or the form may be a computer file that can be tailored to the new account. For some items, it may be appropriate to set deadlines for completion, especially if there are known due dates related to them (e.g., payment of real estate taxes without penalty, expiration of insurance coverages or service contracts). It may also be appropriate to establish specific priorities and list some items in order of precedence. Sometimes an asterisk or other symbol will be used to distinguish items that are to be completed *before* official take-over or within a certain time period (e.g., 30, 60, or 90 days) *after* take-over. In particular, notification of tenants, vendors, and other parties may have to be completed prior to actual take-over.

Exhibit 4.1

Sample Management Take-Over Checklist (partial)

Construction	Assigned To	Start Date	Due Date	Date Completed
Construction agreement forms				
Landlord/tenant work specifications				
Building permits for all developed tenant improvements				
Approved vendors				
company, contact name, phone number				
certificates of insurance				
Other construction information				

Excerpted with permission from *Transition: Taking Over a Management Account,* which provides a comprehensive description of the take-over process and includes sample checklist forms. Copyright 1993 by the Institute of Real Estate Management.

The Take-Over Process

Management take-over is a complex process. The new manager will be gathering information about the ownership of the property as well as the property itself, the tenants, and the on-site staff. Financial data, leases, and tenant information will be collected along with information about risks at the property and their management and how the property is maintained. Following are some points to consider in compiling different types of information.

- *Ownership*—Who owns the building and the business form of that ownership will affect many aspects of day-to-day management and decision-making. In particular, they affect the types of reports to be prepared and their frequency as well as how the investment proceeds (cash flow) will be distributed. Also important are the owner's objectives for the property and how they are to be achieved (a management plan), whether debt service payments are to be made by the manager (from property income), and how real estate taxes and property insurance premiums are to be paid.

- *Property data*—Scale drawings are a must. These should include a site plan showing all structures in relation to the property and its surroundings, as-built drawings or blue prints or both showing structural details (utility connections and controls, interior plumbing and wiring), and floor-by-floor layouts showing leased and vacant space with dimensions (rentable and usable areas). A thorough inspection of the building and grounds using a comprehensive inspection checklist will verify details shown on the drawings and provide a baseline assessment of the property's condition. Documentation of compliance with building codes, environmental laws, and accessibility requirements under the Americans with Disabilities Act (ADA) should be requested and verified by inspection.

- *Site employees*—There may be an on-site staff employed by the owner. The prior management should be able to provide complete records on the individuals' employment status, wages, and benefits, as well as a table of organization showing lines of responsibility and reporting. If they were employees of the former management, take-over will include an assessment of staffing needs and a plan for employing new staff, contracting for specific services, or providing services using staff from the new management firm.

- *Financial data*—Since preparation of an operating budget will be a priority, the new manager will need specific information about the property's income and expenses and how they are accounted. The management firm's standard chart of accounts may differ from what has been used previously at the property so it is important to know how specific income and expense items have been accounted in the past.

- *Leases*—Leases determine the property's income stream which, in turn, is used to determine property value. There should be a valid lease for each occupied space showing the base rental rate and stating how operating expenses are passed through to the individual tenant. If there are retail tenants, there may be percentage rents to be collected as well. There may be separate leases for storage space or for parking, especially if these lessees include non-tenants. (Other records will indicate delinquencies or nonpayment of rent.)

  It is also important to know the status of ongoing efforts to lease vacant space and how those efforts are to be compensated. If new management is also assuming responsibility for leasing, there may be leasing agreements in place that have to be honored or canceled. These agreements may be a paragraph in the lease or a separate agreement attached to the lease.

- *Maintenance*—It is important to determine the condition of the exterior and interior of the building at take-over. A thorough property inspection will include examination of the interiors of occupied and vacant office spaces as well as all common areas. It should identify maintenance that has been deferred, safety features and security measures that are in place or absent, and any noncompliance with building codes or other regulations. (Use of a written checklist will

Management Take-Over in Adverse Situations

Not all changes in management are easy transitions. The managing agent may have been appointed by a court of law to safeguard the property and its income until a loan default is cleared or the property is foreclosed *(receivership).* Alternatively, the manager may have been contracted by a financial institution to manage a foreclosed (real estate owned or REO) property. A change within the ownership entity (e.g., removal of a general partner) may necessitate a change in management of a property. The property itself may be distressed, and the goal of new management may be only to preserve and maintain the property until it can be sold. In these types of situations, advance notification of take-over is unlikely. New management will have other priorities initially, and notification may be handled on an as-needed basis.

Even a straightforward change of management can have negative aspects. If new management was sought because the property had been managed poorly, it is unlikely that there would be any valid historical data to use as a basis for budgeting. In such cases, a zero-based budget may be the only alternative. There may also be problems acquiring information about the property and its operations because on-site personnel who remain loyal to the prior management may not be forthcoming with information needed to expedite the take-over process.

While such adverse take-overs are rare, real estate managers and management companies need to be aware of and prepared to deal with these situations when they occur.

ensure that all components are inspected and provide documentation of the results.) Contracts for preventive maintenance and repair services should be reviewed to determine the costs related to them and whether or not they should remain in effect (or be renewed when they expire).

- *Risk management*—The take-over process should identify the types of emergencies that can possibly occur at the property, both natural and manmade. Other potential risks relate to injuries to people and damage to others' property. All these risks should be properly addressed by specific insurance coverages, and take-over should evaluate the adequacy of those coverages. There should be a list of emergency contacts that includes on-site staff members and tenants' personnel as well as local fire and police departments, hospitals, and ambulance services. An emergency procedures manual should be prepared if there is none.

A major thrust of the take-over process is the determination of what operational tools (policies, procedures, documents) are already in place and whether they are adequate or need to be changed. Some changes will be made to accommodate requirements of new management; others may be necessary to ensure regulatory compliance or to facilitate achievement of the owner's goals. Take-over includes discovery of issues that are not being addressed (e.g., specific risks), assessment of their importance, and development of strategies to deal with them as may be necessary or appropriate. The latter may include a decision *not* to deal with certain items.

Notification of the Assignment. To ensure a smooth transition, new management should be announced to affected parties well in advance of the actual take-over. Following are some of the persons or groups that must receive formal notification.

- *Tenants*—All current tenants should be advised to change the payee for future rent checks and where to mail them. If any changes are expected in the handling of operating expense pass-throughs (e.g., a change in the timing of the adjustment for actual expenses compared to estimated values currently being billed), it may be well to include this information in the notice. Whom to contact for building services and how to make specific arrangements should be included along with a sample service request form, if appropriate. If a tenant is a subsidiary or division of a larger entity, it may be appropriate to notify the corporate headquarters as well. This group should include any retail tenants and those who lease parking spaces if such arrangements exist for a particular property.

  It is a good idea to advise tenants that their insurance policies should be updated to show the new management as an additional named insured party and remind them to arrange for corrected certificates of insurance to be submitted to the manager as soon as possible. It may also be desirable to request that tenants provide updated information on their employees, including names, addresses, telephone numbers where they can be reached, and whom to notify in case of an emergency. (In buildings with large populations of workers, it may not be practical to maintain updated contact information on all tenants' employees. In such situations, tenants should compile and maintain this information for their own use and make it available to the building manager when asked to do so.)

- *Vendors*—All current vendors and contractors, including utilities and other service providers, should be advised of the change in management, the preferred form of billing, and where invoices should be sent. If the management firm handles payments on a fixed schedule, it is prudent to include that information as well.

  Contractors who do work on the property should be asked to update their workers' compensation and liability insurance policies to include new management as an additional named insured party, including a due date for submitting corrected certificates of insurance to the manager.

- *Insurance contacts*—The owner's insurance agent and the insurance carriers need to know about the change in management, and they should be asked to include the building manager and the management company as additional named insured parties on all property policies (as provided in the management agreement). It may also be appropriate to request a review of current coverages so that any needed changes can be made immediately or when the next premiums are due to be paid.
- *Financial institutions*—If debt service is to be paid by management, the lender will need to know about the change of payment authorization. It may be appropriate to request a report of payment status, including principal paid down, in order to have a complete record or to verify information provided by the property owner or the prior management. If existing operating bank accounts or trust accounts are to retain the account names but change the signatories, the bank should be asked about their procedures and to supply appropriate forms for making these changes.
- *Local government*—Emergency services (fire and police departments and possibly an ambulance service and the nearest hospital) should be advised of the change in management and specific contacts. If there has not been a fire inspection or fire drill recently, the fire department might be asked to schedule one.

  The real estate taxing authority should be notified of the change in billing. It may also be appropriate to request information on the basis of the assessment for the building. City services for water and sewer utilities should be notified to change the billing name and address. If trash removal is a city service rather than a direct vendor contract, it should be included in this notice.

  The building department is another entity that should receive notification. This relates to operating and occupancy permits as well as outstanding building permits for ongoing tenant improvement construction. It may be necessary to arrange for various permits to be updated to identify new management as the agent of the owner.
- *Employees*—Site personnel also need to be advised of the change in management. The manner in which this is handled will depend on the specific situation. If the staff are employees of the property owner, it is likely that they will be expected to be retained. In this case, a blanket written notice may be sent to all of them welcoming them as members of the new management team. It may be appropri-

Exhibit 4.2
Sample Notification Letter with Variant Information

ABC Management Company
555 Main Street
Anytown, USA
(phone: 555-555-5555; fax: 555-555-5554)

[date]

Addressee Name
Company Name
Address
City, State, Zip

Dear *[Name of Contact]:*

We are pleased to announce that ABC Management Company will be managing the City Office Tower effective *[insert commencement date].* As with any such transition, there will be some needed changes.

[Information Specific to Tenants]
This is to notify you that effective on the date shown above, all rents and other payments should be made payable to *[name of property/account]* and mailed to the following address *[insert specific mailing address or refer to main office address shown above].* Please also advise your insurance carriers of the change in management and arrange for inclusion of ABC Management Company as an additional named insured party for each policy as appropriate. Revised certificates of insurance should be submitted to the manager by *[insert due date].*

ate or desirable to include a statement regarding new management's approach to employee relations as well.

Savvy office building managers know that long-term site employees develop loyalties to their previous managers, and it is a good idea to determine early whether such loyalties are likely to interfere with the transfer of management or future operations of the property or both. Early review of each employee's record and job performance may be advisable regardless so that an effective management team can be established quickly.

If on-site staff are employees of the prior management company, it may be desirable to send a formal notification that invites their cooperation and assistance in effecting a smooth transition. They should also be advised that employees from the new management company will be on site to collect information about the property and when these visits are expected to take place.

Exhibit 4.2 *(continued)*

Requests for maintenance and other services may be submitted using the ABC Management Company service request form (copy attached). Requests may also be submitted by telephone *[insert phone number]* or e-mail *[insert e-mail address of person or department].*

[Information Specific to Vendors]
This is to notify you that effective on the date shown above, all invoices for goods sold or services rendered to City Office Tower should be sent to the attention of *[name of the manager and property street address].* Invoices should include the ABC Management Company purchase order number, the quantity ordered/shipped, a full description of the goods or services, and the unit and extended prices. Payment will be made only from original invoices.

Any invoices for purchases ordered under the prior management should be submitted to them for payment.

[General Closing Information]
We at ABC Management Company look forward to working with you as a *[tenant of or supplier to]* City Office Tower.

Sincerely,

[name of manager, allowing space for signature]

- *Public notice*—A news release or announcement should be prepared and sent to local news media (print and broadcast) as well as local and national real estate publications.

The foregoing list comprises the parties that are typically notified of changes in management of an office building. Notices should be tailored to the category of recipient and addressed to a specific person if at all possible. (An example of a notice with variant information for tenants and vendors is shown in Exhibit 4.2.) Each property may have some unique entities that require specific notice of the transition, and these should be identified as early as possible to ensure they are included in the notification process.

Property Tasks. A thorough evaluation of an office building will include inspection of the property and the exterior and interior of the building. In addition to these physical aspects, it is important to collect information about occupied and vacant spaces, existing tenants and the particulars of their leases, and all aspects of the property's operations. The following sections describe the types of information that are gathered under the auspices of a management take-over checklist. Some unique situations and aspects that may be encountered are identified as well.

Property Inspection. As indicated at the beginning of this chapter, the manager should obtain copies of architectural drawings and site plans and verify equipment and utility connections via a property inspection. These drawings should be available on site from prior management. If not, they should be requested from the owner, or arrangements should be made to have such drawings made.

Inspections of the building exterior, interior common areas, and leased office (and retail) spaces should be done as part of the take-over process to determine the current condition of the property, identify examples of deferred maintenance, and outline specific actions to be taken. Inspection of occupied spaces is particularly desirable because it provides an opportunity to introduce the new management team to the tenants.

During this initial inspection, it is important to assess the status of general maintenance, including janitorial work normally done at the site. Scheduling of maintenance work depends on how much is to be done by on-site staff and the complexity of the facilities and equipment in place. Scheduling of janitorial maintenance depends on required levels of cleanliness and the size and complexity of the common areas to be cleaned. In office buildings, janitorial maintenance is often contracted out. While large buildings are likely to have an on-site staff to perform routine maintenance and repairs, small properties may contract with specific tradespeople for these types of work.

The take-over inspection should identify safety features and security measures that are in place or notably absent, and observations of actual or potential problems or violations should be noted. Safety concerns include torn carpeting, broken stair treads or handrails, areas where lighting is inadequate or absent, wiring or cabling that is inadequate, and whether fire and smoke alarms, extinguishers, and sprinklers are appropriately located (or if they are absent).

Another issue is workplace safety, which is regulated under the Occupational Safety and Health Administration (OSHA). A take-over checklist should include a review of maintenance tools and their storage, protective equipment and clothing and its appropriateness and condition, and the adequacy of staff safety training. Keep in mind, too, that things like painted ladders and splices in extension cords are among the violations OSHA inspectors seek out specifically, and the penalties OSHA can assess are stiff.

Security measures vary with the type of tenant uses and will change over time. Locks on main entrances and doors of leased premises and doors that open inward are standard today, and a controlled-access entry system may already be in place. Urban high-rise office buildings often include closed-circuit television (CCTV) monitoring of loading docks and all means of ingress and egress as well as lobbies and public corridors. This may also be desirable in multitenant buildings in suburban office parks. Off-hours janitorial work will require access to leased spaces by on-site management personnel or contract service providers, and the take-over inspection should address this issue as well. If keys are used on site, key control should be a take-over checklist item. Employment of security personnel, either directly or as a contracted service, is another related item to include in the checklist.

The initial inspection should also establish the location and condition of all utility meters (water, electricity, etc.) and incoming telephone and telecommunications lines (wiring, cable). There may also be satellite dish installations that should be inspected. Heavy-duty wiring is typically installed during construction of new office buildings. For an older building, however, the condition of the existing wiring should be evaluated to determine whether it is adequate to accommodate computers, complex phone systems, and other high-tech equipment currently in use or likely to be installed for future tenants. It may be desirable or appropriate to recommend upgrading the wiring as a way to make an older building more competitive.

All of the mechanical systems and equipment in the building (HVAC, elevators, etc.) should be individual checklist items. Such equipment requires regularly scheduled preventive maintenance, and the way this is being handled should be recorded as part of the initial inspection. New equipment is warranted against defects for a limited period, and warranty statements and maintenance instructions are provided by the manufacturer or installer. These items should be requested as part of the take-over and, if they are not available on the property, the manufacturers or installers should be contacted to obtain copies for the files. Manufacturers' recommendations are useful guidelines for establishing maintenance schedules.

A particular point to cover in the inspection is the issue of indoor air quality (IAQ). In an office building whose windows are sealed, the HVAC system may retain moisture that can grow toxic molds or a fouled water-cooling tower may be growing *Legionnella* species bacteria (the cause of Legionnaires' disease). While IAQ is not currently regulated by the federal government, the American Society of Heating, Refrigerating, and Air-Conditioning Engineers (ASHRAE) has established IAQ standards, and their guidelines may be helpful in determining whether there are problems and how to address them.

While compliance with building codes, zoning restrictions, environmental regulations, and other governmental requirements (e.g., operating permits) is incumbent on the owner and the individual tenants, the office building manager will likely be the first person to know of any actual or potential noncompliance. The results of the take-over inspection may commend consultation with professional architects, environmental specialists, or engineers to determine the level of compliance and what is needed to overcome noncompliance.

Environmental compliance issues for a take-over checklist would be specific to the building's tenancy. Hazardous materials (e.g., organic solvents) may be used in maintenance and cleaning tasks. Health care professionals can generate biological and toxic wastes (bloodborne pathogens, dental amalgams). Food wastes support a variety of pests (insects, rodents) that can pose health problems. Inspection should reveal how various types of wastes are being disposed and whether the procedures comply with environmental requirements and existing building policies. If there are problems, new management's operations manual should address this issue specifically by developing policies and procedures and sharing the information with all affected parties.

Compliance with accessibility requirements under the Americans with Disabilities Act (ADA) of 1990 is yet another take-over issue. The initial inspection should address specific requirements for the public accommodation areas of the building and whether and how well they have been met to date. This will facilitate development of a plan for making additional changes as necessary or appropriate to ensure full compliance with this important law.

Finally, the inspection should document fixtures and equipment that may be inefficient or costly to operate in their current configurations. This information can be used to develop recommendations for changes to improve efficiency and cost-effectiveness. Energy conservation is increasingly important for office building operations, especially as tenants continue to expand their use of electrical and electronic equipment.

Leases. Because leases define the types and amounts of income ownership will derive from the office building, the new manager should obtain signed leases for all established tenancies during take-over. These should be reviewed to find out who the tenants are, the terms and conditions of their individual leases, and their performance of lease obligations. If there are no *lease abstracts,* it may be necessary or appropriate to prepare these as part of the take-over process to ensure that information about escalations, lease expirations, and other financial terms is immediately available. (Preparation of new lease abstracts may be desirable, regardless, since it allows the manager to confirm the accuracy of the information and become familiar with the particulars of the leases at the property.)

Rents for office space are typically based on a specific measure of the square footage in the tenant's leased space, and that *base rent* may be adjusted to accommodate economic concessions granted to the tenant or to pay back funds the landlord advanced for finishing the tenant's premises (i.e., a tenant improvement allowance). Alternatively, a tenant improvement allowance may be structured as a loan and paid back as a separate reimbursement item. Real estate taxes, insurance premiums, and the expense of maintaining the building and the common areas are typically passed through to the tenants on a pro rata basis in some type of "net" lease. Definitions of "net" leases differ among geographic areas, single-net often meaning taxes only are passed through, double-net being taxes and insurance, and triple-net including taxes, insurance, and common area maintenance. It is important to know exactly what expenses are being passed through to the tenants and how they are prorated. It is also important to find out if there are provisions for limiting the amount passed through to certain tenants (stated as caps or ceilings) and whether and how operating cost increases are passed along.

Leases for office space are usually negotiated for long terms—three, five, or ten or more years. Such leases typically include provisions for increasing the base rent on a specific schedule, either by applying a percentage escalator or by using a standard index of inflation such as the Consumer Price Index (CPI) reported monthly by the U.S. government. Note, however, that downward pressure on the CPI in the 1990s has reduced its use as a standard escalator in new leases. Rent escalation rates and schedules are negotiated with each tenant, so it is rare to find identical escalation provisions in more than one tenant's lease.

Long lease terms allow for continuity of office tenancies and provide economic stability for both tenants and landlords while escalation provisions ensure that the owner receives a specific return on investment (ROI). On the other hand, long lease terms can make it difficult to remove a tenant if that is desirable, and leases written to include renewal options increase that difficulty. In taking over management of an office building, it is important to know and understand all the variant terms in the individual leases and their impact on the property's income and value. If scheduled rent escalations do not keep pace with market rates, the landlord's income may not grow sufficiently to enhance the property's value. (Space measurement is addressed in Chapter 7. Lease terms are described in detail in Chapter 8.)

Tenants. Information about the existing tenants is critical to planning for current and future operations at the property. Leases are the primary sources of certain types of information about tenants. Among them are business names and individual contacts, identification of the specific spaces they occupy, their lease terms (durations), base rents, provisions for rent escalations, and any requirements for security deposits or other financial guarantees that may be required (e.g., a line of credit) and the amounts set for them. These types of tenant information are used to generate reports to ownership covering occupancy and vacancies (rent roll), rents and other payments collected (collections summary), late payment of rents (delinquency report), and disposition of security deposits. The take-over checklist should anticipate development of the reports typically submitted to ownership each month so that the required tenant information can be collected up front.

Office leases may allocate specific responsibilities to tenant and landlord in regard to maintenance. Typically it is the landlord's responsibility to perform the maintenance and the tenant's responsibility to pay for it. In a small office building with only one or a few tenants, it will likely be the tenant's responsibility to perform the maintenance as well as pay for it. The landlord's and the tenant's separate responsibilities must be determined during take-over because the manager will be acting for the landlord and monitoring the tenant's performance of the lease.

Leases for office space typically require tenants to carry insurance coverages appropriate for their business operations and to identify the property ownership and management as additional named insured parties in their policies. Tenants should also be required to provide proof in the form of certificates of insurance to be submitted to management. In addition to adequate property damage and liability coverage, tenants' businesses should be insured against loss of income so they will be able to meet their financial obligations, including those required under the lease. In some situations, the lease for a particular business operation may require additional, special types of insurance. Businesses often own sophisticated equipment, particularly computers and photocopying machines, and such costly equipment should be properly insured. Retail tenants may be required to carry theft insurance and plate glass coverage. The lease should be clear on what is required of each tenant, and the take-over checklist should require the manager to validate appropriate insurance coverages. The change in management will require revision of tenants' certificates of insurance, and this requirement should be emphasized when the tenants are notified of the transition. Note, too, that periodic renewal of tenants' insurance policies will require submission of new certificates of insurance to management, which will be an item to monitor long term.

Site Employees. Management take-over may mean assuming responsibility for on-site personnel who are employed by the building owner. For a new building, the manager may have to determine the amount and types of work to be done, develop job descriptions for positions to be filled, and actually hire the personnel. Even at an established property, actual personnel needs should be evaluated to determine whether it is more efficient to employ on-site staff or contract for specific services.

New management should request and review the employment records for all on-site staff members, including job applications, employment references and screening results, hire dates, work assignments, and documentation of performance reviews, wage rates, and the like. The manager may have to check with several sources if prior management has not maintained separate files on individual employees.

The take-over checklist should request information about workers' compensation insurance (carrier, scope of coverage, and claims data). It is important to determine whether the current coverage is up-to-date and whether any changes are required. If the owner is the employer, documentation of employee benefits and accrual of annual vacations and sick leave should be available from the prior management company. However, if new management is assuming responsibility for the existing staff, the manager will have to create new employment records and obtain documentation from prior management that accrued benefits have been paid to the employees.

Yet another consideration is compliance with equal employment opportunity (EEO) laws. These include state and local laws in addition to federal civil rights legislation. New management should find out what practices have been followed at the property and determine the need to make specific changes in procedures related to hiring, performance evaluation, and termination of employees. Sexual harassment and ADA employment requirements are related issues that should be reviewed, not only for compliance with the laws, but to determine whether there are outstanding claims or lawsuits. These latter should be the responsibility of ownership and prior management but may have implications for how new management handles personnel issues.

Emergency Contacts. A list of emergency contacts should be compiled. In addition to the name of each tenant, information should be collected about who owns the business, who is managing it (if not the owner), and the headquarters location and key contacts there (if the tenant is a franchisee or a subsidiary). Tenants should also be asked to provide a list of their key employees (names, addresses, telephone numbers where they can be reached outside of the office in an emergency).

An emergency contacts list should include names, titles, home telephone numbers, and emergency phone numbers (if different—i.e., a cellular phone) for all site employees. Telephone numbers for outside emergency services (local fire and police departments, hospital or clinic, etc.) should be compiled, copied, and distributed to both staff and tenants. To expedite handling of emergency situations on site, telephone numbers for insurance carriers and agents as well as tradespeople and service vendors (e.g., plumbers, electricians, fire restoration contractors, board-up services) should also be compiled. This information should be kept in the management office on site and at the management firm's main office.

Risk Management Assessment. New management needs to know the kinds and amounts of insurance coverage in place for the property as a whole and whether any other approaches to risk management have been taken. (See Chapter 12 for a detailed discussion of specific risks and their management.) Office building owners usually carry two types of insurance coverages—casualty and liability. *Casualty insurance* offsets losses due to damage to the property itself. While fire insurance is basic to this coverage, other specific coverages are normally carried as well. Specific policies and dollar values are based on the types of risks. *Liability insurance* protects the property and its ownership from financial losses arising out of injuries to other people (e.g., visitors) and damage to other people's property. The types and amounts of coverages vary with the type of property. The insurance needs of a downtown high-rise office building with lobby retail will differ from those of a suburban office park with multiple low-rise buildings and on-site parking.

The manager also needs to know the names of the company that issued the insurance and the agent or broker who wrote and services the policies along with their addresses and phone numbers and an emergency phone number for the carrier's authorized claims agent. The following should be noted for each policy:

The period of coverage,

Whether premium payments are up-to-date,

When the next premium is due, and

Whether the manager or the owner will make the payments.

Although the owner is typically responsible for insuring the property, the manager may be asked to recommend applicable coverages (prior consultation with a qualified insurance agent is recommended) and to hold the policies and pay the regular premiums from operating income. The manager may also be responsible for filing claims when losses occur.

The new management company and the manager assigned to the property should be identified as additional named insured parties on all property policies. This may be requested in the notice of new management sent to the insurance agent.

Marketing and Leasing Plan. While a certain level of vacancy should be anticipated, it is important to find out how long each space has been vacant and what has already been done to lease it. A high vacancy rate and problems inherent in the vacant spaces are likely to be among the early leasing challenges for a new manager and important components of the management plan for the property. (Chapter 5 briefly describes the use of a management plan, and Chapter 13 focuses on its preparation.)

The future is an important consideration in this regard. In a soft market, where an excess of vacant space can lure tenants away with rent concessions and other inducements, it is prudent to begin planning a tenant retention program immediately. This means all tenants, not just those whose leases are expiring soon. To be effective, tenant retention efforts should begin early in the landlord-tenant relationship, and they should be continuous, consistent, and sincere. While the management firm's leasing policies will apply to prospecting for, negotiating with, and moving in new tenants, the new manager should find out what policies and practices have been followed in the past and determine how they differ from those of the management firm. The goal should be to ascertain what has to be done to effect necessary changes with established tenants.

Acquiring new tenants requires the property to be marketed to appropriate groups of prospects. While a small established property may use the same basic classified ad to acquire new tenants periodically, large professionally managed office buildings require a comprehensive marketing program—including specific advertising—to maintain desirable levels of occupancy by appropriately qualified tenants. As part of take-over, the manager should obtain records of past promotional efforts (e.g., institutional and classified advertisements, brochures, and any marketing support materials such as photographs or drawings) along with records of their success. Marketing activities at office buildings typically include direct prospecting (i.e., cold-calling) and detailed and comprehensive qualification of a commercial prospects' ability to fulfill lease obligations. Ownership's goals for the investment may necessitate establishing additional criteria to qualify prospects.

A marketing plan should be developed based on a thorough evaluation of the property and its features, its rental schedule, and the marketplace in which it competes. (Development of a marketing plan is described in Chapter 7.) This should include a comparison grid analysis that identifies comparable properties in the area that have similar tenancies and are of the same size and scale. Most important are the features of the property, its location, and variances among rental rates and other negotiable items. Such data will help the manager determine what is unique or better at the property compared to its competition and should therefore be promoted specifically. For example, low-cost or free parking is a particularly attractive feature at an office building and one to be promoted as an advantage for the subject property. The comparison should also identify any obstacles to the leasing process, indicate whether rents at the property are at or near market levels, and suggest ways to add value for tenants allowing for increased rents. Features of the property or of the vacant space may suggest qualities to be sought among prospective tenants (the target market). For example, if vacant space was previously used by medical professionals or a food service, it is often practical to seek the same type of use for the space. This will not only preserve the existing tenant mix but may also save on costly tenant improvements. Demographic data about the population immediately surrounding the property (its neighborhood) and the larger area of which it is a part (the region) may be needed to demonstrate that there is an adequate pool of potential employees for prospective tenants. It is also imperative to know whether appropriate prospects are available in the market area or if leasing activities will have to be extended beyond the neighborhood and the region. (A more detailed discussion of marketing and leasing strategies is provided in Chapter 8.)

Accounting Records. Assumption of new management requires specific information regarding income and expenses and how these have been accounted. Income at office buildings typically includes operating expense pass-throughs in addition to base rents, and tenants may be required to reimburse the owner for tenant improvement construction costs. Parking and storage fees may be additional sources of property income. Office rents and other scheduled revenues are the primary source of income for operating the property. The manager should find out the current rental rates building tenants are paying, how they vary for different sized spaces and different locations in the building, and how they were established.

Operating expenses include payroll, building maintenance, common area utilities, marketing and tenant retention programs, real estate taxes, and insurance premiums. For an established property, it should be possible to obtain records of expenses for at least the past year (preferably longer) in the form of paid bills and invoices, and there should be ledgers accounting for current receipts and expenditures. It is particularly important to know how specific expense items have been accounted historically (e.g., whether snow removal has been included in the overall maintenance expense or listed separately). Such records are helpful in setting up new records as well as preparing an operating budget. While there may be an established chart of accounts for the property, the manager may be required to use the management firm's chart of accounts to ensure timely payments and proper categorization of income and expenses.

The operating budget should match the items in the chart of accounts. It is also the predictor of cash flow from which debt service on outstanding loans will be paid. Whether debt service will be a management responsibility or is paid directly by the owner, the manager needs to know the terms and payment requirements of all mortgages and other instruments.

Because the value of a rental property is often founded primarily on its income-generating capacity, management's goals in operating the property will usually include efforts to maximize income (or at least optimize it) and minimize or strictly control expenses. While the objectives of ownership for the property may encompass more than income generation, income will be a primary goal. If the owner has been planning a renovation, and the prior management had been accumulating reserve funds for this work, the new manager should determine the status of those plans and arrange for transfer of funds that were already set aside.

Other important checklist items are payroll data (e.g., federal, state, and local income tax deductions; payroll deductions for savings or contributions

Frequently Contracted Services

- HVAC inspection, maintenance, and repairs
- Roof inspection, maintenance, and repairs
- Elevator (escalator) inspection, maintenance, and repairs
- Janitorial services (may be for specific items on a fixed schedule)
- Specialized cleaning of interior and exterior finishing materials (wood, marble, brass or other metal)
- Window washing
- Waste disposal (trash removal and recycling may be separate arrangements)
- Security (electronic surveillance, personnel, or a combination)
- Payroll processing (for a sizeable staff)
- Legal services
- Fire and life safety system inspection, maintenance, and monitoring

At a suburban office park, landscaping or groundskeeping (lawn care, tree trimming) and parking lot maintenance (sweeping on a regular schedule plus occasional restriping and repairs) are likely to be contracted services. For small properties, plumbing, electrical, and other skilled trades are often contracted. Pest control and snow removal services may depend on location and climate.

to benefits costs) and employee benefits (what has been provided to individuals; what individuals contribute toward them) because they affect the property's financial picture. It is also important to know the status of any withholding taxes. The manager should find out whether reports have been filed and when payments are to be made and arrange to transfer any accumulated withholding funds to new management's accounts.

Contracted services are yet another economic item to be accounted. Office buildings often contract for inspection and preventive maintenance services that can only be provided by people who are licensed to do the type of work (e.g., pest control) or when the work requires specialized skills or equipment (e.g., elevator maintenance). The actual services will depend on geography and climate as well as the size of the property and the installed equipment (frequently contracted services are listed in the accompanying box). Contracts define specific expenses of operating the property, often identifying large, fixed amounts that are paid on a regular schedule. Therefore it is important for new management to know the types of services contracted, who provides them on what schedule, and the particulars of the financial arrangements (rates or fees, billing and payment schedules) and other terms of the contract (duration of the agreement, provision for renewal or cancellation). It is also important to note any automatic rate increases and whether higher rates or differential fees apply when services provided exceed what is specified in the contract. At the same time, new management may want to evaluate whether specific contracts should be continued for the present time or renewed when they expire. As a protection for the property and its ownership, contractors should be required to provide insurance certificates as proof they have adequate and appropriate insurance coverage for the work they do, including workers' compensation insurance for their employees. A request for such proofs may be incorporated in the notices sent to contractors.

Previous management records of monthly reports to ownership and their various attachments should be obtained from the prior management and analyzed. Other financial records include a current balance sheet, the current and prior year's operating budgets, last year's operating expense reconciliations for pass-throughs, and prior records of common area costs and how they are being prorated and passed through to tenants.

The new manager should also set up a *tickler system* that provides a reminder of contract renewals, insurance reviews and premium payments, renewals of permits and licenses, rent increases, changes to pass-through billings, and lease renewals as well as follow-up of prospective tenants. Today, most tickler files are created in a computer software program that will not only send e-mail reminder messages but also allow management to generate any notices that have to be sent to other parties. (Tickler files are discussed in Chapter 10 as a component of lease administration.)

Fiscal Responsibilities

Since real estate owners' goals are primarily or predominantly financial, the office building manager's responsibilities include attention to a variety of fiscal matters. First and foremost will be accounting for the property's income and expenses and reporting the financial picture to the owner each month. Budgeting and record keeping are other key activities. Although there are mechanical systems of record keeping, and an owner-manager might be able to account for the financial activity of a small property adequately using a manual system, it is assumed that most real estate managers will use a computer and appropriate software to maintain the accounts and records for an office building.

Trust Accounting. Because the management agreement creates a fiduciary relationship between the owner and the managing agent, one of the office building manager's responsibilities is to protect the owner's funds. This is done by setting up a separate bank account called a *trust account* to ensure that there is no *commingling* of the owner's funds with those of the management firm. (Commingling of owner's and agent's funds is unethical and illegal.) It may also be necessary to establish a separate bank account for tenants' security deposits, especially if security deposits are required by law to be held in *escrow*. (These issues are regulated by local governments.)

In some situations, the management firm may establish a single trust account, maintaining the separation of individual property owners' funds solely through accounting and bookkeeping procedures. If this practice is followed, care must be taken to avoid using one owner's funds to pay expenses for another owner's property. This can be accomplished by maintaining a journal or log record of all receipts and payments for each owner's account. By monitoring this record carefully, the manager can prevent the issuing of payments that would exceed the account balance. If the records indicate a potential shortfall, the owner should be notified immediately and asked to provide additional funds so that property operating expenses (or debt service or other extraordinary expenses) can be paid in a timely manner. This is part of the owner's obligation under the management agreement to maintain a contingency reserve in the property account.

Strict policies and procedures regarding the handling of funds and use of computer accounting programs are specific safeguards that can be employed to avoid commingling. Obtaining *fidelity bonds* on all employees that handle management clients' funds is also recommended and is usually a specific requirement under the management agreement.

Accounting Methods. Accounting is the systematic classifying and recording of financial information and transactions. There are two basic methods of accounting. *Cash-basis accounting* records income and expenses only when monies have been received or paid. *Accrual-basis accounting* recognizes income when it is earned and expenses when they are incurred regardless of when the money is actually received or paid. The accounting system established for a property should conform to one of these two methods. A modified cash system is sometimes used when recurring items of expense are not paid every month. Real estate taxes and insurance premiums are examples of expenses that would be accounted on an accrual basis within a cash-basis system. Today, however, most property accounting is done on an accrual basis, which provides a more accurate financial picture at any given time.

Accounting records are used for different purposes. The owner and the manager need certain types of information about the property and its tenancy for purposes of planning, decision making, and control. They are interested in details of transactions and analysis of specific aspects. Reports are prepared monthly or more often if necessary. The gathering of information and preparation of reports for such internal use is called *managerial accounting*. (The monthly *income statement* sent to the property owner is one of many managerial reports.) Accounting records are also used to prepare reports for other entities who are more interested in the overall financial picture. Reports sent to lenders, shareholders in corporations, and investors in REITs are standardized in format and conservative in their projections. They are usually prepared annually at the end of the calendar or fiscal year. Preparation of reports for external use is called *financial accounting.* (A year-end *balance sheet* is an example.) The office building manager may contribute information for such external reporting and should be familiar with the types of reports and their contents. However, the manager will be more intimately involved with the day-to-day records of property activities and the data that are compiled and reported to the owner each month.

Income Statement. The primary report to the owner each month is an income statement that shows rental income and other receipts and an itemized listing of major operating expense categories. Expenses are totaled and deducted from the total receipts to show net operating income (NOI), and debt service is deducted from NOI to yield cash flow. The income and expense categories usually follow the listing in the budget to facilitate comparison of line items over time. A more complete picture may be presented by including a comparison of actual amounts to budget projections for the month and for the year to date, with variances from budget shown as both dollars and percentages. This latter type of report is more correctly called a *statement of operations.*

An income statement is also prepared for external use. This statement usually covers a period of one year and is presented in a slightly different format. In particular, it includes information related to tax liability, which is a major issue in external reporting. Revenue categories reflect the various income sources and expenses are simplified. Operating expenses are presented as a total along with depreciation (the non-cash tax deduction for investment cost recovery) and interest paid on loans. (The monthly income statement prepared for ownership includes both interest and principal in the debt service payment deducted from NOI.) Total expenses are subtracted from total revenue to yield income before taxes. The owner's income tax obligation is computed and deducted to yield after-tax net income or loss.

Balance Sheet. Another report typically prepared at the end of the fiscal year is a balance sheet that shows the overall financial viability of the property at a specific point in time. This lists the property's assets and liabilities and balances one against the other. *Assets* are economic resources. Current assets include cash on hand (operating funds), accounts receivable, money in escrow, and capital reserves. Long-term assets are the value of the land and buildings (less depreciation on the latter). *Liabilities* are monies that can be claimed by creditors. Current liabilities include security deposits that have to be returned, accounts payable, and taxes owed, while long-term liabilities would be the outstanding mortgage amount. The difference between total assets and total liabilities is the owner's *equity.* (The balance sheet shows the same dollar amount for "total assets" and "total liabilities and equity.")

Information on a balance sheet can be used to measure a property's financial health. For example, the difference between current assets and current liabilities is the amount of *working capital* available. Current assets divided by current liabilities gives the *current ratio,* which is a measure of liquidity. A ratio greater than one (i.e., when assets exceed liabilities) indicates the property is able to pay debt and other obligations within the course of the year without infusion of additional cash by the owner. A ratio less than one is a warning sign that the amount of working capital may be inadequate. The owner's equity is also the *net worth* of the property. If the current-debt-to-equity ratio (current liabilities divided by owner's equity) is greater than one, the amount of debt may be high compared to the property's net worth. The total-debt-to-equity ratio (total liabilities divided by owner's equity) is a measure of the ability to pay long- and short-term obligations from property-specific resources. (Exhibit 4.3 shows an example of how a balance sheet would be configured.)

Chart of Accounts. The key to classifying financial transactions is a comprehensive chart of accounts that identifies all the categories of income and expense at a property. In order to provide a complete picture of a property's finances, the chart of accounts will usually include additional categories to account for assets and liabilities. (Typical income and expense categories for an office building chart of accounts are listed in Exhibit 4.4.)

Usual practice is to assign a number to each category, and it is common to create subcategories within the major categories, depending on the level of detail needed for preparing reports. For example, payroll is often divided into wages and benefits, and separate subaccounts may be assigned for employee income taxes and other withholdings. Maintenance might have subcategories for individual building systems, or the systems themselves might be major categories with subcategories for maintenance, repairs, and contracts. The purpose of a chart of accounts is to facilitate analysis of financial data; it should differentiate key items that need to be monitored closely, but excessive categorization should be avoided. The chart of accounts for a three-story building that has two storefronts and half a dozen office suites upstairs will have fewer and simpler categories than that for a 30-story building with multiple amenities and more than 100 tenants in specially built out office suites.

Budgeting. A budget is a statement of the financial position of a property, covering a defined period of time and based on estimates of income and expenses for the period. Budgets are prepared to serve specific purposes.

A planning tool and guideline for operating a property

A measure of the property's financial health

A projection of future income and expenses as a decision-making tool

A measure of the achievement of ownership's financial goals

A measure of the manager's and the management firm's performance

Exhibit 4.3
Sample Balance Sheet Format

BALANCE SHEET			
ASSETS			
Current Assets			
Cash		______	
Accounts Receivable		______	
Tenant Deposits		______	
Tax Escrow		______	
Capital Reserves		______	
Total Current Assets			______
Long-Term Assets			
Land		______	
Buildings	______		
Less Depreciation	(______)		
Net Buildings		______	
Total Long-Term Assets			______
Total Assets			______
LIABILITIES			
Current Liabilities			
Tenant Deposits Payable		______	
Accounts Payable		______	
Tax Payable		______	
Total Current Liabilities			______
Long-Term Liabilities			
Mortgage Payable		______	
Total Long-Term Liabilities			______
Total Liabilities			______
Owner's Equity			______
Total Liabilities and Equity			______

BALANCE SHEET MEASURES
Current Assets − Current Liabilities = Working Capital
Total Assets − Total Liabilities = Owner's Equity (net worth)
Current Assets ÷ Current Liabilities = Current Ratio
Current Liabilities ÷ Owner's Equity (net worth) = Current-Debt-to-Equity Ratio
Total Liabilities ÷ Owner's Equity = Total-Debt-to-Equity Ratio

Exhibit 4.4
Typical Income and Expense Categories in an Office Building Chart of Accounts

Income Accounts
Rent
Operating Expense Pass-Throughs
Parking Fees
Other Income

Operating Expenses
Payroll
Management Fee
Maintenance and Repairs
Supplies
Electricity
Trash Removal
Water and Sewer
Legal and Accounting
Administration
Insurance
Real Estate Taxes

The use to which the information will be put determines the components of a particular type of budget.

Types of Budgets. Real estate managers prepare and use a variety of budgets. Perhaps the most comprehensive of these is the *annual operating budget*. An operating budget is prepared to forecast annual net operating income (NOI). It lists planned income and expense amounts for each month for each account plus a total for each line item at the right (Exhibit 4.5, page 62, is a representative example). Typically, the line items follow the income and expense categories of the chart of accounts. Fixed items of income and expense may be divided equally into twelve identical monthly amounts. However, items that vary from month to month or are received or paid once or twice during the year should be distributed appropriately. In other words, heating costs would be divided across the winter months (in most northern states, October through April); likewise, air-conditioning costs would be divided across the summer months (May through September). Insurance premiums that are paid twice a year would be entered in the months when payment would be made. This approach gives a more realistic picture of expected expenditures and helps control the amount of variance from month to month.

Exhibit 4.5

Sample Operating Budget Format

Account/Category	**Jan**	**Feb**	**Mar**	**Apr**	**May**	**Jun**	**Jul**	**Aug**	**Sep**	**Oct**	**Nov**	**Dec**	**Total**
Office Rent													
Operating Expense Pass-Throughs													
Other Scheduled Income													
GROSS POTENTIAL RENTAL INCOME													
less Vacancy and Rent Loss													
plus Miscellaneous Income													
EFFECTIVE GROSS INCOME													
Payroll													
Management Fee													
Maintenance and Repairs													
Supplies													
Electricity													
Trash Removal													
Water and Sewer													
Legal and Accounting													
Administration													
Insurance													
Real Estate Taxes													
TOTAL OPERATING EXPENSES													
NET OPERATING INCOME (NOI)													
less Debt Service													
CASH FLOW													

Gross potential rental income is the income the property would generate if it were 100-percent occupied and all rents were paid in full and on time. The annual operating budget should include in this figure the amounts of scheduled rent escalations per tenants' leases. Pass-through expense increases should also be accounted. If there are any other scheduled sources of income, such as parking fees or base rents for retail space, these should be included as line items of income.

Vacancy and rent loss is a deduction to account for rental income that is not collected, either because there is no tenant in a particular space or because a tenant did not pay rent as scheduled. Another adjustment adds in *miscellaneous or unscheduled income* from sources that generate varying amounts of income. Revenues from vending machines in the building and retail percentage rents are examples. If parking is not a regular source of revenue—e.g., the parking facility is open to the public but tenants' employees use most of the available space and pay no fees—it may be more appropriate to consider parking fees as unscheduled income. The adjustments for vacancy and rent loss and miscellaneous income yield *effective gross income,* the actual amount collected.

Operating expenses are itemized according to the chart of accounts. The annual operating budget may show only major expense categories (e.g., utilities, maintenance, payroll) or the components of the categories may be identified individually. For example, payroll wages may be differentiated from employee benefits costs; maintenance may be separately listed as common area maintenance, HVAC maintenance, etc. The number of expense line items depends on the level of detail needed for this annual planning exercise. The operating expense amounts are added together and the total is deducted from effective gross income to yield *net operating income (NOI).*

While the budget can conclude with NOI, the manager is often responsible for making *debt service* payments. The payment amount includes interest on the loan or loans and a portion of the principal. Money may also be set aside from NOI to provide for future *capital expenditures.* Deducting these items from NOI yields the owner's pre-tax *cash flow.* The owner is responsible to pay income taxes on the proceeds received from the investment. The owner's profit—return on investment (ROI)—from the property is what remains after income taxes have been paid (i.e., after-tax cash flow).

An operating budget for an office building is a plan, an estimate of how much income the property can be expected to generate on a regular schedule and a projection of what it will cost to operate and maintain the building during that period. In preparing the annual budget, it is wise to anticipate some inflation. This will help minimize unfavorable variances. It is also a good idea to check with utilities and other suppliers to find out if they expect changes in their costs and rates. Utility rates (electricity, natural gas) may vary seasonally unless a contract for a set rate has been established previously.

Types of Budgets

- Annual operating budget
- Capital budget
- Long-range budget
- Pro forma budget
- Lease-up budget

Another important strategy is to use round numbers in budgeting. If a single item is expected to cost $1,239, it is wiser to budget for $1,300. If it is known that a service contract will be up for renewal at a five-percent higher rate in May, the budget should show the old rate for January through April and the new rate for the remainder of the year. Rent escalations should be handled similarly on the income side. If debt service includes a variable- or adjustable-rate loan, this should be monitored so the timing and amount of change can be reflected in the budget.

In addition to the annual budget, the manager may be asked to prepare quarterly updates, especially during periods of high inflation or when a soft market is affecting occupancy levels and rent collections. This is a good business practice regardless because it can help the manager and the owner plan for needed adjustments. The owner may have to provide some cash out-of-pocket in order to pay operating expenses on time, or it may be desirable or necessary to postpone a planned purchase or find other ways to control costs.

The real estate manager may also prepare a *capital budget,* which shows the amount to be set aside each month to build a capital reserve for major work that is expected to be done at a future date (e.g., roof replacement). Reserve funds are usually deposited in an interest-bearing account, and deposit amounts are calculated to account for the effects of inflation (increased costs of materials and labor when the work is actually done). Funds are transferred from the reserve account to the operating account when specific capital expenses are to be paid. Development of a reserve fund is more likely for a property whose owner expects the rental income to cover all expenditures related to the property. Managers who work for institutional investors do not often accumulate reserve funds because the owners have access to other capital sources and can usually fund major expenditures directly. Instead, they use capital budgets to anticipate expenditures for specific capital projects, tenant improvements, and leasing commissions.

Real estate managers also prepare and use *long-range budgets* to forecast income and expenses for more than one year into the future. Typically, such projections are made for a period of five or more years to facilitate making decisions related to the owner's investment goals.

Whether to renovate or rehabilitate the property (feasibility, timing)

Whether and when to increase rents (new leases, lease renewals)

Whether and when to refinance

Whether and when to sell the property

A long-range budget may be used to show the owner what to expect over the holding period of the investment. It can project the financial gain or loss from a change in market conditions or anticipate rent increases after a renovation. The goal is to determine whether property income will be sufficient to cover the costs of day-to-day operations or if additional cash infusions will be necessary.

Yet another tool for planning future projects is a *pro forma budget.* This type of budget is used to evaluate the feasibility of a project to be undertaken (major rehabilitation, new development) and make sound business decisions about it. Pro forma budget projections estimate the costs of undertaking such a project and the revenue that is likely to be generated from it. They may compare different scenarios. For a new development, different floor sizes might be compared; for a rehabilitation, different time periods for achieving maximum occupancy might be examined. The impact of including or omitting certain amenities might be explored, as might different financing strategies and costs.

At a newly constructed building or following a major rehabilitation, a *lease-up budget* is used to estimate income and expenses for the first year of operation or longer, depending on how long it takes to stabilize occupancy. This type of budget is designed to reflect the changes that occur month to month as space is leased and occupied and is likely to be adjusted frequently as leasing and occupancy goals are or are not met. It also includes special costs for marketing and advertising that are usually at higher levels during this period of initial lease-up.

Budgeting Methods. During take-over, the new manager should have acquired copies of the various income and expense records for the property for the most recent twelve-month period if not longer. Such documents provide a *historical basis* for projecting income and expenses when creating the annual operating budget in particular. Review of the prior year's actual costs for goods and services will provide a starting point for projecting dollar amounts for these line items for next year. Past experience can be a fairly good predictor of the future.

It is important to keep in mind, however, that other factors must also be considered. Inflation is a constant factor that increases the costs of both goods and services. In fact, it is axiomatic that expenses will increase. While some costs may go down, this is a rare occurrence. Just as office leases are written with periodic rent escalations, a multi-year contract for maintenance

Typical Components of a Monthly Management Report

- Income statement
- Rent roll
- Collections summary
- Delinquency report
- Budget variances
- General ledger
- Cash journal
- Check register
- Capital expenditures report
- Bank statements
- Bank account reconciliation
- Narrative summary

The narrative summary usually is presented first in the report, with the various statistical reports following it as backup. While vacancies may be noted in the rent roll, excessive vacancies may warrant a separate vacancy report. A report of leasing activity and a related marketing budget may also be components of the monthly report, especially during periods of high vacancy or during lease-up of a new building. While a balance sheet may be submitted monthly, it is more likely to be prepared annually at the conclusion of the fiscal year.

services may have built-in fee increases that should be accounted in the budget. Real property is reassessed periodically, and a reassessment can mean substantially increased real estate taxes. Utilities often announce rate increases several months before they take effect, and the new rates may not be reflected in the available records. The National Weather Service may be predicting extremes of temperature or precipitation or both that could signal higher costs for heating or air-conditioning or both for the next year. On the other hand, last year's weather may have been anomalous, and cost adjustments can be made in the other direction.

Real estate markets change and historical data can be incomplete or inaccurate. Historical property data might be suspect if they show extreme variances from period to period. There may be no historical information. This is definitely the case with a new property and sometimes happens when a new management account is taken over. To overcome these types of problems, real estate managers will prepare a *zero-based budget.* This approach is also used as a check to ensure that projections based on historical data are not out of line.

Zero-based budgeting forces the manager to take a hard look at the property and its operations and consider alternative approaches to managing the property and achieving the owner's goals. Each expense item is examined carefully, and no assumptions are made. In order to come up with realistic numbers, the manager may contact various vendors to obtain prices for supplies and parts. It may be necessary or appropriate to rebid service contracts. Checking with utility companies, the local tax assessor, and the property owner's insurance agent will yield current pricing information and avoid guesswork. The goal is to create a realistic budget without relying on past budget figures to make projections for the future.

Reporting. The manager is required to report the property's financial status to the owner on a regular schedule, usually at monthly intervals. The timing of such reports will have been negotiated as part of the management agreement. Often reports are submitted late in the calendar month after all expected revenues have been collected and expenses, including payroll, have been paid.

As stated earlier in this chapter, the primary report to the owner will be an *income statement* showing specific items of income and expense consistent with the chart of accounts. While this may conclude with NOI, it is also accepted practice to show the deduction for debt service to yield pre-tax cash flow. When that is the case, the report is often referred to as a *cash flow statement*.

The income statement is supported and accompanied by a number of statistical reports that give a more complete picture of the month's activities. Typical accompaniments include the following:

- *Rent roll*—This is a list of occupied and vacant office spaces that identifies tenants, the spaces they occupy, their monthly rents and other payments due, and other financial terms of their leases including the lease term and expiration date (Exhibit 4.6, page 68). Vacancies are also typically listed in the rent roll. However, excessive vacancy may warrant submission of a separate *vacancy report* showing the duration of each vacancy and what is being done to lease the space.

- *Collections summary*—This is a report of monies collected from each tenant. It will list the tenant's name and suite number, the rent due, and specific amounts received in payment of rent, pass-through charges, and other items. Information about lease expirations and deposits being held may also be included (see the example in Exhibit 5.1 in the next chapter).

- *Delinquency report*—On-time payment of rent is imperative to maintain cash flow at the property. Tenants whose rents are not paid on time should be identified along with the amount owed and any period of extended delinquency. Often there are columns to indicate the type of action being taken to ensure collection and whether eviction for nonpayment of rent is being pursued. In an office building, the delinquency report would also show operating expense pass-

Exhibit 4.6

Sample Rent Roll Form

Rent Roll

Building ______________ Owner ______________ Report Date: From ________ To ________

Suite No.	Tenant	Lease Term		Sq Ft Occupied	Rent $/sq ft (yr)	Base Rent		Base Rent Increase		Pass-Throughs		Gross Rent	
		From	To			Monthly	Annual	Date	Amount	Monthly	Sq Ft / Yr	Sq Ft / Yr	Mo. Total

In most applications, there would be multiple entries for scheduled rent increases. It might also be appropriate to differentiate specific pass-through expenses.

throughs and tenant improvement allowance reimbursements that are delinquent. Tenants' leases should identify these items as *additional rent* so that they would be included in the total amount of rent due in any eviction proceedings.

- *Budget variances*—Variances from the budget are typically reported for the current month and for the year-to-date. These reports show both the dollar amount of variance and the percentage, often also indicating whether the variance is favorable (F) or unfavorable (U) with regard to the particular expense or income item. (Budgeted amounts for the current full year and budgeted and actual figures for the prior full year may also be included for comparison.) Some nominal amount of variance is expected from one month to the next because billings and payments may not match budget projections exactly. The manager is usually required to explain variances that exceed a certain percentage. While this information may be incorporated in the variance report, it is more typically addressed in the narrative that summarizes all the activities being reported. (As noted earlier in this chapter, budget variances may be incorporated into the income statement, in which case the report would be called a statement of operations. This strategy yields fewer actual reports for the owner to review and compare.)
- *General ledger*—All receipts and payments should be recorded in a general ledger that shows the current status of the owner's account.
- *Cash journal*—This is a combined accounting record that shows both receipts and disbursements and the separate line item accounts to which they relate. It is also accepted practice to record income received in a separate *cash receipts journal* and payments made in a *cash disbursements journal*. Apart from the management firm's standardized procedures, the owner's requirements and the complexity of the property's finances may dictate the type of journal record that will be maintained.
- *Check register*—All payments drawn against the property operating account should be recorded in a check register showing the date of payment, the check number, to whom payment was made, and the goods or services provided. Deposits to the operating account (rents and other income) should be recorded here as well. Computer software facilitates maintaining this type of record and calculates the new balance as items are added and subtracted.
- *Capital expenditures report*—Capital expenditures are usually budgeted separately in a capital budget, and money may have been paid into an interest-bearing *reserve account* over an extended period to

ensure that there are adequate funds to take care of a planned renovation, a roof replacement, or other major work. Funds are transferred as necessary from the reserve account to the operating account to make specific payments.

- *Bank statements*—When separate bank accounts are maintained for a property, the bank will issue a monthly activity statement showing deposits and payouts. Some banks provide a consolidated account statement when customers have more than one type of account. In such cases, information for interest-bearing accounts would include interest earned.
- *Bank account reconciliation*—The bank statement should be reconciled with the check register, and any outstanding deposits or payments not reported on the bank statement should be accounted so the two will balance.
- *Balance sheet*—This type of report gives the owner a snapshot overview of the property's financial viability, showing the value of the property and assets related to it balanced against liabilities and the owner's equity. A healthy balance sheet will show assets in excess of liabilities, and the owner's equity should increase from one period to the next.

The income statement and its various supporting reports should be accompanied by a *narrative summary* that highlights management's accomplishments, points out achievement of ownership's goals, outlines specific actions being taken in regard to things like construction and delinquent rent, and explains the variances from budget. The narrative summary is usually presented at the *beginning* of the monthly report, with the income statement and its accompaniments bound together with it.

As for the balance sheet, minimally this will be prepared on an annual basis at the close of the fiscal or calendar year, but the owner may ask to have this information more frequently (quarterly or even monthly) if there are concerns about working capital or if ownership is considering refinancing. Balance sheets prepared for owners would follow a similar pattern to those used for external reporting (see the earlier discussion in this chapter and Exhibit 4.3). However, an owner's balance sheet is likely to include more details. For example, accounts receivable may differentiate pass-throughs, tenant improvement allowance reimbursements, and fees for telecommunications access from base rents while accounts payable might differentiate insurance and real estate taxes from other operating expenses. If there are multiple bank accounts, the balances might be listed as separate assets, and loans other than a building mortgage (e.g., separate financing for capital expenditures such as a roof repair or purchase of a computer system) would be separate liabilities. Likewise, added building improvements and operating equipment that is depreciated separately for income tax purposes (cost recovery periods vary substantially) might be shown as separate depreciation items under assets. The owner's equity would reflect the principal amounts paid down to date on all outstanding loans.

A report of leasing activity may be an appropriate adjunct to the monthly management report. This may be prepared by the leasing agent if leasing is contracted separately. The *leasing report* should include agreed-to lease parameters (base rents, pass-throughs, tenant improvement allowances) to be offered to prospective tenants and the status of negotiations for specific spaces. Lease-up of a new or renovated building will definitely require a leasing report, and this may be prepared and submitted on a weekly basis until a predetermined level of occupancy has been achieved. There will also be a separate marketing and leasing budget that will be adjusted frequently during periods of heavy leasing activity. This budget would accompany the leasing report.

While the reports described here are typical, other separate statistical reports may be generated for a particular property. Financial and accounting information may have to be presented in a specific format that conforms to the owner's requirements, or new management may have to acquire and use the same software program as the owner. These types of requirements must be known when the management agreement is negotiated, and they should be anticipated as part of the take-over process.

In addition to the written reports sent each month, *the manager should speak with the owner from time to time, either in person or by telephone.* It is often easier to resolve questions about budget variances or concerns about the property's operations in a spoken exchange. It also helps both parties to understand each other's perspectives and develops a rapport that can facilitate future decision-making under more trying circumstances.

5

Management Planning and Standardization of Operations

Real estate managers work with two very different types of tools to ensure the efficient operation of investment real estate. One of these is a management plan. A management plan is generally intended as a guide for operating the property in the short term. It is also used to measure the performance of the property and the managing agent. The second tool is a set of standard operating procedures that define management tasks and the way they are to be performed. Operating procedures must be designed to work in concert with the management plan to accomplish the owner's goals for the property.

The Management Plan

A *management plan* allows the manager to anticipate problems and opportunities before they happen. In developing a management plan for a particular office building, the manager should:

- Detail the owner's goals for the property,
- Outline specific programs to achieve those goals, and
- Obtain the owner's approval for the plan.

The management plan is developed from an analysis of the property's current physical, fiscal, and operational conditions as well as its competitive position in the marketplace. The purpose of this analysis is to determine how the current conditions relate to the owner's goals. If the analysis reveals that these conditions are not suited to achieving the owner's goals, the result-

Typical Components of a Management Plan

- Regional analysis
- Neighborhood analysis
- Property analysis
- Market analysis
- Analysis of alternatives
- Conclusion and recommendations

ing management plan may recommend physical, financial, or operational changes—or all three—using specific data to support those recommendations. (The management plan is discussed in detail in Chapter 13.)

A comprehensive management plan is usually included in a proposal that seeks to acquire the owner's property as a management account. Once the management account is established, the manager will use that original plan or modify it so the property can be started on the path to achieving the owner's goals. Over the period that the property is under management by a particular agent, there may be several management plans prepared for it. As the original goals are accomplished, the owner may decide to pursue a different course of action regarding the property, necessitating development of a definitive management plan for its accomplishment. A change in market conditions—a sudden excess or shortage of leasable space—is another reason to develop a management plan. Sometimes an owner may have several ideas in mind for a property, and the feasibility or practicality of those ideas may be evaluated using the management planning process.

The real estate manager uses the management plan to determine whether and to what extent the owner's goals are being accomplished. The plan serves as a yardstick for measuring success or identifying needed corrections to get back on track if there are problems. The property owner uses the plan to measure the performance of the management team. In particular, owners are concerned with the value added by the manager through tenant retention and preservation of the revenue stream.

The management plan should be reviewed on a regular basis and revised as necessary and appropriate. For an office building with stable occupancy, review at six-month intervals may suffice. In most circumstances, review every three months may be reasonable. However, if the building is operating on a tight budget or in a period of change, the management plan may be reviewed every two months or more often.

Standard Operating Procedures

Real estate management companies establish standard operating policies and procedures to be followed within their organizations. Having written

Uses of a Management Plan

For the Real Estate Manager
- Market management services to prospective clients
- Establish performance goals for a property
- Measure property performance against those goals
- Identify problems and opportunities before they occur

For the Property Owner
- Determine feasibility and practicality of ownership's goals for a property
- Outline management strategies to accomplish ownership's goals
- Measure performance of the managing agent

policies and procedures compiled in an *operations manual* ensures that the same information is communicated to all those who work for the company and that specific management tasks are performed the same way every time. It serves as a centralized, authoritative information source, communicating the firm's expectations, assigning priorities to management activities, and emphasizing areas of concern. It should also describe the organization of the firm and the interactions between its various departments. An operations manual is usually published in a looseleaf binder so that changes can be made without redoing the entire book, and copies should be distributed to all employees. However, it may be more efficient and cost-effective to distribute certain types of technical information on a need-to-know basis.

The manual should be updated as often as necessary to maintain consistent practices company-wide and ensure compliance with changing laws and regulations. Minimally, it should be company policy to review the manual periodically (every year or every two years), especially if there have been no reasons to make changes or corrections. This practice will keep everyone aware of the value of this important document.

Each managed office building should have its own operations manual. While many of the policies and procedures will be identical to or based on those in the management firm's operations manual, the manual for a property will also have to address its unique features. For example, the firm's operations manual may address maintenance work in general terms, stating who will perform it, the time frame in which it is to be done, and how the work is to be documented. The property manual, on the other hand, would include specific schedules for preventive maintenance of the various systems and equipment in the building. If property accounting and reporting is performed at the management firm's main office, on-site record-keeping policies and practices should be designed to collect needed information and transmit it to the main office in a way that will expedite the work to be done there.

Tips for Creating an Effective Operations Manual

- Be specific in drafting policies and procedures. This will avert problems being caused by uncertainties of interpretation.
- Use plain English and provide explanations when unfamiliar terms (legal or technical jargon) are used.
- Use active rather than passive voice. It allows you to assign responsibility for an action as well as tell how or when something is to be done.
- Organize the information to reflect the divisions of the organization or the on-site personnel assignments.
- Include examples of forms showing how they should be filled out.
- Use date codes to ensure that the most current information is readily identifiable.
- Choose a binding method that will facilitate updating.
- Distribute the manual to all employees or at least to all business divisions or departments.
- Number the books and monitor distribution.
- Require recipients to sign a form acknowledging receipt of the manual and subsequent updates.
- Review the manual and update it on a regular schedule.
- Issue replacement pages with additions and corrections printed on colored paper so users can easily find the most recent changes in their manuals.

The following sections describe some of the most common issues addressed in an on-site operations manual. They identify many of the policies that are commonly followed in office building management and outline procedures for implementing them.

Accounting. A major area of property record keeping is the accounting of revenue collections and disbursements. The operations manual should clearly outline the management firm's policies regarding these areas and require them to be applied consistently. It should assign responsibility for specific accounting tasks to be performed on site, identify the forms and formats (manual versus computerized) that are to be used for each of them, and specify the types of information to be forwarded to the main office. The accounting section of the manual should also indicate the components of the monthly management report to ownership, who is responsible to prepare it, and when it is to be sent to the owner.

As indicated in Chapter 4, funds may be accounted on either a cash basis or an accrual basis. The operations manual should specify which method is to be used. If a mixed cash-accrual system is used, the manual should state which items are accounted by which method—most often, accrual is used for items paid once or twice a year (e.g., real estate taxes, insurance premiums) and cash accounting for everything else.

An important component of the accounting activity is a comprehensive *chart of accounts* that lists all the different categories of income and expense, assets and liabilities, and capital expenditures at the property. The manual should explain the number (or other code) system being used and provide clear instructions as to how the account codes are to be applied. Used properly, a chart of accounts ensures that receipts and payments are identified consistently to create a cumulative record within each income and expense category, providing important information for budgeting and for analyzing the property's financial status.

Collections. Because income is of primary importance, one of the first accounting activities to address is collections. Rent collection policies should state when, where, and how rent is to be paid. Usual practice in real estate management is that rents are due on the first of the month in advance. If the management firm follows this practice, there should also be procedures for addressing exceptions to this rule. It is important to define when rent is considered delinquent. If there is a grace period, the policy should state what it is and how it is applied. State law may require written notification that rent is delinquent and grant the tenant a period of time after notification to make payment. By law, certain governmental agencies pay rent in arrears. To avoid problems, the collection policy should address these issues specifically. Requirements for written notice of unpaid rent and the manner in which notice is to be delivered should be clearly stated and consistent with landlord-tenant law, especially in regard to requirements in preparation for eviction for nonpayment. (All of these policies should be reiterated in tenants' leases.)

It is also fairly common for leases to require payment of a *late fee*—this may be a flat amount, a percentage of the total monthly rent, or an interest rate applied to the unpaid balance—which is formalized by sending written notice of the total amount due. The late fee is intended to encourage on-time payment and discourage tenants from trying to benefit financially from the delayed payment. One day's late rent means one day of lost interest income for an owner who routinely invests excess cash on a daily basis. To be effective, late fees must be applied consistently.

The operations manual should identify who is responsible for collecting rent. This may be the on-site manager or another designated individual. The firm may send the tenants an invoice each month that shows rent due, their pro rata share of pass-through charges, and any other amounts they pay each month (e.g., parking fees, tenant improvement costs). The collection policy should detail when invoices are to be distributed, how many copies are to be prepared, and who is to receive a copy. Minimally, there should be four copies, two for the tenant, one for the on-site manager, and one for the management company office. Tenants may be asked to mail payments to a lockbox or to the management firm's main office; this information should be included on every invoice. The manual should also identify the path the payment must follow from the point of collection to final deposit.

Once rent is collected, it is recorded as property income and as a tenant payment. The property income record is a *collections summary* that lists the tenants by name along with the space they occupy, the amount due for different items (rent, other charges), and the amount collected. Usually there are columns to record a prior balance as well as a new balance, and there may be space to record the lease expiration date, any refundable deposits being held, and the rate per square foot the tenant is paying. It is also appropriate to include space to record the account code (from the chart of accounts) to which the payment is to be credited—e.g., rent. (Exhibit 5.1, page 78, shows a simplified approach to a collections summary form.) The information to be recorded will depend on the property owner's and the management firm's requirements and how important it is to have certain kinds of information together in one place. A collections summary may also document delinquencies and vacancies so that all the leasable space in the building is accounted for. This report may be prepared manually on site (handwritten entries on a paper form), or the information may be entered directly into a computerized form that will automatically calculate the total collections as well as each tenant's new balance. The operations manual should state who is to prepare the collections summary and when it is due to be submitted to the management office. It should also indicate when additional information is mandatory (e.g., delinquencies).

The tenant payment record is a *tenant ledger*. There should be a separate ledger for each tenant, and the form should be designed to serve as a cumulative record of all payments received during the term of the tenant's lease. Typically this form will identify the amounts payable under the lease for rent and other charges and include calculation of future rent escalations. A separate section is used to record actual payments made. (Exhibit 5.2, page 79, shows an example of a tenant ledger.) A computerized form might have the tenant identification and lease particulars at the top followed by a running list of amounts due, payments made (including the date), and the current balance.

If a separate *delinquency report* is used, the operations manual should include a sample form and instructions for completing it. Minimally, this form would provide space to identify the tenant and the leased space with columns to record the amount and period of delinquency—increments of 30 days or one month are typical, and arrearages may be tracked for six months or longer. Spaces to record the total amount past due and the manager's comments complete this form. The latter would be used to document reasons for delinquency and actions taken to collect amounts due. It may

Exhibit 5.1

Sample Collections Summary Form

Collections Summary

Building ______________ Owner ______________ Month/Year ______________

Suite No.	Tenant	Deposit Held	Lease Expiration Date	Rent $/sq ft	Scheduled Rent	Actual Rent	Previous Balance	Payment Received				Current Balance
								Rent	Pass-Thru	Parking	Other	

Exhibit 5.2
Sample Tenant Ledger Form

Tenant Ledger

Building ______ Page ____ of ____
Tenant ______ Suite No. ______
Mailing Address ______ Lease Term From ______ to ______
Contact Name ______ Phone ______ Security Deposit ______

Period					
Regular Monthly Charges					
Base Rent					
Pass-Thru Charges					
Parking					
Totals					

	Charges		Period Covered		Payment Received				Current Balance
Date	**Description**	**Amount**	**From**	**To**	**Rent**	**Charges**	**Parking**	**Other**	

also be appropriate to differentiate between base rent and other items that are delinquent because a tenant may pay the rent but hold back on pass-throughs or other charges because the amount is disputed.

Tenant payments sent to a bank lockbox or to the management firm's main office will be recorded for deposit at that location. If the manager on site receives payments directly and makes bank deposits, a separate *deposit summary* should be prepared. This is a listing of checks to be deposited showing the source (e.g., tenant name and suite number) and the amount. Cash would be listed as a lump sum. Account codes and what a particular payment is for may also be recorded. The original of this form would accompany the checks to the bank, and copies would be retained on site and in the main office. It should be standard policy to make bank deposits daily, and the procedure should require different individuals to prepare the deposit, verify the information, and transport the deposit to the bank. Much of this type of detail can be alleviated by arranging for electronic transfer of funds from tenants' accounts. However, owners and managers of small office buildings may continue to rely on paper records. Even computerized records will be printed so they can be reviewed and validated.

Purchases. The expense side also needs careful attention. Good management policy requires the use of a written *purchase order* for all goods and services except those obtained under specific contracts or purchased with petty cash. The operations manual should state when and how purchase orders are to be used and who is authorized to issue them. While the authorization may be limited to the office building manager, it may be practical to extend this authority to the maintenance supervisor. Limits on management's spending authority as set in the management agreement should be reiterated. The purchase order form should identify the building (or its owner) as the purchasing entity and include specific shipping and billing addresses if these are different. There should be space to show the name and address of the vendor, the date of the order, and shipping instructions. Usually there will be columns to show the quantity ordered, a description of the item or items, a unit cost, and an extended cost. There should also be spaces for an authorized signature and appropriate account codes. Purchase orders should be numbered sequentially and issued in number order. They are usually produced as multi-copy carbonset forms. The original is sent to the vendor, a copy is retained on site, and one or more copies would be forwarded to the accounting department in the management firm's main office.

The manager should maintain a log record that shows the purchase order number, date of issue, vendor, item purchased, and account to be charged. (Exhibit 5.3 is an example of a *purchase order log.*) Use of such a log facilitates tracking of outstanding orders as they are issued. It also provides a ready record of suppliers and costs.

The procedure outlined above may not apply in all situations. A large management firm may have a separate purchasing department, and the manager may be required to submit a *purchase requisition* that will result in a purchase order being issued. In such a situation, it is a good idea to maintain a log record on site so that items purchased for the property can be tracked from requisition to delivery and entry into the supplies inventory.

There should be a specific procedure for verifying that the item received is the item ordered and that the invoice is reviewed against the purchase order before approving it for payment. Usual policy is to pay only from original invoices (not statements). Vendors should be required to submit a separate invoice for each order showing the purchase order number, the quantity ordered, the items shipped, the cost of the goods, and the total amount due (including shipping and applicable sales taxes as separate additional charges).

The most important consideration in determining what to purchase is whether the item wanted will serve the purpose. Cost is also a consider-

Exhibit 5.3
Sample Purchase Order Log

Purchase Order Log

Building ______________________ Page ____ of ____

Order No.	Date	Vendor	Item Ordered	Amount	Account	Date Rec'd

ation. The manager should seek out the best product at the lowest cost. Buying in quantity when appropriate can result in a lower unit price. However, items held in inventory for long periods are subject to damage and pilferage that can reduce or negate any quantity savings. It is important to determine how much of an item is used in a reasonable period of time and use that as a basis for quantity purchase decisions. (Inventory of maintenance supplies is discussed later in this chapter.)

While purchase orders are important for buying supplies and other goods, services are usually provided under a contract. The operations manual should include specific policies and procedures for contracting for services. Usual policy is to require at least three bids from separate sources. The manager may be required to develop specifications for the work or to send out a request for proposal (RFP). Either approach will require a detailed description of the work to be done, materials to be used, special tools or equipment needed, and time constraints that apply. Contractors asked to bid on the job should submit a quotation containing their analysis of the project, how much time it will take, and the cost of materials and labor. If the project is likely to change once work has begun, the contractor should estimate the costs of materials and specify an hourly rate for labor. Charges for services are billed on a regular schedule as stated in the contract, and any deviations from the contracted rates should have to be explained in the billing to be approved for payment. (Ideally, they would have been authorized by the manager, in writing, before the change was made.) Elevator and HVAC

Selecting a Contractor

Office building managers need to develop skills in selecting vendors to bid on contract work. The bids received should be carefully analyzed for adherence to the RFP or job specifications. The final selection of a vendor should not be based on price alone. The lowest bidder may not be able to do the work exactly as specified or within the required time frame. If the lowest bidder is *not* selected, the reasons for choosing someone else should be *documented in writing.* On the other hand, the property owner may insist as part of the management arrangement that the lowest bidder should be selected regardless of any other considerations. In such situations, it is a good idea for the manager to state his or her misgivings to the owner before the contract is signed and to document any specific problems—especially added costs—that arise in the course of the work. Regardless of contractor selection issues, any changes to the contractual arrangements should be stated in writing and approved by the manager (and the owner, if necessary) before they are undertaken.

maintenance may be performed monthly and billed on the same schedule. Contracts for construction of tenant improvements may include a series of payments at different stages of completion; these are particularly subject to change orders requiring prior management approval. (Contracting for space planning and tenant improvement construction is discussed in Chapter 9. Maintenance service contracts are addressed in detail in Chapter 11.)

Payments. It is good practice to establish a regular time for reviewing and paying property bills. Most vendors send out invoices at the beginning (or end) of the month or on a regular billing cycle based on customer accounts. Management firms usually establish a specific procedure for approving bills for payment. If payment is made at a set time of the month, it is wise to let vendors know about it. This will avert questions about late payments. The operations manual should state when bills are to be paid, who will make the payments, and the types of records to be maintained. Regardless of who is responsible for making debt service payments (management or ownership), there should be information about the sources of financing, the terms of the loans, and the manner of payment (use of coupons, electronic transfer of funds).

Invoices should be approved for payment when they are received—this should include the account to be charged and an authorized signature as well as acknowledgment that the goods and the amount due are correct per the purchase order. Approved invoices may be held in an accounts payable folder until payment will actually be made, or they may have to be forwarded to the management firm's main office on a daily basis. (In that case, a copy should be retained on site to account for the expense.) The manager of a small office building may make payments directly, maintaining a handwritten record in a regular bank account *check register*. Minimally, the record should show the date, the check number, the vendor name, the invoice number, and the amount paid along with a running total adjusted for payouts and deposits. If the check register is maintained in a computer, the record might also show what was purchased and received (items, quantity) and the account to which it was charged.

Accumulated bills should be reviewed to determine when payments are due and whether any discounts are allowed. Vendor invoices may say "2% 10 days, net 30" meaning two percent can be deducted from the total amount due if paid within ten days of the invoice date; otherwise, the full amount is due within thirty days. Even small discounts can be a cost savings leading to favorable budget variances, and bill payment should be timed to take advantage of these whenever possible. It may also be desirable to arrange for some invoices to be submitted electronically (or via facsimile) and for some payments to be made directly by electronic transfer of funds. These types of transactions avert delays in the mail and conserve the working capital of the property. The entire purchasing process—purchase order, invoice, and payment—can be conducted electronically provided the Internet sites have proper security safeguards (encryption technology) in place.

Budgets. The office building manager will work with at least two kinds of budgets. The first is an *annual operating budget* that compares expected income from the property to the array of expenses expected to be incurred in its day-to-day operations. Most budgets follow the elements of the *cash flow chart*.

	Gross Potential Rental Income
minus	Vacancy and Rent Loss
plus	Miscellaneous or Unscheduled Income
equals	Effective Gross Income
minus	Operating Expenses
equals	Net Operating Income (NOI)
minus	Debt Service
equals	Cash Flow

An example of an annual operating budget format is presented in the preceding chapter (Exhibit 4.5); it is accompanied by a discussion of the components of the cash flow chart as they relate to the budget. If the office building manager is to set aside reserve funds, the amount would be a deduction from NOI.

The operations manual should specify whether the annual budget should be prepared on an accrual or a cash basis. It should also tell how the various line items of income are to be calculated. These include base rents for office and retail space, operating expense reimbursements (prorated pass-throughs), tenant improvement allowance repayments, and rent escalations. Lease concessions and retail percentage rents are other items to be considered. There may also be specific instructions for calculating gross potential rental income and adjusting it for vacancy and rent loss. This would include anticipation of occupancy changes due to tenant move-outs and move-ins. Methods of estimating different expense items may be spelled out as well. Mathematical formulas and other information may be provided to further assist in budget preparation.

In real estate management, computer spreadsheet programs are routinely used to prepare budgets. Templates can be set up with arithmetic calculations in place. Then all that is needed is to enter the annual totals for individual line items, and the program will divide them across twelve months based on the criteria set in the formulas. A particular benefit of computerization is the opportunity to test different budget scenarios—e.g., different levels of vacancy, a massive increase in utility rates, the impact of deferring selected maintenance work—easily and quickly.

The operating budget is reviewed each month, and favorable and unfavorable variances are reported to the owner. The operations manual should establish the level of variance below which an explanation is unnecessary (this is usually also stated in the management agreement). It may also identify ways to control variances within the budgeting process.

In addition to the operating budget, office building managers often prepare a *capital expenditures budget.* This forecasts major expenditures for the operations year that are funded from sources other than the property's rental income (reserve funds, financing). While the capital budget for an office building should anticipate major repairs and replacements (e.g., mechanical systems, lobby renovations), there is also a substantial amount of tenant improvement construction to be planned and paid for under both new and renewal leases. Leasing commissions are often included in the capital expenditures budget as well. The operations manual should provide specific information and instructions regarding capital items.

- Whether a reserve fund is to be maintained and how it is to be funded.
- When capital items are financed, what loan terms should be sought.
- How property improvement costs are to be estimated and what to allow for inflation.
- How leasing commissions are to be computed and when and how they are paid.
- How tenant improvement allowances are determined and whether and how they are reimbursed, including interest rates to be applied.

Note: Usual practice is for capital expenditures to be amortized over the useful life of individual items. Tenant improvements are amortized over the term of the lease.

The operations manual should indicate who is responsible for preparing, reviewing, and approving budgets, including the degree of involvement of the on-site manager, the management firm, and the property owner. If long-range budgets are also to be prepared, the manual should provide guidelines and assign responsibilities for them as well. The discussion of budgeting in Chapter 4 includes additional information that can serve as guidance in establishing policies and procedures regarding budget preparation.

Other Aspects of Accounting. The management office on site should maintain a *petty cash* fund for use in expediting small-value purchases of office supplies, postage stamps, and the like. There should be a specific policy regarding the amount of cash to be kept on hand, how it is to be used, and what records are to be maintained (e.g., a petty cash log). As with all purchases, the record should include information about what was purchased and appropriate account codes. Store receipts should be required when cash is advanced for purchases. Staff members should sign a receipt when they are reimbursed for out-of-pocket purchases for which no store receipt was obtained. The fund should be replenished when it reaches a minimum dollar amount or percentage of the total. Best practice is to have only one person in the office responsible for the petty cash fund.

Many of the accounting forms described in this section are ultimately components of the management report sent to the property owner each month. The operations manual should also include instructions and assign responsibility for maintaining a general ledger and a cash journal, reconciling bank accounts, and preparing income statements used in managerial accounting and balance sheets used in financial accounting. Here again, the discussions of these items in Chapter 4 may be instructive.

The Management Office. Most large office properties will have a management office on site. When that is the case, it is necessary to have specific policies and procedures regarding office hours, receiving and responding to tenant service requests, and other aspects of the day-to-day conduct of business.

These days, companies tend to offer employees flexible work schedules. As long as sufficient numbers of staff members are present during the firm's "core" business hours, and they work a set number of hours, employees can arrive and leave early (or late). This has been encouraged in urban centers as a way of reducing rush hour traffic—in theory, fewer drivers arriving and leaving at the same time within extended rush periods keeps vehicles moving and averts traffic jams. Where public transportation is available, employees can adapt their work days to commuter train and transit schedules. The result of this change in tenants' business hours means office buildings and their management offices must accommodate an extended work day. Because this affects all members of the management team, the operations manual should address management office hours and management employee work schedules.

The management office is where tenants direct requests for specific services. Policies and procedures should identify the types of services that are provided, the manner in which requests are to be documented, whether a tenant's signature is required before (or after) the work is done, and any specific charges that apply. It is also appropriate to indicate how rapid a response tenants can expect, and management personnel should be able to give a tenant an approximate completion time when a request is received. For example, a request to replace fluorescent lamps may be taken care of within an hour or two, but work that necessitates purchasing replacement parts may not be completed for a day or two or even longer. Good tenant relations are fostered when realistic promises of service are met and exceeded. If something cannot be completed as scheduled, the tenant should be notified of this in advance.

This section of the operations manual should also address the following issues relating to services to tenants, and the policies should be communicated to all tenants and their personnel. (Preparation of a tenant manual is discussed in the context of tenant issues later in this chapter.)

- Building hours of operation (weekdays, weekends)
- Access during nonbusiness hours (sign-in/sign-out)
- Pick-ups from and deliveries to the front desk (requisite documentation and signatures)
- Building access by messengers (deliveries direct to tenant offices)
- Pick-ups and deliveries by postal and courier services
- Access to and use of the loading dock
- Tenant move-in/move-out (advance notice, use of freight elevators)
- Tenant directory listings
- Mailroom, concierge, or other services provided by management (hours of operation)
- Heat and air conditioning availability (business hours, off hours)
- Notification when building equipment (elevators, HVAC) is out of service
- Scheduling of janitorial services during and outside of business hours

- Security patrols of building common areas and tenant spaces
- Building security and emergency contacts

Since the management office is where building staff receive and report on work assignments and tenants contact management staff and request services, the operations manual should address certain details about the office to help keep it running smoothly. These may include the following:

- Scheduling of management office staff to ensure coverage during building business hours
- Appropriate work apparel for office staff
- Uniforms to be worn by maintenance and security personnel
- Staff attitudes in the work place (treating each other and tenants' personnel with civility)
- Appearance of the management office
- Use of office equipment by anyone other than management staff
- Appropriate use of messengers, air couriers, and other delivery services
- Availability of petty cash
- Smoke-free workplace environment

This brief discussion outlines some of the policies and procedures that an office building operations manual should address in regard to the on-site management office. The manager of a property may find numerous other subjects that need attention because they are unique to the property or its tenancy. If on-site services are all provided under contracts with outside vendors—often the approach taken at smaller office buildings—there may be no management office as such. When that is the case, the operations manual may address tenant services in the context of maintenance or tenant-specific issues.

Human Resources. Human resources encompasses all of the actions and activities related to hiring, evaluating, compensating, disciplining, and terminating employees. The management firm will have established policies and procedures regarding all of these areas, but some of these may need to be modified for application at the managed office building. While the management operation for an office building may comprise a handful of unique jobs including maintenance, security, and administrative positions in addition to the building manager, an urban high-rise or a large suburban office park may have several levels of responsibility within each of these work areas plus others.

Personnel policies and procedures must be designed and implemented to ensure compliance with applicable federal, state, and local laws regarding employment. Of particular importance is the issue of discriminatory employment practices, which can result in lawsuits and expensive penalties (fines and damages). There are three specific federal laws that address discrimination in employment.

1. Title VII of the Civil Rights Act of 1968, which is enforced by the Equal Employment Opportunity Commission (EEOC), prohibits discrimination in hiring, compensation, promotion, or termination on the basis of race, color, religion, and national origin; gender as a *protected class* was added later. State and local laws may include other protected classes—e.g., sexual orientation, lifestyle. (Management policies and procedures should be written to ensure compliance with the most stringent requirements that apply locally.)
2. The Americans with Disabilities Act (ADA) of 1990 prohibits discrimination in employment on the basis of physical or mental disability. Employers must make *reasonable accommodations* for qualified applicants or employees who have a disability by improving access, restructuring jobs, adjusting work schedules, and the like.
3. The Age Discrimination in Employment Act (ADEA) prohibits discrimination against older workers.

Sexual harassment in the workplace is considered a discriminatory practice, and this has been and continues to be a hot issue. The operations manual should be adamant about nondiscrimination, and policies and procedures regarding all human resources activities should be written specifically to ensure that discrimination does not occur. This should encompass acceptable as well as unacceptable behaviors and include clear definitions (with examples) of what is considered to be sexual harassment. Specific disciplinary actions should be spelled out up to and including termination of employment. (It is a good idea to have the human resources section of the operations manual reviewed by legal counsel prior to implementation. Periodic legal review should be required after implementation to ensure ongoing compliance with applicable laws because existing laws are modified from time to time and new laws are passed and enforced.)

Hiring Staff. Bringing new employees on board as members of the management team is perhaps the most important aspect of human resources development. The goal should be to hire people who are not only qualified to do the work but will perform well in their respective positions and become team players. The first step in the hiring process is to prepare a comprehensive *job description* for each position. Minimally, this should define the duties and responsibilities of the position and list the skills and education

Components of a Job Description

- Position title
- Position that supervises the work
- Subordinates supervised by the position
- Duties and responsibilities of the position
- Administrative/fiscal authority of the position
- Requisite skills and education
- Other qualification requirements (specialized training, licensure or certification, years of experience or level of expertise)

The job description should also include a reference to "other duties as may be assigned by the supervisor" or some similar statement so that the office building manager can allocate tasks to staff members on an as-needed basis. The exception to this is where collective bargaining agreements are in place. Such agreements are very specific—job descriptions for positions held by union workers cannot include any reference to "other duties."

Job descriptions should *not* include any references to race, religion, national origin, gender, age, disability, or any other characteristics that could be interpreted as discriminatory, and the Americans with Disabilities Act (ADA) limits job descriptions and hiring decisions to a position's essential functions.

required to perform them. Most job descriptions will include the staff person or level to which the position reports as well as any positions it would supervise. A well-prepared job description will help identify the best candidates for a position and is an important component of job training and retraining. By making clear the employer's expectations about job performance in the first place, it serves as a yardstick for measuring that performance, determining pay raises, and awarding promotions. (Copies of all job descriptions should be included in the operations manual, and there should be a requirement to review and update them periodically.)

Hiring must be done with care, not only to avoid discriminatory practices but to protect other people in the workplace (staff members, tenants' employees, building visitors) and to comply with other specific laws. All job applicants should be required to complete an *employment application,* and the same form should be used for all applicants. The application form should request information about current and prior employment, including company names and addresses, dates of employment, positions held, the supervisor's name, and the reason for leaving. Information about the applicant's education, training, and specific skills should also be sought. (A copy of the applicant's resume can be attached to the form when appropriate.) Both business and personal references should be requested. The form should conclude with the applicant's signature and the date following a statement that the information is true and that the applicant authorizes the employer to verify it.

Components of an Employment Application

- Applicant's name, address, and work and home telephone numbers
- Applicant's Social Security number and citizenship status
- Educational background, specific skills, and relevant training
- Current and previous employers' names, addresses, and telephone numbers
- Period of employment, position, wages or salary, and supervisor's name for each job along with the reason for leaving
- Professional and personal references
- Authorization to contact former employers to verify employment information, to contact personal (character) references, and to run credit and criminal background checks (including agreement to submit to drug testing).

The form should have space to identify the position applied for, the date the applicant is available to start work, and the pay desired. It is also prudent to ask about any criminal convictions and to seek specific permission to contact the applicant's current employer. The form should also include a statement that any falsification of information on the employment application is grounds for dismissal.

Information that could be interpreted as discriminatory—e.g., the applicant's age (birth date), marital or family status, physical or mental disability, or religious affiliation—should not be requested on an employment application (or in a job interview).

It should be standard policy and practice that all applicant information is checked. While employment history, education information, and references are often checked via telephone, written confirmation is sometimes necessary. In that case, it is prudent to have applicants sign a separate form that releases various contacts (former employers, references) from liability, such form to be copied and mailed to the contact with the request for specific information. Because real estate management involves handling of the owner's funds, it may be desirable to ask whether applicants have declared bankruptcy and to run a credit check. (The Fair Credit Reporting Act requires specific language regarding release of information and applicant approval to run a credit check. This is often addressed in a separate release form signed by the applicant.) The increasing potential for workplace violence makes it prudent to ask about prior convictions (other than traffic violations) and to run a criminal background check. (A criminal background check may be required to obtain a fidelity bond on an employee who will handle the owner's funds.)

The *Drug-Free Workplace Act* requires employers who contract with the U.S. government (e.g., manage office space leased to or owned by federal agencies) to certify that they maintain a drug-free workplace. In addition, they must have a published statement notifying employees that drug activity is prohibited in their workplace and specifying the actions that will be taken against those who violate the prohibition. Employees are required to abide by the terms of the employer's drug-free workplace policy as a condition of their employment. Such a policy is good management practice regardless, and applicants should be required to pass a drug test before being hired and periodically thereafter. If this policy is established, appropriate authorization should be included on the employment application.

There should be a standard policy and procedure regarding testing of applicants' skills. This should apply to administrative positions in particular. Accounting ability, typing speed, and facility in using specific software programs required for a particular position (spreadsheets, word processing, maintenance management) can all be tested specifically.

The operations manual should provide guidelines for supervisors and others who interview job applicants, including the kinds of questions that can and cannot be asked in an employment interview. Who conducts interviews for what positions, the number of interviews to be conducted, whether co-workers are to be included in the interview process (a good policy and practice for determining "fit" within the organization), and when and how salary and benefits may be discussed are other aspects to be addressed specifically.

Finally, it should be a firm policy that job offers are made in writing regardless of whether an offer was tendered and accepted in a telephone conversation. The written offer should state the position, the start date, and the starting salary. Employment benefit eligibility may also be addressed. The letter should spell out any additional information the new employee should bring on the start date to complete the employer's records. Under the *Immigration Reform and Control Act (IRCA),* employers are required to verify an employee's identity and eligibility to work in the United States, and employees must complete Immigration and Nationalization Service (INS) form I-9 and present proof of their identity and employment eligibility. This is usually handled on the first day of employment.

Evaluating Employee Performance. Employee performance should be reviewed periodically, not only to determine whether and how much of a salary increase will be given, but also to identify areas that need improvement and set goals for future performance. The operations manual should be specific regarding the conduct of performance reviews—when they are to be done (at least annually), what type of documentation is required, and how such reviews relate to merit or other salary increases. Usually performance reviews have two components: First, the supervisor prepares a written evaluation. The employee may be asked to contribute to this as well—a personal assessment of his or her own performance and a list of goals to be accomplished in the next year (or other period). Then, there is an interview between the supervisor and the employee in which they discuss their respective assessments and resolve any differences.

Staff Compensation. The *Fair Labor Standards Act (FLSA),* also called the Federal Wage and Hour Law, regulates hourly workers' wage rates and the number of hours worked and requires overtime compensation for time worked in excess of 40 hours per week. Employees whose role is primarily management of operations, supervision of employees, or administrative office support that is compensated by a minimum weekly salary regardless of hours worked are exempt from the overtime requirement. All positions should be compensated at or above the regulated minimum wage. (State minimum wage laws may be more generous than the federal law.)

In office building management, the managing agent is typically compensated by a management fee. When the agent is an individual, that fee may be his or her sole compensation unless the management agreement provides separate compensation for other services. When the agent is a management firm, the management fee would compensate for all services provided to the property directly by the firm, exceptions to this being those operating expenses paid directly from the property's income stream (utilities, supplies, contracted services), including payroll and benefits for the on-site staff. Under the latter type of arrangement, the office building manager's compensation may be a salary that is included in the management fee. The operations manual should spell out the various personnel compensation mechanisms in effect at the property, including when wages are paid (weekly, biweekly, semi-monthly), when overtime rates apply, and when overtime will be reflected in paychecks.

Leasing of office space is usually compensated on a commission basis. The operations manual should establish the method of determining leasing commissions for both new and renewal leases. This is discussed in detail later in this chapter in the context of lease administration.

Employers often provide a number of employee benefits to their workers in addition to wages or salaries. The operations manual should include information on the specific benefits available to all employees. The following list identifies some of the more common benefits and ways they might be administered.

- Paid holidays—Employers typically establish a number of holidays (e.g., Christmas, New Year's, Memorial Day, Independence Day, Labor Day) for which their employees receive time off at full pay. The management of an office building will determine which such holidays the building will be closed. This may be done in consultation with tenants of the building to ensure that needed services can be provided if any tenants do not close their businesses for the holiday. Being required to work on paid holidays should be addressed in the operations manual; compensation is usually overtime (time and a half) or double time. In addition to designated holidays, an employer may allow a set number of paid personal days or *floating holidays* to be taken at the employee's discretion.

- Paid vacation—It is common business practice for employers to grant paid vacation time to employees after they have been on the job for a certain amount of time. The number of vacation days may be increased when employees reach specific service milestones (5 years, 10 years). The operations manual should outline how vacation days accrue, whether they must be taken within a specific time period, any limits on how many days can be taken at one time, and whether vacation time can be taken as single or half days. The policy should also state any requirements for advance notice or stipulations regarding overlapping vacations within a particular work area (e.g., maintenance). These details are important for scheduling work so that building operations run smoothly throughout the calendar year.

- Paid sick time—Most employers allow their employees a set number of days per year that they can take as paid sick time, after which they would have to use vacation time or take the time off without pay. Sick time is often part of a broader program that includes *short-term and long-term disability benefits,* which may be provided under a special insurance policy. Particulars should be spelled out in the operations manual.

- Other time off—It is important to establish policies regarding time off in special circumstances. A death in the family, reserve military service, and jury duty are just some examples of events that should be given consideration as to whether the time off will be paid or unpaid and specific requirements for notification from the employee so that work schedules can be adjusted.

- Unpaid leave—Extenuating circumstances may lead an employee to ask for a period of extended leave without pay. While the issue can certainly be addressed on an as-needed basis, it is far better to have an established policy that states whether an employee can take unpaid leave, for how long a period the employee's position would be held open, what documentation is required, and who must approve the request. If the building (or management company) staff exceeds fifty employees, the *Family and Medical Leave Act (FMLA)* will apply. This requires companies to grant eligible employees up to twelve weeks of unpaid job-protected leave in the event of a serious health condition or to care for a family member.

- Health care insurance—This usually consists of medical and hospitalization coverages, and it may include dental care and prescriptions. Typical programs cover both employees and their dependents. It is quite common for the employer to pay the bulk of the premium and the employee to contribute a small portion of the cost via payroll deduction. Dependent coverage is usually optional, and the employee might pay a larger share of that cost or all of it. The number of employees may determine the types of coverages that can be written and what the premiums will cost—the more comprehensive the program, the higher the cost. Collective bargaining agreements typically include required health care coverages for union workers. Under the *Consolidated Omnibus Budget Reconciliation Act (COBRA),* employees who are terminated or leave their jobs voluntarily must be given an opportunity to continue their group health care coverage for a period of time by paying the premiums themselves.

- Life insurance—Employers often insure the lives of their employees for the value of their annual salaries. The cost is borne by the employer, and the employee designates the beneficiaries.

- Pension or other retirement program—The *Federal Insurance Contributions Act (FICA)* requires employer and employee to contribute equally to the Social Security fund and Medicare. While Social Security is regarded as retirement income, employers have long been creative in developing retirement benefits for their employees. In order to hire and retain good workers, it is imperative to offer some form of benefit in this category, whether it is a guaranteed pension, a 401(k) investment plan, profit sharing, or some other program. Whether the property owner has a retirement benefit plan in place for the site employees, or the management firm's established program will be extended to the employees of the office building, details of the program should be included in the operations manual. This would include a description of the benefit, when and how employees qualify to participate in it, when they become fully vested, and whether it is employer-paid exclusively or employees are allowed or required to contribute funds. There should also be information about whether funds can be withdrawn by an employee before retirement (e.g., as a loan), when employees are expected or required to retire, whether they can take early retirement, and how that will affect their benefits. Note that establishment of any kind of pension plan constitutes a promise to the employee-participants, and their rights to this benefit are safeguarded under the *Employee Retirement Income Security Act (ERISA).*

- Tuition reimbursement—Many states require real estate practitioners, including property managers, to be licensed and to maintain their licenses via continuing education courses. Regardless of such requirements, employees should be encouraged to continue learning within their area of expertise and beyond it. One way to do this is to offer partial or full reimbursement for the costs of courses, seminars, and training sessions related to the individual's employment. The employee may be required to provide proof that he or she attended and passed the course in order to be reimbursed for tuition, books, and fees. If the employer chooses the course and requires the employee to attend, such training should be at the employer's expense. The manual should spell out any required advance notice of taking a course, what proofs may be required to receive reimbursement, and how much of the cost will be reimbursed. Since both employer and employee benefit from most such education, reimbursing fifty percent or more of tuition and, possibly, book costs may be a good starting point.

- Professional memberships—Membership in trade or professional organizations is a way that real estate managers and others keep up with what is going on in their industries. Real estate managers, HVAC engineers, accountants, and other professionals on staff may benefit from such memberships. Many organizations that serve the real estate management industry also offer professional designations (e.g., the CERTIFIED PROPERTY MANAGER® designation from the Institute of Real Estate Management). Employees can be encouraged to achieve appropriate designations and maintain professional memberships by offering reimbursement of part or all of the costs of tuition and membership dues.

Also a benefit for employees, but not perceived as such, is *workers' compensation insurance*. Employers are required by state law to carry this type of insurance, which pays replacement wages and costs of care when employees become ill or are injured on the job. The operations manual should address requirements for filing workers' compensation claims.

The foregoing list is representative of benefit types but is not intended to be all-inclusive. Accepted practices at the local level may exclude some of these while adding others. The benefits offered to on-site staff members will depend on whether they are employees of the property owner or the management firm and how such benefits can be funded. It may not be possible or practical to offer some kinds of benefits to employees if the staff is small.

Discipline and Termination. In addition to the duties and responsibilities of their jobs, employees are also expected to follow the employer's rules regarding the workplace. To ensure that this happens, the employer's rules and expectations should be spelled out in the operations manual. In particular, unacceptable behaviors should be identified along with their consequences for the employee. Discriminatory behaviors, sexual harassment, drug use, and violence in the workplace warrant special attention. Theft must be dealt with specifically. In the event of an economic loss, polygraph tests may be used (subject to notification and other restrictions), and employees need to know that such tests will be done. Otherwise, the *Employee Polygraph Protection Act (EPPA)* prohibits the use of lie detector tests in most business situations. Employees should be required to use protective

Some Federal Laws That Affect Employment

- Immigration Reform and Control Act (IRCA)
- Civil Rights Act (Title VII)
- Americans with Disabilities Act (ADA)
- Age Discrimination in Employment Act (ADEA)
- Fair Labor Standards Act (FLSA)
- Federal Insurance Contributions Act (FICA)
- Federal Unemployment Tax Act (FUTA)
- Family and Medical Leave Act (FMLA)
- Occupational Safety and Health Act (OSHA)
- Drug-Free Workplace Act
- Employee Polygraph Protection Act (EPPA)
- Worker Adjustment and Retraining Notification (WARN) Act
- Consolidated Omnibus Budget Reconciliation Act (COBRA)
- Employee Retirement Income Security Act (ERISA)

Information about specific laws and changes in workplace requirements can be obtained by contacting the U.S. Department of Labor or on line at www.dol.gov. States often institute laws covering the same aspects of employment, and these may be more stringent. The appropriate agency should be contacted for information on requirements in individual states.

clothing and equipment when necessary or appropriate for the type of work being done, especially when such is mandated under the *Occupational Safety and Health Act (OSHA)*. They should be expected to work safely, report any hazardous conditions they encounter, and avoid creating new ones. On-time arrival at work, the work day, coffee breaks, lunch periods, and notification of one's supervisor if the employee is ill or will be late for work should also be addressed.

Most employers establish a program of *progressive discipline* that provides ample opportunity for the employee to change the unacceptable behavior. Details of how this works should be explained in the operations manual. The severity of the infraction should determine how it is handled. Policies usually address requirements for specific types of notice (oral, written), whether a problem may be kept out of the employee's record if corrected promptly, whether and how long a period of probation will be given for the employee to correct the problem, and when an infraction warrants outright dismissal. Requirements for specific documentation of notices, meetings, and outcomes should be spelled out in detail. Any meetings between the supervisor and the employee who is being disciplined or terminated should be attended by a third party (a member of management) who can attest in writing to the conversation that takes place. A program of progressive discipline should be administered consistently to avoid claims of discriminatory practices or wrongful termination.

There are also consequences for *not* taking appropriate action: If a pre-employment background check would have revealed a prior conviction for assault (a felony), the employer of an individual who assaults a co-worker or anyone else on the property could be sued for *negligent hiring*. If an employee shows a weapon, makes threats, or exhibits any other dangerous behavior on the job and is allowed to repeat the behavior, which leads to someone being hurt, the incident could result in the employer being sued for *negligent retention*. If an incident in the workplace that results in injury to another person (co-worker, tenant's employee, building visitor) can be attributed to inadequate training or oversight of an employee, the employer could be sued for *negligent supervision*.

If employment is terminated by the employer, the employee is entitled to file a claim for unemployment compensation. The *Federal Unemployment Tax Act (FUTA)* requires employers to contribute funds to compensate employees who are laid off or terminated, but most programs are administered within the individual states. While most claimants receive their benefit payments, there may be circumstances in which a terminated employee is denied unemployment benefits, and the dismissed employee could file suit against the employer because of it. To avoid being sued for any reason related to a termination, reasons for dismissal should be recorded carefully. In the event of a mass layoff, the *Worker Adjustment and Retraining Notification (WARN) Act* requires sixty days' notice if the layoff will affect fifty or more employees and they represent one-third of the employer's work force. It is rare that this would apply to the staff of a single office building.

In states where employment is "at will," either the employer or the employee may terminate the relationship at any time for any reason, with or without cause. There are exceptions to this, however. These include specific contractual arrangements (including collective bargaining agreements) and antidiscrimination (protected classes) and antiretaliation (whistle-blower) statutes. Before adopting specific employment policies—especially ones regarding unacceptable behaviors and their consequences—the manager should consult with an attorney.

Other Human Resources Strategies. Because it is expensive to hire and train employees, a savvy employer will establish programs aimed at employee retention. Compensation and benefits are of immediate concern to all employees. High wages and generous benefits are always attractive. In particular, they allow office building managers to hire and retain the most qualified workers for each job. Acknowledgment of employees' employment anniversaries, awards for long service, bonuses, and other incentives are ways to motivate employees to continue good performance and improve on it. Incentive programs should be addressed in the operations manual so that everyone knows how to qualify for them.

The workplace environment needs attention as well. An atmosphere that fosters camaraderie and teamwork makes it pleasant for everyone.

Sponsoring social activities for employees outside the office—holiday parties, summer picnics, a softball or bowling team—changes the focus from business to fun. The only limits are one's imagination. While such socializing may be encouraged in a variety of ways, social activities would not necessarily be a component of an operations manual.

Marketing and Leasing. When marketing and leasing are the responsibility of the office building manager, the operations manual should address this activity in detail. There should be specific procedures for analyzing the market at different levels—the regional level, the neighborhood, the competition, and the property itself—including the basic methodology and a list of sources of relevant information. The manager (or leasing agent) should be required to visit the competition as part of the analytical process.

A market analysis should begin with a survey of the marketplace to identify existing and potential competitors. Minimally, this should collect building names and locations, age and classification (A, B, or C), and details regarding total square footage, vacant square footage and percent vacancy, asking rent (base rate per square foot), and concessions being offered at a large number of properties that could be considered comparable to the subject property—i.e., the building under management. Information about tenant improvement allowances might also be sought along with data on property operating expenses and their impact on tenants' occupancy costs. This type of survey should be repeated at regular intervals so that rental information on existing buildings is kept up-to-date, and data about new buildings can be added as appropriate.

Buildings that are identified as specific competitors should be visited to collect more detailed information, including the following:

- Building ownership, management, and leasing
- Gross and net rentable square feet and how they are measured
- On-site amenities, including parking
- The number of tenants and average occupied square footage
- Major space users and general mix of tenants
- Location particulars, including available transportation
- Building systems (HVAC, electrical) and standard finish
- Services provided to tenants, including security and building cleaning
- Numbers of lobby and freight elevators
- Occupancy and current rental rates
- Vacancy and asking rental rates
- Lease terms (tenant improvements, escalations, concessions, options)

These types of details are used to set up a building (comparison grid) analysis that compares the features, amenities, and rents at the subject property to several other buildings, preferably at nearby locations. The operations manual should spell out how and how often market surveys are to be conducted and who is to do them. The goal should be to ensure that the manager (or leasing agent) becomes familiar with alternatives in the market that could serve potential tenants as well as or better than the space available in the subject building. (Market analysis is covered in more detail in Chapter 7.)

The data gathered in the survey and analysis should be used to develop a specific marketing plan for the office building. A comprehensive marketing plan will address various advertising media to be used and include a specific schedule that indicates when, where, and how advertising is to be placed. This will require development of a marketing budget that allocates funds for advertising and other promotional activities included in the plan. The marketing plan for a new building may call for additional support materials—brochures, a presentation book, a model office space showing standard finish materials—as well as periodic news releases. The operations manual should include guidelines for the content and use of such materials, including policies regarding public relations.

Responsibility for coordinating and approving the various marketing activities should be assigned specifically. The manual should also address the image to be projected by the building. (The owner should be consulted regarding this.) The image must be presented consistently throughout the entire spectrum of advertising and marketing materials, including building signage. Signage should be dealt with specifically, including policies regarding the content, design, placement, and use of signs in and on the building. Because local ordinances may impose restrictions on signage, information on those requirements should be included.

Development of leasing aids such as standard lease forms, building floor plans, aerial photographs, and architectural renderings should also be addressed. Representations and pictures of the building may be used more prominently during initial lease-up; leases and floor plans will be needed regardless of building age.

The manual should indicate who is to receive the completed marketing schedule. Minimally, the distribution list should include leasing, public relations, and management office personnel and the property owner. Leasing agents need to be able to anticipate increased calls after ads are run. Those handling public relations will want to coordinate press coverage with major promotional efforts. Management office staff need to ensure that promotional events do not interfere with daily operations. Others on the management team may be added on a need-to-know basis. Whether the schedule is included in the monthly report or sent separately, the owner has a right to know what is being done to market and lease office space in the building.

In an established office building, leasing activity may focus on renewal of existing leases. The operations manual should include procedures for developing a computerized data base of information about current tenants, the size of their leased space, lease commencement and expiration dates, and the rents they pay. (These data may be compiled from lease abstracts.) The data base should identify specific vacancies (suite number and square footage) and the asking base rate for each space. These data can be used to generate reports on vacancies and lease expirations. The latter can be used for scheduling contacts with tenants regarding lease renewals. If a tenant is planning to move out or will not be offered a new lease, that information should be noted in the data base as well. A large amount of vacant space or an extended period of vacancy may warrant development of a specific marketing campaign. The operations manual should define the level of vacancy that would trigger such a campaign.

Apart from any marketing or promotional activities that attract prospective tenants, office space is most often leased by contacting prospects directly as part of an aggressive canvassing strategy. The operations manual should outline how prospects are to be approached and what records are to be maintained for each such contact. This is an important issue. Because leasing agents are usually compensated on a commission basis, it is imperative to be able to link the leasing agent to a specific prospect who ultimately signs a lease. The manual should also address the timing of follow-up with prospects, showing of vacancies (timing, access to the building and the space), and the lease terms to be offered (base rent, tenant improvements, pass-through charges, escalations, and other terms may vary based on location in the building, square footage to be leased, and duration of the anticipated lease term).

As a measure of leasing progress, leasing agents may be required to prepare a summary report on the status of inquiries, active prospects, proposals and leases submitted to prospects, and signed leases, documenting prospects' space requirements, rental rates and lease terms quoted, and when they would be ready to move in. Details to be reported and how often reports are to be submitted should be outlined in the operations manual. If an advertising campaign is under way, it may be desirable to track the number of inquiries received and the source of those inquiries. The manual should identify the types of information to be collected and the manner in which they are to be reported so that the effectiveness of different advertising media and strategies can be measured. (The specifics of marketing and leasing are detailed in Chapter 8.)

Lease Administration. The operations manual should outline specific policies and procedures regarding qualification of prospective tenants, negotiation of leases, and approval of negotiated lease terms.

Evaluation of the creditworthiness of prospective tenants should be addressed specifically, including when in the leasing process a credit report should be initiated, what information is to be requested from prospects and verified, what credit bureaus and other information sources are to be used, and what standards determine whether a prospect qualifies for a lease.

Other considerations are assignment of responsibility to verify credit information and when and whether written proofs are required. Requirements for security deposits and personal or other guarantees should also be spelled out, including the circumstances under which these might be waived.

The operations manual should specify which lease clauses are negotiable and the types of changes that are permitted. Alternate clauses may be provided to accommodate frequently requested changes. In particular, the manual should be specific regarding lease options, including whether they are granted at all, limitations on their use, and how they are to be administered (e.g., notification regarding a renewal option, required penalty under a cancellation option). It should also address the types of concessions that can be granted and the circumstances in which they are permitted. The manual should clearly define the authority of the negotiator (leasing agent) to make changes to the standard lease, the types of changes that can be made, and when the manager or owner of the building must be involved in negotiations and lease decisions.

After negotiations are completed and the lease terms agreed to, the manager or the building owner may execute the final document. This authority should be stated in the operations manual (and the management agreement; see Chapter 3) along with any requirement for documentation in support of the lease. A lease transmittal package may include a workletter or other documentation regarding tenant improvements, verified credit information, a summary of the lease terms, a security deposit or verification of a line of credit, any rent paid in advance, and information regarding the leasing agent's commission. The operations manual should address leasing commissions, how they are structured, and when and how they are to be paid. Use of outside brokers and the contractual arrangements that can be made with them should also be spelled out.

Apart from any lease data summarized for the transmittal, the manager of the building should be required to complete a standard summary *(lease abstract)* of each new lease that is signed. This type of document facilitates evaluation of information from individual leases so the manager can readily determine the following for each tenant:

- Business name and individual contacts (headquarters location and contact, if appropriate)
- Billing address
- The location and size of the leased space
- When the lease term starts and when rent payment starts (these may be different dates)
- The lease expiration date
- The base rent per year and per month and whether it is based on rentable or usable square feet (including the R/U ratio)

- Any financial concessions that were granted and how they affect payment of rent
- Whether a security deposit, letter of credit, or other guarantee was required and the amount involved
- The amount and timing of rent escalations (CPI or other basis)
- The exact dollar amount of any tenant improvement allowance and how it is to be paid back if not included in the base rent (the lease should specify the interest rate, start date, and period of repayment, which should not exceed the uncancellable portion of the lease term)
- The pro rata basis for billing pass-through charges
- Any unique aspects of the individual lease (e.g., an expansion option, special terms addressed in a lease amendment or rider)
- Any special agreements with the tenant regarding building services (e.g., parking, security)

The manager is the primary administrator of the lease and must be familiar with all of the standard requirements and potential variations that may apply. Collection of rents and other payments has been addressed elsewhere in this chapter. However, lease administration also encompasses dealing with situations when tenants do not comply with other, nonfinancial requirements of the lease. The operations manual should provide specific procedures for notifying tenants who are in default of any lease terms and state the penalties or other consequences of such default. The latter should be incorporated into the lease document as well. (Lease administration is described in detail in Chapter 10.)

As discussed in the context of management take-over, tenants should be required to list the managing agent as an additional named insured party on their insurance policies and to submit proof of this to the building manager in the form of certificates of insurance. These requirements should be reiterated in a specific operating policy. (Note: If a tenant is reluctant or unwilling to add the managing agent as an additional named insured on its primary policy, an option may be to secure a policy exclusive to the tenant's occupancy.)

If tenant improvements are to be governed by a *workletter,* the operations manual should spell out the terms and conditions that apply. (Tenant improvements are discussed in the next section as a tenant issue.)

Tenant Issues. One way to ensure that tenants know and follow building rules is to prepare and distribute a *tenant manual* (see Chapter 10). A tenant manual is easy to prepare when tenant-specific issues are addressed in the operations manual.

Tenant Improvements. It is common practice for office building owners and managers to develop uniform specifications for finish work to be done in tenants' leased spaces. Referred to as *building standards,* these specifications define the quality of construction and quantity of finish elements the owner will provide. While details of the building standards may or may not be included in the operations manual, several issues related to them need to be addressed. These include computation of the tenant improvement allowance (a dollar amount per square foot or per-unit basis), what material substitutions can be made and who pays the cost differential, the tenant's responsibility for other costs that exceed the allowance, whether and how the allowance is to be reimbursed, and the fact that quality of materials and their installation is controlled by the building manager.

Rent and Other Payments. If the tenant's perspective on rent payments is not addressed in the context of accounting, it should be included here. Other policies and procedures in this section should include calculations of tenants' pro rata shares of common area expenses, interest to be charged on tenant improvement allowance funds advanced by the owner, and how these items are to be paid. It may be building policy to bill tenants each month for their rents and related payments. Reconciliation of common area billings—actual versus estimated—should be addressed, including when this is to be done, how tenants will be notified of the adjustments, and tenants' access to cost information if they dispute the adjustments. Billing for specific services provided to tenants (i.e., whether these will be invoiced separately when the work has been completed or added onto the monthly rent bill) may be addressed here or in the context of service requests.

Service Requests. There should be specific procedures for requesting various building services. Policies may address types of requests that can be accepted by management over the phone as opposed to requests that must be made in writing. The procedure may require use of a standard service request form (discussed later in this chapter in the context of maintenance). The ability to transmit requests via e-mail can expedite performance of the work while also starting the process with a written record. Basic janitorial services that are provided to tenants should be defined along with an explanation of what would be considered additional or special janitorial services and a procedure and time frame for requesting them in advance. (In addition to the topics discussed here, the tenant manual should include the tenant services policies discussed in the context of the management office earlier in this chapter.)

Other Tenant Issues. If the building has parking facilities available, there should be a policy regarding use of those facilities by tenants' employees.

Related issues include how many spaces would be allotted per tenant (perhaps based on leased square footage), whether parking spaces are assigned individually, any fees that would be assessed, and how they are to be paid.

Sometimes an office building will have a large conference room that can be rented by tenants on an as-needed basis. Perhaps the conference room will have audiovisual and telecommunications equipment in place. Management will need to develop policies and procedures regarding use of such facilities, how much advance notice is needed for scheduling, and what charges apply for space and equipment use. Management may be responsible for setting up the room and cleaning it afterwards, but tenants should be required to follow rules about bringing in food and disposing of wastes.

It may be appropriate to address tenants' responsibility for their employees' security within their leased premises. Management policy might be to encourage behaviors that enhance personal safety and security in and around the building, perhaps compiling a list of "do's and don'ts" that are included in the tenant manual and publishing reminders from time to time in a tenant newsletter. (Note: While tenants may be "responsible" for security within their suites, the building owner may be held liable if negligence is involved.)

Nowadays, office buildings and tenant spaces are required to be smoke free. Policies regarding smoking in and around the building might include assignment of designated smoking areas, what kinds of smoking materials are allowed (cigars and pipes may be limited or prohibited outright), and whether any time or other limitations are imposed on the use of these facilities (a smoking room might be locked overnight as a building security measure).

It is axiomatic that retaining tenants is more cost-effective than leasing the same office space over and over again, albeit at three- or five-year intervals. The operations manual should include specific tenant retention policies and procedures for implementing them. These can range from "feel good" activities (serving donuts and coffee in the building lobby for a "tenant appreciation day") to following up on service requests to determine whether the work was performed satisfactorily. (Tenant retention is discussed in detail in Chapter 10.)

Maintenance. An office building has a large number of components that require special attention to their maintenance. The operations manual should outline policies regarding different levels of maintenance and when they should apply. It should also identify maintenance work to be contracted and outline procedures for contracting:

When to use specifications versus a request for proposal (RFP),

How many bids should be obtained, and

What criteria to use in evaluating bids and making a decision.

The office building manager's authority to contract for services may be subject to the owner's approval when the contract value exceeds a stipulated maximum amount. The details of this portion of the management agreement should be reiterated in the operations manual. (Policies regarding contracting are also addressed in the context of purchasing earlier in this chapter.)

Janitorial maintenance—basic cleaning—applies to all common areas of the building as well as the interiors of tenants' leased spaces. The manual should spell out the types of tasks included in regularly scheduled janitorial services, the time of day when they are performed, and how often each is to be done. This might include detailed *janitorial specifications* to be provided to the contractor who performs this service.

Corrective maintenance and repairs are usually performed by on-site staff. The types of work that comprise this category of maintenance, their assignment to specific staff members (by position title), when repairs should be performed (how quickly), and how costs are to be allocated should be spelled out in detail. Classification of work to be done during the work day as opposed to that which has to be done outside of business hours is another consideration. The issue of charges and payment when these types of work are performed in leased premises should also be addressed. It should be standard policy to follow up with tenants after repairs have been made to evaluate the quality of the work and assess the tenant's satisfaction with the service.

It should be standard operating policy that all systems and equipment are to receive appropriate *preventive maintenance* on a timely basis. Owners' manuals and manufacturers' warranty requirements often spell out the types of preventive maintenance to be performed and how often they should be done. The office building manager or the maintenance supervisor should be responsible for developing a comprehensive preventive maintenance schedule for the building that identifies all the equipment to be maintained and includes all the specific tasks related to each piece of equipment, when each task is to be performed, and who is to do the work.

For reasons of safety, the need for specialized tools or equipment, or because special skills or licensing is required, certain types of maintenance work are usually contracted. Unless the size of the building, the extent of its equipment, or the amount of work warrant it, the staff at an office building would not usually perform maintenance on elevators, escalators, or HVAC equipment. Maintenance of these components requires special training and sometimes special tools. Other types of preventive maintenance are unlikely to be performed by on-site staff regardless. Exterior window washing is dangerous; landscaping and groundskeeping require special equipment that itself must be maintained. Tuck-pointing of brick and masonry exteriors is performed very infrequently and requires special skill and knowledge of materials. Cleaning or refinishing of exterior surface finishes is another infrequently performed task that requires specialized knowledge of the finish materials and the cleaning agents. The same applies in regard to metal surfaces, especially brass and stainless steel on lobby door and window frames and revolving doors.

Businesses that sell packaged foods and restaurants that prepare and serve food need to arrange for pest control services for their leased premises. The fact that such businesses are operating in an office building creates a potential problem for the common areas and for other tenants. In truth, there are no barriers to the movement of insects and rodents within a building. When pest control is needed for the building, it should be contracted because application of pesticidal chemicals requires a special license. Applicators are often required to wear special protective clothing and devices as well.

The need for specific maintenance work is determined by performing a comprehensive inspection of the building using a detailed inspection checklist. The checklist should identify every building component and system, every piece of operating equipment, and all of their component parts. The form should include space to describe the character and condition of each element, identify specific work that is needed, and estimate the cost. While the manager of the property should inspect the entire building on a regular schedule, members of the maintenance staff may be assigned to inspect certain areas more frequently and to follow up on work that was scheduled to be done.

The operations manual should spell out how often different areas of the building are to be inspected, who is to perform the inspections, when different types of required maintenance work are to be performed, and who is to perform them. It should also indicate when or whether and for how long some types of maintenance can be deferred. For example, it may not be practical to repair potholes in an open black-topped parking lot during the winter because of cold temperatures and frequent snowfall. However, repairs should be scheduled for the earliest date when it is likely that the patches will stay in place. *Deferred maintenance* should be kept to a minimum. While it is sometimes prudent to defer an item of maintenance as a way of controlling costs in the short term, deferred maintenance will reduce the value of the property over the long term, both as a desirable place for tenants to locate their businesses and as an investment for the owner. (Specifics of maintenance management are covered in Chapter 11.)

An important adjunct to performing maintenance tasks is keeping accurate records. The operations manual should state who is responsible for maintaining various maintenance records, what forms are to be used, and in the case of a supplies inventory, how frequently a general inventory should be taken.

Work to be done in tenants' leased spaces may be requested using a *maintenance service request* form or by telephone or e-mail. Work to be done in common areas may be requested by the building manager follow-

Exhibit 5.4

Sample Work Order Form

Work Order

Date ____________ Work Order No. ____________ Assigned to ____________________
Tenant Name ____ Suite No. ________
Tenant Contact ______________________________ Phone No. ______________

WORK REQUESTED ____

PARTS/SUPPLIES/EQUIPMENT NEEDED ________________________________

WORK DONE ____

Date Work Done __________ Start Time __________ End Time __________ Total Time __________
Parts Cost ________________ Labor Cost ________________ Total Cost ________________
Tenant Expense: YES _____ NO _____ Account Code ________________________
Work Performed by ____
Manager Approval ______________________________________ Date __________
Tenant Approval _______________________________________ Date __________

This example is suitable for on-site use. A work order for a management firm that sends maintenance workers to different buildings would likely include spaces to identify the property (name, address) and its manager (including a phone number). There might also be spaces to record mileage charges and service charges as well. Work to be done by an outside contractor would need information about the company (name, address, contact, and phone number).

ing a routine inspection. Regardless of how requests are received, a specific numbered *work order* should be generated for each assignment (Exhibit 5.4 is an example). This should identify where the work is to be done (tenant name and leased space or other building location), note the date and time of the request, and list the work to be done. Space should be provided to list replacement parts (including costs) and any special tools or equipment needed to do the job, when the work is scheduled to be done, to whom it was assigned, and when it is completed. There should be space to record reasons why requested work was not completed at the time and whether any additional work is needed. Finally, the individual who performs the

Exhibit 5.5
Sample Maintenance Supply Inventory Form

Maintenance Supply Inventory

Item Description ______

Part No. ______ Quantity: Min ______ Max ______ Unit Cost ______

Manufacturer ______ Vendor ______ Delivery Time ______

Ordered			Received		Inventory	
Date	**P.O. No.**	**Quantity**	**Quantity**	**Back Ordered**	**Quantity Used**	**Balance on Hand**

work should sign the form. If a tenant signature is required, there should be space for that as well. The manager or the maintenance supervisor may be required to follow up on all such work to find out whether it was done to the tenant's satisfaction.

It is common practice to list each work order in a *maintenance log* that provides a cumulative record of work done, when, and by whom (staff member, contractor). The location should be noted along with a brief description of the work requested, when the request was received, who is to do the work, and a work order or purchase order number if appropriate.

A running inventory of supplies should be maintained. This may be done using a separate *maintenance supply inventory* form for each item (Exhibit 5.5 is an example). This should track individual maintenance parts with space to name and describe the item, assign a part or stock number, define inventory quantities to be maintained (minimum and maximum counts), and note a current unit cost. Manufacturer, local supplier, and delivery time should also be recorded. A grid is used to record the date, purchase order number, and quantity ordered; list the quantity received and account for any amount that is back ordered; and document items removed from stock and the balance on hand. It may also be desirable to maintain

Some Emergency Services Resources

- Fire Department
- Police Department
- Closest hospital and/or medical center
- Private ambulance services
- Bomb Squad
- Hazardous Materials Team
- Poison Control Center
- Utilities (electricity, gas, water/sewer, telephone/cable)
- Fire/casualty insurance agent/claims adjuster
- Workers' compensation insurance (agent; physician)
- Federal, state, and local emergency management agencies
- State and local environmental regulatory entities
- U.S. Environmental Protection Agency

Some of the listed services are more likely to be available in large urban centers than in suburban areas although there may be mutual assistance agreements between city and suburban fire and police departments regarding certain types of emergencies. A bomb squad may be a separate group in the fire or police department or both while a hazardous materials (hazmat) team is likely to be part of a fire department. Poison control centers are usually based in the pharmacy at a major medical center. It may also be appropriate to include contact information for local social service agencies (American Red Cross, Salvation Army, city-sponsored human services) to provide support services, including counseling, in the event these are needed. Tradespeople, reconstruction contractors, and board-up services are other contacts to identify; it is appropriate to list more than one of these latter to ensure a rapid response in a particular emergency.

an ongoing record of items removed from inventory. This might be recorded on a *stock use log* that lists the date, the item and stock number, the quantity removed, where the item was used, and the person responsible.

Emergency Procedures. Emergencies are distressing events, and they usually occur at inconvenient times. While specifics cannot be foreseen, it is possible to anticipate and plan responses to a variety of situations. In planning for emergencies, one should assume that if something can go wrong it will. Carefully thought-out emergency procedures can safeguard human lives and minimize financial losses. While the operations manual should include specific emergency procedures, it is also good practice to maintain the same information in a separate emergency procedures manual. Specific information on emergencies should be included in the tenant manual as well.

Emergencies the office building manager should prepare for are fire, power failure, crime, bomb threats, and civil disorder. Weather-related emergencies and natural disasters should also be addressed. Management should establish an emergency response team comprised of staff members and volunteers from among tenants' employees. A comprehensive listing of emergency contacts should also be compiled and distributed to management staff and tenants. This should include emergency (home) telephone numbers for management personnel, executives of tenant firms, and other tenant personnel as may be warranted plus various local governmental agencies (fire and police departments) and related services as may be appropriate (private ambulances, hospitals, medical centers). In addition, the manager should maintain a separate list of tradespeople or contractors who can be called upon to help protect the property from further damage between the time of the emergency event and the arrival of the insurance adjuster. Here again, home telephone numbers are vital. Otherwise, if an incident occurs outside of regular business hours, these people could not be reached.

Emergency situations are out of the ordinary, which makes them potential news items. Because of this, it is a good policy to designate one person who is authorized to deal with the media, not only to ensure that the property and its ownership and management are presented in the best light, but also to minimize dissemination of inaccurate information. The management firm may have a separate public relations department responsible to handle media relations in all kinds of situations and most especially in an emergency. (Additional information on emergency preparedness can be found in Chapter 12.)

It is also a good policy to work with local police and fire departments to educate tenants' personnel. Some police departments will send an officer to talk about personal safety and security, how to report a crime, and what to do if a bomb threat is received. The fire department may offer a similar program of talks on fire hazards, fire prevention, evacuation strategies, and the specifics of how to report a fire. Informed workers can respond more appropriately in an emergency, allowing police or fire personnel to do their work more effectively. Not only do such programs educate building occupants, they benefit tenants directly because their workers know how to handle different types of emergency situations, and they benefit management and ownership indirectly as part of a tenant retention program.

Fire. Fire is a special concern to people who work in high-rise office buildings. Everyone who works in the building must be prepared to act quickly in the event of a fire. Both staff and tenants' personnel should know how to report a fire—first call the fire department then the building management office. The fire department must be notified immediately so that equipment can be dispatched to the building.

The manager should consult with the fire department before developing a fire and evacuation plan. Often the fire department will require only floors in the area of the fire to be vacated rather than order a complete building evacuation. The written plan should be reviewed and approved by the local fire department. Once approved, copies of the plan should be distributed to building occupants and reviewed with them periodically. (To minimize liability, all tenant communications regarding the fire and evacuation plan should refer specifically to actions "the fire department requests or suggests or directs" that building occupants take.) At a minimum, everyone who works in the building must know the location of fire exits (stairwells) and how to use them. All exits should be identified with lighted signs and directional arrows. Use of elevators should be strictly prohibited. (Elevators should be programmed to go to the lobby immediately when a fire alarm is initiated.) Regular fire drills conducted under the guidance of the fire department reinforce the evacuation procedure.

Each tenant business should be asked to assign one or more of its staff members to participate on the *emergency response team* (see Chapter 12). Team member assignments will vary from directing people to the emergency exits to assisting in the evacuation of handicapped individuals to checking that all personnel in a tenant's space have been evacuated. The manager should develop a detailed table or chart listing all such personnel and their duties, and the chart should be updated as management staff and tenant personnel changes affect the emergency response team.

The manager should make sure that the fire department knows the exact location of the building and that there is agreement with the department regarding use of building entrances (when there is more than one) and establishment of staging areas (for fire trucks). At any time of the day, depending on building hours and staffing, there should be one management staff member who has access to a complete set of keys or door codes and who can explain the fire situation and guide the fire department personnel into the building.

The plan should provide for establishing a command post where fire and police department personnel can use telephones to communicate with the outside. This might be the office of the building manager or the security supervisor. In a fire, the fire department should be in command. While building staff should be available to assist fire department personnel as may be needed, the manager should not authorize or implement any action.

The office building manager and staff need to be familiar with the firefighting equipment installed in the building. Usually there is a fire hose and pump system in the stairwells. Most buildings have sprinkler systems in common areas and tenant spaces. Local fire codes may require carbon dioxide or dry chemical systems in specific areas of a building. Dedicated spaces that house computer equipment and systems may have special gas fire-suppression systems. (Information on these types of systems can be obtained from the National Fire Protection Association.) Sprinklers are common in new construction; local life-safety codes may require retrofitting them into older buildings. In addition, there may be fire extinguishers

Public Address Systems and Their Use

Modern office buildings may include an emergency voice communication system that can deliver messages to all tenants' spaces. When such a building-wide public address (PA) system is in place, it is important to establish policies and procedures for its use. In particular, the management firm's public relations department or service should develop written announcements or scripts to be used in the event of specific types of emergencies. The announcements should explain the situation that has occurred and provide instructions for tenants and their employees. The operations manual should also identify the person or persons among the building staff who will be authorized to access the PA system and make announcements.

Because there may be potential liability for lost productivity if building occupants are evacuated without adequate cause, it may be necessary or desirable to seek advice of legal counsel regarding the content of such announcements. A review of liability insurance coverage may also be appropriate.

throughout an office building, in both common corridors and tenants' leased spaces. They may simply be mounted on wall hangers, or they may be installed in niches or in cabinets with glass doors. All personnel who may be called upon to use fire extinguishers or other equipment should receive proper training under fire department direction. All fire-extinguishing equipment (sprinklers, hand-held extinguishers, portable or permanently installed) should be inspected and tested from time to time (as mandated locally) to ensure that everything is in good working order.

It should also be management policy to arrange for periodic inspections of the building, including tenant areas, to identify potential fire hazards. (This may be required by the fire department.) In particular, the inspector should look for improperly stored flammable and combustible materials, a situation that must be corrected immediately. Equipment and building inspections should be part of a larger fire prevention program that includes educating building occupants about fire hazards and life-saving behaviors in the event of a fire.

Power Failure. A power failure (blackout) can occur at any time, interrupting building operations and possibly causing damage to sensitive electrical equipment. When demand for electricity exceeds what the utility's system can deliver, the utility may urge a curtailment of usage (brownout). Major urban areas often experience brownouts on the hottest summer days due to high demand for electricity to operate air-conditioning equipment. The office building manager should address this possibility by developing specific procedures for evacuating the building and elevators and protecting mechanical equipment. Sad to say, it is also necessary to address ways of dealing with vandalism, looting, and pilfering.

Most large high-rise office buildings will have emergency power-generating equipment to operate emergency lighting in selected areas of the building (stairwells, exit signs) and other vital equipment—sump pumps, fire pumps, smoke ventilation fans. If there is a building-wide public address system, that should be connected to the emergency generator. If its capacity is sufficient to do so, the emergency generator should be used to bring elevators down to the first floor so people trapped in them can be evacuated safely. It is wise to determine the generator's capacity and set priorities for connections to it based on that information. Like all mechanical equipment, emergency generators can malfunction. To avoid problems, emergency equipment (generators, lighting systems) should be tested periodically to make sure it will work when needed.

In addition to evacuating the building, there should be recommendations to shut down electrical equipment that was in use when the blackout occurred. This should be done to avoid damage to the equipment due to heavy line loads when power is restored. Photocopy machines, computer peripherals (printers, scanners), and desktop computer hard drives should receive special attention. To avoid memory loss and equipment damage, tenants should be required to provide their own backup power for mainframe computers and network systems that cannot be shut down.

Crime. Office buildings are subject to a variety of criminal activities, from petty thievery (e.g., pilfering office supplies) to assaults resulting in bodily injuries or even death. Tenant reception areas, public washrooms, elevators, and stairwells are some of the most vulnerable areas. Unless a building is uniquely situated in a low-crime area, it is prudent to establish policies and procedures for handling different types of criminal acts. The manager should consult with the local police department for advice on dealing with specific crimes. In addition, a security survey should be conducted to determine and correct weaknesses in the building security system.

All criminal acts should be reported to the police and the building management office. It may be appropriate to develop a form for recording specific information about crimes that occur in the building. At the very least, management staff and tenants' employees should be given instructions on how to report crimes, including the types of observations that help police find the perpetrators.

- Location and time of the incident
- Type of criminal act (vandalism, theft, assault)
- Physical characteristics of the person (height, build, hair color)
- What the person was wearing (apparel, shoes, jewelry)
- Distinctive features (eyeglasses, scars, tattoos, a missing finger)
- How the person entered and exited the premises

People also need to be reminded not to touch anything at the crime scene until the authorities have completed their investigation. It may be necessary for police to collect fingerprints from some people so those of the perpetrator can be more easily identified.

Most office buildings maintain a security checkpoint in the lobby. People who work in the building may be required to show identification when they enter. Visitors should be required to sign in and out and wear a badge or label that identifies the tenant or person they expect to visit. Messengers and delivery services may be required to make pick ups and deliveries at the front desk, or they may have to be escorted while making deliveries in person. If closed-circuit television (CCTV) monitoring is employed, building occupants need to be informed that they are being observed. Such systems often include videotape recording equipment. When that is the case, there should be policies regarding retention of the tapes for a set period so that any documentation of criminal activity can be preserved. Regardless of security measures provided by building management, tenants' employees should be reminded periodically about steps they can take to protect themselves. (Security measures are discussed in detail in Chapter 12.)

Because stairwells are fire exits, they need to be accessible from every floor. Common practice is for doors to open into the stairwell from each floor and automatically lock on closing, thereby preventing re-entry to the corridor. In buildings where tenants occupy space on two or more adjacent floors or where washroom facilities are not provided on every floor, electronic locks are often used on stairwell doors. These may require people to enter an access code by pressing buttons or touching a keypad, or the locks may include a device that "reads" information in or on a "key card." Access to shared restrooms may be controlled with similar devices. As added protection, access codes should be changed periodically.

Bomb Threats. A bomb threat is a difficult emergency to deal with because there is no way of knowing up front whether the threat is real. Best policy is to consider every such incident as real until or unless it is proved otherwise. When a bomb threat is received, the building manager should immediately contact the local agency that deals with this type of incident. Most often a bomb squad will be part of the police department, but in some locales, it may be part of the fire department. After the bomb squad has been notified, tenant decision-makers should be informed of the situation so they can decide whether to remain in the building; they can consult directly with the authorities when they arrive on the scene. To avoid potential liability for losses (life, property) resulting from an explosion or for the cost of lost work time if the threat is a hoax, the manager should defer to the local authorities for a decision to evacuate the building.

Nevertheless, an emergency chain of command should be established to deal with bomb threats. Staff should be trained so they can assist the bomb squad in searching the building for a bomb and evacuating the premises. (It may be preferable to have staff concentrate on building common areas and have tenants search their leased premises.) Because bomb threats are usually delivered by telephone, management personnel should be trained to identify and respond to such calls. In particular, the person who takes the call should try to keep the person on the phone and obtain as much information as possible in the meantime. The caller should be asked what the bomb looks like, where it is located, when it is set to explode, what type of explosive was used, and why the building was targeted. To the extent possible, the recipient should note whether the caller is male or female, young or old. Voice characteristics (high-pitched, slurred), speech patterns (nasal twang, stuttering), and demeanor (calm, irrational) are other aspects to be noted along with any background noises (voices, music, machinery). A specific, silent signal should be arranged so that any staff member taking such a call can alert a supervisor or security person to the nature of the call.

Apart from overt threats, everyone who works in the building should be suspicious of any parcel, briefcase, or luggage that is left unattended in an elevator, a corridor, the lobby, or a tenant's leased space and report it to building management.

Civil Disorder. Incidents of civil disorder rarely disrupt office building operations, but even small, peaceful demonstrations can erupt into violence. Incidents that impact an office building directly usually are related to its tenancy. Consulates, trade missions, and other entities that represent foreign governments are a potential source of problems. Political unrest in their home countries or international frictions related to those countries may lead to demonstrations (picketing) at their office location, or the building may receive bomb threats. Agencies of the U.S. government and subsidiary or branch offices of major U.S. corporations may be similarly targeted. A company that employs union labor may be picketed if those employees go on strike. Office building managers need to be aware of certain tenants' potential for problems. Reading newspapers is one way to stay alert to this potential. The building and its other tenants can be provided some measure of protection by checking out this aspect when prospects are being qualified for a lease, discussing the potential for problems before the prospect signs the lease, and including special clauses in the lease itself. Such a lease clause might require the tenant to reimburse the landlord for any additional security (or other) expenses arising out of any demonstrations (picketing) against the tenant by its employees or customers.

Management should work with the police department to develop procedures that will protect the building and its occupants in the event a peaceful protest turns violent. The procedures should be communicated to management personnel and tenants' employees. New buildings can be designed so the lobby can be sealed off in the event of forced entry, thereby preventing intruders from gaining access to other areas of the building.

Natural Disaster. Geography and climate will dictate the types of natural disasters that should be addressed in an operations manual. Flooding can result from heavy rainfall locally or rapid snow melt at a location upstream. There can be wind damage from tornados and hurricanes; the latter also result in water damage. Earthquakes, land slides, and volcanic eruptions are other potential sources of damage to an office building. A natural disaster may cause structural damage, and this could lead to the building being closed for repairs for an extended period or demolished if it cannot be repaired. Emergency procedures should address each type of natural disaster that is likely to occur at the property. Many such procedures will be the same as those for a power failure—evacuation of the building, shutting down equipment.

Other Related Issues. It is appropriate to anticipate other kinds of situations where one may have to call upon the fire department for assistance. Management should also have some minimal procedures in place for dealing with them. Automobiles crash into buildings, often causing structural damage in addition to breaking windows. As well as the driver of the vehicle, people on the sidewalk may be injured in such an accident. An airplane or helicopter might crash onto the roof of the building or into the side of it. A person could slip and fall in any area of an office building. The person might sustain only a few bruises, or the incident could involve broken bones or a concussion. Someone in the building might have a heart attack or similar medical emergency. To ensure that any injuries that occur on the property are attended to quickly, management staff and tenants' employees need to know whom to call in these types of situations.

Most fire departments include among their personnel emergency medical technicians (EMTs) who drive ambulances and transport injured people to hospitals or designated trauma centers. In most areas of the United States, emergency assistance from police and fire departments is obtained by calling 911. There are separate numbers for use with cellular telephones. If a regular seven-digit phone number must be dialed, this can be programmed into a telephone that has a "speed dialing" feature; in most cases, the number is automatically dialed when the caller presses two digits plus the star or pound key.

It is also helpful if members of the management staff are trained in first aid and cardiopulmonary resuscitation (CPR). This should be on a strictly voluntary basis. These people, as well as any tenant employees who are similarly trained, should be identified specifically in emergency contact lists for the building. However, it is prudent to check with legal and insurance advisors beforehand, since there may be liability for the property owner and the manager if problems arise from a staff member's first aid ministrations.

Emergency procedures should include provisions for dealing with handicapped people who work in the building. These may encompass:

- Preparation of a list that identifies all handicapped personnel who work in the building, the nature of their disability, and the type of special assistance they would need in different types of emergencies.
- Methods of providing assistance for evacuation of mobility-impaired individuals who may or may not use a wheelchair.
- Special means of alerting vision- or hearing-impaired workers (adjuncts to the claxon and flashing lights of contemporary building alarm systems).
- A requirement that tenants assign personnel from their staff to be responsible for notifying and evacuating their handicapped co-workers.

It is also important to have in place procedures for dealing with hazardous materials incidents. An electrical transformer might leak polychlorinated biphenyl (PCB) heat transfer agents; HVAC equipment might leak chlorofluorocarbon (CFC) refrigerants. If there is a dry cleaning establishment on the premises, volatile cleaning fluids might be spilled. Medical practitioners may spill biological wastes contaminated with bloodborne pathogens. Each of these types of contaminants must be cleaned up and disposed in a specific way. Management staff need to know whom to contact for assistance in cleaning up certain hazardous materials, methods for cleaning up spills when they can do it themselves, and whom to notify in the event that an incident could lead to broader environmental (air, water, soil) contamination. The tenancy of the property will determine what types of hazards are likely to be encountered and the types of related problems that should be anticipated.

Last, but not least, it is important to establish procedures that ensure continuity of building operations after an emergency has passed. The office building manager should identify property records and other documents that must be kept secure at all times and should be removed from the building in the event of an emergency. Routine backup of computer files is essential regardless. Backup records of both data and software programs should be stored securely and easily accessible for removal from the management office. Off-site storage is preferable. Important papers such as leases, contracts, and payroll information should also be easily collected and removed. Another good practice is to keep a camera loaded with film in the on-site management office. A photographic record of incident sites and specific damage will facilitate filing insurance claims. Photographs are also helpful in establishing an inventory of building improvements, equipment, and other items—including the owner's personal property—for insurance identification. This is another area improved by technological advancements. Digital cameras allow direct downloading of images to a computer, saving the time needed to develop film and make prints; and computer files can be copied onto compact disks (CDs) or other high-capacity media for storage or transmittal.

6

Staffing and Team Management

Savvy office building managers have long known that they manage people as well as real estate. In order to operate an office building efficiently and effectively, the manager must have in place specific programs for recruiting, training, and retaining qualified employees. The details of these programs will vary with the size of the property that is being managed, but the underlying principles will be the same. The goal is to create a team of professionals whose abilities allow them to perform their assigned roles and, with time and experience, to move into positions of greater responsibility. For purposes of this book, it is assumed that the office building manager is responsible for staffing at the property.

Determining Personnel Needs

The first step in staffing an office building is to determine the roles individual staff members will play. A small building may have a minimal staff, perhaps a manager (who may not be on site all the time) and a handful of part-time employees or independent tradespeople who are called in as needed. A large building, on the other hand, is likely to have numerous full-time employees in addition to a full-time manager on site. Often the staff of a large building will be divided into teams—a management team, a maintenance team, and a leasing team.

The Management Team. In a larger sense, every person employed to operate and maintain the office building is a member of the management team.

Staff for an Office Building

Management Team
- Building manager
- Assistant manager *or*
- Administrative assistant
- Bookkeeper

Maintenance Team
- Building superintendent (or maintenance supervisor)
- Building engineer (or maintenance technician)
- Janitorial supervisor
- Cleaning personnel
- Security supervisor
- Security personnel
- Contractors

Leasing Team
- Leasing supervisor
- Leasing agents

Position titles shown here are representative; actual titles may vary from one geographic area to another. (Specific roles have been described in the text.) Building or property size will dictate the differentiation of responsibilities and the numbers of individuals in each position. Often there is a separate position of tenant finish coordinator. This person may be assigned to the leasing team at a large property but is more likely to be a member of the management team in other situations. There may also be some overlap of responsibilities, especially where the total staff is small. For example, the administrative assistant might serve as receptionist and maintenance coordinator in addition to performing general office work. In the latter role, he or she would be the person who receives and records service requests and distributes them to the maintenance supervisor or, perhaps, directly to the technicians.

More specifically, however, the management team may consist of the building or property manager and whatever personnel are needed to handle administrative responsibilities. The building manager has overall responsibility for accounting and budgeting for the property, building and equipment maintenance and janitorial services, leasing and tenant relations, building insurance and real estate taxes, and advertising and public relations. In general, the manager establishes programs, policies, and procedures that are implemented by others then supervises the personnel and approves the relevant paperwork.

An assistant manager might be responsible for many of the day-to-day management duties (e.g., coordinate maintenance and contractor activities) as well as general office work (e.g., receive and record service requests, take telephone messages, type correspondence). On the other hand, specific office duties might be the domain of an administrative assistant.

A bookkeeper may be employed to prepare the payroll, bill tenants for rent and other charges, process bills for payment, and maintain appropriate accounting records related to these activities. In some situations, the bookkeeper may actually issue checks for payroll and bill payments and make bank deposits. It is more likely, however, that bill payments and payroll checks would be issued by the management firm's main office. Rent payments would be sent to the main office, and bank deposits would be made from there.

The Maintenance Team. Supervisory oversight of the maintenance function may be the responsibility of a building superintendent, or the position might be titled maintenance supervisor. This team leader position is responsible for all building maintenance, including janitorial services and building security, and may also coordinate tenant improvement construction and move-in. This person supervises and oversees work done under service contracts, including elevator and HVAC preventive maintenance and janitorial services. If janitorial work is performed by on-site employees, there may be several cleaning personnel whose work is directed by a janitorial supervisor who reports to the building superintendent. If security personnel are building employees, this position might be responsible for supervising them. However, if security is contracted and there are several security personnel on site, the contractor may provide at least one security supervisor who would report to the superintendent or the building manager. Skilled tradespeople and licensed or certified technicians may be called in on an as-needed basis (possibly under a specific service contract), and it is likely their work would be supervised by the superintendent. Oversight responsibilities of the position may also include tenant improvement construction done by on-site staff although the building manager may supervise work done by outside contractors.

Responsibility for maintaining the building's mechanical, plumbing, and electrical systems may be assigned to a building engineer or maintenance technician. This person performs needed or scheduled (preventive) maintenance and maintains records of operation and maintenance of various equipment. There may be a chief engineer who supervises several engineers or technicians. Engineers and technicians may be differentiated in their roles, with the former working exclusively on building systems and the latter responsible for responding to tenants' service requests. Work assignments are likely to define the specific positions, and position titles may vary.

Responsibility for maintaining an inventory of maintenance parts and supplies and authority to issue purchase orders for replacements would be vested in the building superintendent although specific record keeping may be done by all team members as part of their work assignments.

The Leasing Team. When a building is new, leasing will be a major activity. Several people may be employed as leasing agents, and they may report to a leasing supervisor who reports to the building manager. After occupancy is stabilized, renewal leasing and replacement of tenants who move out may be handled by the manager, perhaps with the help of a leasing agent. However, during periods when numerous leases are due to expire within a short period of time, additional leasing personnel may be brought in, and a leasing supervisor might be appointed. If the managing agent is a management firm, there is likely to be a fully staffed leasing department, and its personnel would be assigned to individual properties on an as-needed basis. Leasing may also be done under contract, in which case the leasing agents' activities would be coordinated or supervised by the building manager.

Leasing agents' main role is contacting prospective tenants and successfully leasing office space to them. The owner and the building manager establish specific parameters for leases, and the agents negotiate with tenants' representatives within those parameters. In particular, there will be a minimum base rental rate per square foot and a maximum dollar amount per square foot allowance for tenant improvements. The agents also need to know how pass-through expenses will be prorated and whether a ceiling or expense stop can be negotiated. Another consideration is whether and to what extent options and rent concessions can be offered to help close a leasing deal. Agents are expected to meet agreed-to leasing goals (square footage and time frames), and they are responsible for verifying the creditworthiness of prospective tenants. They are also required to document their contacts and successes in negotiating leases in order to receive commissions. (Leasing agents' role and compensation are covered in more detail in Chapter 8.)

Leasing personnel also play a role in marketing the property to prospective tenants. Responsibilities of leasing agents may include evaluation of the marketplace, the property, and its competition to facilitate development of a marketing plan. They may contribute ideas and strategies for using advertising and public relations. They follow up on promotional activities by contacting prospective tenants directly. The extent of individual agents' participation in the marketing effort may vary, depending on the leasing requirements at the property and the skills they bring to the job.

Team Coordination. The operations manual should establish the authority and responsibility of individual team positions and provide guidelines for making management decisions. This information should be reiterated in a job description for each position. To ensure consistent performance of the work to be done, the manual should include policies and procedures that state how specific tasks are to be performed and who is to do them (details are provided in Chapter 5).

The office building manager is the primary coordinator of all management activities on site. If the various types of tasks are to be carried out by a small group—i.e., one bookkeeper, one leasing agent, one maintenance engineer—the manager would be the sole team leader. In most large buildings, however, there will be a sizable staff divided into teams as described above. In such situations, the manager would directly supervise the management office staff who perform bookkeeping and other administrative tasks. Because tenant relations is a major ongoing activity, this is usually supervised directly by the office building manager although it may be desirable or appropriate to appoint a tenant relations coordinator to do this work exclusively.

The building superintendent or maintenance supervisor would be responsible for scheduling maintenance tasks, assigning engineers or technicians to perform them, and ensuring that the work is properly documented. Specific work plans would be approved by the building manager. There may be a supervisor of security who develops the specific schedule for security tours of the building and maintains records of security activities and incidents. Depending on the scale of operations, the supervisor might report to the building superintendent or to the manager. There might be a separate security team.

The leasing supervisor would coordinate the activities of individual leasing agents to ensure that tenants are actively being sought for all available spaces and that negotiated leases conform to established leasing parameters. This leadership position might be titled director of leasing, and the responsibilities might include supervision or coordination of marketing tasks and the personnel who perform them.

The number of people needed to ensure that various tasks are performed to established standards and in a timely manner will determine the number of supervisory positions. When large numbers of people are involved, it is good management practice to appoint supervisors, rather than have all positions reporting to a single entity. For example, a security or janitorial supervisor might be able to oversee the work of half a dozen employees. A chief engineer or maintenance supervisor might direct the work of three or four engineers or maintenance technicians. In these types of situations, only the supervisory positions would report directly to the building superintendent (or the building manager).

It is also good management practice to hold regularly scheduled team meetings. Such meetings afford an opportunity to air grievances as well as discuss changes in work requirements. In the maintenance area, preventive maintenance assignments might be made in the context of a meeting where employees can also report on the completion of prior assignments or ask for assistance with problematic aspects of a task. The leasing team might get together regularly to discuss strategies and share tips. The maintenance and leasing team leaders should report progress and problems to the office building manager, and this may be done in regular meetings. In addition to team meetings, occasional meetings of the entire staff should be part of an overall program of employee communications. Staff meetings help make employees feel they are part of the overall building operations, that they can

Components of a Job Specification

- Position title
- Supervisor title
- Principal duties
- Education/training required
- Skills (specific equipment, computer software; mandatory or desirable)
- Language skills (English facility, bilingualism; mandatory or desirable)
- Tools, instruments, texts (furnished by employee; mandatory or desirable)
- Prior work experience (type, duration; mandatory or desirable)
- Licenses/certifications (mandatory or desirable)
- Professional affiliations/designations (mandatory or desirable)
- Samples of work (mandatory)
- Travel required
- Relocation (mandatory; reimbursed)

A job specification is an in-depth analysis of the characteristics to be sought in an applicant for a particular position. It facilitates development of a formal job description. (See Chapter 5 for a detailed discussion of job descriptions and their use.)

contribute ideas beyond their exclusive work areas. Such meetings also provide an opportunity for the group to applaud each other's successes and recognize service anniversaries.

The Selection Process

A competent staff is the result of hiring qualified individuals to fill well-defined positions. An important preliminary step is development of a *job specification,* which is an in-depth analysis of the work to be done and the attributes of the employee who can best do it. This analysis forms the basis for a *job description* and can be helpful in defining the job parameters for help-wanted advertisements.

Additional research is needed to determine an appropriate salary level or range for the position to be filled. If the salary being offered is too low, it may not be possible to hire the most-qualified applicant. However, too high a salary can skew the salary budget for the property and upset the balance of salaries across the staff as a whole. One of the best ways to determine salaries is to survey the marketplace to find out what is being paid for different types of positions in the local area. Sources of published data include employment agencies, trade and professional organizations, and federal, state, and local governments. Sometimes other real estate management companies will share information. The key is to contact the appropriate data source. For positions specific to real estate and its management, other management firms may be the best source locally. For positions that are common to many industries (e.g., clerical, data entry), information can be sought from any company that employs people in such positions. For positions that require technical skills (e.g., HVAC maintenance), an industry-specific organization should be contacted. If the need is to create or upgrade a compensation program, it may be desirable to work with a human resources consulting firm that specializes in compensation issues. Specific policies related to hiring have been outlined previously in the discussion of human resources in Chapter 5. That discussion is expanded here.

Recruiting. When the job description and salary are established, recruiting can begin. While there are numerous recruitment strategies, the following are considered major sources of job applicants.

- Internal promotion—The most important resource is a building's current staff or, by extension, employees of the management company. Promotion from within—even a lateral move—has little risk because the employee is already a known quantity. This approach is good for staff morale because it offers real opportunities for individuals to advance within the organization. It recognizes and rewards superior performance and enhances the promoted employee's productivity. Promotion usually means that a lower-level position is the one filled from the outside, giving that new employee an opportunity to start up the organizational ladder.
- Personal referrals—Another excellent source of applicants is a referral from an employee or a business associate. Real estate managers who attend local meetings of professional organizations often share information about job openings or people they know who are looking for work in the industry. These prospects are likely to know something about the building and its staff already. Also, they are likely to be capable individuals, otherwise they would not have been referred.
- Help-wanted advertising—These types of ads may be placed in newspapers or trade and professional magazines. Newspaper advertising is effective in reaching the local market, especially when classified ads adequately describe the open position and are categorized properly in the paper. Trade publications are excellent vehicles for reaching people with specialized technical skills. However, they have the potential to generate responses from a wide area. If a respondent outside the local market is considered for the open position, reimbursement of relocation costs may be a consideration in the employer's hiring decision and the applicant's decision to accept the job. Also, long lead times for placing ads in such publications can delay a hiring decision. The advertising medium should serve the need to fill a particular position.

- Employment agencies—Agencies work with an employer's detailed job description to screen candidates for the available position. This is a preliminary screening for a match of job skills, experience, and other requirements. The employer only interviews the most-qualified applicants. This can be a real time saver in the absence of a human resources department or if the position requires specialized technical expertise. If a candidate brought by an agency is hired, the employer will pay a fee. Often the fee is equivalent to a month's salary or a percentage of the annual salary for the position being filled.

  Also in this category are *executive search firms,* which will conduct an extensive search on an employer's behalf, and there is a financial obligation regardless of whether someone they recruit is actually hired. These firms are most often used to fill one-of-a-kind, hard-to-fill, or high-level positions for which it is worthwhile to pay a substantial fee.

- Educational institutions—Colleges, universities, trade schools, and other entities that provide education and technical training usually maintain a data base of position openings as a service to their graduates. Large management companies may recruit directly on these campuses. Many have career days or similar types of opportunities for students to find out about potential employers. This allows one company representative to meet with many potential job applicants in a short time and select potentially qualified applicants for further interviews.

- Trade unions—Trade unions often have apprentice programs and offer job referral services in connection with them. This can be an excellent source for skilled tradespeople.

- State employment commission—Certain government contractors and other employers may be required by law to list positions with the state employment commission. The local office can be contacted by telephone to find out what requirements are in effect. This may also be a source of applicants if the commission administers unemployment compensation in the state and in connection with that maintains a data base of available job openings.

Help-wanted ads should be self-screening. They should list the major responsibilities of the advertised position along with the skill and education requirements. Applicants should be asked to send a resume or letter describing their qualifications and including a telephone number where they can be reached. (Sometimes a salary history or an asking salary will be requested.) These ads may identify the type of business but not give the company name, and they usually use a post office box or a blind box number provided by the newspaper or other advertising medium. This allows employers to follow up with applicants that are of interest without being required to respond to everyone who answers their ads.

Identifying Job Candidates. In most employment situations, a job opportunity elicits a large number of responses, and there are practical limits to how many respondents can be considered for an opening. This is where an employment agency or want-ads with a blind post office box can be most helpful because they partially pre-screen applicants. A blind ad that is very specific about the duties and skill requirements of a position will help job hunters determine for themselves whether and how well their skills and abilities match the job information. If an employment agency is used, it may run want-ads that similarly narrow the field of applicants.

Whether done by a staff person or an agency, preliminary screening of job candidates can be conducted by telephone. Information gathered in telephone interviews should add to the resume data provided by the applicant. In this way, under- or over-qualified applicants can be eliminated at an early stage along with those whose salary requirements exceed the range set for the open position. Each applicant who has been qualified by the initial screening should be scheduled for an interview, at which time a standard *employment application* form should be completed.

In a large organization, someone from the human resources department may perform the screening and schedule interviews. The person who will make the hiring decision becomes involved only after the field has been narrowed. Where there is no human resources department, the decision-maker would do the initial screening and interview scheduling. This is the person who ultimately is responsible for hiring and supervising the new employee.

Interviewing. The employment decision should be based on the candidate's ability to perform the job. Properly conducted interviews enable the employer to determine whether and how well individual applicants qualify for the open position.

Preparation is essential so that the interview will be as productive as possible. The interviewer should study the job description, referring to the job specification as appropriate, and review the applicant's resume immediately prior to the interview. Basics of the interview can be summarized as follows:

- Greet the applicant in a friendly manner.
- Engage in small talk to put the applicant at ease.
- Try to establish a relaxed atmosphere and maintain it throughout the interview.
- After the informal overture, briefly describe the duties and responsibilities of the position.

Sample Questions to Ask in an Employment Interview

Work Experience

- Tell me about your current position (or your most recent job).
- What did you do?
- Why did you choose to work for that employer?
- Which duties did you like best? Why?
- Which did you like least? Why?
- Why are you seeking a new position (or why did you leave your last job)?

Training and Supervision

- What type of training were you given by your previous employer?
- How were you supervised?
- What did you like best about that supervision?
- What did you like least?

Career Plans

- What type of work are you most interested in doing at this time? Why?
- What is your long-term career goal?
- What type of work is involved in other jobs you are interviewing for currently?

Company Interest

- What do you know about *[name of your company or office building]*?
- How did you obtain the information?
- Why do you want to work for *[name of your company or office building]*?

Job Specifics

- What is your understanding of the various requirements of the job?
- Have you performed this type of work before? When? Where?
- Were you successful?
- How was your performance measured?
- What job-specific skills do you have?
- Do you know how to use the equipment required on the job?
- What kind of special training have you had that would help you in this job?
- What type of additional training do you think you will need in order to be successful in this job?
- What is your opinion of the work hours and schedule?
- What is your opinion of the amount of work and variety of duties in the job?
- How do you respond to close supervision?
- What is your opinion of the physical effort involved in the job?
- Do you have any physical problems that would keep you from performing this job but not some other job?

These are suggestions for potential questions to be asked in an interview. They may not all apply to every position at the office building. Other questions may have to be asked to obtain information or the applicant's opinions regarding aspects of a particular position. In dealing with personnel issues, consistency is all-important. To avoid potential claims of discriminatory hiring, best practice is to ask the same questions of *all* candidates for a particular position and to use the same criteria in evaluating each candidate's responses and resume.

Subjects to Avoid in an Employment Interview

- The applicant's race, color, religion, national origin, or gender[1]
- Birthplace of the applicant or his or her parents or spouse
- The applicant's religious denomination or faith, religious holidays observed, or church membership or participation
- The applicant's native language, the language commonly used at home, or how the applicant learned the language[2]
- The applicant's marital status, number of children or other dependents, or spouse's occupation[3]
- The applicant's former name[4]
- The applicant's age or date of birth[5]
- The applicant's height or weight
- The applicant's driving license number[6]
- The applicant's military experience outside of the U.S. armed forces[7]; dates, conditions, or type of discharge; draft classification or other eligibility for military service; an applicant's National Guard or Reserve unit or whereabouts during war years
- Membership in any social clubs or fraternal organizations, except for unions and trade or professional organizations
- Numbers and kinds of arrests[8]
- Any disabilities that have no bearing on the job[9]
- Whether the applicant is a high school or college graduate[10]

Notes:

1. Likewise, a photograph may not be requested at any stage before an applicant is actually hired.
2. Applicants may be asked which language(s) they speak and write fluently if foreign language skills are relevant to the job.
3. *After* employment, information about dependents may be needed for participation in employee benefit programs.
4. Applicants may be asked if they ever worked or were educated under another name if the information is needed to verify their qualifications.
5. Applicants can be asked if they are over the minimum legal age and under a bona fide mandatory retirement age. (Employment ads containing age specifications that might bar workers under or over a certain age are considered discriminatory; however, there is usually a minimum age for driving licenses, and there may be state-imposed restrictions on the types of work that can be performed by teenagers.)
6. If the position requires the individual to drive a vehicle owned by the property, it would be appropriate to ask if the individual has a current driving license.
7. Applicants may be asked if they have received any notice to report for duty in the U.S. armed forces; otherwise, inquiries into an applicant's experience in the U.S. military may be made only if needed for an employment history.
8. It is appropriate to inquire about *convictions* that bear a relationship to the job.
9. It is permissible to inquire about a disability that would prevent the applicant from performing the job.
10. You may ask for the highest grade completed.

- Ask questions that will reveal the applicant's skills and knowledge relevant to the job.
- Use a written list of questions and ask the same questions of each applicant for a particular position.
- Structure questions so they cannot be answered with a simple yes or no.
- Give the applicant a copy of the job description to read and comment on.
- Encourage discussion by asking additional questions that elicit the applicant's opinions; some of these may be answered yes or no.
- Conclude the interview in a way that leaves the applicant with a positive impression of the employer and the open position.

At the end of the first interview, it is appropriate to let applicants know that others are being considered for the position and who will contact them about the outcome of their interviews. If asked, the interviewer may indicate the extent of the hiring process if a second interview is required or if applicants are expected to undergo testing. However, no promise of further interviews or of employment should be made at this time.

Sometimes multiple interviews are conducted, including a meeting with the applicant's future co-workers. If initial interviews are conducted on site, an interview at the management firm's main office may also be required for some positions. Each applicant who will be moved forward through the process should be contacted and asked to return for another interview or for testing.

Hiring Decisions. Before proceeding beyond the initial interview, there should be general agreement among all those involved in the hiring decision that a particular applicant should be seen again. Even if the first applicant interviewed seems an obvious choice, all applicants who passed the first screening should be interviewed before the final decision is made.

Once there is general approval of an applicant, the next step is to check references. It may be preferable to do this by telephone to expedite the hiring process. Requiring written references can delay the decision, possibly resulting in the loss of a preferred applicant to another employer, and the information obtained in this way may be only minimal. (Most employers will verify a job title and period of employment; often they will not provide any other information, even with the former employee's written authorization.) These days, e-mail may offer a viable alternative to telephoning. However, a potential employer is likely to obtain more information, expressed candidly, in a telephone call.

Written reference requests should ask specific questions, and they should be accompanied by a written authorization (release form) signed by the applicant. (It is appropriate to ask for responses to be returned by fax.)

Employers should be asked to verify the employment information the applicant provided on the application form. Personal references should be asked how long they have known the applicant and the context of their relationship (business associate, friend, member of same professional organization). When references are checked by telephone, there should be a standard form for documenting the results. Minimally, it is important to note the date and time, who was contacted, the information requested, and the response received.

In some situations, it may be desirable or appropriate to verify data about education or training. When hiring for a technical position that requires specialized knowledge or skills and, perhaps, a specific license or certificate, it is prudent to check whether an applicant has the requisite skills or certification as stated on the application. There could be problems if someone is hired based exclusively on the application data, and it is discovered later that the individual is not properly qualified to do the work. Equipment might be damaged or a co-worker or other person might be injured if the worker is not competent, or there may be a penalty or fine if he or she is not properly licensed. In addition to authorization to verify the application information, the employment application should include statements (1) that the individual certifies that the information is true and correct, (2) that the individual understands that incorrect or misleading information may void the application, or (3) if the applicant were employed, that employment could be terminated.

Assuming everything checks out, the next step is to determine the compensation to be offered to the individual. While the salary must conform to the employer's policy on wages and salaries, it should also be competitive within the local job market as noted earlier in this chapter. More information on compensation is presented in the next section.

The hiring supervisor or other decision-maker should extend the offer of employment to the applicant. If someone is being promoted from within, it is a good idea to make the offer in person. For outside applicants, the offer can be extended via telephone. However, the offer should always be confirmed in writing. A copy of the letter should be kept in the employee's personnel file along with the employment application and any documentation that application information was verified.

Once a decision is made and a person has been hired, the remaining candidates who were interviewed should receive a letter thanking them for their interest in the position. It may also be desirable to keep their resumes on file for awhile in case a similar position becomes available since these candidates have already been through the screening and preliminary interview steps. State law may mandate that applicant information be retained for a specific period of time regardless.

The Issue of Compensation. Compensation has already been mentioned in the context of determining the salary or wage for a position. In addition to specific monetary compensation, employees almost always receive an adjunct compensation package that includes paid time off for vacation and sick leave and may provide health care insurance and other nonmonetary benefits. The specific benefits employers offer will depend on what they can afford as well as what competing employers in their local area are offering. Some firms provide a variety of insurance programs (life, health care, long- and short-term disability) that are fully employer-paid. Today, however, most employers ask their employees to share the cost of health care insurance in particular, with the employee's share handled as a payroll deduction. (Specific benefits are described in Chapter 5.)

The compensation for individual positions must be viewed in the context of salaries and benefits for the entire staff. When there are others on staff who can train an inexperienced employee, it may be possible to offer below-market wages to start. However, the problem with low starting salaries is that they discourage more-qualified applicants from taking a position and lead to increased turnover of existing employees because incremental increases never quite catch up with the market. It may be necessary to pay a higher-than-market salary to hire or retain a highly skilled employee, especially in a market where there is heavy competition for the employee's skills. Sometimes a high salary is necessary to offset a less-than-competitive benefits package. However, a high salary will not compensate for poor supervision or an unsafe work environment.

Because wages and benefits represent a substantial portion of a property's operating budget, employee compensation should be considered in the context of meeting the owner's investment goals for the property. The objective should always be to establish salaries and benefits that allow the manager to hire qualified people while staying within budget. The overall compensation program for the office building should be communicated to all staff members because they are directly affected by it. Employees need to know what policies affect their salaries and the basis for receiving raises and promotions. In addition, they must be made to realize that, while their qualifications were the basis for their being hired for their positions, on-the-job performance and personal contributions to the management effort will determine their salary increases and career advancement.

Staff Training and Supervision

New employees need to be welcomed to the work place. They will also need some training to get them started in their jobs. Likewise, existing employees need ongoing training to keep their skills up-to-date. To avoid turnover, the manager should develop programs that motivate employees to increase their productivity and continue their employment. As an employer, it is important for the manager to evaluate employees' performance and reward them with salary increases.

Orientation. New employees should be provided with an orientation to the job and to the organization. This should include an explanation of the management firm's mission and how it is being accomplished if that was not covered during the interview. A history of the firm, the range of services it provides, and how it is organized should also be addressed.

Some small companies introduce new staff members to all the other employees. Minimally in a large organization, the newcomer should be introduced to everyone in the department and then to those in other departments with whom the employee will interact on a regular basis. A tour of the workplace—in an office building, the relevant portions of the building itself—is also in order. Minimally, the new employee needs to know where fire exits and restrooms are located and where other management staff members work in the building. This is also an opportunity to point out security requirements, safety rules, and other matters of importance that can prevent injuries, minimize errors, and avoid embarrassment in the future.

Some companies prepare an *employee handbook* that outlines the firm's policies regarding work hours, attendance, employee benefit programs, performance evaluations, rules of conduct, and other details related to the workplace. In addition, or instead, new employees may be given copies of the operations manual (or at least the sections relevant to their specific work).

The supervisor may review the job description with the new employee to be sure any outstanding questions are answered. If the newcomer will receive on-the-job training, a schedule should be worked out in advance so the training can begin as soon after the first day as possible. Administrative or clerical employees need to learn how office equipment (fax machines, photocopiers, computer components) works. Maintenance workers need to know the locations of tools and supplies as well as building systems and equipment. The orientation should be tailored to the employee's position. In today's high-technology work environment, most if not all new employees need to be shown how to log on to the computer in their work area and how to access e-mail. Maintenance technicians may need training on the software that is used for scheduling and documenting maintenance work. An accounting professional may not have explored all of the capabilities of the management accounting software used on site. There may be differences in computer hardware (drives, peripherals) or an internal network that should be explained.

The first days and weeks in a new job can be confusing and stressful. The orientation should be designed to make the new employee feel at ease in the work environment and help him or her become a productive member of the management team as quickly as possible.

Training. Continuous training should be provided for all employees. It should not be exclusive for new staff members. The amount and type of training will depend on individual employees' skills and knowledge and their position within the management organization. For a large staff, it may be practical to consider training programs for groups of employees who perform similar work and have similar skill levels. Whenever possible, however, training should be part of an overall development plan for the individual employee. The approaches to training are many and varied. Some of the types of training used in real estate management include the following.

- On-the-job training—Usually conducted in the workplace during normal business hours, this one-on-one learning situation is the most common approach to training. Employees gain first-hand knowledge and experience by observing and listening to an experienced co-worker or supervisor and then performing the tasks themselves. They have an opportunity to ask questions and receive answers while being shown the proper way to do the work.
- Classroom instruction—If there are several employees to be trained and the subject can be presented as a lecture or via film or videotape, classroom instruction may be appropriate. This assumes the building manager or supervisory personnel are qualified to serve as instructors or facilitators. (Having knowledge and experience is not a guarantee that someone can present information effectively to others.) Otherwise, since classroom instruction permits the training of a maximum number of employees in a minimum period of time, it may be cost-effective to bring in a subject matter expert to conduct a half-day or one-day seminar.
- Outside education and training—When employees need specialized knowledge or have to develop specific skills, it is often better for them to attend professional seminars or to take courses at a college or trade school. Because the content of such programs is often wide-ranging and general, outside education should be considered as a supplement to on-the-job training rather than as a replacement. These types of courses are often expensive, and that is an important consideration. However, it may be cost-effective to have a training entity develop in-house courses for a large staff and tailor the content to the property's operations.

Staff meetings can also be used as training opportunities, especially when discussion sessions led by the manager provide opportunities for participatory learning and a free exchange of ideas.

Encouraging employees to pursue additional education and training on their own is another way to foster employee development. Reimbursement of tuition for courses and payment for memberships in professional associations are often among the benefits included in a comprehensive employee compensation program (see Chapter 5).

Motivation and Employee Retention. Managers need to be aware that not all employees respond the same way to the same motivators. When employees are asked what is most important to them in regard to their jobs, money is seldom listed first although it is ranked high. (In fact, surveys of managers indicate that being appreciated is what employees desire most; salary usually ranks third or lower.) Apart from its purchasing power, a particular salary level gives an employee a certain status and recognition within the workplace, and that can motivate some employees to succeed. However, money is not the only motivator. The manager must find out what motivates individual employees and use that information to maximize the employee's performance.

The tools of motivation include praise and challenges in addition to promises of financial rewards. Praise may be given in the form of awards, letters of recognition, or acknowledgment before their peers. Employees may be challenged by assigning them additional tasks, increasing their responsibilities, or promoting them to the next level in their work area. Salary increases are the most common form of financial reward, although bonuses and commissions may also be appropriate, depending on the position. The overall work environment is also a key motivating factor. Employees like to feel that they and their ideas are valued and that they are contributing to the success of the management operation. The following are some tips on motivating employees.

- Make sure performance expectations are clearly stated up front.
- Welcome staff members' suggestions.
- Acknowledge others' ideas and accomplishments.
- Foster teamwork but also help individuals achieve personal goals.
- Encourage creativity.
- Reward excellence.
- Be consistent.

Because jobs in real estate management are very different from each other, performance expectations should be based on the duties and responsibilities of the individual job. A bookkeeper may be expected to prepare and issue reports on a regular schedule. A building engineer might be expected to perform certain maintenance tasks within established time limits. A leasing agent may be expected to obtain signed leases for a defined amount of office space within a specified period of time. Communicating expectations in specific terms helps employees do their jobs to the best of their abilities.

In the past, involvement in employees' personal lives was discouraged. Today, however, employers design benefit programs that respond to workers' personal needs. Flexible or part-time work schedules, sharing of jobs (two people may each work half days or alternate days), day care for em-

Components of an Employee Evaluation (Review Factors)

- Quality
  - —Accuracy of work performed, or
  - —Content of work produced
- Productivity
  - —Amount of acceptable work produced
  - —Ability to meet time schedule
  - —Self-direction
- Cooperation
  - —Willing to accept assignments
  - —Able to be flexible in various jobs
  - —Works with others effectively
- Oral communications
- Written communications
- Responsibility
  - —Performance of duties
  - —Utilization of time
  - —Care of equipment used
- Dependability
  - —Attendance
  - —Punctuality
- Attitude
  - —Toward work goals
  - —Toward co-workers
- Personal appearance

This list identifies the typical broad categories for a basic review format, including some component elements that might be commented upon within individual categories. It may be desirable or appropriate to give supervisors specific guidelines for conducting an evaluation. For example, they might be encouraged to comment on initiative and innovation in evaluating an employee's demonstration of self-direction as part of productivity. The review form should be applicable to all positions within an organization, with instructions to omit categories that do not apply to specific positions.

Often the information is organized in a table or grid format with the review factors in a column at the left followed by columns for the supervisor's ratings and space for comments on each factor. Supervisors may be asked to rate employees on a scale of 1 (unsatisfactory or needs improvement) to 5 (superior or excellent). A simpler system might use only three ratings: Unsatisfactory (corrective action needed), satisfactory (meets the requirements of the job), and excellent (consistently exceeds expectations). In addition to the factors listed here, supervisory personnel might be evaluated on their skills in planning, organizing, and decision making. There should be space for the supervisor to summarize his or her overall review and recommended actions as well as spaces to record the date of the interview with the employee and the signatures of both employee and supervisor. The employee should be given a copy of the completed form, and a copy should go into the employee's personnel file.

ployees' young children (either as an on-site service or facility or as a subsidy that defrays part of the employee's cost) are among the options being explored by today's employers. Rather than being summarily fired for substance abuse that interferes with their work, employees may be given an opportunity to receive counseling and allowed to stay in their jobs as long as they attend the sessions regularly, improve their work performance, and stay "clean." There are costs and risks in such a strategy, but it is also an investment in the person which can foster loyalty and maintain stability among the staff. (To minimize liability, it is wise to confer with an attorney and a risk consultant before initiating this type of program.)

Performance Evaluation. Evaluation of employees' performance should provide the employer with an overview of the individual's progress and accomplishments while also helping the employee understand how well he or she is (or is not) doing the job.

A particularly valuable strategy is to have the employee do a self-evaluation at the same time and compare the two evaluations. Most often, the employee will be more outspoken about his or her shortcomings than the supervisor will. If both employee and supervisor recognize a particular weakness, it is easier to effect improvement. Without the employee's own evaluation, weaknesses noted by the supervisor alone may only elicit a defensive response from the employee. Usually the results of this type of dual evaluation are fairly similar, making it easy for the supervisor to discuss individual points with the employee. If the two evaluations are substantially different, it is likely that there may be serious problems; however, the evaluations provide a basis for addressing identified problems. Clear communications in the work environment and making sure employees understand what is expected of them from the beginning will go a long way toward minimizing problems in the workplace.

Employee reviews should be scheduled regularly and carried out when promised. The supervisor and the employee should be able to focus on the expected level of performance and identify and measure specific achievements. This forms the basis for improving the employee's performance in the next review period, which may be stated in terms of specific goals and time frames.

A formal evaluation program also provides support documentation in the event that a reprimand or other corrective action is needed. In such situations, the supervisor should discuss the problem with the employee in a personal interview and document what was said in their meeting. (There may be a specific form or format for such personnel action reports, a copy of which should be kept in the employee's personnel file.)

In real estate management, employee evaluations may actually be carried out at two levels. The first is one-on-one personal evaluation of the employee by the supervisor, and the second is evaluation of the performance of the building management team as a whole by the management firm's executives. The latter is an overall assessment of how well the team achieved its goals, what might have been done better, and what needs to be done in the future to improve the team's performance.

The timing of performance evaluations should be stated in the operations manual, which should also prescribe the written format or form to be used. It is a widely accepted practice among employers for a performance review to be scheduled after an initial period of employment, which may be as little as three months or as much as six months. The idea is to assess the employee's early progress so both employer and employee can decide whether to continue or terminate the employment relationship. During this period, the employee may not receive full benefits (paid sick days may be limited; vacation time may accrue but cannot be taken). Upon favorable review at the end of this period, an individual becomes a "regular" employee. (The term "permanent employee" should be avoided because there are legal ramifications if an employee is terminated and he or she decides to pursue a claim of wrongful termination.)

Personnel Records. A personnel file should be established for each employee of the office building at the time of hiring. The file should be added to as appropriate throughout the period of employment (performance evaluations, salary increases, documentation of disciplinary actions). Minimally, the following documents or information should be in every employee's personnel file.

- Employment application form (with resume attached, if appropriate, and verification of application data)
- Employment confirmation letter
- Job description of starting position
- Proof of identity and work eligibility (INS form I-9)
- Payroll paperwork with appropriate signatures (including tax withholding forms)
- Performance evaluations
- Salary adjustment forms showing reasons for changes
- Personnel action forms or other records of disciplinary actions
- Confirmation letter, new job description, and other documents relating to promotions or in-house job changes
- Disciplinary or complimentary letters or memoranda
- Records of participation in continuing education programs (courses, seminars, training sessions) and any reimbursement from the employer
- Termination documentation (letter of resignation or memo to file stating reason for termination, payroll change form, exit interview/questionnaire, termination checklist)

These records should be retained for at least five years after employment is terminated or whatever period is required by law.

Employers are obligated to ensure the privacy of their employees. Personnel files should be kept in locked cabinets in a secure storage area, and no one other than immediate supervisors or staff members with specific business requirements (e.g., payroll department) should have access to these records.

Terminating Employment

In the past, an individual might have an entire career with one company, often starting in an entry-level position and being promoted several times. Today, however, office building managers must recognize that employees do not stay with one employer forever, and periods of employment with a single firm are getting shorter and shorter. Some employees will leave by choice to pursue a more-challenging job in their field, a higher salary, or a complete career change. Others may be discharged by the employer because of inadequate performance or misconduct on the job. (Employee discipline and involuntary termination are discussed in Chapter 5.) Regardless of why people leave their employment, the office building should have in place defined policies and procedures that ensure the employee will be treated fairly while also protecting the managing agent from false unemployment benefit claims and/or lawsuits.

Employees who leave voluntarily should be required to submit a written resignation to their supervisor. This is to verify for personnel records that their termination is voluntary. Most employers also conduct an exit interview or ask departing employees to complete an exit questionnaire. Usually they are asked to state why they are leaving and what improvements in the organization or the work environment might have kept them on the job. This information could prove valuable in regard to individuals' perceptions regarding employee benefits, working conditions, and other aspects of the work place. At a minimum, it may be prudent to use an *employee termination checklist* (Exhibit 6.1 is an example) to ensure that all necessary information is obtained, wages and other monies due the employee are paid, and any business property in the employee's possession is returned to the employer.

Staffing Alternatives

The size of the staff will depend to some extent on what is being managed. For a small building with only a few tenants, tenant services may be provided by outside contractors; the office building manager may do all of the relevant accounting and record keeping, conduct periodic inspections, and arrange for services that tenants request. A firm that manages a portfolio of small office buildings may employ real estate managers, leasing agents, maintenance workers, accountants, and administrative support personnel and provide services directly to each managed building. In this situation, routine building maintenance, janitorial services, and regular preventive maintenance might be performed on a rotating schedule while some aspects of elevator and HVAC maintenance, for example, would be handled on a contract basis, and tenants would contact the management firm to request specific services. A high-rise office building may employ its own staff and

Exhibit 6.1
Sample Employee Termination Checklist

Employee Termination Checklist

Employee Name ______________________ Position Title ______________________
Dates of Employment: From __________ To __________ Termination Effective: __________
Reason for Termination: ____
____
____

Compensation Due: Wages/Salary _____
Vacation Pay _____
Sick Pay _____
Severance _____
Other _____
Total _____ Paid: Check Number _______ Date _______

Building/Employer Identification Card Returned: ______________________
Keys/Access Cards Returned: Office __________ Building __________ Other __________
Tools Returned: ____

Resignation Letter (if voluntary): Date Received _______ Termination Interview Held _______
Forwarding Address: ____
____
Forwarding Telephone No.: ____

Note that it may be desirable to include a deduction for money owed to the employer before the total compensation due is calculated. Additional line spaces or a blank area may be provided for explaining the reasons for termination. The form should be initialed or signed by the person who completes it. The completed checklist becomes a part of the employee's personnel record.

have one or more people in each of several positions—e.g., administrative support and maintenance personnel. There may be only one leasing agent, but there might be a maintenance supervisor as well as several technicians reporting to that supervisor. There might also be contracts for elevator maintenance and for janitorial services that are performed during nonbusiness hours. For reasons of liability protection, building security is usually a contracted service as well.

Management of low-rise office buildings in a suburban setting may be handled somewhat differently. A suburban office park comprising several discrete buildings might have a management office in only one of the buildings or not at all. There may be no lobby attendants unless this role is filled by security personnel. Lawn care and groundskeeping may be provided as contracted services. There may be no elevators to maintain, and building HVAC systems may be less complicated. Janitorial services may be less comprehensive or provided on a less-than-daily schedule. On the other hand,

Outsourcing to Independent Contractors

Another approach to outsourcing is to hire independent contractors to do certain types of work on the property. This type of arrangement is often seen in working with skilled tradespeople. For example, in maintaining an office building, the tasks requiring a licensed electrician may be few in number and infrequent. While it is not practical to employ a licensed electrician directly, it may be desirable to have in place a contract under which such an individual performs specific electrical maintenance tasks on an as-needed basis.

It is especially important for the contractual arrangement to define the relationship between the independent contractor and the managing agent of the office building to avoid creating an employer-employee relationship. Determination of work hours and methods of performing tasks, who supplies materials and tools, independence of initiative and/or judgment, method of payment for services, and continuity of the relationship are among the issues that differentiate between independent contractor and employee status. (The U.S. Internal Revenue Service is very specific about the difference.) To protect the managing agent and the property owner, potential arrangements with independent contractors should be reviewed by legal counsel before the contract is signed.

there is likely to be infrastructure (roads, sidewalks, water and sewer lines) to maintain along with parking lots or garages. Here again, a management firm with a large staff might provide all of the needed maintenance and administrative services, scheduling staff assignments from the firm's main office.

To some extent, the staffing needs of an office building will depend on tenants' expectations as agreed to in their leases. Also, tenants' expectations will be higher if they leased space in a Class A building as opposed to Class B or Class C. Building age is also a factor. A new building will require less-intensive maintenance than one that is five or more years old. On the other hand, maintenance of a single-tenant building might be the responsibility of the tenant rather than the building owner or a managing agent. Lease-up of a new building or one that is newly rehabilitated will be more intensive than renewal and turnover leasing at a stabilized property.

To ensure that needed work is done in a timely fashion and within budget allowances while also operating the property to meet the owner's financial goals, the office building manager must plan carefully. As indicated in the foregoing discussion, employing on-site staff is not always the most practical strategy. Sometimes it is appropriate to explore alternatives for providing needed services. Contracting has been mentioned specifically. Employee leasing or outsourcing is an increasingly popular approach to staffing when a small number of employees is involved. For short-term projects or to cover staff vacations, it is often more practical to bring in temporary workers with the needed skills than to hire additional personnel. Internships and work/study programs are another way to fill positions on a part-time or temporary basis while at the same time having an opportunity to train potential full-time employees.

Contracting. The variety of services that may be contracted in office building management has been listed previously (see box in Chapter 4). Contracts usually ensure that specific services are provided on a set schedule at a given cost for parts and labor (hourly rate), with any deviations to be approved in writing before work is done. The contract is also a guarantee that the workers have the necessary skills, tools, and/or certification to do the job correctly. Any default by the contractor means the contractor bears the cost of making corrections (both labor and replacement parts).

The contractor should be required to carry workers' compensation insurance for its employees and to maintain appropriate liability insurance, with proof of coverage to be provided to the office building manager in the form of certificates of insurance. Contract workers may need to be bonded (fidelity bonds for accounting or administrative personnel who handle the owner's funds; payment and/or performance bonds for construction contractors) or licensed to do certain types of work, and the manager should verify that such bonds or licenses are current.

The advantages of contracts include known costs and reduced liability for ownership and management. Also, if the amount of work changes, a contractor can easily and quickly provide additional personnel as opposed to the manager hiring additional staff. Employee record keeping is minimized—payroll and withholding taxes are the contractor's responsibility. Dealing with outside contractors may also minimize or avoid union pressures. The disadvantages also need to be considered. Contracted work may cost more overall than hiring staff to do it. Generally, contracts provide specific services under specified terms; there may be no provision for contract personnel to assume additional duties, and emergency services provided during nonbusiness hours may require overtime charges. Likewise, the workers will be supervised by one of the contractor's personnel; management staff cannot give direct orders to contract labor.

Advantages and disadvantages of contracting should be weighed carefully in each situation. Frequency of tasks, liability, and the availability of skills and equipment are the kinds of things that should be weighed in determining whether work should be done by site employees or contracted out. Maintenance work that is done only occasionally (e.g., window washing), work that requires specific skills, tools, or licensing (e.g., elevator maintenance, pest control), and services that have inherent liability or hazards (e.g., provision of security) are often contracted for just those reasons.

Employee Leasing. In order to operate more efficiently and cost-effectively, companies often consider *outsourcing* (also called employee leasing) some of their business activities. In office building management, possibilities for outsourcing include groundskeeping, maintenance, and janitorial services, space planning and architectural design, and secretarial and accounting services. The concept of employee leasing has been around since 1852, when the founder of the Pinkerton National Detective Agency began to provide security guards to other businesses under a contract for services. The guards were Pinkerton employees who worked at another company's place of business. Employee leasing has evolved into what is known today as the professional employer organization (PEO) industry. Contracting with a PEO is one way to provide staff for a property when the number of people needed is small and there are financial limitations on the benefits that can be provided directly.

The arrangement with a PEO allows a small staff to receive high-quality benefits that the building owner or managing agent could not afford to provide independently. It also relieves the manager of the work of processing payroll, paying withholding taxes, and administering other aspects of employment. The contract creates a *co-employer* relationship under which the office building manager retains responsibility for supervision of the employee's work while the PEO assumes many of the risks and responsibilities of employment administration and handles most if not all of the relevant paperwork. Both entities share liability for hiring and termination of employees, workers' compensation insurance claims, and compliance with employment laws and regulations. The workers are considered employees of the building, but the PEO serves as the "employer of record" for purposes of payroll and benefits administration and payment of withholding taxes.

Contracting with a PEO is like having the services of a fully staffed personnel department in a large corporation, including the expertise of adjunct professionals (doctor, risk manager, financial planner). Depending on the company, PEO services can include recruiting and screening job applicants, evaluation of employee performance, safety assessment of the work site, and development of employment policies and procedures and an employee handbook. The main advantage of the PEO arrangement is reduced employee turnover. It gives an office building manager the ability to cultivate employee loyalty and retain valuable expertise that would be lost if employees left voluntarily because their compensation and benefits were inadequate. There are time and cost savings as well.

Temporary Help. Occasionally there will be situations for which time is the defining element. One person being off for a sick day may have little impact because co-workers can do some or all of that person's work along with their own, or the work can be deferred for a day. However, a week or more of vacation or an extended leave of absence may not be as easily covered. When the need arises, temporary workers can be brought in to ensure that building operations and other management activities are not interrupted.

Qualified temporary workers can be found to fill just about any position today, from accountants to building engineers. The temporary agency will want to know particulars—e.g., skills needed, type of work to be performed, hours of work—so they can assign a qualified individual to the job. Usually, the agency charges a fee (an hourly rate) that covers the temporary employee's wages and benefits plus a profit for the agency. Employing temporary staff allows an office building manager to fill a short-term need, whether a week or six months, with as little as 24–48 hours' notice. Different agencies may have to be used to fill different temporary positions, but when particular agencies prove satisfactory, it may be prudent to maintain a relationship with them. Such relationships will make it easier to fill positions quickly in the future because the agencies are already familiar with the building's staffing requirements.

It is also possible to hire someone directly to fill a position on a temporary or part-time basis. Such a strategy can be used to determine if an additional position is needed at all and whether an individual is a good match for a particular job and for the organization. If the position becomes permanent, there is already someone in place who can potentially move into it full time.

Participating in Work/Study Programs. As a way of developing future employees, it may be worthwhile to partner with a local high school or college that offers a work/study program. High school programs typically have students attend their regular classes for part of the day and work on site the remainder of the time, although class work and job scheduling may be alternated on full days. College programs may alternate two semesters of full-time class attendance with one semester of full-time work. In either case, the student is paid a wage or salary but may not receive the usual employee benefits. Such programs vary, of course, but they offer students an opportunity to experience the real world of their career choices. They also provide employers with low-cost, part-time or temporary workers who have potential to become full-time regular employees. Apprenticeship programs sponsored by technical high schools and trade unions similarly offer a combination of classroom learning and on-the-job training in the skilled trades and are another possible source for future employees.

7

Market Analysis and Rental Schedule

Rental rates determine office building income which, in turn, determines the property's value and its capacity to repay borrowed funds. Existing tenants as well as prospects measure the value of office space by comparing rental rates from one building to those of another. An understanding of how rental rates are set and the factors that are considered in setting them is fundamental to leasing success. Rents that are too high may discourage tenants from leasing space in the building and thus reduce its potential to yield an acceptable revenue stream. Rents that are too low may result in a high level of occupancy, but the amount of rent collected may not be sufficient to pay operating expenses and debt service for the building. In either situation, property value will be reduced because of the resulting reduction in NOI.

Understanding of rental rates begins with a market analysis that allows the manager to position the property in its correct market and evaluate it according to the standards of that market. Market analysis provides a basis for creating an effective marketing strategy, determining lease terms and provisions, and developing an accurate rental schedule for the office building.

Market Analysis

In order to analyze the office market, one must understand what a market is. Inherent in the concept of a market is the exchange of goods or services between willing buyers and sellers. For purposes of this discussion, the office market has two components: (1) a group of office space users with specific needs to be satisfied, money to spend in satisfying those needs, and a willingness to spend it and (2) buildings that compete with the subject property, their characteristics and amenities, and the lease terms they offer. Analysis of an office market looks at both prospective tenants and competing products to develop the information needed to set rental rates that will maximize occupancy levels and income for the office building. This requires knowledge of economics, finance, and statistics coupled with an understanding of psychology, sociology, and politics—because leasing decisions are made by human beings.

Defining the Market Area. The first step in market analysis is to define the market area. This begins with an examination of the area surrounding the building because it includes the buildings that compete directly with the subject property. This neighborhood must also be evaluated within a wider region. The objective at this level is to identify trends that affect the supply of office space in the area and the demand for that rental space. Regional analysis may reveal changes elsewhere in the region such as mergers and layoffs by major companies that do business with building tenants as clients or suppliers. Such economic shifts can affect those tenants' ability to pay rent and reduce overall demand for office space. Analysis of the neighborhood may reveal that many competing buildings are undergoing rehabilitation or renovation, decreasing the local supply of office space, though only temporarily.

While the region or neighborhood may be readily identifiable, exact boundaries may have to be defined on the basis of the form in which market data can be obtained. An area may be defined by its population in the form of a Standard Metropolitan Statistical Area (SMSA) used by the U.S. Bureau of the Census. An area may be defined by its geography based on natural or manmade barriers (a river, a hill; a rail line, a highway). Sometimes political boundaries such as zip codes define a data set. The most important factor in defining the boundaries of the region and the neighborhood is its impact on the subject building with regard to locating potential tenants and identifying competing properties.

Regional Analysis. The region of an office building is the area in which changes in the local economic situation (population, employment, etc.) are likely to affect the subject property. The size of the region will vary with the size of the subject building. For a very large building, the entire SMSA may apply. In some parts of the United States, however, the SMSA includes surrounding counties, in which case the city boundaries may provide the best definition of the region for a downtown office building. The region for a large suburban office park might include the entire county or more than one county. The region would be much less extensive for a small building in either setting.

A building's region may be defined more or less narrowly for different factors. Because vacancy rates can vary in different parts of a metropolitan area, a narrower definition may be more appropriate for an analysis of supply and demand. On the other hand, regional climate, which affects heating and air-conditioning costs, can be related generally to the area of the country. In general, a regional analysis should encompass the following:

- *Economics*—The national economy as well as the regional economy should be examined to determine whether they are stable (little or no change) or, if they are changing, whether the changes signal growth or decline. Economic conditions influence rental rates. They also affect the choice of marketing techniques. This portion of the analysis should include money, labor markets, types of businesses in the region, and the governmental policies that affect businesses. Financing methods and the nature of the mortgage market determine the availability of funds for construction of new buildings and rehabilitation of old ones. Businesses planning to stay in the area or relocate to it will be attracted by the availability of a pool of qualified workers. A healthy economy includes a variety of businesses so that the impact of one company moving out of the region or experiencing slow sales will not be widely felt.

  Governmental controls related to real estate must also be considered. Property tax rates are likely to be stable in areas where new development provides a continually widening tax base, but they may increase as the cost of local government increases if there is little or no new development to add to the tax base. Also, more and more local governments are imposing constraints on development in order to control urban and suburban sprawl. Knowing how local government affects real estate at this stage allows the property owner and the office building manager to confer with legal counsel and take appropriate action (e.g., develop information to protest real estate taxes).

- *Demographics*—A region's economy is controlled by its residents and businesses, so it is important to learn about the population of the area. Demographics is the study of the various socioeconomic factors related to populations (age, sex, race, education, occupation, income, family size, nationality, religion, etc.). It also measures changes in population size and density resulting from births, deaths, and movement of people into and out of the region. Businesses are interested in population data that relate to their labor needs.

- *Psychographics*—Psychological factors are also a component of leasing decisions. To enhance their image, attorneys in private practice and new law firms may seek office space near courthouses and established, successful law firms. Investment counselors, accounting firms, and brokers may want to be near financial institutions. Health care professionals usually want to be near a hospital or medical center. Knowing what appeals to different businesses helps office building managers identify prospective tenants and develop marketing strategies to appeal to them.

Regional data can be obtained from a variety of sources. State and local governmental agencies can identify sources of information on the local economy if they do not compile it themselves. Local newspapers usually publish economic statistics on a regular basis. Demographic data compiled by the U.S. Bureau of the Census are available on the Internet (www.census.gov). Private companies often compile and publish demographic data focused on very small geographic areas. Trade organizations and local chambers of commerce are potential sources for psychographic data as well as information on the local economy.

Neighborhood Analysis. An office building's operations and productivity are affected directly by its immediate surroundings. This is the area in which the building competes for tenants, its so-called neighborhood. The neighborhood may be a large geographic area for a building in a suburban or rural location, while the neighborhood of a building in the CBD may encompass only a few blocks. Within the CBD, neighborhoods may be defined by their predominant tenancies (a financial district surrounding banks, a legal district adjacent to a courthouse). In many cities, local newspapers (often working with office industry professional groups) define specific business districts to subdivide rental advertisements for commercial space, and that same type of division can be used to identify a building's neighborhood if others in the market follow the same practice. A neighborhood analysis should identify the selling points of the surrounding area as well as its undesirable features and the types of prospective tenants that will be attracted to the location.

A neighborhood analysis is similar in content to a regional analysis but more narrowly focused. It should explore the economy of the area, including the local employment base, rent levels, and vacancy rates. New construction is a sign of growth while high vacancy rates indicate decline. Business expansion or contraction, movement of businesses into and out of the neighborhood, and company mergers, closings, and bankruptcies are other factors to be considered. They also signal potential changes in the supply of and demand for office space.

Accessibility is an important consideration. Public transportation from residential areas to the neighborhood of the office building is vital for any location but particularly for buildings in the CBD. Even when neighborhoods are well served by trains, buses, and rapid transit, cumulative travel times, frequency of operation, and cost will determine whether they will be used. Where there is no public transportation, there must be ample parking at a reasonable cost and easy access to major highways. Within the neighborhood, street layout (cul-de-sacs, one-way streets) and traffic restrictions (time limitations for on-street parking, prohibitions against over-sized trucks) affect location desirability.

Governmental restrictions within the neighborhood should also be identified. Zoning ordinances that prohibit laboratories and manufacturing entities from locating in office buildings can preclude certain types of tenancies. Proposed zoning changes that would result in incompatible land uses affect the locational value of a neighborhood. Urban renewal projects and major development can affect utility services, forcing major capital investment by building owners to accommodate the changes. A city may create a special improvement district and levy special assessments against private property in order to repay bond indebtedness or to cover the cost of maintaining parks and green areas in a neighborhood. Such a financial obligation must be known for purposes of budgeting.

The overall quality of the neighborhood encompasses things like city services, utilities, and aesthetics—the general appearance of buildings and thoroughfares, compatibility of architectural styles, and distracting noise, dust, and odors—all of which affect a building's competitiveness.

Nearby amenities should also be explored. Tenants prefer office space in locations where their employees have access to restaurants, shopping, and other facilities. Proximity to hotels and airports may be a consideration for companies whose employees travel frequently. Easy access to cultural facilities (museums, theaters) and educational institutions also adds to a neighborhood's desirability.

Once the first market survey is completed, the inventory of office space should be updated regularly to account for the impact of new construction (including remodeled space), construction that is planned but not yet started, and tenants who withdraw from the market or whose space requirements are reduced. Space removed from the market (demolition, change of use) must also be taken into account. Maintaining an up-to-date inventory of office space in the local market should be a standard operating procedure (see Chapter 5).

Analysis of Supply and Demand. As an integral component of the market analysis, demand for office space must be projected and related to supply. In a particular real estate market, the *supply of office space* is the total amount of occupied and unoccupied space in that market, including buildings under construction and in the planning stage. In that same market, the *demand for office space* is the amount of occupied space plus the amount of vacancy that is expected when market rents are stable. As a general principle of economics, rents are likely to be lowered when supply exceeds de-

The Laws of Supply and Demand Applied to Office Space

When supply is greater than demand (including vacancy), rents decline.
When demand (including vacancy) is greater than supply, rents increase.
When demand (including vacancy) equals supply, rents tend to be stable.

These rules apply to *effective rents;* an excess of office space in a market may not change quoted rents, but it could increase the use of rent concessions to secure leases. As stated, these rules also do not account for inflation. In the real world, if supply exceeds demand, rents would be expected to rise more slowly than the inflation rate, and if demand exceeds supply, rents would be expected to rise more rapidly than the inflation rate. If the market were in equilibrium, rents would increase at the same rate as inflation.

Note: While it is appropriate to include buildings in the planning stage when analyzing supply, it is important to know when they are expected to be ready for occupancy. A supply analysis could be skewed if it included properties that will not be constructed and occupied for three or more years into the future. The figures could also be distorted if the analysis does not account for space that has been or is scheduled to be removed from the market, either due to demolition or to a change of use (i.e., from office to residential).

mand and to be raised when demand exceeds supply. When demand equals supply, rents remain stable, but this state of equilibrium rarely lasts long because supply and demand are constantly shifting.

Supply and demand determine the strategies for marketing an office building. Excessive supply creates a market in which competition for the few available tenants will be very strong, and marketing must be aggressive. In a stable market (equilibrium), a fair number of tenants will be looking for rental space, but marketing need not be overly aggressive. The effort should be focused on getting the attention of available prospects. When the number of potential tenants is greater than the amount of space available to fill their needs (i.e., demand far exceeds supply), marketing efforts may be scaled back, emphasizing institutional advertising and other means of ensuring that prospects are aware of the building and what it has to offer.

Likewise, supply and demand are important considerations in setting rents. When demand outstrips supply, rents can be set at rates that favor ownership because the lack of supply increases the property's rental value. This happened in the late 1970s, when demand for office space far exceeded supply, and rents skyrocketed. In a situation of excess supply, as happened in the early 1980s when many U.S. office markets were overbuilt, rents tend to plummet. In developing a rental schedule, the supply of office space must be compared to the level and strength of demand for rental space.

Measuring Supply. The supply of office space in a market consists of existing buildings, new buildings under construction, office buildings in the

Categories of Data

Care must be taken in using statistical information. Data sources can be categorized as primary or secondary. *Primary data* are gathered firsthand via a specific survey. The data source is usually a participant in the activity being surveyed or an official data repository. Primary data are usually gathered by conducting mail surveys or personal interviews or by consulting official records and are therefore verified by the data-collector as coming from a knowledgeable or authoritative source. Collection of primary data is time-consuming and expensive. *Secondary data* are usually available in published form (e.g., the U.S. census, statistics published by trade associations). The reliability of the data depends on the care taken in the collection process. While using secondary data may save time, effort, and money, the user may not know how the data were collected, what sampling technique (if any) was used, and whether numbers have been rounded.

planning stages (future construction), and space that is available for sublease.

To determine the supply of existing office space, managers must rely on local information sources. Real estate brokers, appraisers, and leasing companies monitor the office market and keep current records of the total space inventory in their local marketplace. Vacant space may be available in a few buildings with large blocks of space or in a large number of buildings with small amounts of space for lease. Also a component of existing supply, but often difficult to estimate, is the amount of sublet space. It is not included in vacancy figures because it is being paid for. Nevertheless, it is being marketed to prospective tenants, often at below market rates. Large amounts of sublet space can appeal to small space users who may be willing to take the space "as is"—i.e., without any new tenant improvements—and thereby negotiate more favorable rents for themselves.

Information about planned projects can be obtained from local governments, financial institutions, chambers of commerce, and public utilities. When a building is scheduled to open and when that opening actually takes place can be very different. Grouping new buildings by year of opening will identify how much new space can be expected to come on stream in the near term (those under construction) and somewhere down the line (planned but ground not yet broken). The location of planned new office space is also important for identifying trends. Downtown office buildings may have to compete with new suburban office parks and the amenities they offer tenants. New commercial construction as part of an urban renewal project may change the boundaries of a CBD neighborhood and the quality of the space within its boundaries.

Office building managers must keep in mind that all office space is not equal. There are many types and grades of office space, and the inventory

Classification of Office Buildings

Office buildings are classified on the basis of a combination of factors that include location and accessibility, building finishes, system standards and efficiency, building amenities, and market perception in addition to the rents they receive. (Specific classification factors are described in detail in Chapter 2.) Sought-after amenities include elevator systems, parking, restaurants or other food services, copying services, express mail (USPS) and air courier collection on site, physical fitness centers, and child care facilities. The most prestigious buildings are Class A. They compete for premier office users by offering high-quality finishes, state-of the art systems and amenities, and exceptional accessibility in return for above-average rents. Most buildings in a competitive environment are considered Class B or Class C. Buildings in Class B offer fair to good quality finishes, systems, and amenities and receive average rents. Buildings in Class C offer functional office space at below-average rents.

Class A varies from market to market, depending on what is desirable at a particular time. Construction materials, exterior finishes, building height, and architectural design are important aesthetic considerations for prospective tenants. Competitive pressure from new construction often changes existing Class A buildings to Class B, unless a Class A building is maintained to the highest standards and renovated to keep it up-to-date.

On the other hand, the class system tends to be somewhat misleading because it often ignores the issue of space usability. Some tenants prefer lobby atriums and other features that enhance building common areas and willingly pay for their upkeep. However, in competitive markets and when money is tight, prospects may be less willing to pay common area maintenance costs on large amounts of unusable space. In such situations, space in a Class B building may be more desirable than that in a Class A building.

of market supply should reflect the quality of the space and the services and amenities offered. The local market of prospective tenants will determine what factors affect the quality of office space. Building age and location will have a major impact in almost all situations. However, a number of other factors—rental rates, vacancy rates, tenant mix, accessibility (transportation, parking), standards of maintenance, amenity packages, and pass-through charges—are also carefully weighed. The importance of individual factors will vary with building type (high-rise versus low-rise), age (old versus new), and location (downtown versus suburban). Quality factors are a component of the competitive pressure on a building.

Office buildings are also categorized as Class A, B, or C. The most prestigious buildings—often also the newest structures—in the best locations with the most-desirable amenities are considered Class A, and they command the highest rents. Older buildings in less-desirable neighborhoods often have deficiencies and command much lower rents; they are considered Class C. Buildings whose quality and rental price is in between these two

Exhibit 7.1

Calculating Office Space Demand

Demand = Occupied Space ÷ Stabilized Occupancy Rate

The formula is derived mathematically as follows:

Demand = Occupied Space + Enough Vacancy to Keep Rents Stable
Demand = Occupied Space + (Demand × Stabilized Vacancy Rate)

Demand−(Demand × Stabilized Vacancy Rate) = Occupied Space
(1−Stabilized Vacancy Rate) × Demand = Occupied Space

Solving for demand, you get the following:

Demand = Occupied Space ÷ (1−Stabilized Vacancy Rate)
Demand = Occupied Space ÷ Stabilized Occupancy Rate

extremes are considered Class B. Office buildings generally compete for tenants against buildings in their same class. Existing Class A buildings must be maintained to highest standards in order to retain their Class A status. Vacancy rates may not be the same for all three categories.

In measuring supply, it is also important to differentiate between competitive and noncompetitive space. *Competitive space* is space comparable to that of the subject property that is competing for the same prospective tenants. *Noncompetitive space* is occupied by long-term tenants or building owners and is usually not available to absorb current market demand. A building may contain both competitive and noncompetitive space: The owner may occupy twenty floors of a 30-story building and lease the remaining ten floors to other businesses.

Estimating Demand. There will always be some vacancy in a marketplace, otherwise tenants would not be able to move. To compensate for this when estimating demand, the actual amount of space needed by tenants should be increased by the "stabilized" vacancy. As the laws of supply and demand imply, *stabilized occupancy* is the occupancy rate needed for market rents to remain stable (i.e., occupancy at market equilibrium). If rents are increasing sharply, supply is less than demand, and the estimated stable occupancy must be higher than the actual occupancy rate. In other words, the vacancy rate in the market is so low that rents are rising rapidly. Demand is calculated by dividing the amount of occupied space by the stabilized occupancy rate (see Exhibit 7.1).

Demand for office space is a natural consequence of growth in office-based types of businesses. The main sources of office space demand are:

- Tenants in the local market who are experiencing internal growth and need additional space.
- Firms seeking to upgrade their office space to reflect business success (a consequence of economic growth within the community).
- Formation of new businesses locally and establishment of local branches of firms headquartered elsewhere.
- Businesses relocating from areas outside the community.

Changes in large industries or major corporations may signal decreases as well as increases in demand. Mergers often lead to reductions of the combined entity's work force and, therefore, its space needs.

Information usable in projecting office space demand includes employment data developed by the U.S. Department of Labor, Bureau of Labor Statistics. Prior to 1997, data were collected by industry type using the Standard Industrial Classification (SIC) system. The SIC has been replaced by the North American Industry Classification System (NAICS), which is designed to standardize the classification of industries throughout the United States, Canada, and Mexico. There is also a technological resource that is useful in evaluating demand for office space. Called Geographic Information Systems (GIS), it is a combination of data bases, software, and hardware that allows users to evaluate rents, vacancy rates, and other factors by showing comparable property information on maps.

Demand is also affected by a reduction in the supply of office space. A building that is functionally obsolete may not be able to lease any of its space. An older structure may be demolished to make way for new construction. A corporation that formerly leased out part of its headquarters building may decide to discontinue such rentals and occupy the space itself. A building undergoing a major rehabilitation may remove some or all of its leasable space from the market supply, though only temporarily. These types of changes are ongoing in every office market.

Calculating the Absorption Rate. A simple definition of absorption rate is the amount of space leased during a given period, usually one year, compared to the amount of space available for lease during that same period. The absorption rate for a given period can be calculated as follows:

	Space vacant at the beginning of the period
plus	New space completed during the period
minus	Space demolished during the period
minus	Space vacant at the end of the period
equals	Space absorbed during the period (absorption rate)

When demand exceeds supply, the absorption rate is positive, reducing overall vacancy. When supply exceeds demand, the absorption rate is negative. Office markets in particular are subject to this phenomenon because financing may have been obtained when demand was high, but demand was beginning to wane when construction was started, and stopping construction would have cost more than completing the project since the financing was already in place. Ideally, there is a small amount of vacancy—supply is slightly greater than demand—so that tenants who need to expand can do so.

Real estate markets are constantly changing, making it difficult to calculate absorption rates. Building booms that respond to a shortage of office space are followed by periods when there is a surplus of space. Nevertheless, historical data are important in the determination of absorption rates. Data for several years allow calculation of an average annual absorption rate. This historical information, coupled with current supply and demand figures, allows office building managers to estimate how long it will take for the vacant space in a given building to be absorbed. For an existing building, the absorption rate can be used in setting rents and budgeting (estimating how much space will be rented during the year). For a proposed building, the absorption rate is useful in predicting leasing activity as part of the development plan submitted to obtain financing.

In calculating current absorption rates, it is helpful to know the kinds of tenants who are moving or expanding—significant numbers of accountants, publishers, associations, or other groups may signal changes in their business activities or the impact of new technologies. Some firms' space needs may be more stringent than those of a company that has merely outgrown its current location. It is also important to consider the types of space being absorbed and the kinds of tenants that are active in the market. Current absorption may be comprised of a small number of large space users or a large number of small users; each can have a different impact on absorption at a particular building.

Absorption rate is one of many factors considered in deciding whether to proceed with construction of a new office building. There are two approaches to estimating absorption for a particular building, and they are usually used together. One approach analyzes absorption at recently constructed properties that are comparable to the subject; the other uses *capture rate analysis* of competing properties. Using the first method, an analyst might find that nearby new buildings leased an average of 25,000 square feet per month, which provides a benchmark for the proposed building. Using the second method, one might assume that each of four competing buildings will capture 25 percent of the market and, accordingly, divide the annual leasing and absorption rates by four to find each building's share. While this approach is straightforward, it may be more appropriate to allocate building shares unequally. If one building has outstanding features or its location is superior compared to the other three, the analyst might consider that building likely to capture a greater share, say 40 percent, and the remainder might be apportioned equally among the other three buildings (i.e., 20 percent each). While neither approach is perfect, together they identify the likely potential absorption rate for a building. A precise estimate will depend on the unique features of the proposed building, the amount of preleasing that can be accomplished, and the ability to negotiate rents (i.e., use rent concessions) to speed the leasing process.

Property Positioning. Because no single building can satisfy the space needs of every office user, the most effective leasing strategy is to focus on users whose requirements can be fulfilled by the subject building. This is done by dividing the overall market into submarkets or segments based on location, space needs, and type of business.

- *Location*—Tenants often relocate from one building to another within the same neighborhood. Such changes may be driven by needs their current buildings cannot fill (e.g., more space, newer facilities, specific services or amenities). However, they do not want to move far because their clients and suppliers are also located near their old offices. Thus, firms that lease space in neighborhood buildings whose rents are comparable to the subject comprise its locational submarket. It should also be borne in mind that tenants paying lower rents in other buildings may be willing to pay higher rent in the subject if the move will improve their status (prestigious address), provide access to newer technologies (new construction or retrofit), or help them attract and retain better-qualified employees (more-accessible location, more pleasant work environment).
- *User size*—The configuration of an existing office building may permit its tenancy to include businesses of various sizes, from a major space user occupying several floors to a number of floors tenanted by small space users. While large space users are often sought after, they also tend to dictate lease terms, demanding economic concessions and special services. Small space users have less clout as tenants, but large numbers of them complicate the management of a building. Medium-sized companies are often preferred as tenants because they are less likely to be offered a lease buyout to move to another building, and if they do move out, the amount of vacant space is often more readily re-leased as is or subdivided.

  Tenant size is an especially important consideration in re-leasing. A large tenant may reduce its staff size and, therefore, its space needs by encouraging work-at-home strategies (home officing, telecommuting) or by laying off a large number of workers. That same tenant might be lured to a nearby building with an offer of a lease buyout. There may be only a few prospects of comparable size who could lease the amount of space vacated by a large user who moves out. It can also be difficult to lease space vacated by a small user unless an adjoining, presumably larger, tenant wants to expand into that vacant space. Segmenting the market based on tenant size will help identify likely prospects to lease specific spaces.

- *User type*—Demand for office space can be related to the type of user—corporate, government, general commercial, institutional, or professional. While corporations often own their own buildings, many become key tenants under favorable lease terms. For example, they may insist that the building carry their name, but this also benefits the building by adding prestige that will attract other tenants whose business is related to that of the major tenant. Advances in communication technology have allowed corporations to separate headquarters and administrative functions from customer service and other back office activities. As a consequence, they can locate executives in high-rent buildings in major urban centers while leasing large amounts of space for support operations in suburban or even rural areas where rents are low.

  The General Services Administration (GSA) in Washington, D.C., controls leasing transactions for the U.S. government, which is the largest single user of office space. Generally speaking, having the U.S. government as a tenant means a building will receive less rent than it would for the same space leased to a private business, and rents will be paid in arrears rather than in advance (i.e., rent is paid for last month rather than next month). On the other hand, the government is a stable tenant who pays rent regularly, and that in itself may be a plus. The GSA uses its own specifications for measuring space and drawing up leases. Agencies' space needs are announced in newspapers and elsewhere—seeking bids from landlords—and site selection is based on cost. Because state and local governmental agencies are usually funded on an annual basis, one-year leases are typical for them. While the presence of some governmental agencies may attract other tenants who serve the same clientele, other such agencies can be a negative factor in regard to a building's tenant profile. An agency that is a frequent target of protesters may require increased security. A strictly bureaucratic office may increase traffic in the building, slowing elevator service.

  Small space users who are more interested in good access and favorable rents constitute the general commercial type of user. They are excellent prospects for suburban office parks and free-standing buildings as well as downtown buildings that are well-located but not necessarily Class A. An office building may target specific types of tenants who would benefit from a specialized location that provides advantageous access to clients or services. Independent insurance agencies, real estate, accounting, advertising, public relations, lawyers, architects, and consulting services are examples. Also in this category are engineering, sales, and administrative functions of manufacturing businesses that are often located in office space near the firm's factories while executive offices may be located in a prestigious building downtown.

Institutional users comprise mostly finance-related businesses such as insurance companies, banks, and brokerage firms. Their offices are dispersed throughout the United States in suburban and rural areas as well as major cities. They tend to be stable tenants, flexible in their office requirements, whose prestige attracts related services to a building where they lease space.

Medical and dental professionals have unique requirements for office space and related facilities. Heavy equipment may require special reinforcement of floors. X-ray machines and other technological tools may need special high-voltage wiring. Some wastes generated by medical professionals are classified as biohazards and require special handling for disposal. Doctors prefer locations near other doctors and close to major medical facilities. While many such professionals maintain small private or group practices, demand for medical office space has decreased in general. In part, this can be attributed to hospitals offering captive office space on favorable lease terms and to professionals joining together to purchase a building through a form of cooperative or condominium ownership. Also, the rise of managed health care programs and their requirement for physicians and dentists to become part of a provider network has made it difficult for many of these professionals, medical specialists in particular, to maintain individual private practices.

Market segmentation allows market analysts to stratify demand for office space and identify an appropriate niche to fill.

Property Analysis

A comprehensive analysis of the subject property itself is critical to determining its competitive status and establishing a rental schedule. The first step is to identify the features and characteristics of the building that are likely to be evaluated by prospective tenants. These typically include the following.

- Location—It has long been held that the three most important factors in real estate are location, location, and location. For an office building, access to business support services is important for tenants. Restaurants, banks, and shopping are important considerations for their employees. In urban centers, public transportation is a must; access to major throughways is vital for suburban locations. A prestigious address or the image associated with a particular building is yet another factor related to location. A well-located building can command the highest rents in the market in spite of an inefficient design, poor maintenance, or both, while the rental income generated by a well-maintained but poorly located building may not be sufficient to pay its operating expenses.

- Age—A new building is highly competitive simply because it is new. By comparison, an older building, even in a choice location, may be at a disadvantage due to *functional obsolescence* unless it has been modernized or retrofitted.
- Efficiency—Building efficiency is a ratio calculated as net rentable area divided by gross area and expressed as a percentage. *Net rentable area* is space occupied and used exclusively by tenants. *Gross area* is the total amount of space in the building, which includes elevators, staircases, ventilation shafts, washrooms, and other core elements as well as tenants' occupied space. A more efficient layout means greater rental value. For example, two buildings may each have a gross area of 250,000 square feet. One has a net rentable area of 200,000 square feet while the second has a net rentable area of 187,500 square feet. The first is more efficient than the second and will generate more rental income (200,000 ÷ 250,000 = 0.80 versus 187,500 ÷ 250,000 = 0.75).
- Design—Architectural design can be both an asset and a liability because design affects building efficiency. An irregular-shaped building may be visually striking but problematic in regard to floor layouts. Corridor width and ceiling height can enhance or limit flexibility in configuring interior space of office suites. Floor-load capacity—the weight per square foot that a floor will support—is an important consideration for tenants who rely on mainframe computers and other heavy office equipment.
- Parking—When public transportation is limited or nonexistent, parking is a necessary convenience for tenants' employees and clients. Also an important consideration is availability. There may be a parking lot or garage next to or within an office building, but the building manager may have little or no control over the facility if it is operated by a concessionaire. For new construction, municipal code may require inclusion of a certain amount of parking space (usually a set number of parking spaces based on the building's rentable square feet).
- Maintenance—While general maintenance of the physical plant is a long-term concern of management, janitorial service has a greater im-

pact on a building's competitiveness. The latter consists of the day-to-day cleaning and upkeep of building common areas and tenant spaces whose results are highly visible to both tenants and prospects *(curb appeal)*.

- Elevators—Quality of elevator service is measured in terms of wait times and door opening speed as well as rapid movement from boarding floor to destination. Elevators are also a highly visible component whose location within the building, level of cleanliness, and overall appearance make a discrete impression on everyone who uses them. While efficient elevator service may be taken for granted, inefficient elevator service may discourage prospects from signing leases and drive existing tenants to relocate elsewhere.
- Mechanical systems—Tenants in modern office buildings expect their employees to be able to work in an environment that is comfortably heated in winter and adequately cooled in summer. Landlords may maintain higher temperatures in summer and lower temperatures in winter or limit after-hours availability of heat and air conditioning to conserve energy or to comply with governmental guidelines. Tenants understand these requirements and are more concerned about HVAC system capabilities than specific temperatures. Increasingly, advances in office technology mean tenants' computer hardware (hard drives, printers, scanners), communications devices, photocopiers, and other equipment place greater demands on building wiring systems. Mainframe computers often require a controlled air-conditioned environment. Large photocopiers require heavy-duty wiring and generate heat during operation. New buildings constructed with state-of-the-art systems can keep pace with user demand. So-called *smart buildings* have computerized controls that monitor and regulate electricity consumption and elevator and HVAC operations; they also include telecommunications systems. While it may be possible to retrofit existing buildings to accommodate technological advances, it may not be practical or cost-effective to do so. In today's world, buildings that do not have the infrastructure to meet the demands of technology cannot compete effectively.
- Security—A building security system should not only monitor employee and visitor traffic and protect property against theft, it should also include emergency procedures with plans for dealing with fires, bomb threats, and various types of crises. If a tenant has special security requirements, the cost of providing extra services should be borne by that tenant.
- Tenancy—A property analysis should include information about its tenancy. Company name, type of business, number of employees,

leased square footage, and potential expansion are among the types of data to be recorded for each tenant. A principal tenant or large space user may determine the types of smaller tenants that will be attracted to a building. Having a major tenant's name applied to the building may make it attractive to certain types of businesses because of that tenant's reputation. As an example, a building with a major advertising firm as its premier tenant will be a desirable location for companies that provide illustrations, photographs, and graphic art services to the advertising industry as well as print and broadcast media representatives and smaller advertising firms. The tenancy of a building is a factor given careful consideration by prospects. Some may prefer not to locate too close to their direct competitors; others will avoid locating in a building whose other tenants could detract from their reputations.

- Lease terms—The contents of individual leases affect a building's competitiveness and desirability. Prospects can easily project and compare occupancy costs (rent plus pass-through charges) for equivalent space in different buildings. Escalation provisions determine how well the property's income stream will keep pace with market rents. Renewal provisions can mean blocks of space are controlled for long periods of time, which can limit space availability to meet a prospect's specific needs. Even the requirement of a security deposit has an impact. Before adopting a policy of collecting security deposits, it is important to be familiar with local practices and check out landlord-tenant laws that may regulate how such deposits are handled. Tenants may be reluctant to lease space in a building that requires security deposits in a market where that is not a standard practice.
- Management—Building management provides tenant services such as security, maintains the building and its equipment, and markets and leases office space or supervises these activities while maintaining good working relationships with the tenants of the building. Savvy tenants can easily differentiate between a well-managed and a poorly managed office building by its curb appeal—a building has only one opportunity to make a first impression. They are also interested in the caliber of the management team, the way the staff treats their tenant-customers, and the availability of extra services and amenities (conference rooms, restaurants, fitness facilities). Local market trends will determine which services and amenities will be sought by prospective tenants and how their presence or absence will affect a building's desirability.

These same criteria should be used to evaluate comparable properties in the neighborhood.

Exhibit 7.2

Sample Office Building Field Research Worksheet

Field Research Worksheet

Building Name ____________ Owned by ____________
Address ____________ Managed by ____________
Contact ______ Phone ______ Leased by ____________

Building Type
___ Downtown ___ High-rise
___ Suburban ___ Mid-rise (elevator)
___ With other uses (retail) ___ Walk-up

Construction Information
Year completed ______
Under construction ______
Completion date ______

Building Size
Gross building area ______ sq ft Owner/prime tenant net rentable area ______ sq ft
Net rentable (office) area ______ sq ft Other commercial area ______ sq ft
On-site amenities ____________

Location Data (Area quality—above average, average, below average—building class, transportation)

____

Tenancy
Major tenant(s) ____________

Number of tenants ______ Average sq ft ______
Tenant mix ____________

Facilities
Heating ______ Air conditioning ______
Special electrical ______ Telecommunications cabling ______
Building standard tenant finishes (describe) ______

Comparison Grid Analysis. In order to determine an office building's competitive status, it is vital to collect information about similar buildings and compare them to the subject building and to each other. There may be many nearby buildings that can be considered competitors. For purposes of evaluation, however, it is imperative to identify which competitors are the most comparable in terms of their specific attributes. Buildings should be of similar type and size; a building with 50,000 square feet for lease is not comparable to one with a million square feet. The space available for lease should be designed for office use; office space cannot be compared to retail space. Also, comparables should be in the immediate neighborhood; a downtown building is not comparable to one in a suburban office park.

To ensure consistency of the data, it is a good idea to compile the same information about each building using a *field research worksheet.* The form

Exhibit 7.2 *(continued)*

Services Provided by Owner

☐ All utilities included in rent ☐ All utilities except electricity ☐ All utilities except ____________
☐ Hot and cold water ☐ Elevator service: ______ cabs ☐ Freight elevator service: ______ cabs
☐ Cleaning service (describe) ____________
☐ Security (describe) ____________
☐ On-site management ☐ On-site leasing ☐ Storage ____________ sq ft
☐ Parking: Garage _______ spaces Open lot _______ spaces Charges ____________ /month

Rental Analysis (as of ____________)
Percentage occupancy ______% Vacancy ______ sq ft ________ % Age of vacancies ________
Average rate for occupied space $_____ /sq ft net rentable area Range: $ ____ /sq ft to $ _____ /sq ft
Asking rate(s) for vacant space $ ____________ /sq ft Workletter ____________ /sq ft
Escalations ____________
Pass-through charges ____________
Other lease terms ____________

Concessions ____________
Method of computing net rentable area ____________

Comments

Prepared by ____________ Date ____________

This sample form is representative of the types of information usually collected about office buildings. Special issues such as environmental concerns (e.g., asbestos) and compliance with ADA accessibility requirements can be addressed in the comments area.

should include spaces to identify the building, its ownership and management, and a specific contact person. The area devoted to the details can be set up as a checklist that itemizes all the pertinent points and includes blanks for details of square footages, dollar amounts, and percentages. Space should also be provided for descriptions where they are needed. Exhibit 7.2 is an example of this type of worksheet. To facilitate comparison, a worksheet should also be prepared for the subject property.

Once all the data for the comparable properties have been collected, each building should be evaluated feature by feature, including rental rates and lease terms. The basic format is usually a table or grid, with building features listed at the left and the subject and comparable properties indicated as column headings (Exhibit 7.3, page 164). Base rental rates should be adjusted for pass-through expenses and other forms of additional rent.

Exhibit 7.3

Sample Office Building Comparison Grid

	Subject	**Comparable #1**		**Comparable #2**		**Comparable #3**	
Property Name							
Base Rental Rate							
− Concessions							
+ Expense Pass-Throughs							
+ Tenant Improvements							
= Tenant Effective Rent							
Categories	**Description**	**Descrip**	**Adj**	**Descrip**	**Adj**	**Descrip**	**Adj**
Location/Accessibility							
Age							
BUILDING CONDITION							
Exterior							
Grounds							
Common Areas							
Office Space							
Other							
BUILDING SYSTEMS							
Elevators							
HVAC Efficiency							
After-Hours Charges							
Life Safety							
Other							
AVAILABLE SPACE							
Location							
Floor Plate							
Storage							
Telecommunications							
Other							
PARKING							
Open/Covered/Garage							
Visitor Spaces							
Parking Ratio							
Cost to Tenant							
Other							
AMENITIES/FEATURES							
Vacancy Rate							
Total Rent Adjustments							
Adjusted Effective Rent/ Rentable Square Foot							
× R/U Ratio							
Adjusted Effective Rent/ Usable Square Foot							

The features listed in this form are among those commonly used for such comparisons. Forms to be used for a specific market comparison should identify features of the subject property selected on the basis of their value to tenants and their value in marketing the property to tenants. Construction materials, lobby features, acoustical qualities, floor-load capacity, and building security are other examples of features that might be compared.

For each comparable property, there should be space to describe individual features and to indicate a dollar amount for adjusting the comparable rents up or down. Assigning a dollar value to each feature—i.e., estimating what a tenant would pay because a feature is present or would not pay because of its absence—allows the analyst to derive a market-level rent for the subject property. If the feature is better in the subject property than in a comparable property, the comparable rent is adjusted upward; if the feature is not as good in the subject as in a comparable property, the comparable rent is adjusted downward. The adjustment amounts are totaled, and the comparable rent is changed to reflect the net adjustments. Comparison grid analysis is best used to evaluate specific rental spaces (a typical office space in the subject building compared to the same amount of space in a similar location in a comparable building). It is also best to use data from at least three competing properties, and preferably more, to ensure a valid comparison of rental rates. Care should be taken in selecting properties for comparison, paying attention to occupancy and vacancy rates as well as features and amenities. Full (100 percent) occupancy is usually an indication that a building's rents are below market rates while a high level of vacancy usually indicates that rents are too high. High vacancy may also signal problems with the building or its management. For a comparison to be valid, adjustment calculations should not be distorted by data from any single property.

Compiling comparison data is always a challenge. Office building managers will be aided in their efforts to collect information about competing properties if they are able to network with other local managers through memberships in professional associations such as a local Building Owners and Managers Association (BOMA) or a local chapter of the Institute of Real Estate Management.

Developing a Rental Schedule. To be valid, rental rates must reflect actual market conditions. As noted earlier in this chapter, rents rise and fall based on supply and demand. With this in mind, an office building manager can establish a base rental rate that reflects the local marketplace. The *base rental rate* is the maximum rate at which space in an office building can be leased on a net rentable square foot basis to yield a satisfactory occupancy level without being underpriced. In most areas of the United States, rents are quoted as dollars per rentable square foot per year although they may also be quoted as dollars per rentable square foot per month.

Base Rental Rate. The base rental rate should be determined from the information gathered in the regional and neighborhood analyses and, more specifically, from the comparison grid analysis. The data should be evaluated in context based on an assessment of the desirability of the subject property, the viability of the neighborhood, and the overall strength of the market. Setting a base rental rate is just the beginning. The rent for a particular space in a high-rise office building is affected by the following.

Exhibit 7.4

Sample Calculation of Base Rental Rate

Suppose you manage a 100,000-square-foot office building for which there are no comparable properties in the neighborhood. The property cost $8,600,000 ($8,000,000 building; $600,000 land) and was purchased with $3,000,000 down (equity) and a loan of $5,600,000 with annual debt service of $800,000. Building operating costs are $5.00 per square foot per year. The owner wants a 10% return on equity.

A base rental rate can be calculated as follows:

Annual operating expenses ($5 × 100,000 sq ft)	$500,000
Annual debt service	800,000
Required return (10% on $3,000,000)	300,000
Total income required	$1,600,000

Base rental rate = total income requirement ÷ building area
Base rental rate = $1,600,000 ÷ 100,000 square feet = $16.00/sq ft/yr

- View—Spectacular views of the city skyline in Chicago, the Golden Gate Bridge in San Francisco, the Rocky Mountains in Denver are building assets that command higher rents.
- Floor level—Higher floors typically command higher rents than do lower floors although demand for ground-floor space may warrant charging more rent for it than for second-floor space. Ground-floor retail space may warrant a premium in the form of percentage rent (a percent of the retailer's gross sales revenue).
- Proximity to elevators—On multitenant floors, spaces closest to the elevators often command higher rents from tenants (e.g., law firms) who want their offices immediately identifiable when clients step from an elevator.
- Climate—Office space on the north side of a building in most parts of the United States receives little or no direct sunlight. Because there is no glare on the windows and the HVAC load is reduced, such space may be more desirable and command a higher rent. Conversely, tenants in the Sun Belt may hesitate to lease space on the west side of a building, even with sophisticated HVAC systems in place, because of the potential for employee discomfort from the intense sunlight and the cost of cooling the space if the tenant pays that directly.

The relative value of these factors is determined by a floor-by-floor tour of the building, and the rental schedule should reflect the individual rates for all the spaces on all the floors.

In the absence of data on rents from other comparable properties, a

Exhibit 7.5

The Impact of Concessions

The office building manager must understand the concept of effective rent to accurately evaluate the impact of a rent concession. *Effective rent* is the cumulative rental amount collected over the term of a lease. If a lease term is sixty months, the effective rent is the total rent collected during the sixty-month period. When a period of free rent is given as a concession, the effective rent for the lease term is less than the quoted rent for the space. However, a period of free rent is preferable to actually reducing the quoted rent because the latter alternative may reduce effective rent for many years, not just one.

As an example, suppose the base rent is $16.80 per square foot per year for 10,000 rentable square feet of office space. On a five-year lease with one month free rent per year, the effective rent for the lease term is calculated as follows: 10,000 sq ft × $16.80 = $168,000 annual rent × 5 years = $800,000 total rent due. $168,000 annual rent ÷ 12 = $14,000 monthly minimum rent × 5 months = $70,000 free rent. $800,000 total rent − $70,000 free rent = $730,000 total effective rent ÷ 60 months = $12,166.67 effective monthly rental income. $14,000 monthly minimum rent − $12,166.67 effective monthly rent = $1,833.33 (approximately 13% lost income). On a square-foot basis for the five-year term, the base rent of $16.80 would be effectively reduced to $14.60 ($12,166.67 × 12 months ÷ 10,000 sq ft).

Instead of giving five months' free rent, suppose the base rent had been reduced to $14.60 per square foot. The total effective rent for the five-year lease term would still be $730,000. However, if the lease is renewed for another five years at a 5% increase, the total effective rent for the new lease term would be only $766,500 ($14.60 × 1.05 × 10,000 sq ft × 5 years) as opposed to $882,000 ($16.80 × 1.05 × 10,000 sq ft × 5 years), a difference of $115,500. In order to achieve the equivalent total effective rent of $882,000 for the new five-year lease term, the reduced rent would have to be increased 20.8% ($882,000 − $730,000 = $152,000 ÷ $730,000).

Note: While this example presents the basic method for arriving at effective rent for office space, it does not take into account the *time value of money,* a valuation concept often used in calculating effective rent for leases whose terms exceed one year. Incorporating the time value of money into the calculation would produce a lower rental rate per square foot than the stated $14.60. The impact of lowering quoted rent is magnified when viewed in the context of the whole office building. The overall effect is a reduction in NOI and property value.

base rental rate can be calculated using the subject property's operating costs and debt service requirements coupled with the investor's desired rate of return. (Exhibit 7.4 presents a hypothetical example.)

In a strong market, it is possible to charge maximum rental rates. In a weak market, however, rents must be competitive, or concessions such as free rent may have to be offered. A period of free rent is usually structured to retain a market rental rate for the space. While such short-term concessions (they may be for twelve, eighteen, or twenty-four months) reduce building income overall, the space will be occupied for a period of years afterward at a high rent. If the concession is a reduction in the rental rate, the building may not recover quickly from the financial loss because rent increases would have to be applied to the lower base rental rate (Exhibit 7.5).

Defining the Tenant's Leased Space—Other Considerations

- The tenant's rentable area can vary. If a tenant occupies an entire floor, areas that are normally considered common area on the floor (e.g., corridors) become part of that tenant's leased premises.
- The load factor for a building may not be based on actual space. Sometimes a lower load factor will be used so that the building will be more competitive in the market, even though a higher load factor would be warranted.
- Regardless of how space is measured and/or a load factor is determined, both tenant (lessee) and landlord (lessor) should be in agreement regarding the load factor stated in the lease.

Method of Space Measurement. An important consideration for developing a rental schedule and for marketing and leasing office space is the method of measuring the space for lease. Measurement of office space is based on the following fundamental concepts.

- Gross area of a building—the entire interior floor area.
- Rentable area of a building—the entire interior floor area *less* vertical penetrations through the floor (elevators, stairways, ventilation shafts).
- Usable area of a building (the space occupied by tenants)—the rentable area *less* certain common areas shared by all tenants (corridors, washrooms, storage facilities).
- Usable area of a tenant's leased office space—the area bounded by the partitions that separate one tenant's space from another (demising walls). This is the area available exclusively for the tenant's use and may comprise a portion of a floor, an entire floor of a building, or a series of floors.
- Rentable area of a tenant's leased office space—the space on which the tenant pays rent. This usually includes certain common areas in addition to the tenant's usable area. Tenants on each floor of a multistory office building pay rent for the common areas on their respective floors.

Each tenant's *pro rata share* of the common area of the floor is the ratio of the tenant's usable area to the usable area of the entire floor (the sum of all defined usable areas on that floor) expressed as a percentage. All tenants in an office building also pay rent for their proportionate share of building common areas. These include the ground-floor lobby and other areas that benefit all tenants mutually (e.g., building core and service areas, conference rooms, mail rooms).

Although there are different ways to measure office space, the *Standard*

Exhibit 7.6
Load Factor Calculation

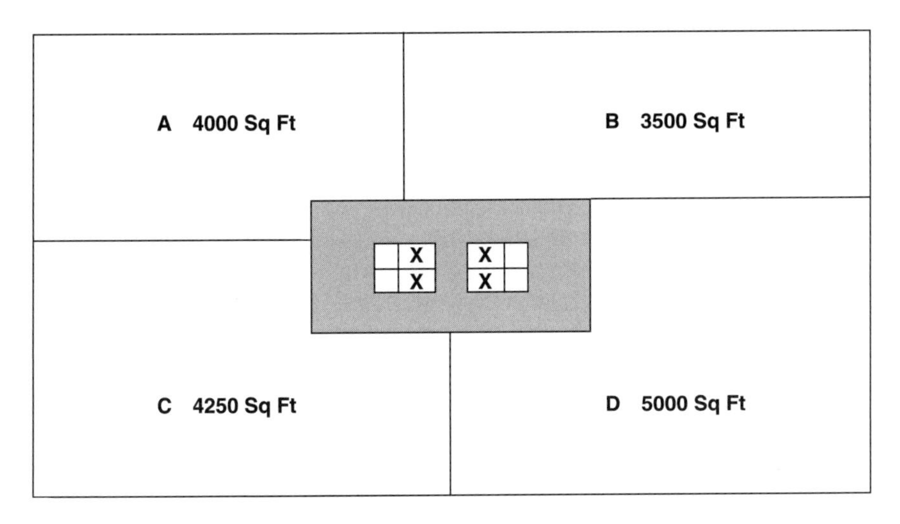

Rentable Area	18,760 Sq Ft
Common Area	2,010 Sq Ft
Usable Area (Total)	16,750 Sq Ft

$$\frac{\text{Rentable Area (18,760 Sq Ft)}}{\text{Usable Area (16,750 Sq Ft)}} = \text{R/U Ratio} = 1.12 \text{ (add-on factor)}$$

Usable Area × 1.12 = Rentable Area

Tenant A:	4,000 × 1.12 =	4,480 Sq Ft
Tenant B:	3,500 × 1.12 =	3,920 Sq Ft
Tenant C:	4,250 × 1.12 =	4,760 Sq Ft
Tenant D:	5,000 × 1.12 =	5,600 Sq Ft
Total:	16,750 × 1.12 =	18,760 Sq Ft

Method for Measuring Floor Area in Office Buildings (ANSI/BOMA Z65.1-1996), developed by the Building Owners and Managers Association International (BOMA), is the one commonly used. The BOMA *Standard* multiplies a tenant's usable area by an R/U ratio to compute the tenant's rentable area. The *R/U ratio* is the rentable area of a floor divided by the usable area of that same floor. A pro rata share of the building's common areas is added to the basic rentable area to arrive at the tenant's total rentable square feet. The larger the R/U ratio, the greater the rent paid for the common areas.

Some markets use a *load factor* (sometimes called add-on factor) to prorate the common areas among individual tenants. This may or may not be equal to the ratio between the rentable and usable areas. (Calculation of rentable area using a load factor based on the R/U ratio is shown in Exhibit 7.6.) In some markets, a standard load factor may be used. For example, if the R/U ratios of buildings in the market range from 10 to 12 percent, an 11-percent load factor may be applied to all usable area rents in the market. Such a practice can effectively eliminate one point of negotiation on a market-wide basis. (Note: Market conditions are also a consideration. An owner may reduce the load factor to make a building more competitive. In a strong market, tenants may agree to pay a higher than warranted load factor.)

Whether the BOMA standard method or another approach is used, it is vital that leases spell out the manner in which rentable and usable areas are determined in order to avoid disputes regarding rental rates and other charges. The method of measurement should be consistent with what is done in the local market area. The market survey (see Chapter 5) and market analysis should identify the method used by other office building managers for determining rentable area as stated in existing leases. (Note: Leases signed prior to 1996 may refer to an earlier version of the BOMA standard or to another methodology.)

Developing Leasing Parameters. Along with a schedule of base rental rates, the office building manager will work with the owner to develop specific leasing parameters. These parameters should address the following issues:

- Minimum rent—The base rental rate per rentable square foot per year for the type of space and location in the building.
- Specific escalations—The required annual increase in rent per square foot over the term of the lease. This adjustment may be linked to an economic indicator such as the increase in the Consumer Price Index (CPI). Periods of low inflation and changes in calculating the CPI have made this approach to escalations less desirable, and it is rarely used in new leases. Existing leases may include a CPI-based escalation provision that might preferably be negotiated out of a renewal lease.
- Lease term—The expected period of the lease for the size of the available space. Office space may be leased for periods of three, five, or ten years or longer. Large amounts of space (a full floor or multiple floors) are typically leased for longer terms because of the investment in tenant improvements made by both landlord and tenant.
- Tenant improvement allowance—The amount of money the landlord is willing to invest to build out the tenant's space and whether it is fully or partially reimbursable by the tenant. This may be stated as a dollar amount per usable square foot or refer to building standard materials and a list of specific items that the landlord will provide at no charge to the tenant (e.g., one door for every 250 square feet, one telephone jack for every 100 square feet). There should be provision

for recovering costs that exceed the standard allowance and assigning responsibility to pay for them. In a slow market, the landlord might assume this responsibility as a lease concession. In other circumstances, the costs might be divided between landlord and tenant or be fully a tenant responsibility, in which case reimbursement to the landlord might be stated in the lease as *additional rent*.

- Leased space—The size of the space to which specific parameters apply may be stated as a maximum rentable square footage or defined as a range.
- Rent concessions—This may take the form of free rent to be granted at the beginning of the lease term and stated as a total number of months or as a month (or other period) for each year of the negotiated lease term.

Rents and escalations should be quoted in the manner accepted in the local market, whether dollars per square foot per year or per month. It may also be appropriate to state how building operating expenses are handled—i.e., use of a gross lease versus a net lease, application of an R/U ratio or load factor that includes operating expenses in the base rent, proration and pass-through of expenses as a separate occupancy cost to the tenant, and/or negotiation of an expense stop to limit pass-throughs.

Leasing parameters provide flexibility for the leasing agent and the building manager in negotiating particular leases or lease renewals. The parameters may also include reference to the leasing agent's commission when leasing is separately contracted.

Marketing Plan

From the information gathered in the market analysis and rental analysis, the manager should be able to design a marketing plan that will effectively attract potential office tenants to lease the vacant space in the building he or she manages. A key component of a marketing plan is the identification of the most likely tenants for the building. This information allows the manager to focus on specific prospects via *target marketing*.

The marketing planning process for an existing building begins with an evaluation of its *tenant mix*—i.e., the types of businesses that are carried out in the building and the stature of the individual tenants. Prospective tenants are naturally interested in who their neighbors in the building will be and what types of clients or visitors come to the building to do business with them. There may be concerns about traffic flow in the building and congestion at certain times of the day. A prospect may also be concerned about the impact of business neighbors on its reputation and image or on the reputation and image of the building.

A building's tenant mix will draw certain types of prospects to it while at the same time suggesting to others that this is not where they want to locate. Various professionals such as architects, attorneys, and accountants may hesitate to lease space in a building whose tenancy includes businesses that are nonprofessional because they do not want their clients to associate them with businesses having less prestige. Sometimes prospects actively avoid locating in the same buildings as their competition.

Ground-floor tenants can be an important factor in establishing a tenant mix. A drug store would be desirable for medical professionals seeking space to lease. A bank is likely to attract other types of professionals. An art supply store would be a boon in a building that houses advertising agencies and other creative ventures. It is most desirable to choose as ground-floor tenants businesses that provide a service to other tenants in the building or otherwise enhance its tenant mix. Examples include an optical shop, a travel agency, or an Internet cafe.

Office building owners and managers should strive to establish a quality mix of tenants who pay rent in full and on time, willingly pay higher rent for space they consider desirable, and contribute to the building's image. The wishes and preferences of such tenants need to be considered in seeking new tenants so that the quality of the building's tenant mix will be maintained over time.

It is good management practice to survey building tenants periodically. This will make ownership and management aware of tenants who are unhappy and the reasons for their unhappiness. Properly written questions will help identify features and amenities that are lacking in the building as well as which of the existing ones are most used and best liked. Including space for comments allows tenants to express specific concerns (e.g., slow elevator service, space configuration inefficiencies) that should be addressed in order to retain existing tenants and attract new ones. (Tenant retention is addressed in Chapter 10.)

8

Marketing and Leasing Office Space

While market analysis is critical to setting rents, it is also critical to marketing and leasing office space. A market analysis should have identified the supply of competitive space available, the level of demand for existing space, rental rates being charged, and the terms of leases negotiated at those rates along with the location and quality of specific competitors. From such a market analysis, an office building manager should be able to anticipate the needs and wants of prospective tenants and develop a marketing strategy to satisfy them. It is easier to do this for an existing building than for one that is under construction.

A survey of current tenants can help identify strengths and weaknesses of the subject building in comparison to other properties. The strengths can be enhanced and used in marketing and leasing available office space. The weaknesses need to be overcome or compensated for in some manner to diminish their negative influence.

The key to getting started is a specific *marketing plan.* The marketing plan should identify target tenant groups (i.e., types of businesses) and develop guidelines for reaching them. It should include a budget developed specifically to fund the planned advertising and promotional activities. While advertising will certainly be a line item in the building's annual operating budget, preparation of a separate *marketing budget* is advisable so that the costs and scheduling of various programs are all known in advance. It is especially important to prepare a comprehensive marketing budget for lease-up of a new building, and this may have to be revised from time to time as leasing proceeds and certain strategies are discovered to be more or less successful. Changes in marketing strategies may require additional funding, or strategies may have to be revised to stay within the budget. The budget should account for every specific advertisement or other promotional material or strategy that will be used. It should also include funds for public relations and adjunct leasing materials (brochures, floor plans, photographs, maps).

Marketing Strategies

The marketing plan should have an integrated or *unified theme* related to the building or its name. This usually involves development of a stylized graphic symbol or logo that will be used on all signage and printed marketing materials, including brochures, advertisements, and stationery. A rendering of a unique architectural feature (a cornice or the building entrance) is a possibility worth considering. Guidelines should establish type faces to be used and a specific color scheme. This might even be extended to color-coordinated staff uniforms. Consistent effective use of the theme creates a lasting impression on the public in general and prospective tenants in particular.

For a new building or an existing one with a large amount of vacant space, leasing will be a long-term activity. If a management firm has an extensive staff that includes graphic designers, it may be possible to design some or all of the necessary materials in house. On the other hand, it may be necessary or appropriate to have an advertising agency create specific marketing materials. Several agencies should be interviewed to find out the following before a contract is negotiated.

- The type and extent of experience the agency has had with real estate clients.
- What success the agency has had in similar assignments.
- Whether the agency handles competitors' properties.
- Who will be assigned creative responsibility for the building's account.
- The caliber of work done by the creative personnel.

As with any potential vendor contract, it is appropriate to ask for and check out references. In this case, the references should preferably be other real estate clients and include office building managers.

Advertising. Specific advertising requires an understanding of various advertising media and their uses and limitations. There are two basic types of advertisements: *Promotional advertising* is used to generate immediate interest in a particular product or service; a newspaper want-ad may be employed to lease a particular block of office space. *Institutional advertising* is

Exhibit 8.1
Sample Want Ad

PARKHURST CENTER
Corner of Park & Main Streets
Spacious office suites available immediately;
1,500 & 5,000 sq ft. High-tech telecom wiring.
Will reconfigure/shared costs. Competitive rent.
XYZ OFFICE MANAGEMENT
555-555-5555
www.xyzmanagement.com

used to establish a company name or image in the marketplace; a display advertisement might be used to establish and maintain the reputation of an office building.

There are countless vehicles for advertising office space for lease. A newspaper want-ad may be the ideal vehicle to find a tenant for an existing space. When leasing up a new building, however, it is often wisest to use a combination of media to announce the availability and opening date. Each advertising medium has advantages and disadvantages in particular uses. The following sections provide an overview of different advertising media and some of their uses.

Newspapers. Newspapers, especially the dailies in major cities, will have a section devoted to real estate for-rent ads. In a large urban center with several defined business areas, the newspapers may position ads based on address (north, south, east, west) or a defined geographic area such as a financial or publishing district. The typical want-ad is one column wide with several lines of copy describing the space for lease. Charges may be based on measured depth or a line count. A *want-ad* (Exhibit 8.1) is usually an effective and economical way to lease an existing space.

Most major newspapers will have a separate real estate section, usually published on Sundays but sometimes also on one or more weekdays. Often there are opportunities to advertise in the section separate from the want-ad portion. This is where a larger *display ad* (Exhibit 8.2) may be practical. Its purpose is to inform the market about the particular office building and the fact that it has space available for lease. Generally speaking, such advertising is institutional in nature; it is not intended to lease a specific office space. This type of advertising is used on an ongoing basis to keep the office building name and identification in front of the leasing public.

Newspapers also rely on news releases as information sources. A properly developed public relations (PR) program will include periodic news releases sent to all appropriate media. Here again, the purpose is not to lease a specific space. News releases may announce the opening of the building,

Exhibit 8.2
Sample Display Advertisement

PARKHURST CENTER
at the corner of
Park and Main Streets

[logo]

- Spacious Class A office suites
- 1,500 to 5,000 sq ft plus full floors
- Available immediately
- High-tech telecommunications wiring
- Will reconfigure/shared build-out costs
- Competitive rent

Prime location close to restaurants and shopping. Public transportation access. Parking garage next door.

XYZ OFFICE MANAGEMENT
555-555-5555
www.xyzmanagement.com

milestones in its lease-up (25 percent, 50 percent, 75 percent), acquisition of a specific major tenant, and personnel changes in the management office. (Public relations is discussed in more detail later in this chapter.)

Other Print Media. Trade magazines, including those directed to the real estate industry, can be good places to insert institutional ads that maintain a visible presence for an office building in the general marketplace. However, ads in local real estate magazines and those directed to company executives are more likely to generate specific rental business. Local real estate magazines may also seek out their advertisers as sources of industry information and related news. They often rely on materials submitted by knowledgeable writers to fill space in issues of their magazines. A well-written article about the building's facilities or a specific problem the current management team solved could be submitted for consideration. Publication of such an article would add to the writer's credentials as well as the building's prestige.

Exhibit 8.3
Sample Billboard Advertisement

PARKHURST CENTER *[photo of building or logo]*	**Office Space Reserved for You!** Call Now! 555-555-5555

Broadcast Media. Radio and television are rarely used to advertise office space for lease although these outlets should receive news releases and announcements for general distribution. Broadcast advertising is expensive and generally reaches a very broad audience although air time can be related to business programming or the business portion of news broadcasts. An exception that may be less expensive and more effective is a local cable channel, especially one that carries business programs and related advertising.

Billboards. While not often used to promote office buildings or space for lease, billboards (Exhibit 8.3) can be an effective way to keep the building's name and location in front of the public. A simple message and contact information—a call to action and a telephone number or Internet address—is sufficient. Drivers and passengers in vehicles on major highways have to be able to get the message in the few seconds when they are passing the billboard. This is where a thematic logo graphic is especially useful.

Signage. Perhaps the most important advertising vehicle is a sign on the office building that identifies the management firm and includes a telephone number. Usually management will negotiate for such signage as part of the management agreement. Most often these are simple metal plaques attached at eye level on a corner of a building. If the building spans an entire block, it is appropriate to have a sign on each end of the building. It may also be appropriate to display a "vacancy" or "space available" sign in a window or other location visible from the street. This should include the name and phone number of the leasing agent (if other than the management firm). Local ordinances may regulate the manner in which signage is displayed on the building or otherwise.

Brochures. Brochures are multifaceted marketing tools. They can be created simply as a trifold using a single stationery-sized piece of paper. Something as basic as black and white photos coupled with a second color ink for titles or headings can be highly effective and produced for a very low printing cost. However, investment in four-color printing and using color photographs to advantage will yield a more-powerful product. As long as basic information in the brochure will not change, a brochure developed initially for lease-up can have a fairly long shelf life afterwards. Even as initial lease-up is being completed, some of the earliest short-term (two or three year) leases will already be coming up for renewal. That is, provided rental rates are quoted as a starting rate or a range or not included at all. A brochure can be designed with a blank area for rental details to be typed or handwritten at the time it is presented to a prospective tenant, or changeable data—available space, rental rates—can be presented on a replaceable insert.

The brochure should characterize the building by size (height, square footage, number of floors), location, features, amenities, and services. It should present basic rental information, including a typical floor plate and a representative small office configuration. It is also appropriate to include information about neighborhood features, such as shopping, restaurants, and entertainments, which are of interest to tenants' employees.

A more comprehensive leasing brochure would contain more details such as demographic statistics and more photographs. It might be designed as four-color front and back covers that would be used to bind together specific information for a prospect, including a preliminary floor plan of the space under consideration, precise measurements of the space (rentable and usable square feet), information about standard building finishes and tenant improvement allowances, and the pro rata share of operating expenses handled as pass-through charges. In this use, full-page photographs of the building exterior, a property map or site plan (if appropriate), and an aerial view of the property might also be included.

A brochure is a useful component of a presentation package to be submitted to a prospective tenant by mail or by hand at the time of showing the space for lease. It is also valuable in a direct-mail campaign. Properly designed, the brochure can be used as a self-mailer.

Direct Mail. While direct mail can be effective, it is not always practical for advertising office space for lease. However, it can be another strategy for keeping the building in the public eye. A mailing list can be compiled as an

Advertising Media

Print Media
- Newspapers
- Real estate publications
- Local business periodicals
- Industry-specific trade magazines

Broadcast Media
- Radio
- Television
- Cable television (local channels)

Other Media
- Internet
- Signage
- Direct mail
- Brochures
- Billboards

Note: The Internet has other potential benefits including opportunities to participate in multiple-listing services.

adjunct to leasing activities. Names and addresses of prospective tenants, company executives as well as particular contacts, can be entered into a data base in a computer. The list can be expanded to include current tenants (marketing to them is a tenant retention strategy). Direct mail is a means of keeping in touch with likely future tenants while it encourages positive word-of-mouth from existing tenants to their clients and business contacts. News releases, promotional flyers for building-sponsored events, and reprints of published articles about the building are examples of direct mail pieces. (Be sure to obtain permission to reproduce and distribute previously published materials.)

The Internet. In today's high-technology business environment, the Internet may be the advertising medium of choice. The key is to establish a web site with a home page that is informative without being all-inclusive. Contact information or a button that takes the user to it is an important component of the home page. At a minimum, the site should include the office building's name, street address, telephone, and facsimile numbers plus e-mail addresses for key personnel (leasing agents, maintenance staff, security personnel, the building manager). For an office building, other web site components might include building news, space available for lease, building amenities and services, and a form for requesting services. It may also be desirable to present statistical information about the building (height, square footage, date opened, etc.). The Internet address should be included on building stationery, forms, staff members' business cards, and other communications vehicles (e.g., a tenants' newsletter).

For a new building, the space-for-lease component might include a virtual office model showing building standard finishes and examples of signage styles. It may also be appropriate to include answers to frequently asked questions (FAQs) about the building, its equipment and facilities, and its tenancy. These should also address what might be called hot button issues (availability of telecommunications cabling, ADA compliance status, etc.).

Once a web site has been established, it must be promoted, and it must be kept up-to-date. Links to other sites can provide additional useful information for current and prospective tenants. Expand the reach of the leasing team's efforts by building a mailing list of e-mail addresses. Broadcast e-mail is another form of direct-mail advertising. Monitoring visitors to the home page and all of its sub-sites will indicate what people are most interested in and yield ideas for making changes and keeping the site up-to-date.

A large real estate management firm may include a web master on its staff to create and maintain web sites for all of the firm's managed properties. For a single office building, however, this is not practical. The best strategy is to contract with a firm that creates web sites, preferably one that has other real estate entities and, better yet, office buildings among its clients. Once the site is active, it may be worthwhile to have an administrative staff member trained to make periodic updates to information on the home page and other web site components. Major content changes, including addition of site components, should be done through the original vendor.

As with any contracted service, it is important to interview several potential web site creators and to check out references. Questions to ask satisfied clients include:

- Was the work completed as promised (on time, within budget)?
- Did you have a clear vision of what the site should look like?
- Did you have to change your goals for the web site?
- Did you have to compromise your vision to get a workable site?
- Did the finished site serve the business purpose you intended?
- Were the vendor's creative people able to understand and implement your vision of the site?
- Were you satisfied with the final product?

The cost of a web site will depend on its complexity. It should be possible to develop a straightforward informational site and include e-mail contacts and a service request form for a modest fee. Virtual tours and complex illustrations will necessarily add to the costs as will any interactive elements.

It may be advisable to develop a *request for proposal (RFP)* to be submitted to three or four or more web site vendors. The RFP should outline all of the types of information to be presented on the web site, in order of importance, differentiating those items that must be included from those that are desirable but could be foregone. The latter should be bid as additional components to be considered separately. In this way, it is possible to control how extensive or elaborate the web site will become and the cost of its development and maintenance. The RFP should also request costs for maintaining the site into the future (this might be a flat charge for each time a change is made or an hourly rate for the time required).

Public Relations. All promotion of the building and office space for lease should be viewed in the context of its public relations (PR) impact. Most people think of PR as periodic news releases. However, all contacts with tenants, visitors to the building, and the general public are part of the building's public image. This is where the element of consistency in using graphic elements (e.g., logos) and setting standards for type faces pays off in presenting a unified theme or image. News releases are an important part of this, and they should be prepared properly to be accepted for publication.

- Include the date of issuance and a date of release (or simply say "For Immediate Release").
- Identify a person to contact for more information (name, phone number, e-mail address).
- Capture the subject in a short catchy title.
- Leave wide margins at left and right.
- Use double-spacing when typing the information.
- Be concise and brief, four pages at most—longer news releases are likely to be edited, and that can result in important information being omitted.
- Close with a brief description of the source (building name, ownership, management).
- Include black-and-white photographs when appropriate.

For those who issue news releases frequently and prepare large numbers of copies for distribution, it is appropriate to invest in a special news release letterhead that includes the building name and address. If news releases will be issued only occasionally, standard building letterhead can be used. Information should be organized for easy conversion to a newspaper or magazine format. While it was a long-standing tradition to use only one side of the 8½ × 11-inch sheet, copying on both sides of the paper is acceptable and more economical in regard to postage.

News releases should be mailed to appropriate contacts at local newspapers, real estate and other trade publications, and radio and television stations. Once issued, news releases can also be included on the building's

Exhibit 8.4

Sample Marketing Schedule

Marketing Schedule

Building ______ As of (date) ______ Prepared by ______ Total Budget ______

	Month/Year																					**Budget $**	**Budget %**
Signage																							
Brochure																							
Newspaper Advertising	Newspaper																						
	Classified Ads																						
	Display Ads																						
Magazine Advertising	Magazine																						
	Design/Art																						
	Dates Run/Billing																						
Reprints	Ads																						
	Articles																						
Direct Mail																							
Public Relations Event																							
Commemorative/Promotional Item																							
Presentation Book																							
Other																							
																					Total	**$**	**100%**

web site and used as components of a direct-mail advertising campaign. Preparation and mailing of news releases can be done by on-site staff if they have the appropriate skills. Otherwise, it is advisable to work with an advertising agency or a PR firm that specializes in this activity.

Public relations also has a negative component. Office building managers need to plan for situations that are beyond their control as manager of the building (e.g., an accident in the building or on the property, a demonstration in front of the building that gets out of hand, a weather-related disaster). This is where it is helpful to work with professionals. A PR firm that specializes in crisis public relations can advise on what information to have immediately available in the event of such emergencies. (Usually an executive of the management company or the property manager will be the designated spokesperson authorized to release information to the media; see also Chapter 12.)

Other Promotional Tools. Advertising includes a variety of materials in addition to the traditional print and broadcast media. Ball point pens, key holders, coffee mugs, T-shirts, and a host of other items can be imprinted with the building name and/or logo. The least-expensive ones (pens, key holders) can be handed out to tenants' employees and anyone who visits the building. More expensive items can be embossed or engraved with the building logo and used as gifts to tenant contacts and prospects. Special giveaways can be prepared for building-sponsored events.

Tracking Results. It is extremely important to measure the success of advertising and promotional campaigns. Before any active promotion is done, it is a good idea to develop a specific *marketing schedule* (Exhibit 8.4) that lists the various media and strategies to be employed along with the amount budgeted for each effort. A separate schedule should be prepared for each campaign, whether the focus is initial lease-up or efforts to re-lease existing space. Each campaign would have its own time frame and budget, and this should be reflected in the individual marketing schedules.

Once a campaign is under way, leasing personnel should be required to keep a running log report of inquiries received at the building. A *leasing traffic report* (Exhibit 8.5, page 184) is used to record each incoming contact and the source of the inquiry. At the end of the week, the total numbers for each type of inquiry and each potential source is shown. Regular review of these reports will indicate which promotional vehicles and strategies are attracting the most-qualified prospects and which are not. This allows management to make adjustments, canceling programs that are not working and redirecting marketing funds to those that are successful. Other forms are used to track specific leasing activities. These are discussed under prospecting later in this chapter.

Exhibit 8.5
Sample Leasing Traffic Report

Leasing Traffic Report

Building __________ Prepared by __________ Week of __________

	Monday	Tuesday	Wednesday	Thursday	Friday	Total
Nature of Inquiry						
Telephone						
Walk-in						
E-mail						
Other						
Referred By						
Classified Ad						
Display Ad						
Building Signage						
Direct Mail						
Telephone Directory						
Word of Mouth						
Tenant						
Inside Broker						
Outside Broker						
Other						
Space Needed						
Less than 1,000 sq ft						
1,000 to 2,000 sq ft						
2,000 to 3,000 sq ft						
3,000 to 5,000 sq ft						
5,000 to 10,000 sq ft						
10,000 to 50,000 sq ft						
50,000 to 100,000 sq ft						
More than 100,000 sq ft						
Comments						

Leasing Strategies

No matter how much and what type of marketing is done, most office leases result from leasing agents contacting prospective tenants directly. Successful leasing requires understanding of the building's features and amenities and the ability to translate them into benefits that will be realized by the individual prospective tenant. Other selling points relate to other tenants of the building, who themselves constitute an amenity that can be used to attract prospects.

Prospecting. Prospecting encompasses all of the strategies used to inform the marketplace that the building has space available for lease and to ensure that the information is being delivered to potential tenants. One of the most effective approaches is *canvassing,* which is the process of directly contacting likely prospects, providing information to them, and showing them the space for lease.

Canvassing involves contacting local office space users or representatives of large companies outside of the local area who are looking for space to lease. Savvy leasing agents build a list of local and out-of-town tenants with each new leasing assignment. They will create a contact data base that includes company names and addresses, names of contacts (actual and potential), their telephone numbers and e-mail addresses, and information about the company's current office space (location in building, rentable and usable area) and lease (rent, escalations, expiration date). Plans for expansion or reduction of their space needs should also be noted if known. It is important to find out if they are expecting to relocate when the lease expires—and why they would do so (e.g., current location cannot accommodate their space needs, unhappiness with the building or its management). Because of the length of office lease terms (three to ten years or more) and the complexity of negotiations, most tenants planning to relocate will begin actively seeking new space at least a year and possibly longer before their current leases expire. This adds impetus to the need for continually updating a data base of prospect contacts.

Telephone canvassing, also called *cold calling,* is an important prelude to personal canvassing. The goal of the initial contact is to generate interest in the office building and arrange a personal meeting in the next few days. Telephone canvassing also provides an opportunity to assess the tenants in the market and gather additional leads—a contact may not be interested but knows of another business that is looking for space.

The leasing agent's efforts should be directed to the leasing decision-maker. A large firm may have a real estate department that handles its space needs. In a small company, the decision-maker will most likely be the president of the organization or its owner. Before making the first call, the leasing agent should know as much as possible about the company and its business, its space requirements, and its financial status. It is also worthwhile to know what the firm's competition is doing, if that can be discovered. In order to respond to questions, the agent will need facts about market conditions and prevailing rental rates for Class A, B, and C rental space in the area.

Canvassing is hard work. Repeated contacts are needed to identify all of a tenant's needs and desires and generate interest in the office building the agent represents. In the absence of a pre-existing data base of contacts, the leasing agent will have to do some research. Business sections in local newspapers often carry news of impending changes. These may be references to downsizing of staff or creation of new business divisions rather than specific statements that a company is planning to move. Industry trade magazines serving the spectrum of potential tenants are other likely sources. Local chambers of commerce, utility companies, and lending institutions are often in a position to know about upcoming mergers, spinoffs, and plans for changing space needs. Other potential resources are companies that serve the business community (stationery suppliers, office furniture dealers) and real estate developers.

One of the best methods of locating prospective tenants is word of mouth. Most companies try to keep up with what other firms in their industry are doing, including when they are anticipating a move. Current tenants in the building may know of other businesses (clients or competitors) that would be likely prospects. Referrals from known sources are especially desirable. Leasing agents can assume that prospects referred to them will be reliable tenants because they are already known to the referral source, and prospects are likely to be more responsive to an agent to whom they were referred by a business contact or a mutual acquaintance. Networking with other leasing agents and with brokers who represent prospective tenants is yet another way to stay informed about prospective tenants in the local market.

Leasing agents should keep track of referrals and signed leases that result from them. Whether they use a computer or enter information on a paper form, a referral source should be documented in detail. In addition to the person's name, title, company mailing address, telephone number, and e-mail address, personal information about the contact's family and interests (spouse name, children's names, favorite sports or entertainments) should be noted. The latter is especially useful for selecting token thank-you gifts. Notes should be made of all contacts with the referral source, including dates and outcomes. The referral record should also identify prospects referred by the contact, dates they were contacted, and whether the efforts resulted in a signed lease or at least an interest in the building.

Each contact with a prospective tenant should also be documented. Usually the agent fills out a *prospect card* (Exhibit 8.6) that has space for noting information about the company and the contact, its space requirements, desired or required features and amenities, relocation timing, and related details. Data about the firm's current lease arrangements would also be recorded. There may also be space to note financial information and the results of a credit check. When all contacts with a prospect are documented on one form, it is easy to see how a leasing transaction progressed.

Another important record prepared by leasing agents is a *lease summation report* (Exhibit 8.7, page 188) or lease synopsis. Prepared after the lease has been finalized, this form may serve as the main resource for the building manager and others who will be responsible for administering the lease, especially if a separate *lease abstract* is not prepared by the manager. Minimally, it should detail the terms of the lease—commencement and expiration dates, when rent payment starts, the rentable and leasable areas attributable to the leased space, and the tenant's pro rata share for apportioning pass-through expenses. Specific modifications to the lease contents should

Exhibit 8.6
Sample Prospect Card

Prospect Card (face)

Leasing Agent ______ Firm ______ Date ______
Contact Name ______ Phone Number ______
Company ______ Address ______
Type of Business ______ Space Needed ______ sq ft No. of Employees ______
Special Needs: Date Needed ______ Rental Rate (range) ______ /sq ft
Location Preferences ______
Amenity Preferences ______ Parking Requirements ______
Other ______

Other Information: Moving from ______ Reason ______
Expansion ______ Future Needs ______
Current Size ______ sq ft Rent $ ______ /sq ft Per Month or Per Year? ______

Prospect Card (reverse)

Banks/Financial Institutions ______
Credit Report Results ______ Net Worth $ ______
Level of Interest Expressed ______
Contact Initiated ______ Negotiations Commenced ______

Date	Contact Name	Space Shown	Quoted Rent	Comments	Active?

be documented along with exceptions regarding janitorial services or utilities. As in the example shown, space may be provided to document tenant improvement arrangements and costs, specifics regarding move-in, and any special fees to be charged to the new tenant. It may also be important to note on the form the chain of approvals of the lease and their timing. In this way, all the pertinent information regarding a specific tenant will be available in one place for ready reference in billing tenant charges and implementing rent escalations.

In order to ensure compensation for leasing services, the agent should also prepare a periodic report on the status of his or her contacts. This is

Exhibit 8.7
Sample Lease Summation Report

Lease Summation Report

Tenant Name ____________ Lease Signed ____________
Nature of Business ____________ Rent Starts ____________
Suite/Floor ____________ Occupancy Starts ____________
Contact Name ____________ Expiration Date ____________
Title ____________ Phone ____________ E-Mail ____________
Leasing Agent ____________ Firm ____________
Commission ______ % Total $ ______ Payment Schedule ____________

Space Leased/Rent/Terms	Floor	Square Feet	$/Sq Ft	$/Month	$/Year
Gross Square Feet					
Net Rentable Area					
Net Usable Area					
Concessions					
Improvement Allowance					
Other					
Total					

Security Deposit: $ ____________ Received By ____________ Date ____________
Changes to Lease (paragraph numbers) ____________

Rider(s) ____________

easily done on a *leasing activity status report* (Exhibit 8.8, page 190), where each contact is recorded as an inquiry or an active prospect. Submission of leasing proposals, completed negotiations, and signed leases would also be documented along with any prospects that are no longer being pursued. Some forms may include a column for annual rent, and provision can be made for tracking other details.

Leasing commissions are usually substantial, and their computation may be complex (Exhibit 8.9, page 191). Usually they are based on the tenant's total rent and the term of the lease. Often they are paid out over a period of years. Such an approach to commissions is most common in situations where outside brokers are contracted, either for lease-up of a new building or when there are large blocks of vacant space to be leased in an existing building. It sometimes happens that one agent is having difficulty finding suitable space for a tenant-client, and a second agent is unable to lease a particular space on his or her own. If they work together to match the one agent's tenant with the other agent's available space, the resulting lease may require a splitting of the commission. This information must be provided when the commission advice or billing is submitted so that all commission payments are handled in a timely fashion. In such instances, the landlord would pay the separate commissions, rather than pay the full amount to the agent responsible for leasing the space and the building agent then having to pay the split to the tenant's agent.

Exhibit 8.7 *(continued)*

Renewal Option ______ Notification Date ______ Terms ______
Expansion Option ______ Location ______ Terms ______
Cancellation Option ______ Penalty ______
Parking ______
Utilities Exclusion/Addition (describe) ______
Janitorial Exclusion/Addition (describe) ______
Escalation Terms ______
Base Year ______ Pro Rata Share ______ % Escalation Review Date ______

Estimated Construction Costs

Total Cost $ ______ Cost/Sq Ft $ ______ Tenant to pay extra cost of $ ______
Allowed Cost $ ______ Cost/Sq Ft $ ______ Amortization $ ______ /year
Difference $ ______ Cost/Sq Ft $ ______ Amortized Interest Rate ______ %

Move-In Information

Rent Commencement Date ______ Revised Rent Commencement Date ______
Suite Occupied (date) ______ Lease Expiration Date ______
Suite Inspected (date) ______ Tenant Information Packet Issued ______
Signs Installed ______ Directory Listing Completed ______
Parking Permits Issued ______ Keys Issued ______

Move-In Charges to Lessee

Keys $ ______
Directory $ ______
Construction $ ______
Other $ ______
Total $ ______

Lease Finalization/Approvals

Credit Approved ______
Legal Review ______
Tenant Signature ______
Landlord Signature ______
Rent Effective Letter Sent ______

Note: A similar form, minus the move-in and lease approval details, is prepared by the office building manager as part of management take-over and as a record of each new lease as it is finalized. Such a *lease abstract* provides a ready reminder of the lease terms for each individual tenant, especially the particulars regarding rents and rent increases, pass-through charges, and other financial arrangements. (Lease abstracts are discussed in Chapters 4 and 5.)

As has been noted in earlier chapters, leasing of office space may be contracted separately from management of the building. An outside broker may be granted an *exclusive listing,* which gives the agent written assurance that the building owner will not deal with any other leasing agent without paying a fee to the agent. The listing agent is guaranteed a commission if a lease is closed, regardless of who may have brought the tenant to the owner. An open or *nonexclusive listing* allows the owner to deal with other agents. The listing agent receives a commission *only* if he or she closes the deal. (The terms of exclusive and nonexclusive leasing arrangements may be defined by the local real estate commission.) An exclusive listing is much more desirable from a leasing agent's point of view. However, owners are generally reluctant to grant such an exclusive because they would like to maintain an arrangement that provides the greatest number of opportunities

Exhibit 8.8
Sample Leasing Activity Status Report

Leasing Activity Status Report

Building ______________ Submitted by______________ Date ________

	Net Rentable Area (sq ft)	Rate	Term	Projected Occupancy	Comments
Inquiries					
Active Prospects					
Proposals Submitted					
Leases Submitted					
Signed Leases					
Prospects Deleted (Reason)					

for finding suitable tenants. Owners are more likely to grant an exclusive when the market is soft—i.e., there are few potential tenants and a large amount of office space to lease. When outside brokers are used, the office building manager oversees the leasing activity, ensuring that agents understand and work within established leasing parameters and monitoring their progress for the owner.

Selling Features as Benefits. Leasing agents need to be thoroughly familiar with the components of the building and the space available for lease and with the features and tenants of nearby buildings. The market analysis prepared earlier is a major information resource. The comparison grid analysis should have identified features and amenities of the building and its ma-

Exhibit 8.9

Sample Leasing Commission Calculation

Suppose a tenant signs a lease for 10,000 rentable square feet at a base rate of $18 per square foot per year for a five-year term. The resulting annual rent is $180,000 (10,000 sq ft × $18). The leasing agent's commission is based on this information only, and the percentage declines over the five-year lease term—6% for year 1, 5% for year 2, 4% for year 3, 3% for year 4, and 2% for year 5.

Year	Commission %	Rental Income	Commission
1	6	$180,000	$10,800
2	5	$180,000	$9,000
3	4	$180,000	$7,200
4	3	$180,000	$5,400
5	2	$180,000	$3,600

The total commission in this example is $36,000.

Note: Percentage rates and payout of commissions are negotiable and subject to accepted practice in the local market. In some markets, an "over the term" declining arrangement as outlined here would not be used. Instead, a lower rate overall (e.g., 4%) might be applied to the total rent for the lease term and paid to the leasing agent "cash out," either as a lump sum when the lease is signed or in divided payments (one-half on lease signing, one-half on move-in). Commissions for renewal leases are usually lower—e.g., 1–4% of the total rent for the lease term payable on commencement of the renewal term. (Lease renewal is addressed in Chapter 10.)

jor competitors. This collection of data is key to identifying aspects of the building that can be "sold" to prospective tenants as benefits. The following questions suggest ways that leasing agents can capitalize on specifics: Is the building I represent more accessible for the prospect's clients or customers than its present location? Does it provide better access to suppliers and services the prospect uses? Will it allow the prospect to attract and retain more-qualified employees?

The following tabulation shows how some features or amenities can be presented as tenant benefits.

Feature/Amenity	**Benefit**
Building location	Transportation and pedestrian access
Efficient building design	More usable area
Energy management system	Energy efficiency; controlled costs
Telecommunications cabling	High-speed Internet access
Building services team	Timely response to service requests
Abundant parking	Low or no cost to tenants

Other sellable aspects of location include neighborhood features and services. There may be six restaurants within a one-block radius offering dif-

Examples of Amenity Tenants

Restaurant	Tobacconist
Fast food vendor	Travel service
Drug store	Branch bank
Card and gift shop	Automated Teller Machine (ATM)
Day care center	Music and video store
Fitness facility	Mailing/shipping service
Flower shop	Jewelry sales and watch repair
Candy store	Shoe shine stand and repair service
Newsstand	Dry cleaning service
Bookstore	Photocopy or print shop
Beauty salon	Leather goods and umbrellas
Barber shop	Computer technical support service
Convenience grocery	Secretarial/office service

The desirability of any of these tenants as building amenities depends on the space available for ground-floor retail as well as the existence of comparable services in nearby competing buildings. The neighborhood itself is another consideration. Some tenants might do more business if there are residential properties nearby.

ferent menus and pricing. A fitness or workout facility in the building across the street, a day care center in the building next door, or a drug store or other non-fashion retailer a block away are part of what makes a particular building's location desirable. For some buildings, spectacular views are a feature to be promoted. Within the building, a lunch room with vending machines and a microwave oven means tenants' employees do not have to leave the building for lunch or breaks. A designated smoking lounge allows smokers to stay indoors during inclement weather.

Creating a nicely appointed large conference room wired for video presentations and conference calls is something to consider if there is space available in the building. While many tenants will have their own conference rooms, these are usually designed for groups of ten or twelve people. To accommodate a larger group, the tenant would have to go to a hotel. Smaller companies may not have a conference room at all. Availability of a large conference room that can be rented on an as-needed basis allows tenants flexibility in scheduling staff meetings and other group get-togethers without leaving the building.

Availability of office services for a fee—e.g., facsimile machines, telephone answering, secretarial services, bulk photocopying—can be attractive to small space users who may not need certain services on a full-time basis or whose owned or leased equipment is not adequate for large or complicated copying jobs. A building mailroom can be a real boon for tenants whose limited shipping needs do not justify having their own mailing facilities. A mailroom can give them access to United Parcel Service (UPS), Federal Express (FedEx), and other courier services for cross-country and international parcel delivery. For a small handling fee added to mailing or shipping costs, such a service can save a tenant a great deal of money—courier accounts have monthly fees, and maintaining a variety of packaging materials is very expensive for any business. Conference room rentals and business services and mailroom fees add to the building's revenue.

Tenants as Amenities. Many of the building-related benefits mentioned in the previous section can be provided by seeking out specific tenants for ground-floor retail space. If there is adequate space, a drug store that sells greeting cards and cosmetics as well as prescription and over-the-counter drugs would be a benefit to tenants' employees, and it will draw traffic from surrounding buildings. A mailing service might be leased space on the ground floor, and part of the lease arrangement could be the tenant serving as a building mailroom. Space in the basement or on the second floor might be leased to a fitness facility. A day care center might be leased space on a lower floor. Having a fitness facility or a day care center will also serve tenants of other buildings. These types of tenants enhance the neighborhood as well.

If a building's tenancy includes a large number of entrepreneurs and professionals, a financial advisor or investment counselor might be a desirable amenity tenant. Small spaces might be intentionally leased to physicians or dentists to include those services as a building amenity. Workers will use available facilities and services when these are not in plentiful supply generally or when they are not readily accessible outside of the building.

Some office buildings lease ground-floor retail space to a single restaurant, or they may configure several small food-vending spaces around an area with tables and chairs similar to a food court in a shopping center. Either approach will attract workers from other buildings as well. A word of caution is in order here. It may be more desirable to focus on food services specific for lunch and coffee breaks and, possibly, breakfast. While fine dining generates more revenue per customer sale, most workers look for inexpensive places to eat lunch and take coffee breaks.

Some types of amenity tenants also pose specific liabilities. Food establishments must be kept scrupulously clean to prevent infestations of insects and rodents. They also are subject to regular health department inspections and may be required by local law to have separate arrangements for waste removal. Fitness facilities and day care centers need extra liability insurance because of the high potential for physical injuries. Health care professionals have special utility and waste-disposal needs. Some types of tenants may require additional security or HVAC because their business hours differ substantially from those of most other tenants—i.e., they may be open from 7:00 A.M. to 7:00 P.M. or later. All of these aspects of amenity tenants can be satisfactorily addressed in specific lease language.

Another building amenity to consider is a concierge service. This is a one-person operation that will arrange for theater or concert tickets, make dinner reservations, order flowers, arrange for a limousine or a rental car, and perform a variety of similar services for a small fee. In a large building with a varied tenancy, it may be appropriate to hire a staff member to provide these services. In situations where there is unusually high demand for these types of services, an individual might be leased desk space in the lobby in return for a percentage of the fees collected.

An important aspect of all types of tenant amenities is visibility. Retailers need to be visible to street traffic, and some may require direct access from the street. Those that cannot be visible from the street or the building entrance may need additional or special signage. It may be desirable to create a special retail or services directory and locate it adjacent to the main entrance. If amenity tenants are on a floor other than street level, it may be necessary to install directional or other signage. In a large building, second-floor retail might be accommodated with escalators or open stairways.

Consider the neighborhood as well when identifying potential amenity tenants. In a central business district (CBD) that is undergoing redevelopment, vacant office buildings may be converted to rental apartments or condominiums. When office buildings are demolished, they may be replaced with new residential properties. Having residential property nearby suggests an expanded pool of potential employees for tenants. It also means there are additional potential beneficiaries of some types of amenity tenants.

Other Specific Leasing Strategies. When the market is soft, it often becomes necessary to offer prospective tenants some kind of rent *concession* in order to secure a lease. While this may take the form of a rate reduction, most owners are more comfortable with a period of free rent. (Other incentives should be pursued first; a rate reduction should be a last resort. The economics of rent concessions and their impact on effective rent are discussed in Chapter 7.) Usual practice is to start by offering one or two months rent-free, increasing this to one free month for each year of the lease if the first offer is not accepted. It may be possible to negotiate additional time on the lease as compensation; the period of free rent is usually timed at the start of the lease term. For example, a five-year lease with five months' free rent up front might be negotiated for a total lease term of five years and five months. If annual escalations were built into the rental rate, the additional time would be at the end of the lease term and during the period of maximum rent.

Other economic incentives may also be worthy of consideration. A highly desirable tenant under a long-term lease may warrant an offer to pay part or all of the firm's moving costs. In some situations, it may be appropriate to offer to buy out the prospect's current lease to expedite a relocation decision. Other strategies may be applied to renewals. If an existing tenant wants to expand but there is no space adjacent to it, management might offer to relocate the tenant to larger space within the building and pay part or all of the moving costs as an incentive. If a tenant needs less space, perhaps its premises can be divided in a way that allows the tenant to retain its location while giving the landlord an opportunity to re-lease the excess space. This is only practical if a reasonably large space would be subdivided to accommodate the tenant, and all parties can agree on the different rent structure that would apply. If the tenant's rent was initially adjusted because of the large amount of space being leased, the smaller space may have to have a higher rent to be economical. Here again, relocating the tenant within the building may be a practical accommodation of the tenant's reduced space needs. However, moving costs should preferably be a tenant expense.

Another strategy is to negotiate *options.* Although options are usually avoided because they favor the tenant at the landlord's expense, in the real world it is sometimes necessary to offer options in order to lease the space. The long-term economic impact of options must be considered *before* they are offered in negotiations, and the owner must be willing to accept the potential financial losses that they can represent. Lease terms regarding options should be specific, including time limitations when applicable. Four commonly offered options are discussed here. The details of a specific lease arrangement may be somewhat different.

1. Option to renew—The tenant may be allowed to renew the lease for an additional period of time on pre-agreed terms related to rent or on the same terms as the original lease. The option may be subject to negotiation of rent, escalations, and pass-through charges at the point of renewal. This is more agreeable to the owner when it sets the rent at a competitive rate or allows for adjustment to a competitive rate. Renewal on the same terms is clearly not desirable because it can jeopardize the building's rental income and the property's investment value.
2. Option to expand—A tenant may seek this option to ensure that additional space can be leased at some future time. The tenant is granted the right to lease a certain amount of additional space at a specific future date (during the term or after expiration of the original lease). The tenant may ask for the additional space to be adjacent to its current space, but this can be difficult to fulfill when all tenants have different multiple-year lease terms.
3. Option to cancel—A tenant may request an option to cancel its lease before the expiration of the original term. While a sole pro-

Typical Clauses in Office Leases

- Parties
- Premises
- Use
- Term
- Consideration (rent)
- Pass-through charges
- Escalation
- Tenant improvements
- Security Deposit
- Landlord's rights and obligations
  —Habitability of premises
  —Elevator service
  —Janitorial cleaning service
  —Maintenance of building
  —Capital improvements
  —Eminent domain
  —Substitution of premises
  —Change of building name
  —Sale of the building
  —Grant of quiet enjoyment
  —Landlord's right of re-entry

prietor or a professional in private practice may seek this option to protect family or heirs in the event of serious illness or death, it may also be sought to avert problems in the event the tenant has to declare bankruptcy. If the option is exercised, the owner will be faced with an unexpected vacancy, but there will be no confusion regarding the owner's rights to re-lease the space; and in the event of a bankruptcy, the building owner will avoid becoming one of a long line of creditors who will receive only partial payment on the tenant's outstanding debts. (Note: If this option is granted, leasing commission may only be paid on the uncancellable portion of the lease initially, with the remainder being paid when the cancellation date has passed.)

4. Option to own—A large space user may seek equity in or partial ownership of the building, perhaps as protection against having to relocate in circumstances other than by the tenant's own choice. This can be advantageous to the owner because it can generate additional cash flow immediately while also reducing the owner's investment risk. Such a strategy might not be practical in a high-rise building unless the property is in pre-leasing or development financing is difficult to obtain. However, it may be very useful in a suburban office park where there are several buildings on a large parcel of land, and most of the tenants are large space users.

Typical Clauses in Office Leases *(continued)*

- Tenant's rights and obligations
  —Acceptance of premises
  —Insurance
  —Hold harmless
  —Default by tenant
  —Strict performance
  —Alterations
  —Signage requirements
  —Surrender of premises
  —Hold over
  —Assignment and subleasing
  —Estoppel certificate
  —Subordination
  —Destruction of building

Other separate clauses may deal specifically with additional rent (landlord may treat any charges against tenant as additional rent to expedite eviction for nonpayment); insolvency, receivership, or bankruptcy of the parties; death not terminating the lease (lease is binding on successors and heirs of the parties); attorneys' fees; compliance with applicable laws, and periods of notice.

An executed lease will usually also include a number of addenda or exhibits, including a floor plan of the leased premises, a legal description of the building, a work letter (tenant improvements), rules and regulations, and other items that were negotiated separate from the standard lease form.

The Lease Agreement

A *lease* is a contract that transfers from the owner to a tenant the right to use a defined piece of real estate for a specified period of time upon payment of specific consideration (rent). Usually, the manager and the owner will develop a standard form lease that contains the owner's preferred clauses. Although nearly every provision in an office lease is negotiable, use of a standard form to start with precludes the need to prepare a completely new lease for each tenant because the landlord's basic requirements are already stated. It also ensures that all the particulars will be addressed and guards against any oversight that might be detrimental to either or both parties to the lease. Prior to signing, the negotiated lease should be reviewed by attorneys for both parties to ensure that it complies with applicable laws and that changes to the standard form lease will be upheld in a court of law if any of the terms are later disputed.

Note: A standard lease form developed with advice of an attorney may not require legal review for each tenant who signs it. In many instances, changes to the base document will comprise only the particulars of a tenancy (parties, premises, term, rent and other payments), which are entered into blanks provided for them. Legal review may be needed, however, when negotiations result in changes that lead to questions about the validity of specific provisions.

Basic Lease Provisions. There are many standard clauses that are incorporated into a lease document. Among those basic to an office lease are the following:

- *Parties*—The lease should name the parties to the lease (business names of landlord and tenant) and identify the people who will sign the lease and their authority to do so. If the tenant is a division or subsidiary of a large corporation, the name and address of the corporate entity should be included in the tenant identification.
- *Demised premises*—There should be a comprehensive description of the tenant's leased space with reference to the building and the location of the space within the building. It should refer to both rentable and usable area and the manner in which they are to be measured. It should include street address, building name, floor, suite number, and the floor area (square footage) of the leased space.
- *Use*—The leased space is to be used for the conduct of office-type business; any other use (retail sales, residential occupancy, illegal activities) should be strictly prohibited. A lease for retail space in an office building would have a similar restriction imposed on its use. Apart from the need to comply with occupancy ordinances, most office space is not suited to other uses.
- *Term*—The term of the lease should be stated along with specific commencement and expiration dates. This might be stated as "a period of three years, beginning March 1, 20xx, and ending on February 28, 20yy. One reason this type of information is necessary is because the lease term may begin on a date other than the date it was signed. Rent payment may not commence until the space has been built out to the tenant's specifications and the tenant has moved in. A period of free rent might also affect the specifics of the lease term. (Note: If the lease commences on a date other than the first of the month, the anniversary should be the first day of the first full month of the lease.)
- *Rent*—The lease should state the base rental rate, the area to which it is applied, and whether it is per year or per month. Most often the rate is applied to rentable area, so it is important to define the rentable and usable area of the tenant's leased space and state the manner in which they were measured. It is a good idea to state the full amount of rent for the entire lease term as well. Doing so can prevent disputes at a later date. It is also important for computing leasing commissions. The rent clause should include when, where, and to whom payment is to be made. It is customary for rent to be paid in advance on the first of the month.

- *Pass-through charges*—Most office leases are *net leases,* which means that some or all of the operating expenses for the building common areas will be passed through to tenants on a pro rata basis. The tenant's pro rata share should be stated as a specific percentage and referred to the tenant's demised premises and the building area that is available for occupancy (tenant rentable square footage ÷ building rentable square footage × 100 = pro rata percentage).

  Pass-through charges are typically real estate taxes, utilities, insurance, building services, and building equipment maintenance, including specific labor. Items usually not passed through are capital items and so-called paper costs (debt service amortization and depreciation).

- *Escalation*—Because office leases are typically written for periods of longer than one year, it is advisable to include a provision for automatic rent increases. Increases in the base rental rate may be stated as a dollar amount to be added to the base rate each year or as a percentage rate increase. For a very long lease term (e.g., ten or more years), incremental increases may be called for at three- or five-year intervals instead of annually.

  Alternatively, the increase may be based on changes in the Consumer Price Index (CPI). However, this is increasingly difficult for landlords and tenants to agree on, especially when the fluctuations are substantial. At the same time, small incremental changes during periods of low inflation may not cover increases in the owner's operating costs.

- *Tenant improvements*—Landlords typically provide certain standard installations as part of the lease arrangement. As stated earlier in this book, the *tenant improvement allowance* may comprise a certain number of electrical outlets or other fixed installations using building standard materials or it may be stated as a dollar amount per square foot. Specifics are documented separately in a *workletter* that is attached to and becomes part of the lease. This also includes a schedule for completion of the work to meet the pre-determined move-in date. If the actual cost of the installations exceeds the allowance amount, the lease should state who will pay for the difference. The landlord may assume the obligation, especially if the tenant's size and the length of the lease term warrant it. Otherwise, the tenant may be obligated to reimburse the landlord via regular payments of *additional rent* over the full term of the lease or a shorter period (see Chapter 9).

- *Security deposit*—As a means of guaranteeing the tenant's performance under the lease, it is a common practice to require a security deposit, which is often equivalent to one month's rent. Security deposits may be used to compensate the landlord for excessive damage to the leased space beyond normal wear and tear or for the tenant's failure to pay rent. Large space users may refuse to pay a security deposit or demand that it be deposited in an interest-bearing account in their company name. As an alternative to a specific lease provision, the security deposit may be handled on an as-needed basis via an addendum to the lease. An alternative to a security deposit is a *letter of credit* from the tenant's bank or financial institution.

If a prospect's credit rating is not up to requirements, it may be preferable to ask for a guarantor in addition to a security deposit. A *guarantor* is a person or business entity who agrees to pay all of the tenant's financial obligations to the landlord in the event the tenant defaults on the lease. Tenant bankruptcy does not relieve the guarantor of liability.

Landlord's Rights and Obligations. The landlord typically provides specified amounts of heat and air conditioning, hot and cold water, electricity, and janitorial service to the tenant's leased space. The amounts should be stated in the lease along with the method of determining excessive use and how the tenant will be billed for such excess. Landlord also provides elevator service and building directory listings to all tenants.

If ownership is required to install special equipment or make capital expenditures to comply with governmental regulations regarding energy conservation, it is appropriate for those expenditures to be reimbursed or amortized as escalatable expenses. Alternatively, utility usage control devices might be installed at tenants' expense. Heat, air conditioning, and utilities may be provided during specific hours, and tenants will need to know whether these services can be made available during off hours and what charges will apply. Tenants who have mainframe computers may require round-the-clock air conditioning and special air filters and humidity controls. Prospects need to know whether the building can accommodate their special needs. While newer buildings include mechanical systems and appropriate controls to handle such requests, an older building may need a special retrofit. The landlord will not want to be penalized for not providing full service at all times, and provisions will be included in the lease to protect the landlord from having to rebate rents or make other adjustments because service has been interrupted.

The situation with regard to elevators is similar. Maximum elevator service may be provided only during certain hours—e.g., when use is heaviest at the start and close of the business day and at lunch time—and the number of elevators and their travel speeds may be reduced during the remainder of the day. In a small building with few tenants, interruption or reduction of elevator service, with adequate notice beforehand, is not likely to cause major problems. In a high-rise, however, where tenants are visited by clients throughout the day, any interruption or reduction of elevator service could be a hardship for tenants on upper floors. In most office buildings, elevator maintenance is a management responsibility. The lease should allow building services to be interrupted for inspections, repairs, or situations outside of management control (e.g., weather) without liability or abatement of rent.

Janitorial services are typically provided to tenants at cost (included in the base rent) although they may pay extra for cleaning of nonstandard tenant improvements. Knowledgeable tenants may ask to have specific *janitorial specifications* incorporated in their leases as an exhibit. It is a good idea to do this as a standard practice. Janitorial specifications should detail the types of cleaning and trash removal that will be done on a nightly basis and how often more-extensive types of cleaning will be done. It is important to itemize the janitorial costs to be borne by the tenant. It will minimize disputes and can help avoid litigation if everything is specified up front in the lease.

Normally, the building owner is responsible for maintaining the exterior walls and roof of the building. Ownership will usually make repairs to tenants' demised premises and charge the tenant for the cost. However, a tenant may be responsible for some types of repairs or replacements (e.g., ballasts and lamps in light fixtures). This is more likely in a building that does not have full-time management.

The cost of *capital improvements* to the office building may be passed through to tenants if their leases include a specific provision to that effect. Normally, capital improvements are a landlord expense for which funds may have been accumulated in advance (reserves). The reserve fund may be an operating expense item for budget purposes (a deduction from NOI), in which case the cost would be passed through to tenants in advance. Absent a reserve fund, the owner may have to borrow funds to pay for capital expenses, in which case the new debt service may become a pass-through item. The lease would have to include a special provision anticipating such a pass-through charge.

Real estate may be appropriated by federal, state, or local governments in order to build new highways or for urban renewal under condemnation and eminent domain. An *eminent domain* clause describes the parties' options in the event a governmental entity should exercise such authority, which may be temporary, partial, or complete. The typical lease clause terminates the lease upon condemnation, and all tenant improvements and fixtures revert to the owner. This precludes the tenant from sharing in any financial award from a condemnation proceeding and negates ownership from liability for being unable to perform its obligations under the lease.

The owner reserves the right to relocate tenants to comparable offices in the building if circumstances warrant such a change. For example, a large tenant who wanted to expand into adjacent space occupied by a small tenant might move out of the building if such an arrangement could not be made. A *substitution of premises* clause provides for the tenant's rent per square foot to remain the same, and the owner would pay the cost of relocating the small tenant within the building. The owner may receive reimbursement for those relocation costs from the tenant who is expanding.

Ownership should reserve the right to *change the building name* if the need arises. This is an important point to negotiate, especially with large space users who want to be identified with a building by its name or who seek prestige through association with a prestigiously named building. Addressing this issue in the lease can preclude liability of the owner for damages (i.e., compensation for lost business, reimbursement of the cost of reprinting stationery).

A building may be named for its owner (e.g., Sears Tower in Chicago, anything built by Donald Trump) or for a tenant who leases several floors. In the latter case, the lease for the named tenant may include a requirement that the tenant consistently lease a certain number of square feet in the building and that the tenant cannot change the building name again independently.

The owner may *sell the building,* assign the tenant's lease to the new owner, and consequently be relieved of all lease obligations. (The purchaser becomes liable for the lease as a result of the sale.)

Finally, the landlord is required to grant the tenant peaceful enjoyment of the leased premises provided tenant fulfills its obligations under the lease. In conjunction with this, the lease should retain to the owner the right to enter and inspect the leased premises at reasonable times *(landlord's right of re-entry)* and with minimal disruption of tenant's business activities, usually with proper advance notice. However, in an emergency, the notice requirement may be waived.

Tenant's Rights and Obligations. Tenants are obligated to pay rent in full and on time and to notify the owner or manager when repairs or other work needs to be done in their leased premises. A number of lease provisions address the tenant's obligations specifically.

- *Acceptance*—Tenant move-in constitutes acceptance of the leased premises in the condition presented. Particulars may be documented in an addendum to the lease that states the specific commencement date and includes a declaration of acceptance of the premises in their current condition ("as built" if improvements are constructed new for tenant; "as is" if not).
- *Insurance*—Office building owners usually procure insurance on the building and standard improvements to it. This includes fire and extended coverage as well as general liability insurance. Crime coverage may also be carried, depending on location. Building insurance

is charged back to tenants as an operating expense. It is also common for both parties to the lease to waive claims against each other for damage caused by insurable casualties *(waiver of subrogation)* and for both parties' insurance carriers to recognize such waivers.

Insurance on the building does not cover the contents of the tenant's leased premises. Such insurance is a tenant obligation. Tenants are also required to obtain premises liability insurance and list the owner and the manager as additional named insured parties. A person who is injured in the tenant's leased premises might sue both the tenant and the owner or management; this insurance protects all parties. Retail tenants may be required to carry plate glass coverage and crime insurance as well.

- *Hold harmless*—The standard hold harmless clause states that the landlord will not be liable for damages for injuries sustained in, on, or about the tenant's leased premises as a result of omissions, negligence, or deliberate acts of the tenant's employees or visitors. Nor will landlord be liable for injuries or damage caused by the tenant's negligence in building common areas.

- *Default*—The lease should clearly define the conditions under which the tenant will have failed to fulfill its lease obligations and thereby defaulted on the lease. Most office leases will refer to a grace period in which the tenant can cure (correct) the default. Five to ten days (with or without notice) is commonly allowed for payment of delinquent rent; thirty days or more may be allowed for curing a default of other lease terms and conditions. The lease may be specific about grace periods for different types of default. Tenants will usually want to receive specific written notice of individual instances of default. It is also desirable to send notices because they provide documentation of each default and whether or not it was cured.

  The landlord's rights to repossess the leased premises follow state (and local) landlord and tenant laws. If the tenant does not cure the default within the allowed time period, the landlord may have the right to:

  Enter and repossess the premises
  Remove tenant's property and hold it as security
  Immediately re-lease the space
  Recover damages from the tenant, including
  —the cost of re-leasing
  —remaining rent due
  —any other money the tenant owes the landlord
  Terminate the lease

Apart from complying with applicable laws, it is important to know exactly what the property owner wishes to do in the event of different types of default. This can save time and money after the lease is in effect because there are costs involved in taking action against a tenant in default. Also, a tenant in default of economic clauses of the lease may not be in a financial position to reimburse the owner let alone cure the default.

- *Strict performance*—This provision states that waiver of one default by ownership does not constitute a waiver of any other default at any time. This is where it is important to emphasize consistency in the handling of default and related issues. If a tenant has paid part of the rent or paid rent late on a regular basis—and those partial or late payments have been accepted—the owner may have difficulty suing that tenant for default.
- *Alterations*—Tenants are prohibited from changing or making improvements to their leased space without the owner's written consent. This is done for several reasons in addition to the fact that the owner needs to maintain control over the investment. Tenant alterations could damage the building structure or equipment, perhaps putting the HVAC system off balance. They could also lower the property value, or the work might violate local building codes. Use of nonunion labor could lead to problems with unions that work in the building. There is also the possibility that substantial improvements could alter the assessed valuation, leading to an increase in real estate taxes. This issue can be addressed by having the lease state that all taxes assessed as a result of a tenant's improvements will be the tenant's responsibility.
- *Signage*—Owner should retain the right to set limits on the type and number of signs and graphics that a tenant can display on the property. There may also be a need to comply with local ordinances regarding signs. Specific guidelines should govern the size of signs, the typefaces used, and where and how signs may be attached to the exterior of the building. It may be prudent to establish a relationship with a vendor who will work with building management to ensure that interior and exterior signage is harmonious. This may make it easier to control company identification on office doors, or on walls in open reception areas that face the elevators when a tenant leases an entire floor or multiple floors. This type of clause helps maintain consistency between tenants' displays and the building's overall image. It also guards against structural damage.
- *Surrender of possession*—This provision states the owner's rights and the tenant's obligations upon expiration of the lease. A lease that does not specify initial ownership of tenant improvements can cause difficulties for both parties when the lease expires (or is terminated).

Usually the tenant is directed to return the space to the owner in substantially the same condition as when it was leased with the exception of normal wear and tear. Under this clause, all improvements to the tenant's leased space revert to the owner although the owner may ask for certain tenant-built improvements to be removed when the tenant vacates.

The departing tenant is required to remove all personal property and to clear away debris. There should be a stated program for dealing with tenants who fail to follow through on this. For example, the cost of cleanup might be deducted from the tenant's security deposit. This clause should also provide for damages to be paid to the owner if the tenant does not vacate on the expiration date.

- *Hold over*—This provision allows the tenant to continue to occupy its leased space after the lease term has expired, upon obtaining the owner's permission to do so. The hold over may extend the terms of the original lease on a month-to-month basis, but it is not unusual for the lease to be specific about a change (increase) in the rental rate for the hold-over period. If the tenant continues to occupy the premises *without* the owner's permission, hold over does not apply, and a fine or other sanction may be imposed on the tenant by the landlord.

- *Assignment and subleasing*—If a tenant subleases its space or assigns the lease to another business, that tenant becomes the landlord for the assignee or sublessee. Tenants acquired via sublet or assignment should be checked out as scrupulously as were the original tenants because a sublessee or assignee might default on the rent or other terms of the original lease leaving the building owner without recourse except through the original tenant. Such secondary tenancies can change a building's tenant mix, perhaps not for the better. Not having a lease directly with the building owner, the assignee or sublessee may create a hazardous situation; its business may be unsuitable to the building, or it might have too many employees for the amount of space. Tenants may ask to have this clause modified to state that, while the tenant cannot assign or sublease the premises without the owner's prior written permission, the owner may not unreasonably withhold permission.

  A long-term tenant may need more space (or less). It may be experiencing financial difficulties or it may be trying to sell the business. These are a few of the reasons a tenant may try to assign or sublet its space. The lease should state that, at the time of any sublease or assignment, the tenant must have fulfilled all of its obligations under the lease. It should require the tenant to serve as guarantor in the event the sublessee or assignee defaults. A tenant may try to sublet its space at a different rental rate, which can lead to dissatisfaction among other tenants in the building if the sublet rent is substantially higher or lower than they are paying. The original tenant should be required to disclose the sublet rent to the building owner.

- *Estoppel certificate*—Tenant is obligated to prepare and submit an estoppel certificate as may be required to secure financing or refinancing or in the event of sale of the building. In its simplest form, an estoppel certificate is a declaration of the rental rate being paid by the tenant, the duration of the lease term, and the amount of any security deposit being held. Reference may be made to the condition of the premises, specific changes made to terms of the lease, and any condition of default on the part of the tenant (e.g., delinquent rent). The completed certificate becomes a part of the lease.
- *Subordination*—In the event the mortgage is foreclosed, the lease is subject to and subordinate to any first mortgage on the property. This is an important consideration because a tenant's lease could be terminated in a foreclosure, resulting in eviction of the tenant by the mortgage holder. Prospects will usually object to this provision, but they will not be able to have it deleted from the lease.
- *Destruction*—The lease should state the tenant's rights in the event the leased premises are damaged or destroyed (e.g., by fire or other disaster) including procedures for handling repairs. If the tenant is found to have caused the damage, directly or through negligence, the tenant would be deemed financially liable. More to the point, a destruction clause is intended to prevent a tenant from terminating the lease because of partial destruction of its premises or because the premises have been made uninhabitable. Usually the lease remains in effect if the owner makes repairs within a specified time frame and rebates rent during the repair period. If damage is extensive, however, the owner may terminate the lease, rather than make repairs, and there would be no liability to the tenant. Total destruction would terminate the lease regardless.

Types of Leases

There are three types of leases—gross, net, and percentage. Under a *gross lease,* the tenant pays a fixed rental rate for the space, and the owner pays all building operating expenses although the tenant may be required to pay increases in specified operating expenses (taxes, utilities, repairs, maintenance). In such situations, the lease may refer to a *base year,* which may be the first full calendar year after move-in, and the tenant will then pay for increases over the amount of actual expenses in the base year. The base year may be changed when the lease is renewed. Alternatively, an *expense stop*

Differences in Net Leases (examples)

Tenant A

Net lease: Real estate taxes only

Net-net lease: Real estate taxes + utilities + insurance

Triple-net lease: Real estate taxes + utilities + insurance + maintenance

Tenant B

Net lease: Real estate taxes + utilities + special assessments

Net-net lease: Real estate taxes + utilities + special assessments + maintenance

Triple-net lease: Real estate taxes + utilities + special assessments + maintenance + some capital improvements

may be stated; in this case, the tenant would be required to pay for increased operating costs over a certain amount (e.g., $4.00 per square foot). Gross leases are not commonly used in office leasing; instead, there is usually some form of net lease.

There are three levels of *net lease*—net or single-net, net-net or double-net, and net-net-net or triple-net. Each extra "net" requires the tenant to pay for more operating costs. However, the meaning of each level of net varies in different locales. For example, a net lease for tenant A in one part of the United States may require payment of real estate taxes only while a similarly named net lease might require tenant B in another part of the country to pay utilities and special assessments in addition to real estate taxes. A net-net lease for tenant A might cover utilities and insurance as well as real estate taxes while one for tenant B might add ordinary repairs and maintenance to the prior list. Under a triple-net lease, tenant A might have added maintenance and repairs while tenant B would be required to pay the cost of some capital improvements.

When retailers lease space in an office building, the landlord may negotiate for them to pay a *percentage* of their gross sales in addition to a low minimum monthly rent. The percentage varies with the size and type of retail business, and percentage rent is usually calculated and paid as *overage*. In other words, the percentage rate is applied to gross sales revenues to determine the total rent due and the minimum annual rent is subtracted from that to find the amount of percentage rent due.

> Suppose, for example, that a retailer has a minimum annual rent based on its gross leasable area (GLA) of $36,000 ($6/sq ft of GLA/yr × 6,000 sq ft of GLA) and a percentage rate of four percent of gross sales. If annual gross sales are one million dollars, the percentage rent calculation would look like this.

$1,000,000 gross sales × .04 percentage rate = $40,000 total rent due
$40,000 total rent due − $36,000 minimum rent = $4,000 percentage rent due

Since minimum rent is paid monthly, percentage rent is likely to be computed and paid monthly as well (although a retailer in an office building may negotiate annual payment to smooth out extreme variances in monthly income). In this case, percentage rent would apply when sales revenue for a given month exceeded $75,000.

$36,000 annual rent ÷ 12 months = $3,000 minimum monthly rent
$3,000 monthly minimum rent ÷ .04 percentage rate = $75,000 monthly breakpoint

The point at which percentage rent equals the minimum rent is the *breakpoint* (also known as the natural breakpoint).

Whether they pay percentage rent or not, retail tenants in both shopping centers and office buildings commonly pay a pro rata share of common area operating expenses as delineated in a net lease.

Retailers' leases may also include an *exclusive use* provision, which grants the retailer the exclusive right to sell a type of merchandise at that location. For example, a drug store might be granted an exclusive for greeting cards and gift wrap that would preclude the owner from leasing space to a gift shop that also sold greeting cards. Such exclusives are rarely granted, even in shopping centers, because they tend to stifle competition. A retail tenant might also be prohibited from opening a similar store within a certain distance from the building. Such a *radius* clause is used in shopping centers to preclude tenants from directing their customers to other nearby stores (within, say, three to five miles) to avoid paying percentage rent. In a downtown office building, the radius might be only a block or two. Except for a drug store or a fashion retailer, most retail shops in office buildings are not shopping destinations; they expect most of their customers to be from within the building. However, if an office building has a substantial amount of retail space—i.e., a lobby corridor lined with shops—the area might be treated as a "shopping center" that is leased separately from the office space in the building.

9

Space Planning and Construction Management

Space planning is necessary because modern office buildings are constructed with large blocks of unfinished space. It is also necessary to satisfy the needs of different tenants, whether they are leasing space in a brand-new building or moving into a space that was previously occupied. In some situations, the leasing agent or the manager will plan tenant interiors personally. In most situations, however, a professional space planner, interior designer, or architect will be hired. This will ensure proper consideration of a tenant's unique design or technical requirements while also maintaining the structural integrity of the building.

Office space planning involves determining how much space is needed, making sure the relationship between space and work flow is balanced, responding to the tenant company's present space requirements, and anticipating its future needs. For the tenant, an effectively designed office interior will improve productivity by streamlining the flow of work and improve efficiency by making the best use of the space. For the office building owner and manager, the result will optimize the leasable space and, thereby, maximize the dollar return. It can also serve to upgrade the property, thereby enhancing its investment value.

Space planning offers other advantages as well. It gives prospects an opportunity to verify, before move-in, whether the space identified for them meets their companies' needs. (Tenants often underestimate how much space they will need.) It can show them how relocating to the building they have chosen will add to their prestige and comfort and/or reduce their operating costs. A good initial plan provides a basis for accurate cost estimates and job bids. Review of the plans helps the building owner's and the tenant's representatives separate the costs ownership will pay from those that will be charged to the tenant. This may lead to another look at the tenant's needs in relation to its budget to determine whether all the improvements are necessary or economically feasible. The prospect may decide to forego some specifically delineated private offices or group work spaces, freeing the space for other uses. It may turn out that certain furniture items are no longer needed or that duplicate equipment can be eliminated.

Space planning is especially important in regard to computers and telecommunications. It can ensure that initial installation and maintenance are orderly and cost-effective and that operating costs remain low while also providing flexibility that will allow for expansion of these vital office components as the company's business grows—without a major investment. Space planning can make it easy to reconfigure work areas to accommodate a growing staff. A well-executed space plan will help the tenant attract and retain quality personnel while helping the staff work more efficiently and enhancing the company's professional image.

The Space Planning Process

Before a space plan can be prepared for an individual prospective tenant, ownership and management must establish building standards for the finishing of tenants' premises. Building standards form the basis for the specifics of the tenant improvement allowance. Tenant improvements are such an important aspect of a lease that they are negotiated in detail, and the agreement regarding them is documented separately in a workletter. The workletter also relies on development of a preliminary space plan that is satisfactory to both owner and tenant. If the owner or the management firm does not employ someone in that capacity, a professional space planner will have to be selected before plans can be developed.

Establishing Building Standards. Before any tenants move into a new office building—in fact, while the building is under construction—the owner and manager will develop building standards that specify the quantity and quality of materials that will be used in finishing the interiors of tenants' leased premises. At an existing building, a new manager will review previously established building standards with the owner as part of the management take-over process, and they may modify those standards to meet market requirements or develop new standards to replace them. Minimally, each tenant office will be provided with demising walls and an entrance door. In most situations, however, tenant improvements encompass a wide array of fixtures and installations.

Because tenant improvements become a permanent part of the building, the owner will want them to be of the same quality as the building itself. The office building manager's goal is to establish standards that will permit construction of an office suite to a prospective tenant's specifications without any extras being needed. This requires attention to materials for components (e.g., doors, partitions, fixtures) and finish items (e.g., floor and wall coverings), which must be compatible with the quality of the building and meet applicable fire code requirements. It is also appropriate to consider what competing buildings are offering.

Components of the building standard tenant improvement package apply to the entire building and are not subject to tenant choice unless the tenant is willing to pay for a substitution. (Substitutions are addressed in the discussion of the tenant improvement allowance later in this chapter.) Having uniform standards for tenant improvements minimizes the amount of work when a space is re-leased; sometimes a previously constructed office suite can be re-leased as is except for some decorating (e.g., painting, cleaning or replacement of finish items). If a tenant requests and pays for fixtures or finishes that vary substantially from building standards, it may be difficult to re-lease the space at a later date. Regardless of whether the previously occupied space would be reconfigured, some installations may be very difficult to remove, complicating the work and costs of subsequent cleanup and repairs. The following sections describe the major components of building standards.

Walls and Partitions. Building standards will be needed for both demising walls that define the tenant's suite and interior partitions that delineate individual spaces within the suite. Local fire codes may specify material type and fire rating requirements for corridor walls. Inside the suite, private offices and selected work areas usually have partitions constructed in place using drywall sheets. Individual work spaces outside the private offices are commonly constructed of prefabricated partitions, which may be configured to accommodate furniture systems (work surfaces, file cabinets, shelving) that result in compact work areas. Prefabricated partitions may come with electrical wiring or other cabling embedded in them with removable plates for installation of outlet connections. The result when such workstations or cubicles are used is called an *open space plan*. Individual workstations can require a smaller amount of floor space per worker than an arrangement without such partitions, and they can be easily reconfigured to change an office layout. The initial cost of movable partitions can be high, but they are generally durable, and sometimes a tenant will already have such workstations and want to move them into the new space.

Apart from dividing the space, walls and partitions also control the noise level in the suite. (Wall system manufacturers usually include sound control ratings among the specifications in their product literature.) Once walls and partitions are installed, it is difficult to overcome deficiencies in sound control, which can be problematic for the tenant. Sound control is not merely a matter of walls and partitions. Sound can transfer through the HVAC system, light fixtures, and back-to-back wall outlets. This means all components used in constructing tenant improvements should be given careful consideration in regard to sound control ratings so the desired results can be achieved.

Building standards for walls should identify the materials to be used in constructing demising and interior walls and the manner in which installation is to be completed (e.g., thickness of drywall, distances between wall studs, and whether they extend to the finished ceiling or to the underside of the slab above).

Doors, Frames, and Hardware. The type of door depends on where it is used. Doors between tenants' spaces and public corridors are usually solid-core construction, 36 inches wide, and sometimes full height to the ceiling line. These doors may be paint- or stain-grade wood, plastic laminate with edges stained to match, or metal with a foam core. Interior doors are typically 30–36 inches wide by 80–96 inches high. Here again, solid-core doors are preferable for sound control and may be required in local building codes. In fact, metal doors are quite common; they offer greater security as well as better fire protection. Metal door frames are common for both interior and demising applications. These are often painted to harmonize with the overall color scheme of the suite.

Door hardware may be polished, brushed (matte), anodized, or paint-grade metal. Locksets on corridor doors should be selected on the basis of their ability to prevent illegal access or make it difficult. Levers are commonly replacing doorknobs to facilitate access by people with disabilities. Locksets as such may be superseded by electronic door controls that use cards or keypads to release the lock. Cards may be swiped through or presented close to a device that reads an embedded chip; keypads require people seeking entry to enter a number code (touch a flush surface or push a button). Access-control systems and devices continue to evolve as greater levels of security are sought. Suite entrance doors should have a door check or closer that will automatically close the door without slamming. A door check is mandatory if local fire codes require corridor doors to be kept closed.

The building standard should specify the type, quality, and finishes of corridor and interior doors (including door dimensions and thickness), locksets, latchsets, door knobs, hinges, and framing. It is also appropriate to identify acceptable access control devices and the manner in which they will be installed. These may be a tenant-preferred option.

To create a more-welcoming atmosphere on multitenant floors, rather than having corridor walls interrupted only by solid doors, the building standard might include glass doors or a glass sidelight on one or both sides of a solid door. These might be tenant options, with the tenant paying the cost differential above that of the basic door.

Ceilings. Most ceilings in office suites are suspended from the building structure. This allows for light fixtures to be flush with the ceiling surface. Various types of wiring and cabling along with HVAC ductwork may also be inserted in the space above the ceiling. There are two basic types of suspended ceilings, one using a T-bar to support acoustical tiles and one having a concealed spline supporting mineral tiles. Components of both types are available in a variety of materials and finishes. The concealed-spline type has a more-attractive appearance but is more expensive than the T-bar type. Also, maintenance in the area above a concealed-spline ceiling is difficult unless a "trap door" access panel is built into the tiles. Building standards should specify materials (including ceiling tile dimensions and suspension system) and finished ceiling height.

Lighting. Building lighting standards should consider energy efficiency as well as illumination of work areas. Where large numbers of computer monitors are in use, lighting levels are usually adjusted to reduce glare and minimize shadows. The building standard should establish minimum illumination levels for different types of work areas. Offices and workers in cubicles need more light (e.g., 50–75 footcandles) while corridors and storage areas need less (15–20 footcandles may be sufficient). The Illuminating Engineering Society of North America (IESNA) publishes lighting standards, and the National Lighting Bureau (NLB) develops guidelines for interior and exterior lighting requirements and publishes comparison data on different types of lights. These sources should be consulted when managers have questions about establishing building lighting standards.

Building standards may specify a number of light fixtures per 100 square feet as an alternative to specifying lighting levels. The type of fixture may also be specified along with the orientation. (Light fixtures should be aligned to give a uniform appearance to all floors when viewed from the outside at night.) Most office work areas are illuminated by fluorescent lamps; alternatives or adjunct lighting may be offered for certain areas (e.g., reception areas, conference rooms). Building standards may also include energy consumption rating guidelines. It may be appropriate as well to indicate whether light bulbs and ballasts for fluorescent light fixtures will be furnished by the landlord at initial installation or if these components will be a separate tenant expense.

Heating, Ventilating, and Air Conditioning. The HVAC system designed for an office suite will often be set up in zones that are separately controlled. A small office area might have a single zone while an office occupying a full floor may be divided into several zones. Most systems will have one mixing damper per zone. This damper controls the flow rates of hot and cold air, which are combined to produce an anticipated comfort level. Each mixing damper is opened or closed by a motor activated by the thermostat for the particular zone. The installed ductwork and dampers should be engineered to provide the required cubic feet per minute (CFM) of air to be discharged in each zone according to building policy. (Local building interior air quality codes may also apply.) Perimeter offices versus interior offices and seasonal sun exposure are specific factors to be considered in setting such policies. These requirements should become part of the building standard for HVAC.

Smoke removal may also be a consideration although many cities have mandated that office building work areas must be smoke-free. If such ordinances do not apply and building policy does not prohibit smoking, conference rooms and perhaps other areas of office suites will need provision for smoke removal. Kitchens and rest rooms should be equipped with odor-exhaust devices. Adequate insulation is also necessary to dampen the noise produced by fans and motors serving each zone.

Building standards should state how HVAC will be provided to the tenant's space (e.g., overhead ductwork and vents, wall-mounted units in private exterior offices, or both). This includes the number and type of vents and other components and the number and placement of thermostatic controls. It is also important to state how air-conditioning zones will be allocated on building floors and whether and how the base pattern will be modified to accommodate individual tenants. The American Society of Heating, Refrigerating and Air-Conditioning Engineers (ASHRAE) is a resource for information on HVAC engineering standards.

Note: Tenants who have mainframe computers housed in a separate computer room will need additional air conditioning for that area. The room will also require a direct, uninterrupted power supply and special wiring. These extras are likely to be a tenant expense.

Electrical and Telecommunications. With increasing use of high-technology tools in offices, the numbers of electrical and telephone outlets needed in office suites has also increased. Where an electric typewriter required one electrical outlet, the computers in individual workstations require at least two (hard drive and monitor), and each additional peripheral (printer, scanner) has to be plugged into its own outlet. Companies often provide a separate power strip to each work station. Similar in concept to an extension cord, this device has heavy-duty wiring and five or more grounded outlets. Most also incorporate a surge protector that prevents high-voltage spikes from damaging the equipment plugged into it (the electrical surge is diverted to a ground). Alternatively, a company may require a dedicated circuit for its computer equipment to prevent electrical interference from other building systems or office equipment.

Many businesses establish a *local area network (LAN)* that links all of their individual computers to each other and to a host computer, which allows for sharing of hardware peripherals, software programs, and data bases as well as electronic mail (e-mail) and access to the Internet. Sometimes network connections are established between computer terminals and photocopying machines, which permits generation of multiple copies of a document without a paper original. Companies with multiple business sites may also have a *wide area network (WAN)* connecting the various locations with each other. Networks use special cabling that is in addition to and separate from the electrical wiring.

The need for telephone outlets has also increased. Separate modems are sometimes connected to computers to permit connection to other computers off site. Computer terminals may have built-in modems or the computer network may include telephone cabling to permit faxing directly from and to individual computers. Separate telephone outlets are needed for free-standing facsimile machines, which also need a power supply. Modern telephone systems are controlled by computers that allow individual telephones to be programmed for a variety of additional functions, including announcement messages and voice mail. A business with a single phone computer may have a separate modem for sending and receiving facsimiles (faxes) and access to the Internet unless the central processing unit (CPU) or hard drive has a built-in modem. Even wireless telephones have limitations on their use, and the handsets must be plugged into a hard-wired unit to be recharged.

While telecommunications cabling once entered office buildings through the basement exclusively, transmissions via microwaves and satellites require rooftop installations. These may be dish-shaped devices of varying sizes, and they have to be positioned specifically to receive the transmissions. Since deregulation introduced competition among telecommunications providers, office building managers are having to negotiate contracts for installation and maintenance of telecommunications risers and rooftop transmission devices with a number of vendors in order to provide services demanded by tenants.

The building standard for electrical and telecommunications installations should include numbers of light switches, duplex outlets, and telephone outlets. It should specify the quality of materials and include provision for special uses (e.g., separate duplex outlets for photocopying machines). Types of special cabling, including fiber optics, should also be addressed along with appropriate housings (e.g., conduit). In addition, the electrical standards should state the amount of power provided to each floor—five watts per square foot is usually the design minimum; eight to twelve watts per square foot may be needed to operate sophisticated computer systems and data-processing equipment—and how individual tenants' special power needs will be accommodated.

As technology creates new tools for office work, the need for ever more sophisticated connections will grow. Building standards for electrical wiring and telecommunications cabling should provide for current technology and anticipate future needs. It is wise to install the best wiring and high-speed cable available and keep up-to-date on changes in cabling technologies. It is also a good idea to establish a tenant improvement allowance for electrical and telephone outlets that has some flexibility built into the relationship between numbers of outlets and tenant square footage.

Wall Coverings. Office walls may be finished in a variety of ways. Paint is a very common building standard finish because it is inexpensive, easy to apply, and easy to change. Often a standard is established offering a range of perhaps a dozen colors in light to medium tones that, when applied, will yield a flat (nonglare) surface finish. While a single coat of good-quality paint may be adequate to cover drywall, building standards usually call for two coats unless the paint is being applied over a darker color used for a previous tenant, in which case a third coat may be needed. It may be desirable to add an option of using complementary colors on some small wall areas to dispel the monotony of a one-color office.

Other interior finishes may also be offered, on a shared-cost basis or totally at tenant expense. Wallpaper, vinyl wall covering, or wood paneling may be used instead of paint. Marble and tile are still other options. These types of finishes may be requested for reception areas, executive offices, or conference rooms. They are more costly than paint and more complicated to apply or install. For example, walls to which wallpaper or wall covering are to be applied must be sized (surface coated) to accept the wall-covering adhesive. Paneling may have to be framed. Marble may require a system of brackets. Tile is applied with special adhesive, and grout is added between individual tiles.

The building standard for wall coverings should identify the type and quality of materials and how they will be applied. This would include a standard number of coats of paint, the type of paint finish, and preparation of wall surfaces for other, non-paint finishes.

Floor Coverings. Floor coverings need to be durable—they receive more wear and tear than any other component of an office suite—and easily maintained. They must also be selected with cost in mind. There are two standard floor coverings used in offices. These are carpeting and resilient flooring. Building standards should be developed for both types because while carpeting may be desirable for all areas, resilient flooring is most appropriate for kitchens, copying centers, and storage areas. Rest rooms included in office suites should also have resilient or other appropriate flooring.

The standard for carpet should specify component material and backing. Newer man-made fibers are wear and stain resistant. Hard-wearing varieties of carpeting have been developed for use in expositions and industrial applications, and that may be a consideration when an office includes a large amount of heavy equipment. Subdued medium to dark tones are preferable to light or bright ones because they tend to minimize the visibility of spots and stains. Padding may have to be installed before the carpeting is laid. As an alternative to wall-to-wall carpeting, carpet squares can be considered. They are especially useful in high-traffic areas because only selected squares would need to be replaced when they are soiled or damaged.

Resilient flooring is available as uniform, square tiles or as sheet goods. Tile is more commonly used in offices because it allows replacement of small areas when tiles are damaged. The standard for resilient flooring should specify the type of material (vinyl is most common) and the adhesive to be used. Light, neutral colors and simple patterns are best.

Wooden floor finishes are rarely used in office buildings because they are impractical. They are expensive to install and finish and difficult to maintain. They would quickly become very shabby looking in any high-traffic area. Because a prospective tenant may insist on wood flooring, it is important to consider such requests and establish a policy regarding them. It is appropriate for such a non-standard finish to be handled on a shared-cost basis or strictly a tenant expense. Maintenance should be a tenant expense regardless.

Regardless of the type of floor covering installed, some type of finish is necessary at the point where floors and walls meet. Usually strips of a rubber or vinyl base are glued to the wall to provide a uniform appearance and protect that area of the wall when the flooring is cleaned.

Window Coverings. Window covering is not only a building standard item, it is usually specified to achieve a uniform appearance when seen from the exterior of the building and across interior office areas. Several alternatives can be considered, including draperies and different varieties of horizontal and vertical window blinds. The chosen covering should be easy to hang, remove, clean, and rehang. The suspension system or mechanism should allow complete closure and maximum opening, the latter being necessary for interior window washing. When setting building standards, consideration should be given to quality of materials, appearance when both open and closed, sun exposure, and fade resistance. Heat and cold insulation are other possible benefits of window coverings and may be worthwhile considerations in setting standards. Minimally, the specification should identify the type and quality of material (e.g., 3½-inch blades for vertical blinds) and the color.

Other Items. Fire sprinklers are installed in a fixed pattern and mounted in the finished ceiling. They are usually pre-existing (i.e., installed before tenant space is finished for occupancy for the first time). The cost of moving sprinklers is considerable and should be given consideration in developing building standards.

Fire exit signs are positioned at ceiling level to indicate entrances to stairwells. When tenants occupy full floors or if their spaces adjoin a stairwell, building standards should include provision for exit signs within tenants' spaces.

A tenant may need a secure storage area for media used for daily backup of a network or mainframe computer. Building standards should at least anticipate such requirements and be prepared to handle them appropriately.

It may also be desirable to set building standards for signage and graphics, particularly if such installations will be part of the tenant improvements provided. Issues to be addressed include the manner in which company identification is applied to glass doors or sidelights or attached to corridor doors or walls. To maintain a uniform or at least consistent appearance on multitenant floors, specifications should be set for materials, fonts and type sizes, and methods of application or installation.

Signage is an even larger issue for retail tenants. Local ordinances may specify size limitations for signs and address their installation on exteriors of buildings. Some jurisdictions prohibit signs that are perpendicular to the building wall. Building standards may set specifications for applications to plate glass windows, attachments to the exterior of the building, sign dimensions (maximum width and height), and use of neon signs. This is important to maintain the appearance of the building. A Class A office building with numerous small retailers will be diminished in value if retailers' signage gives the building a tacky appearance.

Other items may warrant consideration as well. Factors such as property location, market conditions, and finishes offered by competing buildings may govern the extent to which additional items become building standards.

Tenant Improvement Allowance. There are two basic approaches to tenant improvement allowances. One method sets a dollar-per-square-foot amount. The other sets allowances on a per-unit basis. In the first method, the dollar allowance is expected to cover the cost of all demising walls and interior partitions, corridor and interior doors, light fixtures, electrical and telephone outlets, ceiling components, flooring, and window coverings. The second method is directly related to the tenant's usable area, and allowances are expressed as, say, one lineal foot of partition for every 100 square feet of usable area, one electrical outlet per 100 square feet of usable area, and so forth. The unit allowance potentially offers more control over costs.

When working with unit allowances, unit costs must be known in advance. Costs can be obtained from contractors, who usually guarantee quoted prices for a whole year. They will need detailed specifications for materials and work, and their pricing should include labor costs for construction and installation of individual items. The office building manager can seek unit prices for components (electrical outlets, sheets of drywall, gallons of paint) from appropriate vendors and estimate the amount of labor involved in performing the build-out if building personnel do the construction. There are also publications that compile data on construction costs for materials and labor. The R. S. Means Company, Inc., is one source for such information.

As part of the building standards and tenant improvement allowance, it is important to establish a firm policy regarding *substitutions*. This is necessary to control and facilitate allocation of charges when standard allowances are exceeded. Often managers establish a general rule that substitutions within a particular category are permitted, provided the tenant assumes responsibility for the cost differential. If a tenant wanted to substitute a higher grade of carpeting, for example, the dollar equivalent for the building standard carpet would be applied to the carpet cost, and the excess cost would be billed to the tenant. The same approach would apply if vinyl wall covering were requested and paint was the standard finish. On the other hand, substituting between different categories should be strictly forbidden. A tenant should not be allowed to forego interior partitions and apply the value of the partitions to a better grade of carpeting than the building standard.

Managers have other ways of controlling tenant improvement costs. One way is to calculate the standard allowance for a tenant's space using a form or a computer spreadsheet program. (Exhibit 9.1, page 220, is an example of how such a form might look.) Typically, allowance components would be listed at the left, and there would be columns for entering the unit allowance, the actual amount to be installed (based on the space plan), the computed allowance based on the tenant's usable area, and the difference (over/under) between them. This establishes the initial difference for allocating costs. Multiplying the overage by the unit price yields the dollar difference (over/under) from the allowance, which is to be billed to the tenant. Separate columns would show the amount to be paid by the owner and the amount loaned by the owner to be repaid by the tenant. Where the owner provides only minimal improvements at no cost to the tenant (e.g., demising walls and an entrance door), the cost of all other standard items may be structured as a loan to the tenant to be repaid, with interest, as *additional rent* over the term of the lease. Because the standard allowance may have to be computed before the lease is signed, the form or printed spreadsheet should include spaces for signatures of the parties to the lease. The form would then become an attachment or addendum to the lease itself.

Another strategy is to have the tenant sign an authorization form, which states that the tenant acknowledges responsibility and will pay the added cost for all items that exceed the standard allowance. When the work is completed, the tenant is sent a bill for the extra costs.

Exhibit 9.1

Sample Computation of Standard Allowance

Standard Allowance Computation

Building ______ Floor ______ Suite ______ Prepared By ______ Date ______

Tenant ______ Lease Term ______ Rentable Sq Ft ______ Usable Sq Ft ______

Tenant Allowances		No. per 1000 sq ft	Actual	Standard on Usable sq ft	Over (Under)	Unit Price	Over (Under) Allowances	Billed to Tenant	Paid by Owner	Loaned by Owner
Partitions	Demising (lineal feet)									
	Interior (lineal feet)									
Doors	Entrance									
	Interior									
Hardware	Lockset, Outer									
	Latchset									
	Lockset									
Light Switches										
Light Fixtures (Type: ______)										
Electrical Outlets (____V)										
Telephone Outlets										
Floor Covering	Carpet									
	Resilient Flooring									
Plumbing, per Sq Ft										
Other (Extras)										
						Totals				

Some prospects may prefer to pay for finish items of their choosing rather than those the building provides. However, tenants should not have carte blanche in this regard. Management should maintain control over the design and installation of tenant-preferred items, especially when installations such as special electrical and HVAC equipment are connected to building systems. It is important to prevent installation of equipment and materials that are inferior in quality or do not conform to required building codes or whose installation may cause structural or other damage to the building. It is also important to ensure that the tenant's preferred materials can be removed easily. The cost of removing low-quality, improperly installed wall covering or carpeting when a tenant moves out can be very high. It is good policy and practice to require that *all* tenant improvement construction, including tenant-preferred items, be performed by the contractor who is doing the work for the building owner. This will help the manager maintain control over scheduling as well as the quality of workmanship and materials.

Retail tenants in an office building may be given more latitude in regard to tenant improvements, or building standards may not apply at all. In shopping centers and where there are multiple shops, retailers are usually responsible for construction of their own tenant improvements. This is primarily because of the unique ways retail tenants display their merchandise. In shopping centers, the tenant is required to submit a construction or remodeling plan to be reviewed and approved by the landlord. Tenants usually contract for their own construction, and center management sets insurance requirements and parameters for completing the work. A handful of small retailers recruited for ground-floor space in an office building may be treated the same way as office space users in regard to tenant improvement allowances and use of building standard materials. If the retail component is extensive or complex, it may be preferable to make separate arrangements for construction, perhaps similar to those of a shopping center, and establish controls that will protect the building's structure and investment value. Shopping center managers and managers of office buildings with large retail components should be consulted to determine how retail tenant improvements are handled in the local market.

Workletter. A workletter is a separate contractual arrangement between landlord and tenant that spells out the details of the tenant improvement arrangement, including terms and conditions regarding payment for the work. The signed workletter is attached to and becomes a part of the tenant's lease.

A workletter minimally will address the following to enumerate the parties' respective obligations in regard to construction of the improvements.

- The space plan for the tenant's demised premises, a copy of which will be attached to the workletter.

- Preparation of working drawings for the tenant's space.
- Who will pay for the cost of the working drawings.
- What items will be furnished (building standard) and what will be considered tenant "extras."
- A cost proposal for the work, which will accompany the working drawings.
- Tenant approval of the working drawings and cost proposal.
- Modifications to the working drawings and cost proposal.
- Time frames for preparation, submission, and approval of drawings and cost proposal.
- Tenant's approval constitutes acknowledgment of the accuracy of the working drawings.
- Payment for tenant's extra work.
- Use of change orders to authorize deviations from the original plans during construction and how the costs of changes will be handled.
- Timely completion of the work and commencement of rent.
- Tenant overall responsibility for the design.
- Failure to perform and the consequences of such failure.

The workletter will also spell out or incorporate as an attachment the building standard finish items and allowances. It should be specific in regard to what the landlord will provide at no cost to the tenant and whether the tenant improvement allowance constitutes a loan from landlord to tenant, including how that loan is to be repaid (interest rate, payback period) and whether the amount will be simply computed, prorated, and added to the base rental rate or if it is to be repaid separately (e.g., as additional monthly rent for so many months of the lease term).

Paying for Tenant Improvements. Who pays for tenant improvements may depend on the desirability or importance of a particular prospective tenant. A large space user leasing one or more full floors for ten years may be treated more generously than a small business moving into a suite of 3,000 square feet on a multitenant floor under a three-year lease.

When the landlord pays for installation of building standard items, and the tenant is charged for extras that exceed the standard allowance, a bill for the extras will likely be presented to the tenant when the construction is completed. If the landlord only pays for minimal installations (demising walls, corridor doors), construction costs exclusive of tenant extras may be paid by the owner and structured as a loan to be repaid by the tenant, with interest, over the term of the lease.

Market conditions are also a consideration. In a soft market with high vacancies and few prospective tenants, the owner is more likely to pay for all or a larger portion of tenant improvement costs than during "normal" market conditions. When there are few vacancies and prospective tenants are competing for space, the tenant may pay for most or all of the build-out cost. Accepted practice in the local market may also be a factor, not only in determining who pays for tenant improvements, but also in establishing building standards and improvement allowances.

Selecting a Space Planner. Different professionals provide space planning services—architects, space planners, and interior designers. Who will design an individual tenant's space may depend on the nature and complexity of the work to be done. Build-out that will call for modifications to the building's structure or systems may best be handled by an architect in consultation with appropriate professional engineers. A tenant moving its existing furniture and equipment into a previously occupied space that does not require major reconfiguration may only need the services of an interior designer. It goes without saying that an architect's fees will be higher than those of a space planner or an interior designer. Local laws and practices may also be a factor in choosing the professional to plan a particular space.

A developer or a major investor in office real estate may have an architect or space planner on staff. This arrangement is especially valuable for a building in development or newly completed. A real estate management firm that specializes in office buildings may have a division or department staffed by architects, space planners, and construction management personnel. Alternatively, a building owner or management firm may establish a relationship with different types of space planners, perhaps on a retainer basis. In particular, a full-service architectural firm would be able to provide all of the space planning, interior design, and related engineering support required for building tenant improvements.

A manager responsible for selecting a space planner for a new or existing office building will want to investigate various sources for planning services available locally or in nearby cities. The American Institute of Architects (AIA) and the American Society of Interior Designers (ASID) can be contacted to obtain a list of professional space planners who do work in the local area. In particular, they may be able to identify individuals who are qualified to handle the type and scope of tenant improvements that are expected to be needed in the building under management. Specific recommendations can be sought from other office building managers, real estate agents and consultants, financial institutions, and others who may know or work with space planners. Because each build-out is unique, space planning is contracted individually for each leased space.

A good first step is to request information about the space planning firm and its qualifications. This request should be sent to a large number of firms in order to determine the range and caliber of service providers in the area.

Authorization for Space Planning Services

When the building owner pays for the space plans, there is likely to be a formal authorization process to be followed, especially if leasing is contracted separately from management. Documented authorization may come directly from the property owner, or it may be issued by the building manager or the leasing supervisor. A *request for authorization* identifies a firm prospect for those in authority, helps leasing supervisors evaluate the progress of individual leasing agents, and allows the owner to monitor the space planner's work flow and costs.

A basic authorization request form will identify the building and its owner, the prospective tenant, and the specific space (floor level or suite) for which plans are to be drawn. The rentable square footage will be estimated initially (the actual rentable square footage will be calculated before the lease is signed and construction is begun). The form should identify the service provider and the likely array of planning services to be requested (e.g., a space study, architectural and/or engineering working drawings, interior design work), as well as construction supervision and consultations that may apply. There should also be space to list other unspecified services that may be requested. Fees are usually listed on a cost per square foot basis for space studies and working drawings, with an hourly rate (or lump sum) to cover all other services. (Fees should be quoted by the service provider when the authorization process is initiated.) The form should conclude with spaces for signatures, including those of the leasing agent or other requester, the owner or other person who will grant the authorization, and the representative of the service provider. Spaces should be provided to indicate the date of authorization and a date completed plans are due.

To facilitate the planning process, the authorization form may have attached to it a layout or plan of the floor on which the space is to be built out. This should show the locations of all pillars, windows, wall-mounted heat and air-conditioning installations, elevators, and service areas on the floor (including occupied tenants' spaces) and identify the suite or area for which the space plan is to be drawn. The prospect's requirements, if known, should also be included as an attachment. The attachments will facilitate the decision to authorize the particular space planning. Once the approvals are in place, the authorization request form with its attachments may be forwarded to the space planner as an authorization to begin work. Otherwise, a detailed purchase order may be issued for the work or a specific contract may be drawn up and signed.

Building owners generally dislike paying for space plans before a prospect has made a strong commitment to the space and has been thoroughly qualified for a lease. Tenant qualification should also take into account the prospect's requirements and space needs as well as its ability to meet the lease obligations (i.e., pay rent). There should be a good potential match between the prospect's needs and the space to be leased since it may not be possible to configure the space to accommodate all of the prospect's personnel and equipment in the manner requested. Such difficulties should be identified before the leasing process has progressed to development of space plans.

Most firms that provide this service will have a comprehensive brochure or presentation package that should include the following types of information.

- A brief history of the firm, including identification and photographs of recent successful planning assignments.
- A statement of design philosophy.
- Facts that demonstrate the firm's capacity to provide the services being sought within the established time frame.
- Biographical data on the firm's principals and key staff members and how long they have been with the organization.
- A list of key clients, including those for whom work is being done currently.
- A statement of the firm's financial condition.
- A general schedule of fees and pricing policy.

In evaluating such brochures, one should also take into account the way information is presented and the quality of the graphics and printing. These can be suggestive of the firm's approach to space planning assignments and the quality of the work it produces.

A large request-for-qualifications mailing is likely to yield responses from a dozen or more firms that are qualified to do the work. The next step is to narrow the field for the bidding process. Usually no less than three and no more than five firms will be asked to submit bids on the work.

A prospective tenant's requirements in regard to a particular space in the building will already have been identified (specifics of this process are discussed later in this chapter). Based on that information, a formal *request for proposal (RFP)* should be developed. This document should outline the work being requested, the time frame for the project, how fees should be presented (charges for materials and services, schedule of payments), and whatever other specific requirements must be met by the bidding firm (e.g., personnel qualifications, professional liability insurance coverage), including a deadline for submitting bids. Usually the space planner will prepare the working drawings and make the copies of the drawings that will be used by the construction contractor and subcontractors. This should be a component of the RFP and the bid. The RFP package should include the details of the tenant's requirements and the building standards that apply to the construction of tenant improvements. As bids are prepared, the bidders may have questions about the RFP or ask for clarifications. Any specifics that result from such questions or requests should be communicated to all participants to ensure they are all bidding to the same specifications.

The decision as to which bidder will be selected for a job will be based on the proposals received from the various space planners. The proposals should be evaluated individually to determine whether and how well they responded to the RFP. They should also be compared to each other because each planner's approach may be slightly different. In particular, fees for services may be stated in different ways. It is important to determine which items are included in a base fee and which are listed as reimbursable expenses. Fees for some elements of the work may be stated as an hourly rate or a per diem separate from a base fee. The manager should request clarification on a bidder's statements regarding job components and fees if there is any difficulty making a valid comparison. In the end, the planner chosen for the job may not be the low bidder but rather the one whose approach to the work and schedule for completion best meet the needs of the job within the allowed budget.

Payment for Space Planning. Typically, the landlord hires or contracts with a space planner and pays for the initial space plan. If the prospective tenant subsequently requests modifications to the plan or wants more detailed plans that show improvements in excess of the standard allowance, the cost of such drawings is likely to be borne by the prospect. After there is agreement on tenant improvements and the lease has been signed, working drawings will be prepared. Who will pay for working drawings is negotiable. In an owner's market (i.e., there are more tenants seeking space than there is space available for lease), the tenant will likely pay for working drawings. Space planning may be at the tenant's expense regardless, this is especially so if the prospect hires its own space planner. Sometimes the owner will pay for space planning and deduct the cost from the total tenant improvement allowance. Acceptability of this practice will depend on the market and local practice.

Prices for space planning services vary by locale. One should expect price differences between east and west coasts and the middle of the United States. Pricing may also vary with the size of the job, with plans for smaller areas commanding higher fees. Often the price will be stated on a cents-per-square-foot basis and include one or two minor revisions at no additional charge. Sometimes an architectural firm will bid very competitively on space planning, viewing it as an opportunity to work with a property owner or developer who may retain the firm for additional work later.

Space Planning for Individual Tenants. Space planning often begins early in prospecting, when a prospective tenant signals interest in details of the lease arrangement, including, and especially, the tenant improvements aspect. Skillful, efficient space planning means office space can be leased, finished, and occupied quickly. It is also a major marketing plus for the building. A good space plan offers assurance to a strong prospect company that its operational and aesthetic needs will be translated into a comfortable,

The Impact of Company Culture

Increasingly, businesses are looking for ways to foster teamwork among their employees. They want their work places to express their company culture—the organization's identity, its values and attitudes. Personnel involved in space planning need to consider what a prospective tenant's current office says about the company and find ways for the new space to better communicate the intended message. Following are some questions that may be helpful in this regard.

- Are there places for employees to gather informally?
- Does work flow in paths that lead to and intersect with the informal gathering places?
- Does the work place support and encourage collaboration and team work?
- Are individual workstations easily reconfigured to change departmental layouts?
- Can workstation panels be set at different heights to enhance visibility and communication?
- Does the ceiling height allow for expansion of mechanical systems overhead?
- Can different surface materials and lighting effects be used to enhance the work environment?
- What will best express the company's culture for its employees, its suppliers, and its customer-clients?

functional work environment for its employees *before* the lease is signed and the plan is finalized—i.e., before working drawings, construction specifications, and interior designs are prepared. Finalization of the plans depends on negotiation of who will pay for costs that exceed the standard tenant improvement allowance. Who pays for tenant improvements depends on market conditions, the building owner's and the prospective tenant's requirements, and what is being offered at competing buildings.

Developing a space plan for a particular prospect involves several steps, including an evaluation of the prospective tenant's space needs and a review of the limitations set by the landlord in regard to construction and installations. Based on those data, the space planner will develop a preliminary plan for the prospect's approval, and the manager will estimate the cost of constructing the tenant's new office space.

Evaluating Prospective Tenants' Needs. In terms of the prospect's needs, the information to be gathered includes subjective impressions as well as facts. Both are important. When the leasing agent or the building manager visits the prospect's existing offices to start the planning process, the following actions should be taken.

- Examine the layout and work flow of the prospect's current space.
- Count the number of employees.
- Define each person's work space requirements based on his or her job.
- Make a list of file cabinets, computer peripherals (shared scanners, printers, etc.), office equipment, and furniture, including which job or jobs they relate to and where they are located.
- Measure the floor space occupied by nonstandard furniture and equipment (know the dimensions of standard items so that space for them can be allotted accurately).
- Define the work relationships within each department, among departments, and with the company's public (clients and suppliers).
- Find out what types of specialized facilities and service areas are needed (mailrooms, storage, conference rooms, computer rooms, photocopying areas, non-work-specific gathering places such as a kitchen or break room). To use space efficiently, some companies may create banks of file cabinets or storage shelves, two or more layers deep, with items in front being able to slide back and forth to provide access to items at the back.
- Develop a clear picture of the company's plans for growth of the business (and, therefore, staff size) and future need for additional space.

It is also important to determine what image the company wants to project and evaluate how the desired image would affect design and construction of the prospect's new space.

All of this information is necessary to determine the total square footage required by the prospect. Other factors may have to be considered to accommodate a prospect's unique requirements. Once the work areas and equipment have been identified and inventoried, the square footage needed for each area can be estimated. (An example of a form for collecting these types of prospect information is shown in Exhibit 9.2, pages 230–231.) The prospect may indicate square footage preferences for some or all allocations for private offices, shared equipment areas, and individual workstations. A large firm with offices in many locations may have a standard layout or specific square footage allocations for different positions within the organization. (Governmental agencies must work within specific space allocation standards established by the General Services Administration. They may do their own space planning, and the building owner may not be shown the plans until after the lease has been signed.)

If workstations are modular cubicles constructed of movable panels, panel thickness (usually at least two inches) must be accounted in the measurements. The thickness of constructed interior walls must also be considered. An allowance for aisles between cubicles and offices as well as clearance for open file drawers is added to the estimated total requirements. Such a *circulation factor* is usually ten to fifteen percent. An example of a space requirement calculation is shown in Exhibit 9.3 (page 232).

Meeting the Landlord's Requirements. The building owner will want to control the space planning process in order to protect its investment. Details of what the owner considers acceptable (and unacceptable) in space plans are incorporated into the original leasing plan. Basic requirements are straightforward and usually include the following:

- Materials, equipment, and installations to complete the tenant's space plan must not damage the building.
- Finished improvements must conform to other building features and not lessen the building's value.
- The tenant must be able to pay for its share of the construction costs and not create any lien's against the building.
- Work on the tenant's space must not disturb other tenants unduly.

To make sure these requirements are met, many owners employ space planners themselves or have outside experts on retainer as noted earlier in this chapter.

Space planners often use computer-aided design (CAD) software, which can analyze the prospect data, draft multiple space plan alternatives, and estimate the costs of each plan. This is both a time- and cost-saving strategy because the software can also quantify linear wall space, electrical and telephone outlets, light fixtures, and other building standard items based on the plans—information that is useful in determining prices for discussion during lease negotiations. While prospects may be allowed to use their own space planners and interior designers, the owner will expect the specialists who perform these services for the building to monitor all stages of improvement construction and move-in. (Selecting the space planner is discussed earlier in this chapter.)

Developing Preliminary Plans. The space planner will need specific information about the prospect and its space requirements, the kinds of information mentioned previously (see Exhibits 9.2 and 9.3). Sometimes a visit to the prospect's current offices will be necessary so the planner can observe the existing layout and work flow and consult with the prospect about details. Such visits are more likely for large space users than small ones and

Exhibit 9.2

Sample Tenant Space Requirements Questionnaire

Tenant Space Requirements Questionnaire

Building ______________________ Floor/Suite/Exposure ______________
Tenant Name ______________________ Length of Lease Term ______________
Contact/Title ______________________ Phone ______________
Present Address ______________________
Reason for Move ______________________
Present/Future Employees ___/___ in Offices ___/___ in Cubicles ___/___ in Open Area

General Space Needs		**Estimated Sq Ft**
Mail Room	No. and Type of Machines ______	
	Freight Access Needed ☐ Yes ☐ No	
	Floor Site Important ☐ Yes ☐ No	
	Traffic ☐ Heavy ☐ Medium ☐ Light	
	Comments ______	______
Copy Center(s)	☐ Room ☐ Alcove No. and Type of Machines ______	
	Location ______	______
Computer Room	☐ Yes ☐ No Special Needs ______	______
Lunchroom/Lounge	☐ Yes ☐ No Special Needs ______	______
Library	☐ Yes ☐ No Special Needs ______	______
Conference Room	☐ Yes ☐ No How Many ______ No. of People ______	______
	Table Size/Shape ______ Special Needs ______	______
Central Files	☐ Separate ☐ Not Separate Special Needs ______	______
Vault	☐ Yes ☐ No Special Needs ______	______
Closets	How Many ______ Size each ______ Special Needs ______	
Additional Storage	☐ Yes ☐ No Special Needs ______	______
	In Basement ☐ Yes ☐ No Comments ______	
Reception Area	Switchboard ☐ Yes ☐ No Furniture ______	______
	No. Visitors/Day ______ Special Needs ______	
Parking	No. of Spaces ______	
	Subtotal of Estimated Square Feet	______

Equipment

Communications	No. of Telephones ___ No. of Incoming Lines ___ Intercom ☐ Yes ☐ No
Office Machines	Personal Computers ______ Electric Typewriters ______ Photocopiers ______
	Computer Printers ______ Other Peripherals (No./Type) ______
Special Needs for Equipment	Water ______ >125 Watts Electricity ______
	Special Soundproofing ______ Special HVAC ______ Auxiliary Power ______

for those whose build-out requirements are complex. The planner should focus on the following:

- Operations and aesthetics—This includes details of the evaluation of equipment, personnel, and space requirements discussed earlier and attention to the prospect's business image and reputation.
- Current efficiencies and inefficiencies—Familiarity with the prospect's current office layout will help the planner maintain or improve the company's efficiency and try to solve problems caused by layout or work-flow inefficiencies.

Exhibit 9.2 *(continued)*

Name/Title	Old Office Size	New Office Size	Contents	Special Requirements	Estimated Sq Ft

Number of Offices Private _____ Semi-Private _____

Subtotal _________

Subtotal from Previous Page _________

+ 15% for Traffic Flow _________

Total Square Feet _________

- Circulation—The allowance for office traffic flow is typically ten to fifteen percent added to the space requirements; it is important to determine whether this standard allowance will be adequate for the particular tenant.
- Budget—It is important to know which tenant improvements the building owner will pay for and which will be the tenant's responsibility and to ascertain what funds the prospect has allocated for its new office space. Planners are expected to meet design requirements while staying within budget guidelines and avoiding unnecessarily costly materials and installations.

Exhibit 9.3
Sample Computation of Space Requirements

Work Area		Sq Ft
Reception—6 chairs, 2 tables, 96 × 24 90° counter/desk, computer terminal, telephone/switchboard		160
Administrative Assistants—4 each, 72 × 30 desk in 72 × 90 cubicle, w/24-in runners and 2-drawer file, 1 chair, telephone, computer terminal w/printer		180
Executive—private office, 72 × 30 desk, 24 × 60 credenza, 3 chairs, endtable, telephone, computer terminal w/printer		200
Executive—private offices, 2 each, 72 × 30 desk, 24 × 60 credenza, 5 chairs, 48-in round conference table, telephone, computer terminal w/printer		300
General Staff—25 each, 72 × 30 desk in 72 × 90 cubicle, w/24-in runners and 2-drawer file, 1 chair, telephone, computer terminal		1,125
Shared Equipment—3 each, 72 × 24 counter w/cabinets or drawers, 2 computer printers, 1 facsimile machine, 1 electric typewriter		36
Mail/Copy/Storage Room—10 file cabinets (sliding tiers), photocopying machine, mailing machine, 60 × 12 shelving for sorting mail, 60 × 36 counter work surface		120
Conference Room—96 × 48 oblong conference table, 10 chairs, 60 × 24 credenza, telephone		300
	Subtotal	2,421
	Plus 15% for Traffic Flow*	363
	Total	2,784
	Rounded Up to	2,800

*Local building or fire codes may dictate the widths of aisles between desks or workstations, which may alter the added allowance for traffic flow.

Using the foregoing types of information, the planner prepares a preliminary plan for the space under consideration. The planner will need a layout or plan of the floor showing where the prospect's space is located. This floor plan should include all vertical penetrations (elevators, stairwells, ventilation shafts, electrical and plumbing risers) and all pillars, windows, wall-mounted HVAC vents, rest rooms, and service areas on the floor (e.g., fan foom, electrical closet). Occupied tenants' spaces should be indicated to provide overall orientation.

The preliminary plan drawing should represent the tenant's new space and its relationship to adjacent common areas. Private offices and other work areas should be clearly delineated, with doors and windows indicated and room dimensions noted. The scale of the drawing should be indicated as well. Typically this is ⅛-inch = 1 foot, but for small areas, ¼-inch = 1 foot may be preferable. A legend should define any symbols that are used, especially if they are likely to be unfamiliar to the prospect. The best plans will represent the prospect's furnishings and equipment in place (potted plants and other decorative items may be omitted). This will help the prospect's personnel visualize the new work space. It will also give a clear idea of how people and work would circulate in the space.

Reviewing the Preliminary Plan. The planner will usually prepare several copies of the preliminary drawings so that all parties—the prospect, the building owner and manager, the leasing agent—will be looking at the same thing. The drawings will be reviewed before they are presented to the prospect to make sure they represent the prospect's requests and requirements and that the costs are within the estimated budget. This review may be the responsibility of the building manager or the leasing agent.

When the preliminary plan is presented to the prospect, it should be accompanied by a request for approval or information regarding changes to be returned by a certain date. A small space user may need a few days to return a decision or request changes. More time should be allowed for a large space user to respond. At this stage, the prospect may ask for minor changes to the plans, and these may be made at no charge. If the requested changes require a second plan or the tenant asks for a completely new plan, part or all of the added cost may have to be borne by the prospect. (Policies at the office building should address the number of plan revisions allowed at no charge. This may be guided by accepted practices in the area. Allowing two such revisions is fairly common.) Everyone involved should keep in mind that drawing a new plan or changing the initial one may necessitate revision of the estimated costs of tenant improvements. All plan revisions should be approved in writing by the appropriate parties and state who is responsible for the added costs, if applicable.

When the preliminary plan is complete, the demising perimeter of the tenant's space can be drawn, and the total area of the space can be remeasured. This is the tenant's usable area. The tenant's net rentable area (the square footage on which rent is paid) is determined by multiplying the usable area by the building load factor. The *load factor* (also called add-on factor) is the percentage of the total space in the building that is occupied by common areas and equipment, including lobbies, corridors, rest rooms, mechanical systems, elevators, stairwells, and the like. Load factors are often in the range of ten to fifteen percent. Newer buildings that include atrium lobbies or other space-consuming design features may have higher load factors. A one-story suburban building will likely have a load factor near zero because space allocated to common areas and equipment is limited. The lower the load factor, the more efficient the building. (Space measurement and rentable and usable areas are discussed in detail in Chapter 7.)

Acceptance of the preliminary plan by the prospect is the signal to develop working drawings and determine the cost to build out the space. The

Exhibit 9.4

Sample Construction Cost Estimation Form

Tenant Construction Cost Estimate

Building Name ______________________ Date ____________

Tenant Name ______________ Suite No. __________ Square Footage __________

The following estimates are based on plans and specifications identified as follows: __________

		Estimated Cost $	Actual Cost $
Demolition		______	______
Demising Partitions: ½ of ____ linear feet = ____ linear feet		______	______
Interior Partitions		______	______
Doors, Frames, Hardware:	Entrance—Single	______	______
	—Pair	______	______
	Interior—Single	______	______
	—Pair	______	______
Electrical Wiring		______	______
Light Fixtures (type: ______________)		______	______
Electric/Telephone Outlets:			
	Duplex, Wall	______	______
	Telephone, Wall	______	______
	Telephone/Electric, Floor	______	______
	Dedicated Circuits	______	______
	Other ______________	______	______
HVAC		______	______
Exit Lights		______	______
Fire Horns		______	______
Wall Covering:	Paint ______________	______	______
	Vinyl/Paper ______________	______	______
	Paneling ______________	______	______
	Special Soundproofing ______	______	______
Floor Covering:	Carpet and Pad ______________	______	______
	Resilient Flooring ______________	______	______
	Hardwood ______________	______	______
Painting		______	______
Plumbing		______	______
Sprinklers		______	______
Ceilings		______	______
Window Covering		______	______
Graphics/Signage		______	______
Carpet Cleaning		______	______
Carpet Repair		______	______
Cleanup		______	______
Architectual Design		______	______
Building Department Filing and Permit Expense		______	______
Miscellaneous:	______________	______	______
	______________	______	______
	Subtotal	______	______
	Contingency: ________ %	______	______
	Management Service Charge: ________ %	______	______
	Estimated Total	______	______

lease may not be finalized until the parties agree on the cost of tenant improvements and who is to pay for them. Details of the preparation of the space for occupancy and the respective responsibilities of landlord and tenant regarding tenant improvements will be spelled out in a workletter that is signed by both parties and attached to the lease. (The workletter is discussed earlier in this chapter.)

Estimating Construction Costs. Construction costs are estimated based on the final working drawings. These are detailed drawings and specifications showing the exact nature and extent of the work to be done. Usually drawn to a standard scale (i.e., ⅛-inch = 1 foot), the working drawings represent the agreed-upon specifications, including location, materials, and quantities. These drawings should show everything—demising walls, interior partitions, structural frame and floor construction, and layouts and controls for HVAC, electrical wiring, telephone, and plumbing. (Exhibit 9.4 shows an example of a form that can be used to estimate construction costs.) It may be desirable to consult with a mechanical engineering firm for preparation of electrical and HVAC drawings.

Construction drawings must conform to many laws and regulations—local, state, and federal. This means the architect or space planner must keep up-to-date on building codes and other governmental restrictions that may apply. The local building department must review the drawings for conformance to safety and life-support provisions of the building code and approve them before a building permit will be issued. The building department must also inspect and approve the completed construction before issuing a certificate of occupancy. Federally mandated requirements regarding energy conservation and accessibility may also have to be followed. It may be necessary or desirable to abate asbestos-containing material (ACM) such as resilient flooring or equipment insulation as part of demolition. This work, in particular, will add a whole new dimension to the construction process and the cost of the project.

The tenant must approve the working drawings (in writing) before construction can be started.

Tenant Improvement Construction

Tenant improvement construction will have a different meaning in different situations. The tendency is to think in terms of constructing an all-new office suite in a new building. However, similar major improvement construction is involved when an older building is *rehabilitated* or as part of a change of use. Some tenant improvements may be needed for a new tenant moving into a previously occupied space. These may be classified as *remodeling* or *renovation*. A tenant renewing a lease may negotiate for nominal or even

Types of Construction

Remodeling—The process of changing the appearance and functional utility of a building or a constructed space by painting, repairing, and/or replacing fixtures and equipment.

Renovation—The process of making changes to an existing building, adding or replacing items to upgrade the building and/or extend its useful life.

Rehabilitation—The process of restoring a (usually older, rundown) building to a sound and efficient condition.

extensive improvements to its existing space. In order to retain a tenant who needs to expand or one whose space needs have been reduced, tenant improvements will likely be an issue. Each of these situations poses some specific challenges.

A New Tenant in a New Building. Preleasing is a common requirement to obtain financing for new commercial buildings. Preleasing of buildings under construction means space planning is often completed before the building is ready for interior finishing. The challenge here is selling a prospective tenant a particular space in the absence of any floors or walls or windows to provide a real-world perspective. Managers and leasing agents use color renderings, models, and a variety of other visual aids to demonstrate the advantages of preleasing. Floor layouts are available early because they are part of the construction drawings, and these can be shown to prospects along with building specifications. If construction is in progress, it may be possible for the tenant to tour a representative floor.

While new construction may seem to offer a blank slate for planning office space, the owner will establish specifications or guidelines for what can and cannot be done with the leased space. The costs of tenant improvements and who will pay them will also be a consideration. As indicated earlier in this chapter, the owner may provide a dollar-per-square-foot allowance based on the area leased or a quantity allowance for various items, again based on square footage, or a combination of the two. Some items may be provided as a building expense and not included in the tenant improvement allowance. In a slow market, the owner may pay more for tenant improvements as a means of obtaining a tenant. (This will require more careful scrutiny of the prospect's financial status and business references to ensure payment of the lease obligations.) In a strong market, prospects may have to pay for tenant improvements themselves.

A New Tenant in a Previously Occupied Space. While it is possible that a prospect moving into a previously occupied space will find that it fits the firm's needs exactly, such situations are rare. Even if the space configuration will work, cleaning and a coat of paint are likely necessities, and the company's name will have to be displayed.

The prospect may ask for some specific changes. For example, creation of a special-purpose area is likely to necessitate changes in the interior partition arrangement; and space planning will be required to accomplish this. Other work will also be involved (i.e., moving electrical and telephone wiring, new ceiling and floor finishes). Before the new ones can be built, existing partitions will have to be demolished. The owner will have to consent to the changes, and the parties will have to agree on who will pay for the work. In a slow market, owners may be willing to pay for some tenant improvements in existing buildings; in a strong market, however, those same owners usually allocate fewer dollars for tenant improvements.

The Renewing Tenant. Lease renewal is an opportunity for landlord and tenant to reaffirm their commitment to what has already been a long-term relationship. A renewing tenant may not wish to change its office layout, so no space planning will be required. However, the tenant may ask for some improvements to freshen the space for continued use. Repainting, applying vinyl wall covering to some interior walls, and new carpeting are examples of such refurbishment. Of course, if the tenant wants to alter the existing space by adding or removing some exterior offices or constructing new enclosed space for a special use, a space plan will be needed, and relocation of electrical and telephone connections and other such adjuncts will have to be considered in scheduling and performing the construction. While it may be possible to construct such improvements with the tenant in place, more than likely it will be necessary to relocate the tenant temporarily to expedite completion of the work. This is practical only if there is vacant space in the building that can reasonably accommodate the tenant for the construction period.

If the owner-tenant relationship is good, the owner may agree to pay the costs of improvements. This is especially true in a soft market because the owner will want to retain the tenant. Relocation costs may be strictly a tenant expense although, in a soft market, the owner may share these costs or absorb them. In a strong market, however, the owner may not pay for improvements. Tenant size and reputation will also be important considerations. The owner will be more likely to pay improvement costs for a large space user than for a small one.

Tenant Expansion. A tenant's need for larger quarters may coincide with the expiration of its lease. However, it is more likely that a tenant will need to expand before the current lease term expires. Good space planning initially would have given consideration to future space needs, making expansion easier and precluding the tenant relocating to another building.

Expansion of an existing space is usually predicated on availability of sufficient space adjacent to it. A tenant occupying a full floor is likely to want its expansion area on an adjacent floor and may have a preference for whether that is the floor above or below. Space planning will be required, and it may be necessary or desirable to demolish the demising wall between the adjacent spaces or to provide access across it by creating one or more openings, with or without doors. Ideally, the new space plan will be designed not only for more efficient work flow, but also to be consistent with and complimentary to the tenant's original space.

Market conditions and the size of the expansion area are likely to be considerations in determining who pays for the expansion planning. In a soft market or for a large expansion area, the owner may willingly pay for space planning. However, in a strong market or for a small expansion area, space planning will most likely be a tenant expense. The same considerations may apply to construction costs.

When expansion takes place before the lease term ends, either or both of the parties may require the lease to be extended. In the tenant's case, an extension may be necessary to guarantee it will get full benefit from its expanded space, especially if it is to pay most or all of the construction cost and the remaining lease term is short. If the owner pays any of the expansion costs, an extension will certainly be in order.

If there is no adjacent space, the owner may be able to relocate an adjoining tenant to another suite in the building if that tenant's lease included an appropriate provision to allow this. Depending on the desirability of the expanding tenant and the strength of the market, the owner or the expanding tenant may pay the relocation cost, which can include space planning, tenant improvement construction, and moving. If the rent for the space to be occupied by the relocating tenant is higher than its current lease rate, the difference may have to be absorbed as well. There may be other considerations for the relocating tenant that are less easily accommodated. The tenant may have leased the space originally because it offered a compelling view or its entrance was the first one seen by visitors as they step off the elevator. An employee lounge or other amenity that was unique to its original floor may be lost as a result. These kinds of changes have the potential to generate hard feelings. However, good planning for the relocation space can help dispel such feelings, especially if the tenant needs additional space, and this need can be accommodated in the relocation. The cost of improvements to the extra space would have to be paid by the relocating tenant. However, this might be a small price to pay to stay in the building and not have to plan and build expansion space after the relocation. There is also an upside for ownership and management—the relocation will have placed additional space under lease and thereby increased the property's revenue stream.

Tenant Contraction. Reorganization, a need to relocate part of the organization (a division or subsidiary) to a completely different geographic area, or financial cutbacks are some reasons a tenant may require less space than originally contracted under the lease. For a tenant who has been reliable, the owner may agree to reduce the space or relocate the tenant within the building. In fact, the owner may view this as an opportunity to accommodate expansion of an adjacent tenant. The excess space might also be welcome as a temporary location for a tenant whose space is being remodeled or to accommodate other building renovations.

If the tenant is having financial difficulties, the owner may permit reduction of its space to lower the monthly rent rather than risk default by the tenant. This is more likely to occur in a soft market. If the tenant can afford it, the owner may accept a lump-sum rent payment for the excess space for the remainder of the lease term. Alternatively, the owner may agree to rewrite the lease to cover the lesser amount of space for a longer term in exchange for freeing the tenant of its obligation on the space it no longer needs. In a strong market, an owner may prefer to terminate the lease (rather than reduce the space), especially if the entire space can be leased to another tenant at a higher rent. In truth, the owner can disallow the reduction altogether, which will force the tenant to retain liability for all of the space for the full term of the lease. The only option that may provide relief for a tenant is the possibility of subletting the space or assigning the lease if these are allowed under provisions of the lease.

For a tenant attempting to compress operations into a smaller area, space planning will be critical. It is likely that tenant improvements needed to reduce the space will be costly, and that may be a potential hardship for a financially strapped tenant. Since all of the construction costs are going to be the tenant's responsibility, the space planner and those involved in the construction must make every effort to control costs. Space planning for a sublessee or assignee will require the permission and approval of the original tenant as well as the owner, since the tenant will be paying for both planning and construction. For obvious reasons, the tenant will not want the improvement costs to exceed the amount of rent for the remainder of the lease term; and because the lease term is likely to be short, it is important not to tie up the space for construction any longer than absolutely necessary.

Construction Management

There are three ways to handle construction of tenant improvements—hire a general contractor, hire a construction manager, or subcontract the work directly (i.e., serve as the general contractor). The manager's choice will depend on the circumstances of individual projects. Local practices may also be a factor.

If the manager decides to hire a *general contractor,* selection should be based on bids from several contractors, each of whom has been given a copy of the working drawings for the project. Several contractors whose reputations and quality of prior work are well known should be asked to submit bids. As with other contracting, the bid request should include the scope of the work, materials and methods of installation, and fees and payments. Most general contractors have working relationships (or even contractual arrangements) with subcontractors who can install drywall, electrical wiring, HVAC ductwork, and plumbing. Carpenters and painters would be part of this group as well. In a brand-new office building, a single contractor may be used for all tenant improvement construction rather than obtaining bids on a job-by-job basis. In such situations, general contractors are usually asked to submit bids that include unit prices (i.e., for materials), which can be reasonably guaranteed for a certain amount of time. The manager who has not worked with general contractors before or who wants to add new contractors to a pool of bidders can follow a process similar to the one used in space planning—i.e., send out a request for qualifications to obtain information about local builders and contractors. As with all contracting, references—including previous clients—should be checked. An important selection criterion should be the contractor's past performance in completing projects on time.

There are firms that specialize in *construction management.* Some space-planning companies also offer construction management services. The construction manager who supervised construction of the building might be hired to oversee tenant improvements. With this approach, the manager controls the selection of subcontractors and thereby controls construction costs.

General contracting and construction management fees may be established in different ways. One approach is to base the fee on the cost of the job, adding a percentage of the cost for overhead and supervision plus a separate percentage for profit. Another approach is to set a fixed price for the work, to be paid in installments as specific work is completed. This method gives exact specifications of the time needed, procedures to be followed, and expenses—before the work is started. Any deviations from working drawings or materials specifications are handled as specific *change orders* that will account for cost overruns. (Change orders are approved in writing by both the manager and the tenant. They should also be dated so that everyone will know which change is the latest.) Yet another approach is a cost-plus arrangement under which the contractor is paid actual costs plus a fixed fee, and these may be billed and paid monthly.

In an older building, the manager may *subcontract* construction work directly. The contractual arrangements may be for labor only, and the manager may purchase the building standard materials and supplies to be used in constructing tenant improvements. In actual fact, the manager may serve as general contractor for all tenant improvement construction. Most office building managers are familiar with the work involved in establishing specifications, obtaining bids, and overseeing installation of finishes and equipment, and they deal personally with many of the vendors who supply building standard items (e.g., window coverings, carpeting). Their skills in this area often qualify them to supervise construction of tenant improvements. This role should be kept separate from that of property management, and the manager should be compensated separately for this service. Usually such arrangements are anticipated and incorporated in the management agreement when it is negotiated.

Whether the manager assumes the role of general contractor or hires others to oversee the construction, the goal should be to control the cost of the project while maintaining the quality of materials and workmanship and completing the work on time.

A key tool in tenant improvement construction is a carefully thought out schedule. While a detailed schedule may not guarantee specific results, it will certainly provide a means of measuring performance of the work while also facilitating coordination of the many subcontractors involved. All those involved in the construction project—general contractor, subcontractors, on-site job superintendent—must work with the office building manager to develop the work schedule. The first step is to identify the work to be performed and the order in which component tasks must be completed. The time to complete each task must also be estimated. Once the time required for each task is determined, the work can be scheduled.

A construction schedule may be developed on a paper form in a grid format. This will encompass all aspects of the work from overhead rough-in to hanging of drapes and everything in between. Usually tasks are listed in the order in which they are to be performed so that electrical wiring and other installations are in place between the studs before drywall is to be installed, and so forth. Apart from subcontractor work, installations by utility companies (e.g., telephone wiring) must also be scheduled. More likely today, a computer spreadsheet program will be used. In this way, tasks can be itemized and scheduled very precisely, materials can be ordered and received in advance of when they will be installed, and progress of the entire project can be mapped. The advantages of a detailed construction schedule include:

- The manager knows which subcontractors will be in the building at different times.
- It identifies which items must be completed before others can be started.
- On-site personnel who may have a role in the construction (maintenance workers who will clean up the work site and remove con-

struction debris; security personnel who need to allow access for deliveries of materials) can know the specifics of their duties in advance.

- Other tenants can be notified in advance that construction will be taking place in a particular area of the building between specific dates.
- Tenants can be alerted to days and times when elevator service may be modified to accommodate construction workers and movement of materials.
- The new tenant has a time frame in which to plan and make arrangements for move-in.

The schedule should include time before construction begins to obtain permits and order materials. Time should be included after completion to allow for building department inspections necessary for issuance of certificates of occupancy. Requirements for building permits and occupancy certificates are determined by local governments. If a previous tenant's interior has to be demolished before construction can be started, time should be allocated for that as well. (Demolition, core drilling, and other noisy work should be scheduled before or after normal business hours to minimize disruption of other tenants' activities.) Arrangements should be made for delivery of construction materials via freight elevators or a passenger elevator that has appropriate protective padding installed. Elevator access will have to be coordinated so as not to disrupt tenants and other material movement within the building. Mats and other protective materials may need to be in place to protect the building against wear and tear during the construction period, and placement or installation of these items requires time that should also be accounted in the schedule. If the tenant is planning to re-use workstation partitions and furniture systems, the construction schedule must include time to move these from the old location and assemble them in the new office. Cleaning or refurbishment of the components may also be needed.

When construction is completed, the manager—preferably accompanied by the tenant—will conduct a final inspection using a *punch list.* This form lists the various types of work to be done in the different areas of the office at the left, with columns to indicate whether the work has been completed and whether it is included in the contract. There should also be a column to indicate an estimated cost for items still to be done that are not included in the contract. A column for comments allows the manager to indicate details that need attention, such as cleanup of specific areas and missing light bulbs, as well as work items that have not been completed. Here again, it may be preferable to create a basic punch list form using appropriate computer software. Not only can it be printed as needed, but it can be tailored to the individual job by adding and deleting work items. In particular, a tenant occupying a whole floor will have additional types of work done beyond what would normally be done for a small space user on a multitenant floor. The tenant will be asked to approve the items on the punch list by initialing it.

The punch list becomes the work order for the completion of the outstanding work. When all the items have been addressed, the manager will make another inspection using the old punch list as a checklist to verify that all the unfinished items have been completed.

Whether work is done by a general contractor who subcontracts with various tradespeople, or the office building manager contracts with the tradespeople directly, all construction-related contractors (including vendors delivering materials and supplies) should be required to provide proof of adequate insurance, including liability and workers' compensation coverage. For the work that is being done, they should have their insurance carriers include the property owner and the building manager or management firm as additional named insured parties on their policies. Verification of coverage is usually in the form of a certificate of insurance that names the insured parties and identifies the types and amounts of coverages being carried.

In addition, provision must be made for accumulation and removal of construction wastes. Any removal of pre-existing hazardous materials (e.g., asbestos-containing floor tiles or insulation) will have to be addressed specifically from the planning stage forward. Special provisions will have to be made for enclosure (encapsulation) of the construction space and for collection and disposal of the hazardous material. Workers must wear special protective clothing and devices as well. Best practice is to have planning and implementation handled by a properly qualified asbestos removal contractor.

The Construction Contract

As with space planning, the choice of a contractor should be based on several factors and not strictly on the lowest bid. A contractor's reputation for quality work and on-time completion of projects within the available budget should be the dominant considerations. Access to or contracts with subcontractors and ability to obtain required construction materials should also be weighed.

Once a general contractor is selected, the work to be done should be spelled out in a written contract that will be signed by the contractor and by the owner or the manager (as the owner's agent). The contract is usually a standard form presented by the contractor, or the contractor's bid may be submitted in the form of a contract.

The document should be reviewed by the property owner and the manager before anything is signed. In particular, they will want to verify that the contract is specific about the covered work. It may refer to space plans, building standards, and detailed specifications rather than spell out these particulars. Such documents would then be incorporated into the contract as addenda. The contract should state a time frame for completion of the work (this may include a detailed schedule as well as commencement and completion dates), spell out the costs for the project (both direct costs for material and labor and indirect costs such as insurance premiums, employer taxes, and the like), and specify how deviations from the original plans are to be handled (e.g., change orders). It should also address insurance requirements, and an appropriate certificate of insurance should be incorporated into the contract as an addendum. (Insurance requirements for contractors are discussed earlier in this chapter in the context of construction management.)

A variety of other issues should be addressed. In particular, the agreement should include provisions that afford specific protections to the owner and the owner's agent. If the following points are not addressed in the contractor's standard form, appropriate provisions should be added to it.

- *Indemnification*—Minimally, the contractor should indemnify *(hold harmless)* the owner and the owner's agents against liability, loss, and attendant expense arising out of any action or inaction of the contractor. Liability is related to physical injury to people (building staff, tenants' employees, visitors) and damage to property (including the building structure and equipment and belongings of people in and about the building). Any financial losses incurred would relate to the cost of repairing or replacing damaged property or restoring the health and well-being of people injured as a result of being on or near the construction site. Expense would relate to legal fees and other costs (e.g., awarded damages) having to be paid as a consequence of an incident. As an added protection, indemnification should survive termination of the construction contract.
- *Bonding*—Contractors often obtain different types of bonds as a protection for themselves as well as the property owner. A *payment bond* is an assurance that the contractor will pay for all materials, labor, supplies, equipment, and subcontractors used on the project. This type of bond protects the owner against liens and claims after a project is completed and the contractor has been paid for the work. A *performance bond* is an assurance that the contractor will perform the work and complete the project as stated in the construction contract. The two may be combined. Performance and payment bonds are designed to protect the property owner from construction risks related to nonpayment of suppliers or others by the general contractor or failure to complete the project as contracted. In some situations it may be necessary or desirable to have the contractor obtain a *bid bond*. This is an assurance that the contractor will furnish payment and performance bonds and enter into a contract with the owner or the

owner's agent in the event the contractor's bid is accepted. Such bonds are three-way contracts between a surety or bonding company (usually an insurance company), a principal (in this case, the contractor), and a beneficiary (the property owner).

- *Payment*—The contract should include an itemized list of parts and unit prices for materials or equipment the contractor will provide. If the building will supply specific finish materials for the work (e.g., some or all building standard items), a list of these items should be appended to the contract. (They should not be included in the contractor's price.) The contract should also state the total cost of the project and list a schedule of payments. Regardless of how payments are structured, there should always be provision for a *final payment* after satisfactory completion of the work. (This may be an agreed amount—called *retainage* and usually around ten percent of the total fee—that is held back to ensure completion of all punch list items.) If change orders will be used, the contract should stipulate how and when the attendant differences in costs will be paid to the contractor. (The structuring of general contracting fees is discussed in the context of construction management earlier in this chapter.)

- *Lien Releases*—Construction work involves many subcontractors and suppliers in addition to the general contractor. If suppliers of materials and/or labor are not paid by the contractor in a timely fashion, they have a legal right to place a *mechanic's lien* against the property as a claim for priority of payment of the amount owed to them. A *lien* is an encumbrance that must be satisfied before the property can be refinanced or sold by the owner. Such liens attach to the land as well as the building and other improvements on the land, which become collateral for payment of the debt, and the creditor may sell the property to satisfy the debt. (A mortgage is a lien against the property in the event of default on a loan.)

  The agreement should require the contractor to execute a lien release for each payment received from the owner, including partial and final payments. A *conditional release,* which becomes effective upon payment of a stated amount, may be issued for partial payments. A *full release,* which states that the contractor has been paid in full for the work, should be executed after final payment. If the agreement is silent in regard to lien releases from others, the contractor should be encouraged to obtain appropriate lien releases from all subcontractors, tradespeople, and materials suppliers as a protection for itself and the property owner.

  A lien release form should identify the parties involved and include a description of the project and the address of the building where the work was performed. The form should state whether it is a conditional release or a full release and the amount of any payment involved. Space should be provided for the contractor's signature and the date of the transaction. Space is also usually provided for the executed form to be notarized.

- *Completion*—The contract should clearly define completion of the work, including reference to inspections by the building manager and performance of work identified on the punch list as incomplete. The agreement may also refer to inspection by the local building department and its issuance of a certificate of occupancy. If construction work is not in compliance with applicable building codes and fire safety codes, city officials will not issue a certificate of occupancy until the appropriate changes have been made and approved. This is an important issue and should be covered specifically in the construction contract.
- *Acceptance*—Usually contracts will include a provision stating that signing of the contract by the owner or the owner's agent constitutes acceptance of the terms and provisions of the agreement.

It is common practice in construction work for contracts to include an incentive for the contractor to complete the work on time. This is often a specific clause that rewards the contractor for completion ahead of schedule and calls for a daily penalty for each day construction continues past the scheduled completion date. This is a highly desirable provision and should be added if the base document does not address penalties.

The entire contract should be reviewed by ownership's and management's legal counsel before being signed to ensure that it complies with applicable laws and provides the specific protections sought by the parties. If the tenant is paying part or all of the construction costs beyond what the owner pays for, there should be a separate contract between the tenant and the contractor or construction company for the tenant's share of the work.

10

Lease Administration and Tenant Retention

The manager's first contact with the tenant—whether as a prelude to direct lease negotiations, at some point during negotiations that are being conducted by a leasing agent, or later still—will shape the tenant's perception of the office building and the management team. Savvy office building managers realize that tenant retention begins with that initial contact, and they try to make a strong, positive first impression.

Throughout the term of a tenant's occupancy, there will be countless other contacts between members of the management team and the tenant's employees as well as its designated representatives. Most of these contacts can be expected to relate to the tenant's leased space and, therefore, to specific provisions of the lease signed by the tenant. Because the contents of all the leases for space in the building will determine how specific situations are handled, it is imperative to develop an appropriate lease administration program, keeping in mind the needs of individual tenants. Much of the office building manager's job will revolve around understanding tenants' needs and striving to meet those needs while also staying within the owner's operational guidelines and complying with the provisions of individual leases.

This chapter covers various aspects of tenant relations, from move-in to move-out.

Moving the Tenant In

It is important to establish an effective line of communication between building management and the tenant at the earliest possible moment. If there has been no previous contact, the building manager should begin laying the groundwork as soon as the lease is signed. If the tenant company has a large staff, it is likely that the person who negotiated the lease on the tenant's behalf will not be the main contact after move-in. The manager should find out who will represent the tenant during and after move-in so that an ongoing relationship can be developed with the appropriate person or persons.

Tenant Move-In Information. As construction of the improvements to the tenant's space nears completion, the tenant will need to know details of the building's move-in procedures. The tenant will also be asked to provide certain information in advance to help effect a smooth move-in. While this exchange of information can be initiated in a telephone or face-to-face conversation, details should be spelled out in writing. This early communication has three specific goals:

1. *To obtain routine tenant information.* It is desirable to have the tenant's name and suite number incorporated into the building directory on the day of move-in. Directory information is needed in advance to accomplish this. The tenant's name should also be displayed on the door of the leased space at move-in. The building should have a set of guidelines for such signage, including who is responsible for paying for the work and how requests for nonstandard signage are to be handled. If nameplates can accommodate company logos, appropriate logo artwork must be obtained from the tenant in advance. Numbers of keys to the suite and specifics regarding parking (if applicable) should also be addressed.
2. *To coordinate the tenant's move.* The exact move-in date must be known in advance so that use of freight elevators and loading areas can be scheduled. If the building does not have a separate freight elevator, a passenger elevator will have to be taken out of service and its interior protected for the move. If the office property is a complex of low-rise or garden office buildings, it is important to have a cleared area in the parking lot for the moving van or vans. This may require blocking off a number of the parking stalls closest to the building entrance. (Care should be taken not to limit handicapped parking and access.) It may be appropriate to notify other tenants in the building in advance that parking and building access will be limited by a move-in on a certain date, or it may be enough to post signs identifying the affected area. Arrangements for removal of moving-related trash (boxes and other discarded items) should also be made in advance. A firm move-in date is especially important for a new building where many tenants are moving into the building in a short period of time and careful coordination of the multiple moves is required.

Building passes will have to be arranged for the move-in day for employees of the tenant as well as moving company personnel. The tenant may want some passes prior to move-in so that its staff members who have responsibility for the move can have access to the building during and after business hours. Special permits may be required for on-street parking of moving vans, and these will have to be obtained in advance.

When a new tenant has thousands of employees, it is important for those employees to become familiar with the building *before* the move. This might be handled by preparing a slide show, perhaps provided on a computer disk or CD-ROM, or a collection of photographs the tenant can use as an employee orientation. The pictures should show all of the entrances and approaches to the building (and the garage if appropriate), the building lobby (from multiple perspectives if possible), the location of elevators and identification of those that serve different levels of the building, plus whatever other building features and amenities would be appropriate. The orientation images become a marketing tool if pictures of ground-floor retailers and service tenants are included.

3. *To inform the tenant of building operating procedures and rules and regulations.* The tenant should be given certain information about the building in advance so the firm's employees know what to expect regarding mail delivery and building security procedures and how to arrange for off-hours HVAC or special janitorial services.

An example of a tenant move-in information letter is shown in Exhibit 10.1. Note that the sample letter does not address parking. If the building includes parking facilities and the tenant's lease provides for a certain number of parking spaces, these types of details should be noted with the other move-in information. Also, the letter is very straightforward about locks and keys. In many situations, tenants will have electronic access control devices for their entry doors. If a new electronic system has been installed for a tenant who is moving in, the tenant should have made arrangements in advance for its employees to have cards or numeric codes that will allow them to access their work spaces. (These electronic systems are in addition to standard locksets that are needed for janitorial and management team access to the leased premises.)

The sample letter takes a very basic approach to building security. Typically in high-rise office buildings, all people who work there are required to have and carry with them a building identification card or badge that includes their picture, their signature, and the name of their employer. When such a system is in place, arrangements will have to be made, in advance, for a new tenant's employees to have identification cards prepared and issued to them. (The same would apply if electronic cards or devices are needed to access the building outside of regular business hours.) In the

Exhibit 10.1
Sample Tenant Move-In Information Letter

[Date]

Dear *[Tenant/Contact Name]:*
Your new space is scheduled for completion on *[date],* and there are a number of details that need attention before you move in. Note that items #1 through #5 ask for specific information that should be sent to my attention as soon as possible.

1. Entry Door Graphics—Please indicate, line-for-line, how your company name should appear on the entry door. *[It is appropriate to indicate the building standard for company names or refer to the tenant's lease if an alternative graphic presentation has been agreed.]*
2. Directory Listing—Please provide a list for display in the building directory. This should include your company name and the names of key individuals and all departments/divisions to be listed there. *[If there are limits on the number of list entries or the number of characters per line in the directory, the specific parameters should be spelled out for the tenant here.]*
3. Keys and Locks—Please state the number of keys you desire for your entrance door and the number of keys desired for interior doors that lock. If there are any changes to the number of locking interior doors, please indicate them so that the changes can be implemented while your premises are being constructed.
4. Move-In Date—Please specify the date and time you want to move in so that freight elevators and loading areas can be reserved for you and conflicting schedules can be avoided. *[Many building managers prefer to handle move-ins on weekends or after 5:00 P.M. on weekdays. Any such scheduling limitations should be stated up front in this letter. Also, if the tenant is moving into a garden office building, the arrangements for parking of moving vans and expedited access to the building—including the specific location, possibly marked on a site plan—should be spelled out along with time limitations if appropriate.]*
5. Coordination with Movers—Please provide the name of the moving company you are planning to use and ask them to contact the building to arrange a pre-move visit to (a) become familiar with the loading areas and elevators and (b) walk your space so they will know where to place your furniture. *[Some building managers ask that movers take specific steps to prevent damage to carpeting, floors, and walls during move-in. Building policy should be stated here with a request that movers be asked to comply with it.]*
6. Insurance—Any company or persons doing work for your firm, including the movers, must be fully insured as outlined in your lease. Please collect appropriate certificates of insurance from movers or other contractors before they perform any work and send me a copy for the building files.

absence of such identification, it may be advisable to have the tenant provide a list of the names and position titles of all the firm's employees so they can be checked in by lobby security personnel in the first few days after move-in. Such a list is especially appropriate for a new tenant who occupies a full floor or multiple floors, regardless of any building identification system that is in place. It may also be appropriate to mention other aspects of

Exhibit 10.1 *(continued)*

7. Mail Delivery—Please notify the U.S. Postal Service and your customers and suppliers of your new mailing address before the actual date. *[It is a good idea to recommend inclusion of their suite number to facilitate delivery. If mail is delivered to a lockbox in the building, the tenant's lockbox number should be included in the address. Tenants should also be advised when they will be given a key to their lockbox.]*
8. Construction Problems—While construction of your office space will have been completed and the work inspected, there may be some items that still need attention. During move-in, please make a list of construction details that are incomplete or not satisfactory and forward it to the management office so that corrections can be coordinated with the contractors.
9. Building Security—*[Here should be stated the hours the building is open on weekdays and weekends, which entrances to the building are accessible outside of regular building business hours, the need to sign in and sign out at particular times, and other standard procedures that apply. If items carried out of the building require a "pass" signed by a company-authorized person, the tenant should be asked for a list of persons within its organization who have authority to sign such passes.]*
10. Heat and Air Conditioning—Heat and air conditioning are generally provided between the hours of *[state the beginning and ending times]* on weekdays and *[state the beginning and ending times]* on weekends. If you wish to have heat or air conditioning during extended evening or weekend hours, please notify the building management in advance. *[Usual practice is to charge for off-hours HVAC at a flat rate per hour. The applicable rate under building policy should be included in this section. Overtime charges should be waived if building policy requires that move-ins take place during off-hours or on weekends.]*
11. Building Rules and Regulations—A copy of the building rules and regulations is attached to this letter. The rules are designed to help tenants and management avoid preventable problems. Please review them carefully and contact me as soon as possible if you have any questions or cannot comply with one or more of the rules for any reason.

The management team looks forward to having your firm as a tenant in *[Name of Building]*, and we will do all we can to make your company proud of its new business location.

[Allow Space for Signature]

[Name and Title of Building Manager]

Note: Assignment of parking spaces and access to the parking lot or garage (if controlled) should also be addressed in the move-in letter if appropriate.

building security. If closed-circuit television (CCTV) cameras are positioned throughout the building, particulars related to public areas and the tenant's space should be noted. If security personnel patrol the building periodically during business hours, tenants should be advised that this is done. The schedule should remain confidential, however.

The last item in the letter refers to building rules and regulations. These typically outline the kinds of things that are prohibited or specifically encouraged to ensure that all tenants and their employees and visitors have pleasant experiences in the building. In addition to reiterating requirements related to building security and advance requests for HVAC services outside of normal building operations, the following are some issues that are likely to be addressed in rules and regulations.

- Elevator operations (identified periods of heavy traffic; reduced operations for regularly scheduled maintenance)
- Use of freight elevators (or of passenger elevators to move freight)
- Use of loading areas (shipping and deliveries)
- Keeping public corridors free of litter
- Keeping fire exit doors closed (and locked, if appropriate)
- Ensuring ready access to fire-fighting equipment (extinguishers, hoses)
- Fire drills and evacuation procedures
- Janitorial services (what is provided; how to request additional or special services)
- Separation of recyclables from trash and organic (food) garbage
- General housekeeping (preventing fires, accidents, and infestations by insects and other pests)
- Use of space heaters and fans
- Keys (or access codes) for washrooms on multitenant floors
- Items prohibited from being disposed in toilets and washbasins
- Tenants' responsibility for security within their demised premises

Rules and regulations may also address emergency procedures, including what to do in case of fire, power outages, bomb threats, or a natural disaster. However, it may be necessary or desirable to prepare a separate *emergency procedures manual* and provide a copy of that manual to new tenants at move-in. (This is especially appropriate in high-rise buildings.) Office building managers often work with local fire and police departments to develop appropriate procedures for their buildings and to provide proper training to their personnel and their tenants' employees. The move-in information letter should refer specifically to emergency and evacuation procedures that are in place for the building. To emphasize their importance, building rules and regulations may be spelled out in a specific lease clause or listed in an addendum to the lease.

Utilities may be an issue to address in this letter. Established local tenants may be able to retain their current telephone numbers, but new businesses and those relocating from outside the immediate area would need to arrange for new telephone numbers in advance. Tenants whose electricity consumption is extraordinary may wish to make separate arrangements for power supplies. A list of utility companies and related resources might be included in the letter along with recommendations regarding timing of arrangements to ensure that equipment is in place and operational for the tenant's move-in.

The tenant move-in information letter may also be used to request the names and telephone numbers of company personnel who should be contacted in the event of an emergency outside of business hours. It is important to have this information before move-in or as soon thereafter as possible.

Tenant Move-In Packet. Office building managers often prepare an information packet or "kit" to give to tenants when they move in. This might include some or all of the following items:

- Building hours—When the building is open (normal business hours) and when people entering and leaving the building are required to sign in and out.
- Building access controls—How electronic devices work, when they are in operation, and what types of identification cards or devices are needed to operate them.
- HVAC service—Hours when HVAC is provided on regular workdays and procedures for requesting service during off-hours.
- Parking—Assignment of parking space in the building garage (if applicable) and parking-specific rules and regulations. If the building has no parking facilities, a list of nearby garages and information about access and rates would be appropriate.
- Maintenance—How to request maintenance services, including charges for specific services, how they will be billed, and whom to contact.
- Janitorial services—How and when services are provided, including the contractor name if building staff do not do this work, and how to arrange for additional or special janitorial services.
- Floor plan—A small-scale floor plan of the tenant's space showing in particular the locations of light switches and thermostats. This is especially helpful for tenants in large spaces where lighting and HVAC may be divided into "zones."
- Keys—How to arrange for additional keys for entry and interior door locks in the tenant's space. (The tenant should have been asked in advance about keys for staff members as part of the move-in preparations.)

- Deliveries—Building procedures for handling deliveries (and pick-ups) of both hand-carried and larger items. The front desk may handle small parcels, in which case tenants need to know how parcels should be addressed to expedite these exchanges. Deliveries to the building via a loading area should also be addressed. Procedures for courier services (e.g., UPS, FedEx) and mail pickups should be explained. (Tenants should be advised in advance about changing their mailing address and how mail is delivered to the building.)
- Recycling—Details of how the building's established recycling program works, including specifics regarding separation of materials. It is also appropriate to include information about waste management in general. If the building's tenancy includes health care professionals, preferred ways of dealing with certain biohazards (e.g., bloodborne pathogens, heavy metals) should be addressed specifically.
- Rent payments—When rent is due, to whom checks should be made payable, where payments should be sent, and whether tenants are billed each month for rent and other charges. This might include instructions for making arrangements for payment via electronic transfer of funds. If building policy includes a grace period and/or late charges, specifics of the policy and its outworkings (including steps leading to eviction for nonpayment) should be spelled out.
- Common area pass-through charges—How operating expenses are passed through to tenants and when escalations take effect. If expenses are estimated and billed based on annual budget figures, tenants should be advised of when adjustments for actual costs are computed and how the differences (over and under) are handled.
- Insurance—A reminder of the requirement for tenants' insurance on their premises and possessions to include the names of the building owner and the manager or management company as additional named insured parties as required by the lease.
- Estoppel certificate—A form or format for providing an estoppel certificate and an explanation of what it is and why the landlord needs it.

Obviously, some of the information packet contents overlap or duplicate components of the tenant move-in information letter. Since the letter is also a request for advance information from the tenant, it may be set aside before the move is completed. The tenant "kit" serves as a friendly reminder of the tenant's obligations under its lease and provides an opportunity to supply much more detailed information about building operations and rules and regulations.

Other information might be provided to tenants as well. If they are relocating from across town or from out of state, their employees may not be familiar with the neighborhood of the building. A list of nearby restaurants, possibly including copies of menus, and information about nearby shopping and entertainment opportunities would be a nice welcoming gesture. Relocating employees may need information about changing driving licenses or obtaining new license plates for their vehicles, so a list of governmental agencies and services can assist the transition. Tips for personal safety and security in and around the workplace are a helpful adjunct regardless of the neighborhood's crime potential.

Some managers prefer to distribute a *tenant manual* instead of a simple packet. Often presented in a ring-binder, the manual will include extensive information about building rules and regulations, operational procedures, and forms for requesting maintenance and other building services. Such a tenant manual might also incorporate a section on emergency procedures, depending on how extensive that information is. (As noted earlier, a separate emergency procedures manual may also be appropriate.) An important component of a tenant manual is a list of contacts and emergency telephone numbers, including the building manager, the maintenance supervisor, and other key members of the management team.

Supervising the Move-In. A few days prior to move-in, the building manager and the tenant's representative should walk through the built-out leased space to ensure that the work is complete and the space is in good condition. It may be desirable to include a representative from the moving company to familiarize that person with the location of the office and the various spaces in which the tenant's furniture and equipment are to be positioned. Having the mover involved in the inspection provides a unique opportunity to confirm that both tenant and mover fully understand the building move-in policies and procedures, which should eliminate any subsequent misunderstandings among the various parties.

This walk-through might be scheduled as the manager's final inspection, comparing the finished space to the punch list created during a previous inspection. (If the contractor's work is of known quality and few problems are anticipated, this might be the only formal inspection of the construction work.) All incomplete or unsatisfactory work should be noted on a new punch list so any construction deficiencies can be corrected before the move-in. The results of this inspection should meet with the tenant's approval indicated by the representative signing or initialing the punch list. This joint inspection also ensures that any damage that occurs during move-in (e.g., nicks on doors, scratches on walls, chipping of paint) can be identified and charged to the tenant, who can arrange for reimbursement from the moving company.

It is a good idea for someone from the management team (e.g., the building manager or the maintenance supervisor) to supervise the move-in. This is beneficial to both manager and tenant. From a tenant's perspective,

Exhibit 10.2

Sample Tenant Move-In Checklist

Tenant Move-In Checklist

Tenant Name ________ Suite Number ________
Anticipated Move-In Date ________ Net Rentable Area ________
Tenant Contact ________
Tenant Current Mailing Address ________
Present Telephone Number ________ New Telephone Number ________

1. Lease Summation Report (or Lease	____	7. Form Letter to Moving Company Mailed:	____
Transmittal) Received:	____	Certificate of Insurance Received:	____
2. Tenant Ledger Card Prepared:	____	Contact with Mover:	____
3. Construction Schedule Received:	____	8. Construction Punch List Compiled:	____
4. Initial Contact with Tenant:	____	Distributed:	____
5. Tenant Move-In Information Letter Sent:	____	Completed:	____
6. Advance Tenant Information Received:	____	9. Construction Cleanup Scheduled:	____
a. Door Graphics Ordered:	____	10. Move-in Elevator Reservation to Security:	____
b. Directory Listing Ordered:	____	11. Tenant Manual/Information Packet Sent:	____
c. Suite Keys: Number ____ Ordered:	____	12. Acceptance of Space by Tenant—	
Delivered:	____	Form Letter Sent:	____
d. Move-In Date ____ Confirmed:	____	Received:	____
		13. Rent Commences:	____

Details will vary depending on building policies and facilities. Assignment of parking spaces and submission of a list of tenant emergency contacts are other common items for a move-in checklist. If special parking permits are needed for moving vans, that would be another item to add. Receipt of a certificate of occupancy might be an appropriate checklist item as well.

moving a business means a loss of productive employee time. Having the manager or another building representative supervising the move means building-related problems that arise can be handled quickly, and move-in will not be unduly delayed. From the manager's perspective, on-site supervision can help protect the building and its equipment from excessive wear and tear. In particular, the management representative can facilitate arrangements for protection of elevator interiors or corridor floors, especially if the mover does not have sufficient or appropriate protective materials. Another key role of this person is making sure that freight elevators and loading areas are ready for the move-in—business tenants often schedule moves for evenings or weekends to minimize downtime—and that the mover knows where to park the van, how to bring furniture and equipment into the building, and how to operate the elevators.

To ensure an orderly move, management should create and use a *move-in checklist.* This should include every step that must be taken to move a new tenant into the building, with a space for noting the date each step is completed. In this way, all of the details are anticipated and nothing important is left undone. An example of a move-in checklist is shown in Exhibit 10.2.

Note that it begins tracking activities after the lease is signed and includes advance information needed from the tenant, construction punch list inspections of the leased premises, and the commencement of rent payments.

Follow-Up on the Move-In. The first business day after the move is likely to be hectic for the tenant. The tenant may have concerns about construction items that are unfinished or questions regarding maintenance service requests. It is a good strategy for the office building manager to visit the new tenant during that first day to offer assistance with details related to the building and lend moral support.

This is an opportune time to give the tenant representative a copy of the tenant manual or information "kit" although it may be best to schedule a return visit to review its contents. It may not be practical to deal with construction issues while the firm's employees are setting up their work areas. So the manager should make an appointment to return in a day or two to walk the finished suite with the tenant representative and identify any construction work that is incomplete. While the suite should have been thoroughly inspected prior to move-in, it is always possible that some detail was missed. Using the punch list created during this walk-through, arrangements can be made with the contractor or building personnel to quickly fix any outstanding construction deficiencies. The manager should check back a few days later to be certain everything has been completed to the tenant's satisfaction. On the other hand, if all the construction inspections were conducted as they should be, this post-move-in walk-through will be most helpful in determining the types and amount of damage caused by the movers, which repair costs would be the tenant's responsibility.

Administering the Lease

Leasing involves a large amount of paperwork. Records of contacts with prospective tenants, documentation of lease negotiations, and the resulting lease document are prominent components of this. Once a tenant has moved into the building, it is important to have a record-keeping system that will ensure accuracy of documents and facilitate their retrieval when they are needed.

Lease administration includes a variety of activities. Among the most important is collection of rents. As noted elsewhere in this book, having established policies and procedures will ensure that tasks are performed consistently and that tenants are treated evenhandedly.

Rent Collection Policies. The building should have a standard operating policy that states when, where, and how rents are to be paid, and this information should be incorporated into tenants' leases. Rents are usually due and payable in advance on the first of the month. Often a grace period is allowed between the first of the month and when rents are considered delinquent. Ten days is typical, but local practices may dictate a longer or shorter grace period. The policy should also state how delinquencies are to be handled. Upon expiration of the grace period, usual practice is for the manager to contact the tenant, either by telephone or written notice, about the oversight. If the rent is still not paid, a second (written) reminder notice is sent. This is more strongly worded and intended to warn the tenant that the matter will be turned over to an attorney if the rent is not paid. If a third notice is required, it usually informs the tenant that legal action (leading to eviction for nonpayment) has been initiated as provided in the lease. The manager should have access to an attorney with expertise in the area of eviction and consult with that attorney as necessary when the standard delinquency notices have been unsuccessful.

Building policies and procedures regarding delinquencies may have to be adjusted to reflect existing market conditions. If a building is fully occupied and the local market is strong, rents are more likely to be paid on time, and a short grace period may be all that is needed to accommodate checks in the mail. In a soft market, however, the grace period may have to be extended to allow tenants to maximize their cash flow. Tenants' problems may also have to be considered individually. If a business is struggling, it may be in everyone's best interests to try to work out a payment plan. This might take the form of smaller payments made twice a month or a change of the payment due date to one that the tenant can more easily meet. If such adjustments become necessary, the specifics should be documented in a *letter of agreement* that becomes part of the tenant's lease.

Rent collection policies should also address the form of payment. Corporate and personal checks as well as postal money orders are certainly acceptable. As electronic transfer of funds is increasingly available, tenants may be invited to arrange with their banks for rent to be paid automatically. Apart from some initial paperwork to establish the arrangements, rent payment via electronic transfer automatically credits the appropriate building account while simultaneously debiting the tenant's bank account. The adjustments appear on the parties' respective bank statements; there are no checks to be collected and deposited. This is certainly viable when the rent amount is the same each month. Any changes to the amount must be communicated to the respective financial institutions in advance to ensure accurate and timely payment.

Another consideration is whether tenants will be sent a bill for each month's rent. Here again, if the rent payment is the same each month, there may be no need for billing. However, if there are additional charges to the tenant (e.g., for extra HVAC or in-suite maintenance services), it may be most practical to send a bill for the rent plus the extra charges. Rent bills are also a means of accounting for pass-through charges and differentiating them from the base rent. The need for such bills should be considered in light of the cost of preparing and mailing them. (If rent bills are sent, the

Gross-Up of Expenses in New Buildings

When a building is new, it will be some time before it is fully occupied. If tenants' leases will require payment of some or all operating expenses of the building, the first occupants would bear a disproportionately large share of operating cost increases. To make this assessment more fair, knowledgeable tenants will ask to have the base year or base amount of specific expenses *grossed up* to what they would be at full (e.g., 90 or 95 percent) occupancy. When grossing up is combined with base year or expense stop lease provisions, the tenant is protected from operating cost increases due solely to increased occupancy of the building. At the same time, the landlord is protected from inflationary risks associated with providing services to the tenant.

Grossing up is applied only to variable costs such as utilities and janitorial services that are dependent on occupancy. Landlord and tenant should agree on what expenses may be grossed up. The lease should also stipulate that the grossed-up base year should be recomputed on an annual basis.

tenant move-in information letter should ask where the bill should be sent and to whose attention. This information is vital if the tenant is a subsidiary of a major corporation, and all payments are handled from the firm's headquarters.)

Escalation. There are several different ways that rents on long-term office leases can be adjusted for inflation. An *operating expense escalation clause* might be written into the lease. Under this type of provision, increases in building operating costs are passed through to tenants on a pro rata basis. For example, if operating expenses were $800,000 one year and $875,000 the next, the $75,000 increase would be prorated among the tenants. A tenant who occupied 20,000 square feet of a 200,000-square-foot building would be responsible for ten percent of the building's operating expenses. In the case of the $75,000 increase, that tenant would be responsible for $7,500 in addition to the prior year's expense amount.

The new obligation might be billed as a lump sum or divided into multiple payments over the coming year. Alternatively, it might be structured as an increase in the tenant's rental rate. The ideal strategy in this situation is to collect the full amount in a lump sum because the added amount is being collected in arrears, but that is not always possible.

A more reasonable approach is to estimate increases in operating costs for the coming year and divide the estimated total into twelve monthly payments. At the end of the fiscal or calendar year when the actual cost increases are known, tenants are advised of the difference between the budgeted and actual amounts. If the estimate was less than the actual increases, tenants would be billed for the difference. (It is unlikely that such a lump-sum billing would be as large an amount as noted in the foregoing example.) If the estimate exceeded the actual increases, tenants would be credited for the difference. While this difference might be paid back to the tenants, usual practice is to apply the credit against the tenant's estimated pass-through charges for the new year. As an alternative, the credit might be applied against the next month's total rent bill.

Another alternative is to use an *index escalation clause*. This type of provision bases rent adjustments on changes in an established index such as the *Consumer Price Index (CPI)* published by the U.S. Department of Labor, Bureau of Labor Statistics. The CPI is computed for major metropolitan areas and for the United States as a whole. It is based on changes in the costs of a specific array of goods and services consumed by a typical family and reported as a percentage of the cost of those same goods and services in a *base year* (currently 1982–1984 = 100). The metropolitan indices represent the effect of inflation on the cost of living at the local level. It should be pointed out, however, that large incremental changes make it difficult for tenants to accept the CPI as a basis for rent increases. On the other hand, rent increases based on small incremental changes in the CPI during periods of low inflation may not cover the actual increases in building operating costs. This type of clause was common at one time and is often found in older leases. However, current practice has moved away from CPI-based rent increases for the reasons stated above.

A lease may provide for rent increases by referring to a *base year,* which may be the current calendar year or the first full calendar year after move-in. With this approach, the tenant pays for increases over the total amount of operating expenses in the base year. For example, a tenant moving into an office building in October 2001 would be responsible for increases from the base year of 2002. Under a seven-year lease, increases would take effect in 2003, 2004, 2005, 2006, and 2007, with a partial increase in 2008 when the lease term expires. The base year may be changed when the lease is renewed.

An *expense stop* may be used to limit expense escalations. For example, if the stop is set at $5.00 per square foot per year, the tenant would pay a pro rata share of the increase in total expenses over that amount. (In other words, the owner's liability for expenses would stop at $5.00 per square foot per year.)

Yet another alternative is to increase the base rent a set amount each year over the course of the lease term, or landlord and tenant might agree on specific rates to apply for set intervals. With this approach, annual escalations might be stated in specific dollar increments: Base rent will be $12 per square foot in year one increasing to $13 per square foot in year two and $14 in year three. They might also be stated as a percentage: Base rent will increase 7.5 percent each year of the lease term. A lease for a very long term might state specific increases at three-year or five-year intervals.

The reason for including escalation provisions in leases is to protect the owner's investment by permitting upward adjustments of rents to compensate for inflation. Local practices and market conditions may determine which approach or approaches will be accepted by tenants in a given area.

Proper adjustment of tenants' rents requires complete understanding of the building owner's and the management firm's policies regarding escalation as well as the specific escalation clause used in building leases. Detailed records of each tenant's base rate against which adjustments are to be made are also a must. Rent escalation calculations and copies of escalation billings should be kept in the files maintained for each tenant. The office building manager should also establish and maintain a master record of all rent adjustments. These data are essential for documenting how well the scheduled rent escalations recover increases in operating costs. These records need to be reviewed periodically so that corrective measures can be implemented to ensure that expense increases do not erode the owner's cash-flow position.

Apart from the management perspective, administration of escalation provisions requires effective communication with tenants. These rent adjustments can be very complicated, and even the most sophisticated tenants may not understand all of the details. To minimize confusion, rent bills that include escalations should be accompanied by a breakdown of how the specific adjustments were calculated and refer the tenant to the appropriate lease provisions.

Tenant Lease Files. A separate file folder should be maintained for each tenant in the building. This should be organized following a standard pattern so that related documents are always kept together. Consideration should also be given to which documents will be retrieved most often; these should be at the front of the folder. If the contents of these files are extremely varied and numerous, it may be desirable to use folders with internal dividers to separate individual documents or categories of documents. Typical contents of a tenant lease file include the following:

- Lease abstract—A completed copy of the form that summarizes pertinent data from the lease (see note in Exhibit 8.7).
- Lease document—An executed copy of the lease agreement.
- Lease amendments—Copies of documents regarding changes to lease provisions, especially those taking place after the original lease agreement was established.
- Escalation information—Copies of all escalation calculations and billings (see preceding discussion).
- Rent roll change instructions—Documentation of rent roll changes and effective dates for the particular tenant (e.g., adjustments to ex-

pense pass-throughs, rent escalations) as they were communicated to the accounting staff or department. These ensure correct billing of tenants when the adjustments are scheduled to take place.

- Miscellaneous billings—Copies of requests for services that are charged back to tenants along with the relevant billings. Usually these are isolated charges and not part of the rent roll.
- Keys and locks—Information on the locksets on the tenant's doors and which master keys will access them.
- Tenant contacts—A list of the tenant's staff members who are considered key contacts, either in regard to building management issues or because of emergencies. This should include names, position titles, daytime and after-hours telephone numbers, and e-mail addresses.
- Tenant improvements—Copies of bids, construction contracts, relevant billings, and other information related to building out the tenant's leased space. (This may become a separate file if the build-out project is large or complex.)
- Floor plan—A copy of the "as built" floor plan for the tenant's space.
- Correspondence—Copies of all written communications with the tenant including those related to the lease and lease negotiations.

The tenant lease file should be the one-source reference for information about a tenant, the tenant's lease status, and various communications with the tenant, including bills. (Tenant payments are typically documented on a tenant ledger form such as that shown in Exhibit 5.2.) Other items that might be included in this file are space plans and related forms and contracts, approved construction punch lists, completed move-in checklists, information related to leasing commissions, and certificates of occupancy.

Tickler Files. Good management practice regarding lease administration will include development of a tickler file. This is a system of reminders of upcoming events that require action by the office building manager, among them:

- Automatic rent escalations
- Lease expirations/renewal negotiations
- When periods of free rent end
- Commencement and expiration of any rent abatements
- Periodic decorating as called for in the lease
- Notification requirements
- Tenant-negotiated options to expand

Exhibit 10.3
Sample Tickler File Record

Critical Date ____________

Tenant Name ____________ Suite Number ____________

Event ____________

Activity Required ____________

____

____

Department or Person to Notify ____________

Person Responsible ____________

Cards are filed in order of the critical date when action should be taken or initiated. It may be desirable to include space for noting actions taken or for signing off on completion.

Other time-sensitive lease issues should be included as well. The same system can be used for building-specific events (deadlines for an internal newsletter, building-sponsored tenant activities, training for evacuation drills). While some managers use index cards to record the particulars (Exhibit 10.3 is an example), others use computer software to set up these types of reminders. Periodic reports are generated, minimally once a month, providing the manager with an action reminder and the necessary backup information to proceed. The key to maintaining a computerized system is keying the pertinent data into the appropriate format so that it can be retrieved as needed.

Other Considerations. The lease requires the tenant to provide certain types of documents at or after move-in. Certificates of insurance should be kept together in a master file. Estoppel certificates, if required, would be in another master file. It may be desirable to compile a master list of tenants' pro rata shares of operating expenses, noting in particular any negotiated differences from the building standard lease form. If any tenants have separate arrangements for telecommunications services or electricity, copies of relevant documents might best be kept in appropriate master files as well as the tenants' lease files.

The Cost of Tenant Turnover

Consider a tenant who occupies 8,000 usable square feet of office space at a base rate of $15.50 per square foot per year (based on 9,200 rentable square feet) and whose lease expires in nine (9) months. Because problems with the HVAC system have contributed to poor relations with this tenant's employees, it is questionable whether the tenant will renew the lease. Current market conditions support the following leasing parameters:

Lease Term:	36 months
Rental Rate:	$17.00/sq ft (rentable)
Common Area Factor:	15%
Improvement Allowance:	$12.00/sq ft for a total remodel; $3.00/sq ft for a renewal—based on usable square feet
Time to Re-Lease:	6 months
Leasing Commission:	$1.15/sq ft for new leases and $0.38/sq ft for renewals—based on rentable square feet and the full term of the lease

Using these data, the following comparison can be made:

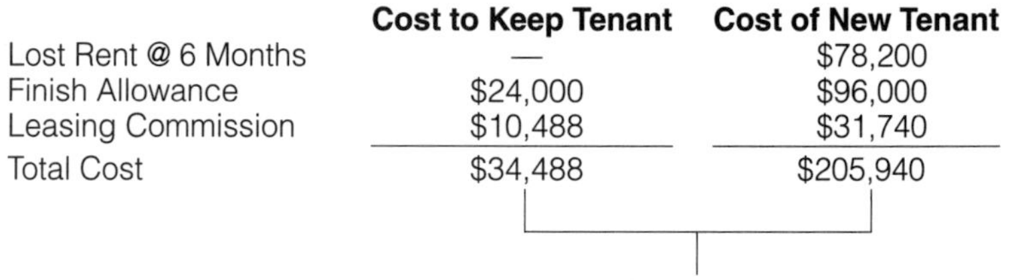

	Cost to Keep Tenant	**Cost of New Tenant**
Lost Rent @ 6 Months	—	$78,200
Finish Allowance	$24,000	$96,000
Leasing Commission	$10,488	$31,740
Total Cost	$34,488	$205,940

Incremental Cost of Losing this Tenant $171,452

It would cost nearly *six times as much* to acquire a new tenant as it would to retain the current one ($205,940 ÷ $34,488 = 5.97).

The distinction between rentable and usable square feet is an important one because of its impact on the dollars involved. In this example, the area on which the rent and the leasing commission are calculated (rentable area) is 1,200 square feet larger than the basis for calculating finish and moving allowances. The difference is the common area load factor (15%).

Adapted and reprinted with permission from *The Tenant Retention Solution: A Revolutionary Approach to Commercial Real Estate Management* by Howard K. Lundeen, CPM®, Laurence C. Harmon, CPM®, and Kathleen M. McKenna-Harmon, CPM®. (Chicago: Institute of Real Estate Management, 1995.)

Tenant Retention Strategies

Tenant turnover is expensive. Not only is rental income lost when space is unoccupied, but bringing in a new tenant has attendant costs for space planning, improvement construction, and leasing commissions. One key to maintaining high occupancy levels is retaining existing tenants. Every member of the management team has responsibilities in this regard. They must understand that every contact between tenants or their employees and management personnel is an opportunity to build a better relationship and foster tenant retention.

In addition to skills that qualify them for the work they perform, management team members must have good people skills. They must listen to what is being said by tenants' representatives and respond appropriately. They should show concern when problems related to the building are brought to their attention. Above all, there should be a timely response to tenant service requests. This issue—response times—will have a major impact on tenants' opinions of the building and its management.

The building manager and the management team are not the only ones who will interact with tenants and their personnel. Management policies regarding personal interactions with tenants, written communications, and general responsiveness must be shared with the service providers and professionals who also have tenant contacts. This includes leasing agents, space planners and architects, construction workers, contracted service providers, and others. All must understand that, while in the building, they are representing the property owner and the building management; and as such, they are expected to foster goodwill with the tenants.

Developing Tenant Contacts. Office building managers need to cultivate a relationship with a representative of each tenant firm. The tenant contact may be the owner or president of the company. In large organizations, however, the representative may be the office manager or another employee of the firm. Regardless of who the contact is, the building manager should visit the person regularly and inquire about building-related concerns or problems that need attention.

To ensure that every tenant is visited on a regular schedule, the manager should maintain a list of contacts and keep a record of each meeting and the topics discussed as well as any actions taken to resolve outstanding problems. How often tenant contacts are visited will depend on the number of tenants in the building. In most situations, once a month would be a reasonable starting point.

The goal of these visits is to develop confidence in the competence of the management team and foster goodwill. Being available to address tenants' concerns and being responsive to specific requests are all-important. It is also helpful to interact with contacts occasionally in a less formal setting (e.g., taking them to lunch or a sporting event).

Handling Tenant Requests. Although service requests are generally a maintenance issue, how those requests are handled is part of the ongoing relationship with the tenant. To expedite service, tenants should be asked to appoint one employee to contact the building staff regarding maintenance service requests. This will facilitate communications and avert mishandling of tenant requests.

Within a few days after move-in, the building manager should follow up with the new tenant to ensure that a maintenance contact person has been named and that all employees of the tenant firm have been informed of that person's role. The manager should also appoint one member of the management team to receive the tenant's maintenance requests. The respective tenant and management contacts should then be introduced in person as soon as possible.

The building operations manual should include specific procedures for handling tenant service requests, including response times. Most office buildings allow service requests to be initiated by telephone, with pertinent information being entered on a *maintenance service request* form by the staff member who takes the call. Where computerized maintenance record-keeping systems are in place, the information may be entered directly into a *work order* form and printed for distribution to those who will do the work (see Exhibit 5.4). Alternatively, tenants may be able to request service via e-mail, either as a message to their management team contacts or by filling out an on-line service request form. Both telephone and e-mail allow for immediate responses indicating when the requested work will be done or if it will be delayed. Sometimes a type of work cannot be done, for whatever reason, and the tenant contact should be given that information up front. If a requested service is out of the ordinary or if additional charges will apply, that information should be shared as well. This type of communication avoids surprises for tenants and gives them an option to not have work performed if they do not wish to pay for it.

Basic requests (e.g., fluorescent lightbulb replacement) can be fulfilled immediately or within 24 hours if supplies are on hand. The goal should be to turn around individual service requests within a reasonable time frame while also performing scheduled preventive maintenance and providing requested services to other tenants. If part or all of the requested work cannot be performed within the normal time frame, the tenant contact should be advised when it will be done. The tenant manual (described earlier in this chapter) should inform new tenants of the requirements for submitting service requests and how they are handled by building management. If paper forms are used, tenants should receive a supply of these forms at move-in.

As noted in Chapter 5, all service requests should be entered in a *maintenance log*. This may be a paper form where entries are written by hand. Today, however, most management offices maintain these records in their computers. The maintenance log serves as a record of the work requested, who requested it, when the request was received, and when the work was completed. This helps the manager monitor tenant requests and facilitates follow-up with tenants after the fact.

Obtaining Tenant Feedback. Tenants will find various ways to communicate when they are *not* satisfied with the service management provides.

This may take the form of complaints by telephone or in writing. When things are running smoothly, however, there is usually little specific feedback. To encourage feedback and to help evaluate management team performance, savvy office building managers will survey their tenants periodically. (Exhibit 10.4 is an example of a tenant survey questionnaire.) While building managers and management companies can conduct their own surveys, results may be more informative if an objective third party (e.g., a market research firm) occasionally conducts the surveys and compiles and analyzes the responses anonymously.

Another useful strategy is to include space on the work order form (see Exhibit 5.4) for the tenant to comment on the quality of the service received. Use of specific questions with boxes for yes and no answers can be even more helpful. Examples of questions to ask include:

Was the service provided promptly?

Was the maintenance worker friendly?

Was the work done satisfactorily?

Is there any other work that needs to be done?

Note that asking for particulars in this way invites additional opportunities to provide service to the tenant.

When it is practical to do so, the manager or another member of the management team should follow up with the tenant directly by telephone to ask if maintenance work was done to the tenant's satisfaction. It is also a good idea to let maintenance workers know the results of such follow-up and to reward them for positive tenant feedback.

Other Useful Retention Strategies. In the traditional office environment, workers were likely to discover a need for maintenance or repairs when there were building personnel available to handle them because most businesses operated during the same hours that maintenance personnel were on duty. Today, however, many tenants offer flex-time schedules to their employees, and the company's work day may extend from 7:30 A.M. to 6:30 P.M. or later rather than the traditional 9:00 A.M. to 5:00 P.M. These tenants' employees are increasingly likely to discover maintenance service needs outside of management's normal business hours. Office building managers have responded to this change by scheduling maintenance personnel to work in shifts coordinated with their tenants' office hours.

These managers have discovered that *visibility adds value*. The opportunity to observe maintenance service being performed makes the work more valuable in and of itself—seeing the work done means the tenants' employees can appreciate the promptness of response, the courtesy of the building employee, the way the work is performed, and the quality of the finished product.

Janitorial work in office buildings has traditionally been invisible. As

Exhibit 10.4
Sample Tenant Survey Questionnaire

Tenant Survey

Tenant Name ______________________________ Suite Number __________
Survey Completed by ______________________________ Date __________

We value your opinion, and we need your help to ensure that the management of *building name* continues to meet your expectations in providing requested services. We therefore ask you to take a few moments to answer the questions below and return this form to the management office. Thank you very much.

Please rate the following service categories on a scale of 1 to 5, where 1 = superior, 2 = above average, 3 = average, 4 = below average, and 5 = unsatisfactory. For items that are not applicable, circle NA.

Janitorial Service—In your office area	1	2	3	4	5	NA
Janitorial Service—Corridors and lobbies	1	2	3	4	5	NA
Janitorial Service—Rest rooms	1	2	3	4	5	NA
Overall maintenance of landscaped areas	1	2	3	4	5	NA
HVAC operations	1	2	3	4	5	NA
Elevator operations	1	2	3	4	5	NA
Security procedures	1	2	3	4	5	NA
Parking—For employees	1	2	3	4	5	NA
Parking—For visitors	1	2	3	4	5	NA
Building amenities*	1	2	3	4	5	NA
Tenant communications	1	2	3	4	5	NA

Please rate the members of the management team listed below, using the same scale.

Building Manager						
Responsiveness	1	2	3	4	5	NA
Courtesy	1	2	3	4	5	NA
Follow through	1	2	3	4	5	NA
Maintenance Team						
Responsiveness	1	2	3	4	5	NA
Courtesy	1	2	3	4	5	NA
Follow through	1	2	3	4	5	NA
Security Personnel						
Responsiveness	1	2	3	4	5	NA
Courtesy	1	2	3	4	5	NA
Follow through	1	2	3	4	5	NA

Please comment specifically on the following areas:

What would you suggest to improve energy management in the building? ______________________________

____

What would you suggest to improve building operations in general? ______________________________

____

Will you need expansion space within the next 6 months? 12 months? 18 months? 24 months? ____

Other Comments ______________________________

____

____

____

*It may be desirable to itemize building amenities for specific feedback.

workers leave the office at day's end, janitorial crews are coming into the building to clean the tenants' spaces and public areas. The old saw, "out of sight, out of mind," applies here. Because such work is invisible, it tends to be taken for granted. Only if it is not done or is done improperly or incompletely is it likely to be noticed. Considering this, the notion of visibility adding value can also be applied to some janitorial activities. Maintenance personnel can be scheduled to wash windows and polish brass in the lobby when tenants' employees are coming to work in the morning or around their lunch hours. Changing light bulbs, freshening greenery in planters, vacuuming carpets, and any number of other common area maintenance tasks can be made visible without hampering people's movement through the lobby.

While it is a truism that a good maintenance program is all-important to tenant relations and tenant retention, there are many human touches that can be implemented to foster good tenant relations and encourage tenants to renew their leases. Among these are:

- Newsletters—Building management teams often produce a monthly tenant newsletter that is distributed to all employees in the building. New tenants moving into the building, major work being done on the building, scheduled maintenance that will impact elevator or HVAC operations, and local (neighborhood) events are the kinds of things communicated in these newsletters. Changes in building management personnel (promotions, new hires) and seasonal safety tips are other possible subjects. The information need not fill more than the two sides of a single sheet of paper.

- Welcome gifts—Some managers send flowers or a pot plant, candy, or some other token gift to welcome new tenants to the building or as a thank you for renewing their leases.

- Move-in party—An alternative "welcome" gift might be a deli sandwich tray or a pizza for a new tenant's personnel on moving day.

- Food for thought—Seasonal changes offer opportunities to treat tenants' employees with appropriate foods. Lemonade or ice cream sundaes served in the lobby by management staff on a hot summer's day can be a nice way to welcome building workers back from lunch. Coffee accompanied by donuts or bagels can be a warming welcome as they arrive on a wintry morning.

- Safety training—Management might sponsor demonstrations or seminars on life-safety topics, personal security in the workplace and beyond, and similar subjects.

- Health fair—Management might work with tenant representatives to organize a health fair where people can have some easily tested parameters checked (e.g., blood pressure) or get a flu shot (for a fee). Often management will sponsor a blood drive every year or in response to local needs. These can be arranged with the American Red Cross or, perhaps, a local hospital.

- Treats—Holidays can be recognized by having janitorial personnel distribute wrapped candies to tenants' employees (heart shapes for Valentine's day, turkeys for Thanksgiving, etc.).

This is an area for creativity. It is also something that requires extensive planning in advance and budgeted funds to carry out the different activities.

Holiday decorations in the lobby, a picnic in the park, and an art exhibition in lobby corridors are other possibilities. Sometimes management and tenants will collaborate in sponsoring sports teams and scheduling opportunities to play together. These kinds of things create positive impressions on visitors as well as tenants and their employees, generating favorable word-of-mouth advertising that cannot be purchased at any price.

As a general tenant relations effort, it is a good idea for the building manager to be a visible presence occasionally. Greeting people as they enter the building in the morning or saying "good night" as they leave in the evening lets them know that management is actively aware of what is occurring in the lobby and not just part of the behind-the-scenes operation of the building.

Planning for Lease Renewals. Lease renewal is not a given for either the tenant or the landlord. It is important to evaluate the desirability of renewing individual leases. In doing so, several factors should be considered:

Should the tenant's lease be renewed?

Has the tenant fulfilled its financial obligations under the lease?

Has the tenant complied with other aspects of the lease?

What is the tenant's financial condition?

Does the tenant need to expand and, if so, can that expansion be accommodated?

What is the current market situation?

In some circumstances, it may be desirable to ask: Is the tenant a good "fit" with the other tenants in the building? It may also be appropriate to ask if a suitable replacement tenant can easily be found for the space.

On-time payment of rent and compliance with lease requirements in general are important considerations. If a tenant has had difficulty fulfilling its obligations to pay rent and pass-through charges (i.e., repeated delinquencies), this may signal other financial problems. The tenant may not be able to handle a rent increase. Is it appropriate to try to structure renewal lease terms to retain this tenant?

Tenants can be problematic in other ways. If a tenant has been very demanding in regard to building services and constantly complains about poor service quality, slow response times, and excessive charges—despite the fact that all the other tenants are completely satisfied and are generally complimentary of the management staff on these same points—the built-in hassle factor may weigh heavily in determining the desirability of renewal. Is it possible to find a way to satisfy this tenant's service demands? Will not renewing this tenant's lease have a major financial impact on the building's income stream?

Future expansion is often planned for when the initial lease is being negotiated, in which case a provision allowing the tenant to expand into adjacent space would have been included in the lease. If expansion was unanticipated, however, a tenant may be lost if its needs cannot be accommodated in some way. Can a tenant in adjacent space be relocated to allow for this tenant's expansion? Is there a larger space elsewhere in the building that might serve this tenant's needs as well as or better than the adjacent occupied space?

Also a consideration is the state of the local office market. In a strong market, it may be fairly easy to replace a problematic tenant. In a slow market, it may be desirable to keep a marginal tenant to maintain the property's income stream. The current situation will dictate leasing strategies and renewal lease terms. A strong market is likely to support higher rents and longer lease terms, and improvements to demised premises may be at the tenant's expense. A soft market may warrant smaller rent increases, shorter lease terms, and landlord-paid improvements.

A complicating factor in regard to lease renewals is the need to begin negotiations before the current lease term expires. Advance preparation for negotiation of renewals may have to account for notification requirements stated in existing leases. The tenant is required to notify the landlord within a certain time period before expiration whether it will or will not exercise an option to renew that was negotiated for the original lease. The landlord may be required to notify the tenant in advance if a renewal lease will not be offered. Typically, an office building manager will begin the process at least six months in advance of any notification requirements. For large space users with long-term leases (ten or twenty years), negotiations may be started a year or more before the lease expires. (Renewals may have to be negotiated by outside leasing agents, which may alter the time frames involved.) As with a new tenant, negotiations will encompass base rent, pass-through charges, escalations, and tenant improvements. The manager and the property owner will develop specific leasing parameters that encompass renewals as well as new leases. These parameters would also include leasing commissions. (Leasing parameters are discussed in Chapter 7. Leasing strategies and lease terms are covered in Chapter 8.)

Timing is important for several reasons. The early notice gives the tenant an opportunity to evaluate the renewal terms and respond in a timely fashion. (Usual practice is to require notice of nonrenewal at least 90 days before the current lease expires.) Too little time to make an informed decision to renew may lead to frustration and the loss of a valued tenant. Lease renewal almost always means higher rent, and a substantial increase in rent and pass-through charges is likely to meet with resistance. However, if the new rates are accompanied by data on rents and other occupancy costs in the local market, the tenant will be able to make comparisons and weigh the financial and other consequences of staying versus moving out. If the tenant has been served well by members of the management team and the renewal terms are consistent with current market conditions, it should be an easy decision to stay in place.

As mentioned elsewhere in this book (see Chapter 3), leasing to new tenants may be contracted separately from property management; however, the office building manager may be responsible for lease renewals, especially at an established office building. When that is the case, the management agreement should provide for additional compensation to the manager in the form of a leasing commission.

Move-Out Procedures

No matter how well a building is managed, tenants will eventually move out. When that happens, it is the manager's responsibility to see that the move-out proceeds smoothly. This can be approached as a reverse of the move-in procedure, and use of an appropriate *move-out checklist* will ensure that important details are not overlooked.

As with move-in, the manager will need specific information regarding the transition, including the expected move-out date and the name of the moving company. The freight elevator must be reserved and arrangements made for access to loading areas. A parking permit may have to be obtained. Management team members, including security personnel, have to be notified. Keys to the leased space must be collected, and the tenant's name must be removed from the entrance door and the building directory.

The manager should also be certain that all rents and other charges have been paid by the tenant prior to move-out. Any escalation amounts incurred through the move-out date but not yet billed should also be collected. Having collections up-to-date before move-out is imperative. Once the tenant vacates the premises, it will be difficult to collect unpaid amounts due.

Whenever leased space is vacated, the manager should conduct an inspection to determine whether the space is being left in good condition (normal wear and tear excepted). If the inspection indicates that the tenant did not leave the space in satisfactory condition, a list of damage charges will be presented to the departing tenant. Alternatively, these repair costs may be charged against the security deposit collected at the start of the lease term. If that is done, the tenant should receive an itemized statement of the deductions taken along with a check for the remainder of the deposit. Charges for damage should be reasonable and appropriate. If a tenant was in a space for several years and no additional improvements were made to the space, one would expect to replace carpeting and repaint the walls for a new tenant who does not require a completely new build-out. However, damage to window coverings and their operating mechanisms, installations that were not part of the original build-out, or removal of built-in items that has left unsightly or potentially hazardous conditions should certainly be cited. Damage assessments are a sensitive issue, and most situations will not require them because the space is likely to be built out differently for a new tenant.

Whether a space is to be re-leased as currently configured or built out to a new tenant's requirements, the manager should ensure that it is in leasable condition as soon as possible. Maintenance personnel should remove all the debris, vacuum carpets, mop vinyl floors, and wash the windows and any interior glass walls or sidelights. Lights and HVAC should be in working order, and the space should be generally presentable for a showing. In order to lease the space, it may be desirable to remove interior walls, tear out old carpeting, and replace ceiling tiles. This will facilitate installation of improvements for a new tenant and is especially appropriate if the departing tenant's space configuration was not consistent with current office layouts.

Move-outs should be handled with the same consideration and courtesy as move-ins, keeping in mind that a departing tenant is also a source of word-of-mouth advertising about the building and its management.

11

Maintenance Management

The financial success of an office building largely depends on the quality of its maintenance. Maintenance not only ensures optimal function; it also preserves (and sometimes improves) a building's condition, thereby enhancing its value. Building condition is also a measure of the quality of a building's management.

Office building managers generally do not perform maintenance tasks. Their role is primarily administrative. They must know how to recognize problems and be able to find effective ways of dealing with them. Because maintenance costs usually represent a major portion of a building's operating budget, decisions regarding maintenance must also anticipate a financial impact. A sound maintenance program begins with a thorough inspection of the building.

Building Inspection

The office building manager should perform a comprehensive inspection of the building and its systems and equipment as part of the take-over process (see Chapter 4). Subsequently, the entire building should be inspected on a regular schedule to identify the types of maintenance work needed to maintain or upgrade the building. Most management firms will have a generic *inspection checklist* that identifies specific building components and includes columns to indicate the general condition of individual items, the type of repairs needed, and an estimate of the cost to do the work, with blank spaces to add items unique to a specific building. It is also appropriate to include

Exhibit 11.1

Sample Office Building Interior Inspection Checklist Format

Item	Condition			Description	Repairs Needed	Est. Cost
	Good	Fair	Poor			
Office Interiors						
Walls						
Floors						
Ceilings						
Lighting						
Fixtures						
Switches						
Electrical Outlets						
Radiators						
Air Conditioning						
Doors						
Locks						
Hardware						
Baseboards						
Windows						
Window Coverings						

This is representative of the list of items inspected in an occupied office suite. Checklist contents should be tailored to the specific building. For example, types of floor coverings might be differentiated (carpeting vs. vinyl tile). An older building might have transoms above corridor doors; newer buildings may have different types of telecommunications outlets.

An office building exterior checklist will include such elements as the roof, the four exterior walls, the building entrance, the loading dock, and exterior fire escapes, with appropriate subcategories under each component to help pinpoint problem areas. An interior checklist will have major categories that identify areas of the building or specific types of facilities, with subentries for all the component elements to be inspected. For example, checklist items under windows would include things like frames, glass, weather-stripping, and window treatments. Caulking, sills, and locks might be listed, too, if appropriate. An elevator inspection would include the pit, surfaces and fixtures inside the cab, and the various switches and indicators, as well as other considerations such as floor numbers on the doors and the elevator shaft. The lobby, stairwells, men's and women's rest rooms, and specific types of equipment (water heaters, pumps, compressors, HVAC components) would be other major categories on an interior inspection checklist.

a column for indicating a time frame to do the work. (Exhibit 11.1 shows an example of an inspection checklist format.) Inspection forms usually include spaces to record information about the building (e.g., building name and age) as well as the name and signature of the person conducting the inspection and the date it was done. The accumulated inspection reports form a record of the condition of the building over a period of time.

Typical Frequency of Selected Maintenance Tasks

Task	Frequency
Clean windows	Twice a year
Recharge fire extinguishers	Yearly
Inspect common area lighting	Weekly
Wax lobby floors	Three times a year
Clean/replace HVAC filters	Monthly
Inspect and oil exhaust fans	Quarterly
Patch parking lot and other concrete	Yearly

Because the exterior of the building is usually inspected less frequently, separate checklist forms may be used for the building exterior and interior. It may also be appropriate to have a separate checklist for elements of common areas, which are often inspected daily or several times a day. Computers allow managers to create inspection forms tailored to the buildings they manage. While the manager needs to be thoroughly familiar with the condition of the building and its component equipment, it is often most appropriate to delegate inspection of some items to members of the maintenance team who are more knowledgeable about the system or equipment.

A thorough building inspection will yield a list of maintenance tasks to be performed. These should be differentiated into two categories—repairs that must be performed immediately to preserve building components or ensure the safety of those who work in the building and tasks that can be delayed but should nevertheless be scheduled as soon as possible. These two categories of tasks guide the manager in developing a comprehensive maintenance schedule that also includes regular cleaning of building components and routine servicing of equipment and systems. For each inspection item that needs repairs, the manager should prepare a *work order* form (see Exhibit 5.4) detailing the location of the item and the work to be done. If the work requires priority handling, that should be indicated as well.

Note: The Institute of Real Estate Management publishes office building interior and exterior inspection forms that identify features common to most office buildings, with columns to record their condition, work that needs to be done, and an estimate of the cost. They also include blank spaces to note additional unique characteristics of the building.

Types of Maintenance

Real estate managers recognize several different types of maintenance. In office buildings, three types of maintenance tasks are differentiated—janitorial, preventive, and corrective. In addition, some work may be categorized as emergency maintenance (e.g., stopping an overflowing toilet) or deferred maintenance (work delayed intentionally or indefinitely). Work may also be done solely to improve the property's image. This is called cosmetic maintenance.

Janitorial Maintenance. The day-to-day cleaning of building components, common areas, and tenants' leased premises is referred to as janitorial or custodial maintenance. General visibility and the amount of foot traffic through various areas of the building will determine how often different cleaning tasks are performed. High-visibility areas such as ground-floor windows, the building lobby, elevator cabs, and public corridors will require more frequent attention because they are the essence of the building's *curb appeal.* Stairwells and supply closets may receive only periodic spot inspections and cleaning.

Whether janitorial maintenance is performed by in-house staff or under a service contract, the work should be described in detail in a set of comprehensive *janitorial specifications* that lists individual tasks and indicates how often they are to be performed. Sweeping floors or vacuuming carpeting, dusting, and removal of wastepaper are usually done nightly. However, metal and glass surfaces may be cleaned on an as-needed basis—daily in lobbies; less frequently in less-visible areas. Rest rooms may be cleaned nightly, but they may need to be inspected and serviced (e.g., restocked with toilet tissue, paper towels, and soap) two or more times a day. The specifications should account for all areas of the building, including tenants' spaces, and all the types of tasks that are to be performed on a regular basis.

Building type and size and how often different cleaning tasks are to be performed are basic considerations in formulating janitorial specifications. The specifications should also consider quality and amounts of cleaning materials and supplies. These are important components of janitorial costs, which are a major portion of an office building's operating expense budget. (Purchasing of supplies is discussed in Chapter 5.) A good way to develop janitorial specifications for a new office building is to obtain copies of specifications used at buildings whose level of service management wants to emulate. An existing building may already have janitorial specifications in place. These should be reviewed at take-over and modified as necessary to ensure the level of service desired. Because janitorial service is typically included in the base rent paid by tenants, their expectations will be another important consideration. Janitorial services are often a major source of tenant complaints while exceptional service in this area is a major contributor to tenant satisfaction.

When janitorial work is performed by in-house staff, one or more supervisors will usually oversee the work and serve as the communications link between management and cleaning personnel. The supervisors are responsible for the overall productivity of the cleaning staff, and they control the supplies and equipment used in the cleaning process. This arrangement gives the building manager more control over janitorial activities. However, the attendant payroll and benefits costs, the need to rearrange schedules or find last-minute replacements to accommodate individual workers (e.g., vacations, illnesses), and the challenges of training and then supervising a large number of employees working in dispersed locations throughout the building can be considered disadvantages of using in-house staff.

On the other hand, if janitorial services are contracted, there is a single periodic charge, and the contractor has all of the payroll and supervisory responsibilities as the employer of the cleaning personnel. The arrangement may also include cleaning supplies and equipment. Such a total package can be an advantage for the manager of a small building because some types of equipment (e.g., floor buffers) may be used infrequently and therefore not a worthwhile investment for the building (although it may be possible to rent them as needed). Also, the service contractor may be able to obtain the supplies and equipment at more favorable prices because of its size. However, it is important to understand how supplies and equipment are computed into the contract cost. (Most janitorial contracts are bid on a square-foot basis.) This information is vital, not only for comparing bids from different service providers, but also for computing the value received for the fee charged. There may be a markup on supplies (cost plus a profit factor), and equipment costs may be amortized over the period of the contract. The former practice can lead to excessive charges for supplies; under the latter practice, a piece of equipment might be paid for several times over. The savvy manager will monitor labor charges and materials costs locally to be able to negotiate the best possible deal under a contract. In some situations, it may be more cost-effective for the building manager to provide the cleaning materials and invest in equipment for the contract workers to use on site.

Because janitorial work inside tenants' premises is done during off-hours, there are added concerns about the security of business assets (equipment and information) and the safety of tenants' employees who may be working late. Building management should establish a policy that requires a thorough background check, including a criminal history and documentation of the individual's employment eligibility (see Chapter 5 regarding INS Form I-9), *before* in-house janitorial personnel are hired. If janitorial service is contracted, the contractor should be required to provide the same information and documentation for all of its personnel who will work in the building. This will require careful monitoring in regard to replacement workers (employee turnover) and personnel substitutions (illness, vacation).

Preventive Maintenance. Much of the maintenance work done at office buildings is designed to keep building systems and equipment operating at peak efficiency. Preventive maintenance is a program of regularly scheduled inspections, servicing, and repairs that prolong useful life while also helping to avoid major, more-costly breakdowns.

Preventive maintenance should be scheduled so that this work is done in a timely fashion regardless of the building's other maintenance needs. In general, other maintenance tasks should be worked into the schedule so they are completed along with the preventive maintenance. The best way to plan for preventive maintenance is to collect the operating manuals and manufacturers' warranty information for each piece of installed equipment. (If manuals are not available on site at take-over, they should be obtained from the local distributor or the manufacturer. In the absence of manuals, an alternative is to work with the contract service providers to establish appropriate preventive maintenance schedules for building systems such as elevators and HVAC.) The manuals should show how components are to be dismantled for servicing and state how often they should be cleaned or lubricated or both. If a special type of oil or grease must be used, that will usually be indicated as well. Whenever possible, servicing should be planned for a time when the equipment is not being used or when its use is not at peak capacity. Substantive work on heating equipment is often done in summer months, with work on the cooling system being scheduled for winter months.

Many types of preventive maintenance tasks can be performed by staff members who are provided with the information and tools to do the job. Lubrication of fan motors and cleaning of HVAC vents and ducts are examples. However, some types of maintenance work require specialized knowledge (HVAC system repairs) or tools (elevator maintenance). Pesticide applicators have to be licensed, and they may be required to wear special protective clothing. In most situations, these types of services are best provided by contractors unless the size of a building or the extent of its installed equipment warrants having such specialized expertise on staff. (A list of frequently contracted services is included in Chapter 4. Contracting is discussed as a staffing strategy in Chapter 6 and as a maintenance policy in Chapter 5. Bidding of service contracts is addressed later in this chapter.)

Corrective Maintenance. Most of the maintenance work that results from a building inspection will be the types of repairs referred to as corrective maintenance. The dripping faucet, the frayed fan belt, the motor that is running "hot," the area on the roof where the flashing is loose—these are examples of minor repairs that, left undone, can lead to more serious problems. Making corrective repairs as soon as possible after a problem is discovered will prevent further damage to the system or equipment and avert a more costly, more time-consuming repair at a later date.

Cosmetic Maintenance. Some maintenance activities have the exclusive purpose of enhancing the appearance—i.e., curb appeal—of a property and keeping it competitive in the marketplace. Changing the landscaping at a suburban site, installing new floor coverings in the corridors and lobby, replacing building signage, upgrading the directory, and painting something simply to change its color are examples of cosmetic maintenance. These types of work need to be planned, budgeted for, and implemented along with the corrective repairs and preventive maintenance that preserve the property and keep its equipment operating optimally.

Emergency Maintenance. It is virtually impossible to anticipate everything that can go wrong in an office building. In spite of good preventive maintenance, equipment will break down. A severe storm may break one or more windows. Drains become clogged, and sinks occasionally overflow. These and similar types of problems require immediate repairs—i.e., emergency maintenance—in order to prevent structural damage or to protect the health and safety of building occupants or both.

Taking care of such emergencies is likely to disrupt a preset schedule of preventive maintenance tasks unless the office building manager makes a point of scheduling time for the variable tasks as well. This is a matter of establishing priorities so that needed repairs identified during building inspections and specific work requested by tenants can be handled in a timely fashion along with regularly scheduled preventive maintenance tasks—and it still being possible to take care of the occasional emergency repair.

Deferred Maintenance. Sometimes the most practical approach to a maintenance task is to defer it intentionally. Bad weather may preclude scheduling of parking lot repairs when potholes are discovered in midwinter. However, the work should be scheduled when the weather improves. Funds to pay for a repair may not be available when a problem is identified because a more-pressing maintenance need has already consumed the budget allocation for the month, but it may be possible to reallocate funds so the repair is made within a few weeks.

Indefinitely deferred maintenance is potentially problematic from several perspectives. Over time, small problems become big problems that are more costly to correct. Deferred maintenance in visible areas affects the general appearance of the building and the property and diminishes curb appeal. In less-visible areas, it can lead to major equipment breakdowns or structural deterioration. At worst, deferred maintenance is a sign of neglect or poor management and lowers property value. Best practice is to avoid deferred maintenance by careful planning and allocation of resources, including staff time, materials, and money.

Maintenance Strategies

A well-managed maintenance program will be proactive rather than reactive. A proactive approach requires proper planning and scheduling in advance coupled with effective time management and cost controls. Each member of the maintenance team has specific assignments, and the overall maintenance schedule includes time to respond to unanticipated service requests. A reactive approach, on the other hand, wastes time and money because people and materials are not utilized effectively—i.e., personnel are reassigned from tasks they are working on to deal with newly discovered problems.

In spite of planning and attention to preventive maintenance, equipment and systems will occasionally break down. Office building managers can minimize the consequences of breakdowns by attending to them immediately so the initial problems do not increase in size or intensity and cause additional damage.

It is always most desirable to maintain an office building in top condition. This will help attract new tenants to the building and keep existing ones in place while also preserving and enhancing investment value. Office building managers need to employ a variety of management strategies to achieve these objectives.

Making Decisions to Repair or Replace. Not only does equipment break down. Sometimes it wears out. Machines and their moving parts have a finite useful life. A major question to be answered when there is a breakdown is whether the item should be repaired or replaced. Each situation will have to be analyzed individually to determine the best strategy for building operations. The time and cost to make repairs and the nature of the problem must be weighed against the cost (and time) to replace the item. While the results of a time and cost comparison may yield a clear direction, this is not always the case. Some questions that might be asked and answered to formulate a decision are:

Is the damage repairable?

Will repairs extend the item's useful life?

How old is the item?

Can it be replaced with a more-efficient model that will save on operating costs?

What is the full cost of repairs versus replacement (including downtime and tenant dissatisfaction)?

If the problem is with a major building component, replacement may require a capital expenditure, which raises a question of how the capital will be obtained. An institutional owner may have funds available for such replacements, or the building manager may have been setting money aside in a capital reserve fund. However, when there is not such ready access to capital, a major replacement would have to be financed. Investment in capital equipment is easier to sell to an owner if the recommendation is accompanied by a cost-benefit analysis showing the payback period and return on investment (ROI). Examples of these types of calculations are presented in Chapter 13.

The owner's investment objectives will also be a consideration. Owners who intend to hold a property for several years or who want their buildings to be maintained in superior condition are usually willing to invest the necessary funds. On the other hand, an owner planning to sell the building in a year or two or whose main objective is periodic income may direct the manager to perform only the minimum amount of maintenance work needed to keep the building operating. The property itself may determine the parameters of a maintenance program. Tenants' leases may specify the quality, quantity, and frequency of certain maintenance services. On the other hand, if vacancy is high, there may not be sufficient rental income to maintain the building properly.

Bidding Service Contracts. Having maintenance work performed under service contracts has been discussed specifically in the contexts of janitorial and preventive maintenance. The operations manual should provide detailed guidelines for bidding contracts, evaluating bids, and deciding which bid will best serve the building's needs. As a rule of thumb, it is prudent to have at least three vendors bid on each service contract to obtain a cross-section of cost estimates. Each vendor should be provided with a set of uniform *specifications* for the work to be done and asked to return a bid by a certain date.

Each bid should be analyzed carefully. Even though all bidders have been provided the same basic specifications, it often happens that individual contractors have unique ways of displaying their bid information. It is important to analyze the specifics of each bid to ensure that comparisons are valid. As an added safeguard, the office building manager should ask for financial and customer references and check them out. A check with the bidders' banks should indicate the soundness and stability of their respective businesses. Other office building managers who have used the contractors' services should be asked about the quality and timeliness of the service provided and whether there were any problems related to the work being done for the stated price. Some cautions are also advised. In analyzing bids, the manager should keep in mind that the lowest bid is not always the best bid for the job. Some contractors will submit a low bid in order to obtain the job, counting on "extra" charges to make their profit. It is important to look for hidden costs. Also, if a vendor other than the lowest bidder is chosen, the reasons for the decision should be documented in a memo to the file in case the decision is challenged at a later time.

Once a vendor is chosen, a contract should be negotiated. The contract should be specific in regard to the work or service being provided. A maintenance and repair contract (e.g., for elevators) should separate costs for labor and parts. Usually labor is charged at an hourly rate, and the contract may provide for overtime charges outside of regular business hours. Charges for commonly used parts should be itemized. A janitorial service contract should spell out what is to be cleaned, how often each task is to be performed, what cleaning materials are to be used, when the work is to be done (time of day), and the size and composition of the labor force. (This may be done by reference to the building's janitorial specifications, which should then be attached to the contract as an addendum.) The contract should assign the contractor responsibility to make individual work assignments and establish on-the-job safety standards in addition to hiring, training, and supervising the cleaning personnel. The contractor should also be required to provide proof of adequate and appropriate liability and workers' compensation coverages (certificates of insurance). Before the contract is signed, it should be reviewed by legal counsel as a protection for the building manager and the property owner in the event any of the contract terms lead to litigation. If the value of such contracts exceeds the manager's authority under the management agreement, the owner's approval may have to be obtained before the contract is signed. Indeed, the owner or another authorized agent of the ownership entity may have to sign the contract.

Communicating with Maintenance Staff. A frequent challenge, especially at large office properties, is communicating with maintenance personnel on assignment throughout an office building. While *pagers* have been and continue to be popular, all pager services are not equal. Some may only flash a telephone number; in which case, the recipient must find a telephone to return the call or contact the building office. Others may delay sending messages rather than responding immediately. Either of these approaches can lead to inefficiencies as maintenance tasks are repeatedly interrupted, and management office personnel (and others) have to repeat their calls to make contact. There are effective alternatives. *Two-way radios* offer the advantages of instantaneous communication and two-way conversation. However, radios should be selected with care. They often have a limited range, which can be a disadvantage in a large high-rise building or on a suburban office campus spread out over several acres, and other radios in the vicinity can intrude on communications if both are using the same channel. *Cellular telephones* offer the same advantages as two-way radios with longer range and clearer communications. They are often smaller and lighter than radios but require an intermediate device to recharge their lightweight battery packs. (Although technological improvements continue to reduce the size of two-way radios, they often require several standard batteries, which adds weight.) Where cellular services are costly, it may not be practical to issue a cell phone to every member of the maintenance team. Instead, several units might be kept in the office and checked out by the staff on an as-needed basis. With increasing competition in the marketplace, service costs will come down, making cellular phones issued to maintenance staff members the communications device of choice. Wireless technologies make it possible to send written messages using hand-held devices. This may be another means of communicating effectively with maintenance personnel. In fact, there are devices available that combine cellular phone, two-way radio, and text messaging functions.

Computerization. Energy conservation as well as maintenance operations can benefit from computerization. Computer systems can be used to turn equipment on and off at set times and to monitor usage and function. This can provide more efficient operations and energy utilization, with attendant cost savings. Such systems can also make it possible to establish heating and cooling zones and monitor and alter hours of operation. The costs of heating and cooling outside of normal business hours can then be passed on to specific users rather than apportioned among all the tenants. (Energy conservation is discussed in more detail later in this chapter.)

Specialized software can be used for tracking maintenance work assignments (service requests, a maintenance log, preventive maintenance schedules), parts and supplies inventory, and related costs. Computer programs can also generate reports that indicate when preventive maintenance should be performed on specific equipment, with details of what servicing is needed and how often the work is to be done.

In choosing computer software, it is important to check out several programs to find one that will provide all the functions that are needed. Some multifunctional real estate management programs integrate accounting, record-keeping, and maintenance tracking modules. If it is necessary or desirable to work with separate software programs for different functions, compatibility among programs may be an important issue. Some programs may accumulate and analyze data but not generate the specific types of reports that are needed. The reporting software should be able to pull in the needed data and display it in the desired format. Often it is possible to test a demonstration version of the software for a period of time (e.g., 30 days), allowing the manager and others to see how well it fits their needs. It also helps to see the full-scale version in operation. The software provider should be able to identify other local users who would be willing to share their experiences with the program (both good and bad) and, perhaps, even provide a real-world demonstration. Compatibility with the user's existing hardware—in particular memory requirements and operating specifications—and the quality and level of technical support available are also considerations.

Complying with Regulations

Office buildings are required to comply with a variety of regulations. Many originate at the federal level, but state and local laws also apply, and they may be more stringent. The obligation is to comply with the most-stringent requirements in place locally. Workplace safety and the environment are only two such issues.

Workplace Safety. The Occupational Safety and Health Administration (OSHA), an agency of the U.S. Department of Labor, establishes workplace safety standards. It also has the authority to conduct inspections and cite businesses for violations. Office building managers should know what OSHA standards apply to the activities on the property and make sure maintenance and other employees understand and comply with them. Worker training is an especially important aspect of OSHA compliance.

Many of the materials used in and around office buildings are known to pose some type of danger to people who use them. Lubricants and solvents employed in systems maintenance, chemicals used for cleaning metallic and other finishing materials, and pesticides used for controlling insects, weeds, and animal pests are examples. Combustibility and flammability are common hazards of solvents. Pesticides and some formulated cleaning compounds are toxic; even minimal exposure can cause breathing difficulties or skin irritation or both. At an office building whose tenancy includes physicians, dentists, and related testing facilities, there is the potential risk of exposure to bloodborne pathogens. The specific types of hazards should be communicated to workers, and they should be trained in the proper handling of different materials to avoid accidents or injuries. The necessary information is readily available. Materials shipped in bulk quantities (e.g., one-gallon or larger containers), even those that are minimally dangerous, must be accompanied by a *material safety data sheet (MSDS)* that lists the type and degree of hazard they are known to pose, procedures for handling a spill or release, and first aid treatment for exposure. Smaller containers must be appropriately labeled.

Workers should also be provided with safety equipment appropriate to their duties, and they should be trained to use the equipment correctly. Protective clothing, safety glasses, rubber gloves, and respirators may be required for some activities as well.

The *Occupational Safety and Health Act*—the federal law that created OSHA—requires employers to keep their workplaces free of hazards that can cause injuries to workers. Proper grounding of electrical equipment and shields on power tools are examples of specific workplace protections. The Act also requires employers to maintain a log record of work-related injuries and to post the information prominently.

Environmental Concerns. A number of materials once considered safe for use in buildings have since been determined to be harmful to humans or the environment or both. To protect both people and the environment, regulations have been enacted at the federal, state, and local levels. Here, again, state and local requirements can be and often are more stringent than those imposed by the U.S. Environmental Protection Agency (EPA). It is always best to contact local authorities regarding procedures for dealing with environmental issues to ensure that actions taken comply with applicable laws. The materials of particular concern in office buildings include the following:

- *Chlorofluorocarbons (CFCs)* are refrigerants used in chiller components of air-conditioning systems. These compounds, which contain two types of halogen atoms—chlorine (Cl) and fluorine (F)—are being replaced with similar compounds that do not include chlorine atoms. The newer refrigerants are not always compatible with existing air-conditioning systems, but the equipment usually can be modified to use them. The American Society of Heating, Refrigerating, and Air-Conditioning Engineers (ASHRAE) can provide information on specific refrigerant chemicals and equipment modifications and costs.
- *Polychlorinated biphenyls (PCBs)* are heat-transfer agents used in electrical transformers. They are relatively harmless if undisturbed. However, a PCB-containing transformer that catches fire or leaks can release *dioxin* gas. (Dioxin is a known carcinogen.) Transformers containing PCBs must be disposed at a licensed location, and an authorized hazardous waste hauler must transport the material for disposal. State or local laws may require removal of PCBs during rehabilitation of a building. By law, new transformers cannot contain PCBs, and any existing transformers installed after 1976 would be PCB-free. Electrical transformers are usually owned by the utility company, which would be responsible for mitigating any transformer-related environmental problems. However, this may not relieve the property owner of liability for PCB contamination caused by a transformer at the site or even after its removal.
- *Asbestos* is a fibrous mineral that was used in fireproofing, insulation, floor coverings (asbestos vinyl tile), and the mastic (adhesive) used to affix them. Intact asbestos poses little hazard. However, when it is *friable* (crumbling), asbestos can be released into the air; and airborne asbestos fibers are a health hazard. Only appropriately licensed contractors can assess the condition of asbestos-containing material (ACM) in a building and, if the asbestos is friable, remove it *(abatement)* or leave it in place but prevent it from being disbursed *(containment)*.

The office building manager must determine whether there are any harmful materials in the building or on the property and whether they pose a hazard in their current state. Even if there is no potential danger, their presence alone can lower a property's value. In addition, much attention has been given to the issue of liability for leaving such materials in place or removing them, a subject that is beyond the scope of this book.

Of even greater concern than hazardous materials is the issue of *indoor air quality (IAQ),* which can be a constant source of complaints from tenants' employees. Office buildings often have poor IAQ because they have centralized HVAC systems serving large amounts of space, and most of them have been built new or retrofitted as entirely enclosed systems—i.e., windows cannot be opened. The result is poor air circulation. Building occupants may experience symptoms of *sick building syndrome (SBS)*—e.g., dizziness, drowsiness, headaches, nausea—as a result of exposure to *volatile organic compounds (VOCs),* bacteria, mold, and other contaminants circulating in the air. Organic solvents (e.g., acetone, benzene, naphtha, turpentine) are common sources of VOCs, whether used in pure form or formulated in cleaning compounds. *Legionella* bacteria can grow in fouled water-cooling towers and enter the building's air supply. They cause Legionnaires' disease, an often fatal respiratory infection. The federal government has not yet issued any regulations addressing IAQ. However, ASHRAE established an IAQ standard in the early 1990s, and the 1999 updated version ties ventilation rates to the occupancy level of a given space. The ASHRAE standard continues to evolve.

Older office buildings may have had storage tanks on the premises to maintain a fuel supply for their boilers. Because of the potential for groundwater contamination from *leaking underground storage tanks (LUSTs),* there are now regulations that require inspection (and sometimes replacement) of tanks currently in use; a tank that is no longer being used must be made safe by either removing it or filling it with cement.

Other Regulations. Building codes are usually established by the city or municipality. They are used to control the design, construction, quality of materials, repairs and alterations, and the use and occupancy of buildings. Compliance with building codes is an important aspect of tenant improvement construction as well as any remodeling or rehabilitation of the common areas of a building. For guidance regarding construction work in a geographic area where there is no specific building code, managers can refer to a published model code. Several model building codes are recognized in the United States. These include *The Uniform Building Code* published by the International Conference of Building Officials and the *BOCA® National Building Code* published by the Building Officials and Code Administrators International.

The Americans with Disabilities Act (ADA) has had widespread impact on office buildings. Parking areas, routes to and from the building, entrances, rest rooms, drinking fountains, public and common areas and routes

Energy Conservation Strategies

- Install flue gas analyzer
- Install heat recovery systems
- Install controls that allow HVAC operation in economizer mode
- Adjust thermostat settings (lower for heating; higher for air conditioning)
- Reset heated and chilled water and condenser water supply temperatures
- Implement/improve water treatment program to minimize fouling and scale development
- Insulate exposed piping and ducts
- Improve boiler or furnace combustion efficiency
- Return steam condensate to boiler
- Preheat combustion air
- Preheat boiler water
- Utilize outside (ambient) air whenever possible for heating and cooling
- Reduce unnecessary ventilation
- Lower hot water temperature
- Install devices that regulate (restrict) hot water flow
- Reduce lighting levels
- Replace lamps with more efficient (lower-wattage) versions
- Clean light fixtures when lamps are changed

These are a few steps that can be taken to improve energy efficiency in an office building. Many of them have little or no cost while some may require capital investment in equipment or control devices.

to them, and available work areas must be accessible to people with disabilities. If a building undergoes remodeling or rehabilitation, installation or replacement of faucets and relocation or replacement of doorways are among the changes that affect usability and must be made to comply with the ADA. (Specific requirements for elevators and rest rooms are outlined in Chapter 2.) The best strategy is to consult with knowledgeable professionals (architects, building contractors, attorneys) to determine whether a particular building is in compliance with ADA requirements or if changes are needed to bring it into compliance.

Energy Conservation

Office buildings consume vast amounts of energy. A furnace or boiler may burn fuel oil or natural gas, but most of the energy used in office buildings is in the form of electricity. Electricity not only powers all the technological tools used in the conduct of business—e.g., computer networks, computer hardware (central processing units or hard drives, printers, and other peripherals), photocopiers, facsimile (fax) machines—it lights all areas of the building. Electricity also moves elevators, pumps refrigerants and chiller wa-

Electrical Demand

Electric bills of large consumers of electricity often include a separate demand charge, which can represent as much as 25%–50% of the total bill. This is in addition to the charge for kilowatt-hours of electricity actually used. The demand charge is applied to the highest short-term consecutive period of electrical consumption *(peak demand)* during the billing period. The demand charge is based on the fixed costs the utility incurs in acquiring the large electrical capacity required to meet the maximum demands of electricity consumers. Lowering peak demand is one way the office building manager can reduce utility costs. This can be accomplished by implementing specific energy conservation strategies related to HVAC operations and controlling the timing of elevator operations to match the volume of traffic.

ter in air-conditioning systems, and generally runs all of the building equipment and systems, either directly or indirectly.

Deregulation has created competition among utility providers and added the management challenge of comparison shopping for energy. Instead of dealing with a single source, office building managers may purchase electricity or natural gas from one entity (generator) and pay a fee to the original utility company whose infrastructure continues to serve as the local distribution network. Monthly billings will reflect the agreed contract rate for the power provided by the generator and a separate rate for the cost of transmission and distribution by the local utility. Comparison shopping allows large users to lower their energy costs by contracting separately with a power generator. It is also possible for small users to join forces (i.e., aggregate their loads, forming the equivalent of a large user) to purchase power.

While it is important to control or reduce the amount paid for energy, it is also important to improve operating efficiency so that the level of consumption is controlled as well. (Equipment that is kept clean and properly lubricated will function more efficiently and use less energy.) It is a good practice to have an *energy audit* performed when taking over the management of a building and when a major structural or equipment change is being planned. Even more important is to have energy audits done periodically to determine whether changes already made have improved efficiency or if additional conservation measures are needed. Some utility companies will conduct energy audits at no charge.

Even without a formal audit, it is a good idea to maintain a record of energy consumption. This means analyzing utility bills at least once a year, not only to measure consumption, but also to make comparisons over time. It is also appropriate to compare the results with energy data from other office buildings. (Energy cost and consumption comparison data are included in the *Income/Expense Analysis®: Office Buildings* published annually by the Institute of Real Estate Management.)

Gas and electric utilities are a good source of consumption information. In many areas, utility bills provide prior period usage comparison data along with the consumption figures for the billing period. Some utilities offer rebates for reducing consumption or using more-efficient equipment, and these opportunities should be explored. Replacing equipment will likely require a substantial capital investment. Each such alternative should be evaluated, weighing upfront equipment costs against utility cost savings to determine economic feasibility.

Office building managers often take a step-wise approach to measuring energy efficiency. Basically, there are three steps:

1. *Convert amounts of fuel consumed to a single unit of measurement.* The preferred unit is the British thermal unit (Btu). Electricity consumption is billed in kilowatt-hours (kwh); 1 kilowatt of electricity = 3,413 Btu. Natural gas is measured in therms; 1 therm = 100,000 Btu. Fuel oil is sold by the gallon; 1 gallon of No. 2 fuel oil = 143,000 Btu. Steam is measured in pounds of pressure; 1 lb. of low-pressure steam = 1,200 Btu.
2. *Determine the total number of degree-days for the year.* A degree-day represents one degree of difference from the baseline temperature of 65°F for one day. Outdoor air temperatures above 65°F represent *cooling degree-days;* temperatures below 65°F represent *heating degree-days.* (A summer day with an average temperature of 83°F represents 18 cooling degree-days; a winter day whose average temperature is 42°F represents 23 heating degree-days.) Add heating and cooling degree-days together. Degree-day data can be obtained from the local offices of the National Weather Service or U.S. National Climatic Data Center. Often local newspapers publish degree-day data on the weather page. Information is also available on the Internet at http://weather.gov.
3. *Calculate the performance ratio on a per-square-foot basis.* Divide fuel consumption by gross square footage to determine consumption per square foot, then divide the result by the total degree-days to yield the performance ratio. The lower the performance ratio, the more energy efficient the building. (Exhibit 11.2 summarizes the steps and the mathematical formulas.)

Keeping records of energy consumption gives the manager the ability to monitor the sources of supply (utilities and other vendors) as well as evaluate the effectiveness of implemented conservation measures. Routine building inspections and maintenance procedures provide opportunities to identify areas of potential energy waste (e.g., broken weatherstripping or caulking, leaking hot water faucets). It is a good idea to involve tenants and

Exhibit 11.2
Energy Performance Calculations

Step 1: Convert the fuel consumption units to British thermal units.

Source (units)	×	**Conversion Factor**	=	**Btu (millions)**
Electricity (kwh)	×	0.00341	=	
Natural gas (therms)	×	0.10000	=	
#2 Fuel oil (gal)	×	0.14300	=	
Steam (lbs)	×	0.00120	=	

Step 2: Calculate total degree-days (thousands).
Heating degree-days + cooling degree-days = total degree-days

Step 3: Compute performance ratio.
Performance ratio = total Btu (millions) ÷ gross square footage (thousands) ÷ total degree-days (thousands)

Example:
Suppose you manage an office building with 42,000 gross square feet of conditioned space. Last year, building operations consumed 75,000 kilowatt hours of electricity and 28,000 therms of natural gas. During that period, the local area climate report showed a total of 6,500 heating degree-days and 500 cooling degree-days. What is the performance ratio for your building last year?

75,000 kwh	×	0.00341	=	255.75 million Btu of electricity
28,000 therms	×	0.10000	=	2,800 million Btu of natural gas
For a total of				3,055.75 million Btu

6,500 heating degree-days + 500 cooling degree-days = 7,000 degree-days

Performance ratio = 3,055.75 (million) Btu ÷ 42 (thousand) square feet ÷ 7.000 (thousand) degree-days = 10.39

A comparison after a change has been implemented (retrofitting with high-tech controls; replacement of a major HVAC component) should yield a lower performance ratio due to reduced gas and/or electricity consumption.

Note: Performance ratio calculations are limited in their accuracy. Because of variances in solar coverage, numbers for cooling degree-days can be misleading—it will take more energy to cool an office building on a bright day than on an overcast day, even though outdoor temperature readings on both days may be the same. The same is true for heating degree-days because those figures do not account for wind-chill factors. Calculating a performance ratio may be most useful to compare the energy efficiency of a building's operations over time.

their employees in energy conservation by providing energy-saving tips for using building equipment (HVAC, lighting) and their own business tools.

Government regulations have long dictated choices of design elements to conserve energy. Some of these measures can be applied to existing buildings as *retrofits*. Increases in the insulating values of roofs and walls, double glazing for all windows, and overall reductions in the amount of glass in a building dramatically reduce heat gain and loss in office buildings. Enclosing special gases in the void between glass panes helps reduce heat loss from inside buildings while glass with reflective or tinted surfaces can lower the amount of heat gain from sun exposure. Selection of more efficient HVAC equipment, incorporation of heat recovery systems, use of outside air or condenser water for cooling (these are no-cost items), and co-generation of electricity using steam from the turbine exhaust to provide heat or hot water in the building are other strategies that may be employed. Each must undergo rigorous cost-benefit analysis, comparing upfront costs with the potential payback in the short and long terms. (Cost-benefit analysis is discussed in Chapter 13.)

12

Risk Management, Security, and Emergency Preparedness

Office buildings have inherent dangers because of where they are built, how they are built, and how they are used. Many types of problems can be minimized or eliminated by establishing standard operating policies and procedures and maintaining the building and its equipment in good condition. In spite of these types of efforts, problems will arise. Some are more likely to occur than others. It is important to be able to manage them effectively when they do arise. This chapter will discuss various approaches to risk management, including insurance coverages, provision of building security, and emergency preparedness.

Managing Risk

Risk management is a very important responsibility of the office building manager. It includes protecting people and property and, ultimately, the property owner's investment. In order to fulfill this responsibility, the manager must understand the different types of risks that can exist at an office building and how the nature of the property exposes it to risk. In general, it will be the manager's responsibility to identify specific risks and find ways to reduce them.

Types of Risks. Office buildings present a variety of types of risks related to safety, security, emergencies, environmental concerns, employer responsibilities, and liability. Following are some examples.

- *Safety risks*—Electrical extension cords laid across an aisle where people walk, wrinkles in wall-to-wall carpeting that has stretched in place, and slippery surfaces such as wet or freshly waxed floors are potential trip- or slip-and-fall hazards. Tools and equipment used by building employees can pose workplace safety risks if not used properly. Outside the building, ice and snow can create slip-and-fall hazards for pedestrians. Accumulated snow can collapse awnings, and icicles formed on building surfaces and overhangs can fall to the ground; both have potential to cause injuries.
- *Security risks*—Entrance and exit doors and loading areas that are not properly closed and locked during off-hours and appropriately monitored (perhaps even locked) during business hours are potential access points for intruders who may steal valuable items, assault personnel who work in the building, or cause damage to the building through vandalism.
- *Emergency risks*—Emergencies can be natural (high winds causing windows on high-rise buildings to fall out of their frames, a fire caused by lightning, an earthquake) or manmade (a bomb threat, an arson fire, intentional contamination of the building's water or air supply).
- *Environmental risks*—The presence of friable asbestos-containing material (ACM) as insulation on heating ducts, release of a chlorofluorocarbon (CFC) refrigerant from an HVAC system, and contamination with a polychlorinated biphenyl (PCB) heat-transfer agent from an old transformer are examples of potential environmental hazards.
- *Employer risks*—Embezzlement of funds by an employee, sexual harrassment of one employee by another, and violence in the workplace are potential risks an employer may have to address. A disaffected employee may claim infringement of his or her civil rights in regard to hiring, compensation, promotion, termination of employment, or accommodation of a disability and file a lawsuit seeking compensation.
- *Liability risks*—All of the foregoing types of risks include liability because of specific action (or inaction) on the part of the building manager or the property owner. Safety, security, emergency, and environmental risks can lead to bodily injury, death, or damage to property of a third party. Noncompliance with accessibility requirements under the Americans with Disabilities Act (ADA) or with local building codes as they apply to tenant improvement construction and equipment maintenance is another potential source of liability.

Risk Exposure. A variety of factors contribute to the potential for exposure to different types of risks. These include the building's location, its tenant mix, and the manner in which it was constructed.

- Location—The manner in which a building is sited can pose security risks. A suburban office park whose campus is adjacent to a major highway with nearby entrance and exit ramps may be a potential target for burglary, vandalism, and other types of crime. This is especially true if the area around the office park is not built up (i.e., there are no other commercial properties or residential developments adjacent to it). Special attention to security measures such as access control and campus lighting may be required. In an urban setting, a location near or adjacent to a high-crime area will require stricter security measures to protect building workers during business hours and to protect the building itself at all times.

  Geography and climate can create emergency risks. Some parts of the United States are more susceptible than others to tornados, hurricanes, floods, and other weather-related disasters. California, in particular, is subject to earthquakes; parts of Hawaii experience periodic volcanic eruptions. The likelihood of different types of natural disasters occurring should guide the development of specific emergency procedures related to them.

- Tenant mix—Building policies and procedures should outline specific tenant selection criteria. Financial stability is important to ensure that a tenant can meet the obligations of the lease. As noted elsewhere in this book, management should consider carefully the consequences of leasing space to some governmental or social agencies, political organizations, or other potentially controversial entities because they might be targets of protests. Unfortunately, protests can lead to civil disorder and, possibly, damage to the property or injury to people who work in the building.

  Food service tenants can be a fire hazard if they are careless with cooking equipment. Food wastes can attract vermin infestations. Health care professionals need to take special care in disposing of medical wastes, including used needles and syringes. A particular hazard is infections from bloodborne pathogens such as the human immunovirus (HIV/AIDS) and various types of bacteria. Dental amalgams handled improperly can lead to heavy metals contamination. X-ray equipment can leak radiation. Laboratories that use volatile organic solvents pose risks of fire and explosion.

- Construction—Building design and method of construction can contribute to potential risk. Many high-rise building exteriors are mostly glass. High winds and pressure differences between the inside and outside surfaces of the glass have occasionally resulted in upper-story windows blowing out, endangering pedestrians and vehicles at street level. There can also be losses of paper and other items through the window opening, and these can add to the hazard. High-rise windows sometimes attract birds that fly into the glass and stun or kill themselves. They may also break the glass.

Terra cotta has been popular as a lightweight exterior finish for buildings. Glazed white terra cotta gave a clean, polished appearance to many buildings, including the Wrigley Building in Chicago. Unfortunately, the terra cotta on some older buildings has not been properly maintained. Cracks let water in behind the tiles, rusting the metal ties that anchor them to the building exterior. Pieces of terra cotta have broken or become detached from buildings, posing a hazard to pedestrians and vehicles. Some other surface finishes applied to skeletal frames have posed different problems: The marble exterior of the Amoco Building in Chicago developed cracks, which increased in number and size so that the marble could no longer withstand design loads. Eventually the marble was completely replaced with panels of white granite finished to resemble marble. Other potential exterior hazards include ornamental elements (e.g., gargoyles, replica urns), which can become detached and fall off of buildings.

Many smaller office buildings are wood frame constructions. Usually these are low-rise, one- to three-story buildings. Because wood burns easily, fire is a potential hazard. In some geographic areas, wood buildings are subject to insect (termite) infestations, which can cause major structural damage. They are also less able to withstand weather emergencies (hurricanes, tornados, flooding).

Building interiors can also pose risks. Placement of stairwells and the widths of stairways can be problematic in effecting evacuation of buildings with large numbers of people working in them. Elevator and riser shafts can allow noxious gases, hazardous liquids (from large spills), and fire to transfer between floors.

Here again, the dangers of injury or death and potential for damage to other (third-party) property are also accompanied by liability.

Building owners and managers are expected to exhibit "reasonable care" to ensure the safety and security of people inside the building and on the property outside the building. This is important when they are required to defend themselves in a lawsuit. In particular, lawyers for *plaintiffs* (injured parties) and *defendents* (the owner and/or manager) will want answers to the following questions: Could the danger have been foreseen? Is there a connection between the injury or damage that occurred and the owner's or manager's actions (or inaction)?

Identifying Risks. To protect the property, the property owner, and themselves from lawsuits, office building managers should have a qualified professional conduct a risk analysis of the property. The expert can check municipal codes and fire-safety regulations and advise whether an office building and the property as a whole are or are not in compliance. By identifying vulnerabilities (potential hazards, foreseeable accidents and crimes) the expert can recommend ways to reduce liability for their consequences. The evaluation process begins with a *security survey* that encompasses the perimeter of the building and property, the interior of the building, and pedestrian and vehicular traffic patterns in and around the building.

Perimeter Security Survey. Location, design, and age will determine the type and extent of perimeter security. For example, fencing may be appropriate to increase security at a suburban office park; it would not be a consideration for a downtown high-rise. Landscaping, which can conceal criminals along routes to and from buildings, is a feature of suburban rather than downtown office buildings. Exterior lighting, properly placed, can reduce or eliminate shadows that can serve as hiding places. Older buildings often have operable windows and exterior fire escapes that increase vulnerability because they provide additional points of entry. New construction, which features windows that do not open, is more secure by design. A security survey of the property perimeter should identify vulnerabilities that can and should be eliminated such as breaches in fencing, overgrown shrubbery, and inadequate or poorly positioned lighting.

Specific points of access such as entries, loading areas, and garages also need special attention. The perimeter security survey should address the following and document potential vulnerabilities.

Entrances and Exits

- Number, locations, and hours of operation of pedestrian entrances and exits.
- Types and effectiveness of locking devices and/or electronic access controls.
- Use of identification cards to authorize building access (including a photograph and signature).
- Method of handling off-hours entry by authorized personnel (e.g., sign-in/sign-out log).
- Method of monitoring (alarms, CCTV) and responsibility for observing/responding.

Loading Areas/Docks

- Method of operation during hours when building is open and after-hours.

- Method of controlling deliveries and removals.
- Personnel responsible for operations and monitoring.

Parking Lots/Garages

- Number, locations, and hours of operation of vehicular and pedestrian entrances and exits.
- Types and effectiveness of electronic access controls.
- Method of monitoring (patrols, CCTV) and responsibility for observing/responding.
- Placement and level of lighting throughout the facility, especially along pedestrian access routes.
- Adjunct security measures (e.g., after-hours guard escorts to/from cars, TV-monitored call stations).

Interior Security Survey. The interior security survey should focus on building staff, traffic inside the building, and methods of communication. The goal is to identify vulnerable areas and make changes as necessary and appropriate. Among the points to be considered are:

Security Guards

- Number of guards, scheduled hours, and assigned duties.
- Security checkpoints/patrol routes and schedules.
- Monitoring of checkpoints (CCTV, clock devices).
- Supervision of guards on duty.
- Location and use of security control center.
- Guard communications (guard-to-guard; guard to security control center).

Internal Traffic Patterns

- Use of stairways, including floor-to-floor travel by tenants' employees and building staff.
- Heavy traffic areas—where people are going and why.
- Methods of mail and package delivery within the building.

Internal Access Controls

- Number of master keys and method of key control.
- Types and effectiveness of electronic door locks (keypads, card systems).

Ongoing training of security guards and whether they are in-house employees or part of a contracted service are other points that may need to be considered. (Specific security measures are discussed in detail later in this chapter.)

Approaches to Managing Risk. There are four approaches to managing specific risks.

1. *Avoidance* is the elimination of a known risk. For example, buildings can be built without windows to avoid broken glass and window-replacement costs. As this example indicates, avoidance (elimination) of risk is not always practical.

2. *Control* involves taking steps to preserve life and property. For example, fire and evacuation drills help people protect themselves from injury and death; using fire-resistant construction materials and installing sprinkler systems help prevent damage to the building from a fire.

3. *Transfer* involves a shifting of risk to a third-party (a professional risk bearer) under different types of insurance policies.

4. *Retention* may be intentional or unintentional. Intentional or active retention may be chosen when the probability of loss is very low. The owner and manager may decide not to insure for a certain risk or to *self-insure* for some risks by setting aside funds to pay for losses that might occur in the future. Unintentional or passive retention may result because a risk is unknown or unobserved. For example, electrical wiring enclosed in a wall, and therefore invisible, can develop a short circuit.

The most commonly employed strategies are risk control and risk transfer. Risk is most often controlled by actions that reduce risk, and these will be discussed in this section. Specific insurance coverages will be discussed later in this chapter.

The most effective approach to risk reduction is *prevention*. Safety risks can be reduced by educating workers in the building about different types of safety hazards. For example, laying extension cords across aisles where people walk should be prohibited. Building employees should be taught the correct way to use tools and to employ protective devices and wear protective clothing when these are required. Security risks can also be reduced through education and training. Building staff or contracted security personnel should check that access to the building is properly controlled, especially during nonbusiness hours, and workers in the building should be informed of steps they can take to prevent breaches of security in tenants' workplaces. In particular, they should know whom to contact to report a breach of security in their immediate workplace or elsewhere in the building. (Establishment of policies and procedures regarding specific types of emergencies is discussed in Chapter 5. Methods of dealing with some environmental hazards are outlined in Chapter 11.)

Regular inspections of the interior of the building and the property as a whole, using written checklists, are a key component of risk management. Routine maintenance inspections should include the following fire safety-related items and verify that they are in good working order:

- Fire extinguishing equipment (fire extinguishers, fire hoses, sprinkler systems)
- Fire alarms
- Smoke detectors
- Emergency lighting
- Auxiliary electricity-generating equipment

What to do in case of a fire should be spelled out in an emergency procedures manual. Emergency contact information and instructions for reporting a fire and evacuating the building should be included in the tenant manual (see Chapter 10).

Building security requires constant vigilance. Unoccupied office suites and storage areas in the building should be checked daily to make sure they are properly secured. Security devices and systems should be checked frequently to be sure they are functioning properly, and damaged components should be repaired or replaced immediately. Specific security inspections or patrols should be conducted regularly to uncover potential problems.

Insurance companies are usually happy to assist in preventing losses. They may send a knowledgeable representative to inspect the building periodically, and the representative's findings and recommendations will be sent to the building owner and manager. It is important to correct any deficiencies immediately and notify the insurance company that this has been done. If a deficiency is in a tenant's premises, correction is the tenant's responsibility. The tenant should be informed of the deficiency and what must be done to correct it. The outcome should then be reported to the insurance company.

In general, methods employed to control risks and prevent losses can be expected to result in lower insurance premiums.

Insuring the Property

Insurance policies are designed to protect the insured party—in the case of an office building, the property owner—from financial losses due to property damage or liability. In addition, mortgagees (lenders) will usually require that a property be insured in an amount to cover their loan. Office building managers must know and understand the different types of insurance coverages that may apply to the property. The manager's role may include responsibility for purchasing insurance. It will certainly include filing claims when losses occur.

Basic Fire Insurance Policy Components

- Parties to the contract (insurer and insured)
- Term of the policy (effective and expiration dates; three years is common)
- Premium for the specified coverage (payable in advance)
- Description of the property (building, contents, improvements; location)
- Covered losses (and specific exclusions)
- Covered amounts (actual cash value versus replacement cost coverage)
- Suspension of insurance (based on increased hazard or period of total vacancy)
- Cancellation by either party (procedures to be followed)
- Subrogation (insurer can recover damages from the party who caused the loss)
- Apportionment of loss among all companies insuring the property
- Required actions to be taken in the event of a loss

These are components of a basic fire policy. State law usually prescribes the wording. The basic policy covers direct loss from fire and lightning; other perils may be added by endorsement. Exclusions are direct or indirect losses as a result of war, invasion, and rebellion and losses from riot, nuclear disaster, or explosion (unless fire ensues, in which case the fire loss is covered). Specific fixtures or improvements (e.g., foundations, parking lots, sewers or drainage systems) may also be excluded from coverage in a fire policy.

Property Insurance. The basic form of property insurance is a standard fire insurance policy. Various forms and endorsements may be added to a fire policy to extend the basic coverage. They also add to the premium. Some of the most common endorsements are described here.

- *Fire insurance*—The basic policy typically covers losses from fire and lightning strikes. It typically excludes losses caused by war, invasion, rebellion, nuclear disaster, riot, and explosion. However, if an explosion or riot causes a fire, losses attributable to the fire would be covered.

- *Extended coverage*—To provide coverage for perils other than fire and lightning, an extended coverage endorsement can be purchased. This covers direct loss or damage caused by wind, hail, explosion, vehicles, aircraft, civil disturbance, riot (including riot attending a strike), and smoke.

- *Vandalism or malicious mischief (VMM)*—Since damage from graffiti (often spray painted), breaking and entering (burglary), and other acts of vandalism is not covered in the basic policy, specific coverage may be obtained as an endorsement. The level of this kind of activity in the local neighborhood may determine the need for or desirability of such coverage.

- *Building and contents*—This special insurance form may be added to a fire policy to cover lobby or common area furnishings and fixtures that are considered *personal property* of the building owner. (This form does not cover tenants' property, which they should insure themselves as required under the lease. See Chapter 8.)
- *Rent loss*—Because the basic fire policy covers only direct losses, it is advisable to obtain this special coverage in the event the damage to the premises is so extensive that occupancy of the building may be reduced or discontinued for a time, resulting in a loss of rental income. This is usually a lender requirement because mortgage loans are often *nonrecourse* (i.e., the property pledged as collateral is the lender's sole recourse to satisfy the debt). Rent loss insurance—sometimes also called rental value insurance or business interruption insurance—reimburses the rental income lost after the damage occurs and until the building can be occupied again, thereby ensuring, among other things, that mortgage payments can be made. The cost of this insurance is based on the percentage of income value insured (40 percent, 60 percent, etc.). Owners frequently self-insure a percentage of rent loss.

Fire damage can result in unexpected expenses for researching and replacing valuable documents and records as well as removing trash and debris. These types of *consequential losses* may warrant specific consideration in determining required coverage.

A fire policy, even with extended coverage, does not provide coverage for all the possible sources of losses that can occur at a property. The location of the building (geography, climate) and the types of equipment contained within it may warrant additional specific types of coverage. Insurance can be obtained for the following:

- *Boiler and machinery*—The equipment in an office building often includes boilers, compressors, pumps, motors, and various control devices for which additional insurance coverage should be considered. This type of policy covers losses from direct damage to property of both building owner and third parties in the event of an explosion or equipment failure. Separate endorsements can be added to cover (1) repair or replacement of damaged equipment and (2) substitution of equipment essential to building operations. The latter, called *outage insurance,* reimburses at a specified daily or hourly rate for leased or rented equipment. In addition to property damage, boiler and machinery insurance includes liability protection because an explosion or breakdown could result in bodily injury. This is important coverage to have.

- *Water damage*—This type of insurance covers direct loss and damage caused by accidental discharge, leakage, or overflow of water from specific sources, among them plumbing systems and tanks used to store water that supplies the plumbing system, standpipes for fire hoses, and HVAC equipment. It also covers damage from rain or snow that enters the interior of the building through windows, transoms, ventilators, open or defective doors, or defective roofs. Exclusions from coverage include backing up of drains or sewers, seepage through building walls, floods, tidal influx, and rising surface water. It also excludes leakage or discharge from sprinkler systems; however, separate insurance is available for this latter.
- *Sprinkler leakage*—This type of coverage should be considered for buildings equipped with a sprinkler system. It covers direct loss to the building or its contents as a result of leakage from or damage to sprinkler installations and can be written as a separate policy or as an endorsement to a fire policy.
- *Plate glass*—Glass insurance covers damage caused by accidental breakage or vandalism or resulting from acids or other chemicals applied to the surface. Policy details vary according to the size (window dimensions) and thickness of the glass, whether it is tempered or tinted, and whether ornamentation or lettering is present. Policies usually cover repair or replacement of glass and protection of windows (boarding up) when replacement is delayed. If fixtures or other obstructions have to be removed to replace the glass, that is usually covered as well. While individual dollar losses may not be large, the number of windows and likely frequency of damage warrants consideration of this type of coverage for glass in common areas, especially at ground floor level. Above-ground windows are not often insured, and tenants should be responsible for plate glass in their leased premises (as required under the lease).
- *Flood*—Prior to 1968, flood insurance was not available. Even now it is only written in areas declared eligible by the Federal Emergency Management Agency (FEMA). The National Flood Insurance Program provides for government-subsidized insurance to be made available by private insurers. The insurance protects property owners from financial loss due to catastrophic floods and includes damage from inundation by mud slides. This type of insurance is very expensive, and there are specific requirements to be met by the communities in which it is written. The program varies by state, with specific exclusions being stipulated and certain conditions being uninsurable. Policies can be tailored to the needs of the insured by adding appropriate endorsements.

Actual Cash Value versus Replacement Cost Coverage

Actual cash value (ACV) means the insurer will reimburse the current value of an item after it is adjusted for *depreciation.* Thus, if equipment with an expected use life of ten years is destroyed in a fire after being in place only four years, the insurer would probably reimburse only 60% of the cost of new equipment

Replacement cost coverage means the insurer will reimburse a loss at the full current cost of the same or a comparable item (there is no deduction for depreciation).

- *Earthquake*—Damage from earthquakes is often greater than that from other causes. Consequently, the cost of this coverage is very high. The owner and manager should evaluate their situation carefully before making a purchase decision. While earthquake coverage may be written as an endorsement to a standard fire policy, as is done on the Pacific Coast, in most other areas of the United States it is written as a separate policy. (This coverage is required by many lenders in California.)
- *Demolition*—This type of insurance covers the costs of demolishing the portion of a building that was not damaged or destroyed by an insured peril. Local ordinances often require demolition of any property damaged more than fifty percent by fire or other perils. This coverage may be extended to cover the added cost of reconstruction to conform with more stringent building codes and zoning ordinances. Alternatively, such *increased construction cost coverage* may be written as a separate endorsement.

Office building managers should be aware of other property coverages that are available and consider adding them as may be appropriate. For example, commissioned or purchased artwork displayed in the lobby or other common areas would not be covered for full value unless *fine arts insurance* were purchased. If records are damaged, lost, or destroyed, it may be difficult or impossible to collect outstanding receivables; this type of loss can be covered by *accounts receivable insurance.* Along the same lines, a property owner may wish to insure against loss or destruction of financial or mortgage data, tenant lists, construction plans, and the like by purchasing *valuable papers insurance.*

Traditionally, property insurance paid claims on an *actual cash value* basis. The value of damaged property was adjusted for depreciation based on its age. Property owners could add an endorsement for *replacement cost coverage* by paying an additional premium. The latter coverage eliminated the deduction for depreciation and paid a claim on the basis of the current cost to replace the damaged item. Today, insurers typically provide coverage on a replacement cost basis and adjust the limit upward on an annual basis.

Liability Insurance. This type of insurance is often thought of as third-party insurance because the one claiming injury or damage is a third party in a triad that includes the insured (the property owner) as the first party and the insurer as the second party. The nature of rental real estate, including office buildings, and the attendant responsibility to maintain buildings and equipment creates the potential for lawsuits based on actual or alleged bodily injury or property damage experienced by the public (i.e., third parties) because of actual or alleged negligence on the part of the property owner. The need for this type of insurance is based on the premise that if a person is injured or his or her personal property is damaged while on the premises of the office building, the owner may be responsible (i.e., legally liable) for the injury or damage, in particular if the owner or an employee of the owner acted wrongfully or negligently. In the event of a lawsuit, the issuer of the liability policy will pay any monetary *damages* awarded to the claimant *(plaintiff)* against the property owner *(defendent)* up to the limit of the policy. The insurer will also pay the cost of defending the owner against the lawsuit regardless of any damages.

General liability insurance typically covers bodily injury liability and/or property damage liability and/or medical payments. A single policy may be written to cover different hazards such as the following:

- *Owners, landlords, and tenants (OLT) liability*—This form covers liability arising out of the ownership, maintenance, or use of the insured office building and all operations necessary and incidental to it. In addition to incidents occurring on and around the premises, it includes incidents that occur off site while those involved are engaged in the insured's business. Coverage is automatically extended to new acquisitions (equipment, real property) provided the insurer is given proper notice as required by the policy. The OLT liability form is usually the basic policy written for an office building, and other coverages are added to it as necessary or appropriate.
- *Personal injury liability*—This type of policy covers incidents of actual or alleged libel, slander, or defamation of character; false arrest, detention or imprisonment, or malicious prosecution; and invasion of privacy, wrongful entry, or wrongful eviction. Personal injury liability insurance is typically purchased to cover interruptions to a tenant's "quiet enjoyment of the leased premises" by a wrongful entry or evic-

tion or any other invasion of the tenant's privacy. In an increasingly litigious society, it is prudent to have this type of coverage for interpersonal incidents that might be considered libelous or because prosecution of a criminal incident can have negative consequences if the alleged perpetrator has been wrongly accused. This type of coverage should be supplemented by the purchase of *umbrella liability* insurance in amounts much higher than the basic policy.

- *Medical payments*—This coverage is typically added to certain liability policies. Members of the public who are injured on the property are reimbursed for hospital, medical, and funeral costs related to their injuries. The coverage surpasses the medical payments provision in the general liability policy, and payments are made regardless of any negligence on the part of the insured.
- *Contractual liability*—Management of office buildings involves a variety of contractual arrangements, tenant improvement construction and different types of maintenance services among them. Contracts often include hold harmless clauses that, in essence, require one party to the agreement to assume liability for another party's actions in a situation where the first party normally would not be liable. A review of existing contracts should indicate whether this very expensive type of coverage is advisable.

In order to obtain the broadest coverage, property owners may purchase *comprehensive general liability (CGL) insurance.* This type of policy covers premises and operations, elevators and escalators, and owners' protective liability (for negligent acts of others such as independent contractors). Coverage can be broadened further by adding separate endorsements. It is also possible to extend coverage by purchasing an *umbrella liability* policy that provides coverage in excess of the limits of specific liability policies and provides for legal defense in the event of a lawsuit.

Business operations related to the management of an office building commend consideration of additional types of insurance coverages. One example is *crime insurance,* which covers burglary (forcible entry) and theft of property belonging to the property owner by persons other than building employees. Protection from liability for dishonest acts by employees (e.g., theft, embezzlement) can be obtained by purchasing a *fidelity bond* on employees who handle the property owner's funds. (Fidelity bonding should be a requirement under the management agreement, and the amount of such bonds should be agreed to during the negotiations and stated in the agreement. The cost of this coverage is usually a building operating expense.) A fidelity bond is not strictly insurance because it involves three parties—a *surety* or guarantor, which may be an insurance company; the covered party or *principal* (i.e., the employee), and the party to be protected or *obligee* (i.e., the employer). The surety agrees to reimburse financial losses sustained by the employer because of the covered employee's dishonest act.

Garage keepers' liability insurance should be obtained if there is a parking garage in the office building. If the garage facilities are operated under a service contract, the contractor should provide proof of this type of coverage. If the garage is managed by the building management, whether under a separate management agreement or not, such coverage should be purchased as an operating expense of the garage. *Nonowned automobile liability insurance* should be considered if employee-owned or hired (rented) cars are used in management activities. If an employee is involved in an accident while driving his or her own vehicle (or a rental car) in performing a work-related errand, the employer could be held liable for injuries or property damage resulting from that accident. This type of coverage would protect the property owner from such liability. Vehicle owners should have automobile insurance as required by state law.

Employers in most states are required to carry *workers' compensation insurance,* which protects employees who become ill or are injured on the job. It pays for medical costs and provides salary benefits during the employee's recovery, and benefits continue if the employee is partially or permanently disabled. The premium is based on the employer's total payroll, individual job classifications, and the claims experience of the insured employer. The insurer audits the employer's payroll records annually to arrive at an adjusted premium for the next year. This is important coverage to have, even if the number of employees in an office building is below the required threshold for mandatory coverage, because if a contractor working on site does not have adequate or appropriate insurance coverage, liability for injuries to contracted workers could transfer back to the property owner or the building manager or both.

Another type of protection available to employers is *employment practices liability insurance,* which covers judgments resulting from lawsuits filed by current or former employees who claim discrimination (including nonaccommodation of a disability), sexual harassment, and wrongful termination. This is a relatively new type of insurance, and premiums are high.

Because office building managers are exposed to financial risks if they make a mistake or fail to act within the authority granted to them, it is prudent for individual managers to carry *professional liability insurance,* also known as *errors and omissions (E&O) insurance.* This type of policy covers liabilities arising out of administrative and other oversights; however, it does *not* cover gross negligence. Because the financial awards can be very large, this type of insurance is very expensive. In order to exclude small claims, E&O policies are usually written with a large deductible, and the policy carefully states what constitutes an error or omission. (This coverage is comparable to attorneys' malpractice insurance.)

Purchasing Insurance. Traditionally, properties have been insured against specific losses or casualties under a number of individual policies, each with specific limits, exclusions, and premium payments. (The earlier discussion of property insurance suggests the range of possible coverages.) Policies might have been obtained from several different carriers to maximize coverage and minimize costs. Today it is fairly common for insurance companies to offer a single *all-risk policy* that covers all perils *except those specifically excluded.* (This means losses that might be questionable under other circumstances are covered because they are *not* specifically excluded.) War, riot, and nuclear disaster are standard exclusions from this type of policy; other types of exclusions would be spelled out in the policy documents. Special needs can be addressed by adding endorsements and paying extra premiums. Property and liability coverage can be combined in a *special multiperil (SMP) policy* for the type of property. Specialized coverages such as boiler and machinery insurance and crime insurance can be added to the SMP policy as endorsements.

Insurance *premiums* are based on the amount of coverage sought or required and are usually billed annually or semiannually in advance for the period covered. (A property's size, location, and prior claims history may also be considered in quoting premiums.) Rates are usually stated as a dollar amount per $100 or $1,000 of value. This is the cost per unit of exposure. For example, if the premium rate is $1 per $100 of value, the premium for insurance coverage in the amount of $250,000 would be $2,500. Premiums vary by type of coverage and the insurer's estimate of loss potential. They are based on the law of averages for different categories of loss and the frequencies with which they occur in different types of buildings. Usually insurers will inspect the property to assess the risks, and they will recommend preventive measures that can be taken to reduce specific risks. Premiums will be reduced, for example, if a building already has sprinklers in place or if the building can be retrofitted for sprinklers and it is economically feasible to do so. Since most losses are partial, the office building manager may recommend carrying insurance for less than full value of the building, which is another way to save on insurance premiums.

Insurance premiums are also lower if the insured agrees to bear a portion of the loss. This is usually stated as a *deductible* that sets a ceiling on the loss borne by the insured party; losses above that amount will be reimbursed by the insurer. While high deductibles may lower premiums, they also require larger out-of-pocket expenditures before insurance reimburses specific losses. Deductibles can be structured in a variety of ways. The deductible amount may apply to each occurrence (each person injured, each item damaged), or it may apply to the total amount of losses (cumulative or aggregate) in a given period, usually a calendar year. If the policy is written with a straight deductible, losses have to exceed the amount of the deductible before the insurer pays anything. The deductible may be stated as a dollar amount or a percentage of the total loss. By maintaining an accu-

Exhibit 12.1
Sample Coinsurance Calculation

Suppose an office building is valued at $1,000,000. To maintain full insurance coverage with a coinsurance clause, the owner is required to carry 80% of the value or $800,000 worth of insurance. As long as the value of the building is $1,000,000, the insurance will cover 100% of losses up to the policy limit. However, if the coverage is maintained at $800,000 but the property value increases, the insured will be penalized. In essence, the insured will be required to pay the difference based on 80% of the new value versus 80% of the original value. Thus, a $250,000 loss would result in an insurance payment of the full amount of the loss if the property value was $1,000,000 at the time of the loss but only $200,000 if the property value had increased to $1,250,000 when the loss occurred (because the amount of insurance required to cover the increased property value has increased to $1,000,000). The difference is shown in the following calculations.

$$\frac{\text{Amount of Insurance Carried}}{\text{Amount Required at Time of Loss}} \times \text{Amount of Loss} = \text{Amount Paid by Insurer}$$

$$\frac{\$800{,}000}{\$1{,}000{,}000 \times .80 = \$800{,}000} \times \$250{,}000 = \$250{,}000$$

$$\frac{\$800{,}000}{\$1{,}250{,}000 \times .80 = \$1{,}000{,}000} \times \$250{,}000 = \$200{,}000$$

rate ongoing record of all losses and reviewing that record regularly, the office building manager should be able to determine a deductible amount that will minimize insurance premiums while adequately protecting the owner's investment.

Another means of controlling insurance costs is to include a *coinsurance* clause, which requires the insured to carry insurance equal to a specified percentage of the value of the property at the time a loss occurs to avoid a penalty. In return, the insured will benefit from a savings on the premium. Coinsurance is typically stated as 80 or 90 percent of the actual cash value or the replacement cost. If coverage is not maintained at the required level, the insured shares the loss with the insurer. An example of how this works is shown in Exhibit 12.1. Coinsurance has been around a long time, and existing policies may still include this clause. In some high-risk areas where losses due to flooding, tornados, or hurricanes can be massive, coinsurance may still be required. However, current practice leans toward insurers determining the amount of coverage to be representative of the 100-percent value of the building and its contents and stating that in an *agreed amount endorsement.* Under this arrangement, as long as the agreed amount of coverage is carried by the insured, the insurer will always pay the full amount of the loss up to the face value of the policy. Agreed amount coverage may include provision for automatic increases in the amount of insurance to compensate for inflation during the insurance term, with appropriate adjustment of the premium.

Policies written for the property should be in the owner's name as the *insured party*. To protect the manager from lawsuits arising out of insurable losses, the manager should be listed as an *additional named insured party* on the owner's policies for the property. This requirement should be stated in the management agreement. While insurance policies are usually written to cover a single property, an owner of more than one property may wish to cover several properties at different locations under a single policy. This type of *blanket policy* can lower the premiums for all the covered properties and is especially helpful in reducing premiums for any higher risk properties included in the group.

Insurance can be purchased through a variety of insurance producers. These include *insurance agents* who represent specific insurance companies, *independent agents* who contract with several insurance companies, or *insurance brokers* who determine a client's needs and negotiate with selected insurers to obtain the best terms and lowest possible rates. In most states, insurance policies must be countersigned by a licensed insurance agent representing the insurer. The property owner may have a relationship with a particular agent or broker or with a specific insurance company, and the office building manager may be obliged to work with that entity in arranging for insurance coverages for the property. If the manager is starting an insurance program, it may be wisest to seek the advice of an insurance consultant. The consultant will assess the property's risks and insurance needs, developing from that information a specific insurance program to be presented as a request for proposal (RFP) to several insurance producers for competitive bids. If the manager is employed by a real estate management firm, there may be personnel in the firm's office who can develop a building-specific insurance program or even write the insurance. The goal should be to provide the best quality insurance coverage to meet the needs of the building and its ownership and to do this at a reasonable cost.

Once insurance has been purchased, the manager should review the various exclusion provisions to understand what is *not* covered by the policy or policies and under what conditions the exclusions apply.

Handling Losses. Before any losses are experienced, the office building manager can take steps to facilitate claim adjustments when losses do occur. These include creating and maintaining detailed written records of items that are insured. These types of documentation can be very helpful in establishing specific losses and preventing misunderstandings as the loss-adjustment process moves forward. It is also good practice to maintain a photographic record of equipment in place as well as structural and finish elements. Photographs will be invaluable in establishing specific losses by comparing pictures of damage to those of the items in an undamaged state. Still photographs may be most helpful in documenting nameplate data (manufacturers' serial numbers and operating specifications) and similar information for building equipment or to identify works of art. It may be preferable to videotape areas with numerous pieces of equipment or to provide a comprehensive panoramic record of an interior or exterior area. Photographic records should be updated as equipment is replaced or changes are made to the building.

The insurer should be notified immediately when a loss occurs. The time requirement for notification is usually stated specifically in the policy, and the insurance agent or broker is usually the entity to be notified first although a major loss should be reported directly to the insurance company. (Violation of the notification requirements can result in penalties for the insured.) Claims may be adjusted by the insurance agent or by adjusters employed by the insurer. In situations where there are multiple insurers (e.g., very large office buildings where different types of specialty coverages may be carried) and the dollar loss is large, the insured may ask to have an independent professional adjuster evaluate the loss and apportion it among the various insurers. It is very important to have a complete record of all losses along with known costs to repair or replace damaged equipment or structural elements *before* the manager agrees to sign a "proof of loss" statement as the agent of the owner.

It is standard practice for the insured to secure competitive bids for repairs or replacements when losses occur. This is usually a responsibility of the office building manager. If the nature or extent of a loss precludes competitive bidding, the insurer should agree up front to accept a single bid so that work can proceed quickly. When dollar losses are large, however, insurers will usually insist that competitive bids be submitted to them for approval *before* work is started. Because insured and insurer will not always agree on the amount of a loss or whether a particular loss is covered, many types of policies provide for disputes to be settled by arbitration.

In reporting a damage loss, the manager should assemble the following types of information.

- Name, address, and telephone number of the insured. An e-mail address may also be appropriate.
- Name, address, telephone number, and position title of the person to contact for additional information.
- Date and time the loss was incurred.
- Location of the damage (building address *and* exact location within the building).
- Estimated cost of repairs/replacement.
- Identification of who will do the work.
- Original builder of the damaged property or original manufacturer of the damaged item.
- Date of building completion or purchase date of manufactured item.
- Witnesses/notification of authorities (fire department/police department).

- Detailed description of damage and cause (e.g., fire, explosion).
- Signature of person filing report and date of submission.

The management firm may have a standard form for documenting losses and providing notice to insurers. Otherwise, the manager may develop a generic form that can be used to document most types of damage-related losses. The insurance policy should state the types of information to be submitted when filing claims. The insurance company may have a standard form for its agents to complete, and the agent may be able to share an example to use as a model. This will ensure that all pertinent information is documented appropriately and expedite the claim process.

Liability losses require different types of information to be reported. Here again, the management firm may have a standard form for reporting accidents, or the manager might seek guidance (or an example form) from the insurance agent. An accident report should include the following types of information.

- Name, address, and telephone number of the person preparing the report.
- Date, time, and location of the accident.
- Detailed description of the accident.
- If a person was injured—
  —Name, address, telephone number, age, employer, and occupation of the injured party.
  —Description of how the injured party was hurt (what the person was doing when injury occurred).
  —Nature and extent of the injury.
  —Where the injured party was taken after the accident.
  —Whether the injured party resumed work/probability of disability.
- If property was damaged—
  —Name, address, and telephone number of property owner.
  —Description of damaged property and estimated cost of repairs/replacement.
- Who called authorities (ambulance, fire department, police department) and when.
- Names, addresses, and telephone numbers of witnesses to the accident.
- Signature of person filing report and date of submission.

If available, photographs of the damaged property or the area where the injury occurred should be attached to the written report form. Accident reports should also include information about the condition of the building at the time of the accident and any unusual circumstances that would assist an attorney in defending the insured against a lawsuit, if that becomes necessary.

Documentation of accidents taking place within tenants' leased premises should include the tenant name and suite number and identify a person to contact for additional information.

Accidents involving employees of the building (i.e., management employees) are handled differently. If an employee is injured, a report must be filed with the state industrial commission or other agency that handles workers' compensation. Most states will have a specific form to be completed, and copies of the form as filed with the state agency should be sent to the workers' compensation insurance company and any other entities required by law.

Regardless of the size or severity of a damage loss or accident, *all* occurrences should be reported to the insurance company. If damage to the property is minor, or if the amount of liability damages seems likely to be inconsequential and legal action is unlikely, the report can be marked "for information purposes only."

When a major loss occurs, it may be only a matter of hours—but it could be several days—before the insurance agent or an authorized insurance adjuster can get to the property and assess the damage. In the meantime, the building manager should protect the property by taking steps to limit consequential damage (e.g., arrange for broken or missing windows or doors to be boarded up and for utilities to be shut off). To this end, the manager should have a list of tradespeople and other service providers who can be contacted in an emergency.

Property and casualty insurance policies will include a *subrogation* provision that allows the insurer to recover amounts paid to an insured party for damage caused by an at-fault third party. For instance, if an automobile strikes a building and causes damage, the property owner's insurance may pay the claim, but the vehicle owner's insurance should cover the loss. Under subrogation, the property owner's insurer can seek reimbursement from the vehicle owner's insurer. The subrogation provision prohibits the insured from waiving the insurance company's rights in this regard. However, if the insurer is willing to forego this right, a separate *waiver of subrogation* provision will be written into the insurance policy.

Building Security

Security is not only a risk issue for office building managers. It is a very important aspect of the service provided to tenants and their employees. People like to feel secure in their workplaces. Business owners want their business assets (equipment, documents) and personal property to be protected from theft and destruction. Security is an increasingly important consideration for prospective tenants along with building location and quality of office space. In selecting and implementing specific security measures, the need to protect management staff, tenants' employees, and visitors to the building should be considered along with the costs.

The Dangers of Marketing "Security"

In trying to compete effectively for tenants, office building managers may actively promote the level of security in their buildings. This strategy is potentially problematic. Not only is a promise of security likely to create unrealistic expectations, it can also backfire, making prospects think the property is unsafe or has problems that do not exist. Promoting security may also lead to liability that would not ordinarily arise. Ownership and management could be blamed because they did not provide the promised level of security if someone is assaulted, injured, robbed, or killed in the office building. The recommendation against marketing security means *not* mentioning security in advertising space for lease. It also means avoiding the appearance that security is "guaranteed"—e.g., if CCTV surveillance is used, all cameras should be operational.

On the other hand, prospective and existing tenants do need to know the types of security measures that are in place in the building and how different security devices work. In addition, building staff, contract workers, and tenants' employees should be educated about security measures that are in place and how they protect people in the building. They also need to understand that they are responsible for security of their persons and their personal property and that there are actions that should be avoided because they can breach building security.

The range of security measures provided in a particular building will depend on the building's location (e.g., the level of crime in the neighborhood), its tenancy, and the types of security-related problems that exist now or are likely to arise in the future. The available budget for security will also be a factor. Consideration should be given to the adequacy and appropriateness of access control systems, alarm systems, and closed-circuit television (CCTV) surveillance and the role of on-site security guards. If guards are employed, it may be necessary or appropriate to establish a security control center. Regardless of the specific security measures employed, lighting in and around the building is very important to the perception of security as well as the prevention of security problems. The discussions that follow describe the measures identified here. These are all fairly standard. It should be noted, however, that this is *not* the entire spectrum of possible security measures. Buildings that require very high levels of security may warrant installation of x-ray scanning and metal detection devices as additional access controls. Also, the array of security measures is continually expanding as new technologies are developed. Office building managers should keep up with new security products and services to determine when and whether it is appropriate to replace or upgrade existing security measures. It is also important to determine who will be liable in the event a specific security measure is breached. Liability of building ownership and management in regard to security issues should be considered in evaluating insurance needs and purchasing appropriate liability coverages.

Access Control. The simplest access control devices are locks and keys. Because there will be *master keys* for tenants' premises as well as doors in common areas of the building, it is a good idea to develop a key control system to limit access to these keys. Building size will be an important factor in determining the number of master keys and the extent of the system. There may be a few grand master keys that open every door in the building as well as a series of different master keys that open one type of lock or all doors on a single floor or in one area of the building. The problem with master keys is that if one is lost, all the locks it opened will have to be rekeyed, and meanwhile, the security of the entire building may be jeopardized. It is important to keep track of all master keys and maintain a list of all persons who have one. A professional locksmith can recommend an appropriate key control system based on a review of current key-handling procedures in the building.

In addition to master keys, which are important in providing access by janitorial and management personnel to tenants' leased premises, there are many types of electronic door locks that can be installed on building and tenant doors. Electronic door locks provide an additional measure of security. They may be used by tenants to control access by their employees and keep nonemployees out of their premises. They can allow after-hours access to the building by authorized personnel while keeping unauthorized personnel from entering. In particular, they can facilitate enforcement of a policy requiring all doors (except possibly the building's street-level entrance) to be kept locked at all times.

One type of electronic door lock is controlled by a keypad. Keypads use numeric codes to control access. Authorized personnel are required to push a button or to touch or apply pressure to a smooth surface adjacent to the appropriate numbers. Most have a manual override that is controlled by a receptionist or attendant, who can release the lock to admit authorized visitors or part-time workers, and the same code can be used to control multiple doors. The advantage over keys is that the numeric code can be changed more easily and for less cost than changing locks when an employee leaves the company or is terminated.

Another type of door lock uses a card or other device to release the electronic lock. Cards may include a magnetic stripe or an embedded chip to be scanned by a device mounted next to the door. The card may have to be swiped through the device or held in front of it or pressed onto it. Either way, an authorized card will complete a circuit that opens the door lock. Card systems can be used to control multiple doors. Because the programming is more sophisticated, card systems can be used to limit access to specific areas.

Unfortunately, electronic door locks are not impenetrable. A keypad system can be breached by someone giving the code to an unauthorized person or by an authorized person holding the door for one or more additional unauthorized personnel to pass. It is also possible, with enough time and persistence, for someone to figure out the code. While more difficult to breach than keypads, card systems can be breached by passing a card to an unauthorized person. It is also possible to counterfeit some types of cards.

The nature of electronic locking devices warrants consultation with an expert installer. The number of people who will use the system, the type of system programming and its reprogramming capabilities, the areas to be protected, and specific security needs are among the points to be considered in choosing an electronic locking system. Installation should preferably include an alarm mechanism that will signal when the keypad or card reader has been tampered with or when the door is held open too long. Because they rely on electricity, a back-up source of power must be available. Cost is also a consideration. While electronic controls provide greater security, they are more costly than keys and locks.

Alarm Systems. An *intrusion alarm* system will not prevent unlawful entry, it will only advise that an access point has been breached. A variety of technologies have been applied to signal intrusions. Passive infrared motion detectors signal rapid temperature changes, as from body heat. However, being temperature sensitive means these detectors can register false alarms from drafts, sunlight, or HVAC outlets located too close to them. Ultrasonic motion detectors transmit high-frequency sound waves within the detection area to a receiver. (Transmitter and receiver may be combined in a transceiver.) Movement in the alarmed area increases or decreases the frequency of the transmitted sound waves, and an alarm is signaled if the receiver detects a change. These, too, are subject to false alarms, in this case from objects in motion, high-pitched sounds, and air turbulence. Magnetic contacts may be used on doors and windows—one magnet is attached to the moving part, another (the switch) is hard-wired to the stationary doorjamb or window frame. They form a closed circuit when aligned; movement of one of the magnets opens the circuit and activates the alarm. However, incomplete circuits (loose-fitting or warped doors) can result in false alarms.

There are also more-specialized applications. Metallic foil tape may be applied to glass around the perimeter of windows and wired into the alarm circuitry. A break in the tape opens a circuit, signaling an alarm. Shock sensors may be mounted on walls or roofs as well as window frames. Used to detect energy shocks (hammering, chopping, etc.), the level of sensitivity is adjustable, but false alarms can be triggered by loose frames. Safes or cabinets may be equipped with capacitance devices called proximity detectors. The circuitry is highly sensitive and will detect an intruder approaching the protected cabinet or safe.

Fire alarms are part of the overall building alarm system. Pull stations mounted behind glass are commonly installed on individual floors. The glass must be broken to access the pull mechanism and manually activate the alarm. Different types of automatic detection devices are commonly used as well. Smoke detectors may be required by law. These serve as early warning to building occupants and can be set up to close fire doors, trigger extinguishing devices (e.g., sprinklers), notify the local fire department, and stop elevators (preventing their use except by fire fighters) as well as shut down air-handling equipment and start exhaust fans. Heat detectors are used to trigger sprinkler extinguishing systems. There are also devices that detect flames visible to the human eye (ultraviolet type) or invisible to the human eye (infrared type).

Intrusion alarm systems are typically wired to sound an alarm in the management office or the security control center. Fire alarms usually sound where smoke or fire has been detected and at the local fire station as well as in the building management and security offices. Alarm systems should be installed by knowledgeable professionals. This will ensure that the signals and transmissions are appropriate to the building and minimize false alarms. It will also ensure that the alarm system is adequate without being excessive.

For alarm systems to be effective, there must be personnel (in sufficient numbers, properly trained) to respond when alarms sound, and the systems must be inspected regularly and maintained in operating order. For these reasons, managers often choose to have building alarm systems monitored off site by an alarm service. Because this would be a contracted service, it should be bid by several vendors. While the building manager may be able to develop some specifications, it may be more appropriate to have potential vendors evaluate the areas to be alarmed and submit a proposal based on that evaluation. The resulting contract should identify all the equipment to be used (it should be UL-listed), state where different components would be installed, and include a wiring diagram, as well as describe provisions for off-site monitoring. Usually there is a monthly service charge for monitoring, and there may be separate charges for inspecting or repairing equipment; these should be spelled out in the contract as well. Telephone lines are the usual connection between the alarmed site and the service office so it is important to have adequate telephone infrastructure. As with all contractors, references should be checked to determine how other office building managers have been served in regard to vendor response to service requests, quality of service, and monitoring and other charges.

Closed-Circuit Television Monitoring. The purpose of CCTV monitoring is surveillance and deterrence. A basic system consists of one or more cameras, monitors, and time-lapse recorders. More-sophisticated systems include a microphone so guards can speak and listen to someone in camera range as well as observe people and activities. Some systems provide split-screen and picture-in-picture multiple images on a single monitor. The owner's and manager's surveillance goals should determine the choice and placement of equipment. The quality of the equipment chosen will determine the quality of its imaging and the overall capabilities of the system. An economic consideration is that a camera can be positioned at any location where placement of a guard might be considered, offering potential savings in labor costs. Cameras give additional eyes (and sometimes ears) to a single guard who can monitor several screens at once. Primary positioning of cameras would be to monitor building entrance and exit doors, loading areas and docks, elevator entryways, garage entrances and exits, and vulnerable tenant areas, including public corridors.

There is a limit to how many monitors one individual can watch effectively. To overcome this limitation, an audioactivity alarm (a type of motion sensor) can be installed on each camera. An alarm will sound at the monitor station when there is any movement in a camera-supervised area. This provides some visual relief because the guard can do other work at the station rather than watching the monitors exclusively. A timed-sequence cycle of images from several cameras can be directed to a single monitor, allowing comparable coverage with fewer monitors and reducing potential guard fatigue.

It is best to proceed with caution in choosing a company to install a CCTV system. Equipment should be properly installed by company-trained technicians, and there should be round-the-clock technical support to troubleshoot problems. (A comprehensive contract will provide for periodic inspection and preventive maintenance service of installed equipment.) The contract should specify all the equipment (manufacturers' makes and models) and accessories to be used in configuring the system and itemize the costs of equipment, installation, and ongoing service. As with any contractor working on site, proof of insurance should be required.

Security Guards. The first decision is whether or not to use guards, and if guards are deemed appropriate, the more important decision is whether to employ them directly or contract with a guard service. If guards are on-site employees, the building owner and manager will be presumed to be responsible for protecting tenants, their employees, and their property, thereby incurring legal liability they may not have intended. Contracting with an outside guard service limits the owner's and manager's risk while also providing staffing flexibility (a contractor can provide additional guards on short notice or in emergency situations), handling payroll and record keeping, and dealing with personnel problems that arise among the guard force. The service also can replace guards more quickly than a building manager can. Because of the attendant liability, management should confer with legal counsel before hiring security guards as building employees.

As with other building services provided under contracts, the negotiated contract for security services should spell out the quality of service to be provided (number of guards and their duties, training and retraining of personnel, level of supervision) and the cost of providing their service. Guard services usually quote an hourly rate, so it is prudent to inquire about the hourly pay of individual guards, which will determine the quality of service. (Low-paid guards may not be qualified if the required guard duties are sophisticated.) Multiple bids should be sought in response to a request for proposal (RFP). In developing the RFP, the manager should determine the duties required of the guards, the skills required (or desired) to perform those duties, and the desired hours of coverage. The bidding contractors can then recommend a specific number of guards and a range of rates to provide the level of service being sought. The RFP should also require the contractor to guarantee that individual guards will not be changed or relocated without the manager's approval. The contractor should be required to provide proof of adequate workers' compensation and liability insurance coverage and to have the building owner and manager listed as additional named insured parties on the policies. Due to the nature of the work and the need for guards to be on site around the clock—perhaps to have access to tenants' premises as well—the contractor should also be required to provide proof of criminal background checks and employment eligibility for its workers. It goes without saying that the contractor's references should be checked, including and especially other local office building managers who use the security guard service.

The guard service should not be expected to provide 100-percent security (no matter how many guards are used, this cannot be done). Rather, the service should be a *visible presence of security* by patrolling the building and thereby signaling to potential intruders that they are being watched. On the other hand, a guard's presence at the same place and the same times every night indicates that criminal activity in that area would not be observed during the time between those appearances. One way to avoid this situation is to conduct patrol tours at erratic times and change the patrol time and sequence frequently.

A floor-by-floor patrol should cover public corridors, requiring guards to check for unlocked doors and verify that individuals they encounter have proper identification. Guards should also check rest rooms and walk down stairways, noting potential fire hazards and anything else that is out of the ordinary. Patrols should include any garage within the building or attached to it.

Frequency of patrols during a 24-hour period will depend on the types of security concerns. A complete inspection should be made after the cleaning personnel have finished their work, checking to make sure all lights (except code-mandated or emergency lights) have been turned off and all corridor doors have been secured. Other tours should be required as necessary or appropriate. Installation of clock stations at different locations and a requirement to punch the clock at each station along a guard's assigned route will provide an accurate record of patrols. Because guards cannot be in all places at all times, it is usually advisable to supplement patrols with CCTV surveillance.

Security Control Center. The security control center is often a desk or counter in the lobby set up with CCTV monitors and control panels that identify the sources of alarms. Building size, the number and types of alarm points, and the number of CCTV monitor screens will determine how extensive the control center must be. Because there are practical limitations to what a single individual can do, it may be necessary or appropriate to have several persons involved in monitoring building security systems. In that case a separate room in a protected location may be appropriate. Since this will also serve as the command post for the security guards from a contracted service, lockers and washrooms should be readily accessible. Security personnel should wear uniforms that identify their role and the company that employs them. If security personnel are employees of the building, the management office may include space designated as a security control center.

Lighting. Lighting is an especially important component of perimeter security. Street lights in downtown areas usually provide adequate ambient light for pedestrians and vehicles. Outside of the downtown area, however, it often becomes the responsibility of property owners and managers to ensure that lighting levels are adequate, not only on their property but also around it. Lighting is needed for walkways, parking lots, building entrances, and other areas where people typically walk at night. Entire areas should be illuminated, and lights should be positioned so that it is difficult for intruders to hide in the shadows. Lighting inside garages and enclosed pedestrian walkways that are part of the office building require the same level of attention. It is important to change bulbs and clean light fixtures regularly because light intensity diminishes as bulbs age and dirt accumulates on fixtures. Mechanical timers may be used to turn outdoor lighting on and off, but they will have to be reset as the seasons change. Photosensitive devices that respond to changing light levels and motion sensors that detect the presence of activity offer the advantage of being automatic.

Emergency Preparedness

The first step in preparing for emergencies is to establish specific policies and procedures for different situations. Of particular importance in office building management are emergencies caused by fire, power failure, criminal acts, bomb threats, and civil disorder. Natural disasters such as flooding, hurricanes, and earthquakes as well as hazardous materials incidents (e.g., chemical spills) should also be addressed as appropriate for the geographic area and the building tenancy. Specific emergency procedures as components of the property operations manual are addressed in Chapter 5, and inclusion of emergency procedures information in a tenant manual is covered in Chapter 10.

Emergency preparedness means having in place a well-trained *emergency response team* whose primary responsibility is to expedite evacuation of the building in an emergency. Members of the building management team should be joined by representatives from tenant companies. On multitenant floors, team members may represent the floor rather than an individual tenant. It is best to work with the local fire department in identifying the roles and responsibilities of an emergency response team for a specific building. While titles may vary regionally, the positions and roles noted here are representative.

- Fire warden or area captain—This is the team leader for the floor or specific area of the building. Usually an assistant fire warden or area captain is also appointed so there will be a backup team leader if the primary person is not available. This person supervises the evacuation process.
- Floor leader—This person, representing a single tenant on a floor or an entire multitenant floor, makes sure everyone knows where stairwells are and is responsible for orderly evacuation of his or her work area. There may be more than one floor leader for a tenant or floor.
- Searcher—Usually there is more than one searcher who makes sure all areas, including rest rooms, have been evacuated. There may be a requirement that those who work in private offices close their doors as they leave. Alternatively, this responsibility may fall to the searchers who will apply a Post-it® note or other easily removable adhesive label low on the door (around 12 inches above the floor) as an indicator that a room or enclosed area has been checked.
- Stairwell monitor—There should be one monitor on each floor for each stairwell. This person ensures that people evacuating a floor keep to one side going down (or up) so that firefighters can also use the stairwells. If a stairwell is filled with smoke, these monitors prevent people from entering it and direct them to another exit.
- Elevator monitor—Depending on building configuration, it may be appropriate to have one monitor on each floor for each bank of elevators that stops there. The monitor is responsible to keep people from entering elevators because they might not work at all or, if they are working, it is always possible they could stop on a burning floor

because a heat-sensitive call button was activated. (Elevator service should be stopped immediately in an emergency and the elevators returned to the ground floor for use by firefighters if appropriate.)

- Handicap aide—These people are responsible for moving handicapped workers to safe areas in stairwells where they can be rescued by firefighters. A tenant who employs a number of handicapped workers may need several aides; on a floor where there are no handicapped workers, there may be no need for such an aide. Building management should ask tenants to provide details on their handicapped employees—who they are, where they work in the tenant's space, and the nature of their disability. This will assist in emergency evacuation planning for the tenant and for the building.

The local fire department may recommend additional or different roles for team members, and the department's guidance should be followed. To expedite evacuation of multitenant floors or tenant offices with multiple entrances, a member of the evacuation team should have a master key that will open all the corridor doors on the floor.

It is important to conduct evacuation drills periodically to ensure that everyone can get out of the building safely and quickly. Recommended fire department procedures should be followed in this regard. In some cities, evacuation during a fire may be only to clear one or two floors above or below the fire floor. Other cities may require evacuation of three or four floors above or below the fire floor. Having fire department personnel supervise an evacuation drill will ensure that proper procedures are being followed and identify potential problem areas that need to be addressed.

Emergency response team members will need training to be effective. Training should include descriptions of their specific duties and how to perform them as well as a floor plan of the area for which they are responsible. This should include all stairwells, elevator banks, rest rooms, private offices, and other enclosed spaces on the floor. Searchers, in particular, need to know how to conduct a search and verify for fire personnel who follow that an area is clear. Special training may be necessary for handicap aides, especially if any workers in the building have complex disabilities. Vision- and hearing-impaired individuals will require different types of assistance than those who are confined to wheelchairs. If handicapped individuals are accompanied by assistive animals, provision must be made for the animals' safe evacuation as well. Personnel assigned to make announcements over a building-wide public address (PA) system need to know how much information to give and how to present it. The preferred strategy is to develop scripts that address specific emergencies with blank spaces into which details of the current situation can be inserted (see discussion of PA systems in Chapter 5).

Additional Emergency Considerations

National and international events can have an unexpected impact. In the wake of terrorist attacks against the World Trade Center and the Pentagon, office building managers have tightened existing security measures and implemented such additional procedures as may be appropriate for their buildings' tenancies. In addition, local governments have scrutinized building codes and made changes to facilitate evacuation of high-rises. Review of emergency procedures and building insurance coverages may be an ongoing process as a result. Managers should consult with appropriate governmental agencies to facilitate compliance with new requirements. They should also consult with the companies that have written property insurance for the buildings they manage to ensure adequate coverage in the event of losses from acts of terrorism.

Training and retraining should be an important component of the building's emergency preparedness program. The local fire department can advise on particulars and may be willing to do the training. To foster a team spirit as well as identify members of the team, it may be desirable or appropriate to distribute baseball caps or a specially designed name tag to be worn during drills and in the event of an emergency. This will help workers know that they are being directed by designated members of the evacuation team.

Evacuation is a critical response to many crises, among them power failures and bomb threats as well as fire. However, evacuation is not the only issue to be addressed. Specific procedures should be developed for handling different types of breaches of security. Security personnel and members of the management team need to know what to do, whom to contact in addition to police and other authorities, and how to recover from the security breach. Documentation of the incident and reporting to the insurance company should also be covered. Theft of money or property, vandalism, and bringing a weapon into the building are just a few examples of incidents that should be anticipated in emergency procedures.

Yet another important aspect of emergency preparedness is public relations (PR). In any crisis situation, it is too easy for an off-hand remark to be captured by an eager journalist. The next thing the manager knows, he or she is quoted in a newspaper or shown on television. Public relations and media consultants recommend development of a *crisis management plan.* This should be a written plan that includes identification of a designated spokesperson, a list of media contacts, and strategies for handling the reactions of building employees, tenants and their employees, the media, and the community at large. The best way to start a plan is to make a list of possible scenarios along with questions people and the media are likely to ask about them.

Issues to address include any type of natural or manmade disaster and its potential outcomes (likely injuries, even deaths). Many other types of situations should also be considered. An employee of the building or a worker in the building (a tenant's employee) might be arrested on site. Building management might be sued by a visitor for a slip-and-fall injury or because something fell from the building and hurt them. People have committed suicide by jumping out of windows in high-rises. Lawsuits may be brought by former employees for discriminatory employment practices, wrongful termination, or injuries that resulted from negligence related to another employee (e.g., negligent hiring, supervision, or retention). These are just a handful of obvious examples. It is important to consider all the possibilities and develop a strategy for handling each of them. Approaching crisis management from the standpoint of a worst-case scenario will ensure that the less-disastrous incidents are properly addressed as well. It will also ensure that media scrutiny does not add to the crisis and that public perceptions of the building and its ownership will be as positive as possible.

13

Maximizing Value—Analysis of Alternatives

A management plan is the substantive component of a proposal to manage a specific property. Once the proposal is accepted by the property owner, the management plan will guide the day-to-day operations of the property and serve as a measure of the manager's success in achieving the objectives stated in it. Development of a management plan begins with a thorough analysis of the property, its environs, and the marketplace in which it competes. The development process is guided by the owner's financial goals for the property. The market analysis component of the plan is critical to understanding local rent levels and to establishing a rental schedule for the office building. However, property income is not the only focus of a management plan. A longer-term perspective requires assessment of the physical condition of the building, review of property income and expenses as part of the larger financial picture, examination of the way the property is marketed to prospective tenants, and evaluation of the effectiveness of current management. Market analysis and development of a rental schedule have been described in detail in Chapter 7. The focus of this chapter will be on the owner's goals, problem identification, and analysis of alternatives.

The Owner's Goals

As was indicated in Chapter 1, a real estate owner's investment goal may be a regular income, a way to lower personal income taxes, capital appreciation, or all of these. Initially, the owner may want to invest in capital im-

Exhibit 13.1

The Cash Flow Chart

	Gross Potential Rental Income
minus	Vacancy and Collection Loss
plus	Miscellaneous Income
equals	Effective Gross Income
minus	Operating Expenses
equals	Net Operating Income (NOI)
minus	Debt Service (Interest and Principal)
minus	Reserves for Replacement and Capital Expenditures
equals	Pre-Tax Cash Flow
minus	Income Tax
equals	After-Tax Cash Flow

provements and support high mortgage payments that provide substantial income tax deductions for cost recovery and mortgage interest. After the property has been held for many years, the owner may expect it to be a major source of retirement income and prefer to make lower mortgage payments to maximize that income. An owner may plan to hold the investment for a specific period of time and then sell at a profit. During that time, the manager may be called upon to develop management plans that include major as well as minor renovations, especially if the expected holding period is ten years or longer. For that owner, increased value (i.e., capital appreciation) at the point of disposition will be paramount. The income stream from a real estate investment is usually tracked using a cash flow chart. Capital appreciation is measured as an increase in property value.

Cash Flow. For the owner whose goal is periodic income, the bottom line is the property's cash flow. Cash flow from a management perspective is what remains after debt service has been paid out of net operating income (NOI). Also deducted from NOI are monies set aside as reserve funds and direct capital expenditures. The remainder is the *pre-tax cash flow*. However, the owner's actual profits are the money remaining after income taxes have been paid—i.e., the *after-tax cash flow*. The cash flow chart in Exhibit 13.1 demonstrates this.

In office building management, however, the cash flow chart is often expanded because leases typically require tenants to reimburse operating expenses of the property as a separate pass-through charge in addition to base rent. Because of the dollar amounts involved, it may also be important to list loss items or items paid out of NOI separately. Such an expanded version of the cash flow chart might look like the one shown in Exhibit 13.2.

Reserve funds are typically set aside to accumulate money to pay for

Exhibit 13.2

Expanded Cash Flow Chart

	Gross Potential Rental Income
minus	Vacancy
minus	Collection Loss
equals	Net Rent Revenue
plus	Expense Reimbursements (pass-throughs)
plus	Miscellaneous Income
equals	Effective Gross Income
minus	Total Operating Expenses
equals	Net Operating Income (NOI)
minus	Debt Service (interest and principal)
minus	Reserves for Replacement
minus	Capital Expenditures
equals	Pre-Tax Cash Flow
minus	Income Tax
equals	After-Tax Cash Flow

major repairs or replacements planned for the future. Capital expenditures, on the other hand, are amounts paid out of NOI for capital items without regard for prior accumulation of reserves. The owner's (and the property's) cash situation usually determine these items. A sole proprietor who owns a small office building may establish a reserve fund, expecting the property to be economically self-sustaining so that he or she will not have to provide funds out of pocket. However, institutional owners typically do not accumulate reserves; instead they draw on available capital to fund major repairs and replacements.

In developing a management plan for an office building, the manager must anticipate the impact of changes on cash flow as well as NOI.

Valuation. The value of an office building can be determined in different ways. Four methods are recognized within the real estate industry.

1. *Cost approach*—This method bases property value on the cost to replace the improvements on the land (e.g., buildings) plus the value of the land itself. Land value is estimated from recent sales of comparable properties or nearby vacant land. Construction costs are adjusted for *depreciation* of existing improvements (i.e., loss of value due to physical, functional, or economic obsolescence) and take into account the owners intent either to *reproduce* the building using exactly the same materials to build an identical structure or to *replace* it with a structure of comparable function and utility using modern materials. Except for rare instances when it is necessary to

Appraisal

An appraisal is an opinion of value at a specific point in time. It is based on information that includes data about competitive properties, market conditions, the national and local economies, and observed economic trends as well as an in-depth analysis of the property being appraised.

The validity of an appraisal depends on the qualifications of the individual who performs it. When a formal appraisal is needed—e.g., for insurance company adjustment of insured losses, to obtain financing, to make investment decisions regarding an acquisition or disposition, or for such other purposes as taxation, litigation, estate value, and audits—the valuation should be performed by a qualified independent professional appraiser (e.g., someone who holds the MAI designation as a Member of the Appraisal Institute).

reproduce a building exactly—continuity of historical landmark status might be one example—value is most often based on replacement cost. The difficulties of accurately estimating the cost to rebuild and of quantifying depreciation limit the usefulness of this approach. The exception to this rule would be a new office building for which there is little or no accrued depreciation.

2. *Market approach*—In this approach, recent sales of similar properties are used to determine value. Comparison factors include location, construction materials, physical condition, lot size, and zoning, among others; and comparable values are adjusted for differences in these factors. This method, too, has limited usefulness. There is rarely a large enough number of recent sales for the results to be reliable statistically. This is especially true for very large office buildings, for which there may be no recent comparable sales data available.

3. *Income capitalization approach*—This method applies a market-derived capitalization (or "cap") rate to the net operating income (NOI) of the subject property to determine value. This approach may be used to estimate both current and future value. It requires particular skill and experience in determining the capitalization rate because a small error can have a major impact on the resulting value. This method is used by knowledgeable investors and real estate managers as well as professional appraisers.

4. *Discounted cash flow method*—Using this approach, the present value of a property is determined by discounting all the future fiscal benefits (cash flow, capital appreciation, and accumulated equity) of the real estate over a predetermined holding period.

Highest and Best Use

The highest and best use of real property is that use which will develop a site to its fullest economic potential and produce the highest property value. When the investment is in raw land, usually a number of potential alternate uses will be considered for a site. To be considered the highest and best use, the use must be:

- Physically possible—Physical characteristics of the land (size, shape, topography, soil conditions) as well as local climatic conditions may limit the use of a site.
- Economically feasible—Demand for a particular use compared to the available supply, both currently and projected for the near future, will determine whether there is a market for that use.
- Legally permissible—Use of a site may be limited by public restrictions set forth by governmental agencies (e.g, zoning ordinances, building codes, environmental regulations) or private restrictive covenants that are part of the conveyance of title and are binding on all subsequent purchasers (control of lot size, architecture, placement of buildings, cost of improvements).
- Most profitable—This is a measure of maximum return on the owner's investment.

In determining highest and best use for a site with existing improvements, the alternatives being considered may be sale (or purchase) of the property, make improvements (rehabilitate) now or wait till later, use cash or finance the cost of improvements. Other possibilities are to demolish the building and replace it or retain the building and change its use.

The projection showing the largest amount of income that can be expected from the property will indicate its *highest and best use.*

In developing a management plan, an office building manager will usually use the income capitalization approach to demonstrate changes in property value as a result of each potential change that is evaluated. Before implementing a particular change, the owner will want to know whether and how much it will increase or decrease the property's value.

When the income capitalization approach is used, the property income (I) as NOI is divided by a capitalization rate (R) to determine property value (V). The formula is displayed as follows:

$$\frac{\text{Net Operating Income (I)}}{\text{Capitalization Rate (R)}} = \text{Estimated Market Value (V); } I \div R = V$$

The importance of selecting an appropriate cap rate cannot be overemphasized. The higher the cap rate the lower the value and vice versa, as the following calculations demonstrate. For example, if a property's annual NOI is $650,000 and the current cap rate is ten percent (.10), the value would be $6,500,000.

$$\frac{\$650{,}000}{.10} = \$6{,}500{,}000$$

The value will be very different if the cap rate is only one-half percent higher (10.5 percent) or lower (9.5 percent).

$$\frac{\$650{,}000}{.105} = \$6{,}190{,}476$$

$$\frac{\$650{,}000}{.095} = \$6{,}842{,}105$$

Problem Identification

The reasons for seeking professional management in the first place or changing the management of a property are usually related to the property's financial performance—the property is producing less than optimum rental income. A management proposal will likely suggest a number of alternatives that will make the property more profitable. The owner's objectives will determine the ultimate recommendations in the initial management plan. Over the period of management, several management plans will be developed to address the owner's changing goals and increase the property's income. This is how the manager *adds value* to the owner's investment. For purposes of discussion here, it is assumed that increased rental income is the primary objective of the management plan.

In order to determine possible courses of action, the cause or causes of the problem must be identified. A property may yield lower-than-expected income for several reasons.

- *Physical problems*—An existing building may have obsolete equipment or systems that are costly to operate, or its floor configurations may make it less desirable to today's prospective tenants.
- *Operational problems*—The management office may be computerized, but the computer system is not used to its maximum potential for accounting, record keeping, maintenance scheduling, and other activities that would increase management productivity and better control operating expenses.
- *Fiscal problems*—Analysis of the rental schedule may indicate that most tenants' rents are below current market rates.
- *Management problems*—Examples of these include the way the building is marketed (i.e., its ability to attract the types of tenants the owner would prefer), the leasing parameters (base rents, lease terms,

etc.), the distribution of tenant improvement costs (owner's versus tenants' shares), and the way pass-through expenses are calculated and billed. Perhaps when their leases are about to expire, tenants are looking for space in other buildings because they are not receiving the level of service called for in their leases due to inadequate staffing.

There may also be problems related to market conditions—e.g., reduced demand for office space resulting from an overbuilt market *(economic obsolescence)*. Changes in zoning, neighborhood deterioration, and a shift in development from the CBD to suburban office parks are other causes of economic obsolescence. These types of problems are external to the property and beyond the control of the office building manager.

Once the manager has identified the problem or problems, he or she will explore different potential solutions. However, it should be understood that there may not be any specific "problems" to address, a situation that is more likely to arise after management has been in place and implemented previously recommended "solutions." Regardless of whether there are identifiable physical, fiscal, or other problems, lease analysis, tenant retention strategies, and growth and preservation of the property's income stream through aggressive lease renewal efforts should be a continuing part of the management plan.

Analysis of Alternatives

Solutions to a property's problems may take a variety of forms. The changes recommended for a particular property may have little or no cost, or they may require a major infusion of capital. The intent of the changes proposed in a management plan is to increase NOI and thus increase property value. The manager should investigate the range of possible changes and their potential impact on the property. Because each proposed change usually involves a cost, it is imperative to compare the costs and benefits of each proposal in order to determine which one will result in the highest and best use of the property.

Depending on the circumstances, the manager may recommend one or more of the following types of changes.

- *Refinancing*—Sometimes the property or the owner could benefit from refinancing the existing mortgage loan. Depending on market conditions, an existing loan may be refinanced at a lower interest rate, for a longer or shorter term, or for a smaller or larger amount of principal. Refinancing for more than the current principal balance is a way to provide extra cash for operations, but it will also reduce the owner's equity in the property. If the owner needs cash, the same strategy can put cash in the owner's pocket. Refinancing at a lower interest rate can reduce the periodic debt service payments. This also has the effect of increasing pre-tax cash flow and yielding a higher return on the owner's investment.

- *Operational changes*—These may affect office or maintenance procedures or improve efficiency or productivity, which may increase property revenue or reduce operating expenses and thus increase NOI. Operational changes may involve changes in staffing (increases or decreases), implementing a new rental schedule, or renegotiating service contracts. Many such changes have little or no direct cost. For example, implementation of a combination service request/work order form can improve tracking of maintenance work and reduce the amount of paper used. It can also facilitate billing of tenants for services when required. Use of electronic transfer of funds to pay some regular expenses (including debt service) can save staff time as well as transaction fees, and usually there is no cost involved in making the arrangements.
- *Physical changes*—Sometimes physical (structural) changes may be necessary to extend the useful life of an office building. Over time, buildings become out-moded, and equipment becomes less efficient *(functional obsolescence)*. A management plan may recommend *rehabilitation* of an older office building to maximize its marketability. It is especially important to restore a building to a state of functional efficiency when there is *physical deterioration* due to deferred maintenance. In the course of rehabilitation, existing features may be removed or upgraded to reflect newer technology *(modernization)*. Physical changes may be substantial and expensive. Replacing windows to reduce energy consumption, retrofitting for air conditioning, and replacing an HVAC system with more efficient equipment are some examples. Changes such as upgrading electrical wiring, installing additional risers to accommodate telecommunications cabling, and replacing light fixtures to accommodate more efficient lamps may be considered major or minor *renovation*, depending on the size of the building. Simply cleaning *(refurbishing)* the exterior of the building will enhance its curb appeal. In a suburban office park, it is often possible to build an addition to a low-rise building. Space in an urban office building may be increased by adding one or more floors, provided the existing structure will support the added weight. All of these types of changes require capital investment, and if the owner does not have cash available for a rehabilitation (e.g., reserve funds), the project will have to be financed.
- *Change of use*—An especially radical proposal would be to change the use of a building. Conversion of a loft building by adding partitions and infrastructure to subdivide the open areas into functional

office space is an example of *adaptive use*. In order to achieve the highest and best use of a property, it may be desirable or appropriate to recommend conversion of an existing office building to another use (e.g., rental apartments or condominiums). This might be recommended in an overbuilt market where demand for office space is low and not likely to increase while, at the same time, new residential construction is unable to keep up with demand for apartments.

An even more radical proposal would be to demolish the building and replace it with a new one. However, the combined cost of demolition plus construction—new construction must comply with ADA accessibility requirements, current (often more stringent) building codes, and other regulations—means the new building would have to generate a very high level of income to be successful. There are other considerations as well, including the impact on the neighborhood where the building is located and possible implications of landmark status. (When a building is listed in the National Register of Historic Places, demolition is prohibited.)

Cost-Benefit Analysis

Any change at a property will involve costs. How much a particular change will cost depends on the nature and scope of the change. Rehabilitation or other physical change will have a high cost, and the property's income stream may be disrupted while the work is being done, adding to the project cost. Even changing a record-keeping procedure—e.g., the combined service request/work order form mentioned above—will have a measurable cost. Before recommending a specific change, the manager will perform a cost-benefit analysis, evaluating each alternative to determine whether it will yield more NOI and cash flow than if the property is left as is. Also of concern is recovery of the costs involved, including the costs of financing. For a recommended change to be feasible, the benefits must outweigh the costs. This requires evaluation of the *payback period* to determine how long it will take for the change to pay for itself. A cost-benefit analysis should also demonstrate that the change will increase the property's value. An example of a cost-benefit analysis calculation is shown in Exhibit 13.3.

The example in Exhibit 13.3 is simplified for demonstration purposes, with the increased income going directly to the bottom line as NOI. Usually a more comprehensive approach is required to present a complete picture of the scope of the changes being proposed and their costs as well as their benefits so that the owner has a sound financial basis for making decisions as to which change or changes to implement. In most situations where rehabilitation or modernization is being contemplated, the process and the calculations will be expanded. There may be a number of improvements to be made as part of a building upgrade. Listing the individual components

Exhibit 13.3

Sample Cost-Benefit Analysis Calculation

John Jones is the manager of a 20-year-old, 11-story office building, with 100,000 rentable square feet of space, 90,000 square feet of which is currently under lease (i.e., 90% occupancy) at an average rent of $15/sq ft/yr. Both management and ownership are aware that tenants' employees frequently complain about the level of heat or cooling and generally poor air circulation at certain times of the day. Jones estimates that the cost to upgrade the HVAC system, which would improve its ventilation capacity and overall heating/cooling efficiency, would be $250,000. He further estimates that the upgrade will allow a rent increase of $0.50/sq ft/yr. The payback period, return on investment (ROI), and increase in property value (based on a 10% capitalization rate) would be calculated as follows:

$0.50/sq ft × 90,000 sq ft = $45,000 additional annual income as NOI
$45,000 ÷ 12 months = $3,750 additional NOI/month
$250,000 improvement cost ÷ $3,750 additional NOI/month = 66.7 months (payback period)

$45,000 increased NOI ÷ $250,000 improvement cost = 18% ROI

$45,000 increased NOI ÷ .10 (capitalization rate) = $450,000 increase in property value
$450,000 increased value − $250,000 improvement cost = $200,000 net increase in value

This example is designed to demonstrate the calculations in a straightforward manner. It assumes the improvement cost can be paid in full by the owner, either out of pocket or from reserve funds accumulated for the purpose and that any increase in rental income will occur immediately on completion and go directly to NOI. It also assumes little or no disruption of tenants' businesses—i.e., that the problem is with the major central components of the HVAC system and that the distribution system (ductwork and vents in tenants' spaces) is adequate.

The upgraded HVAC system is likely to make space in the building more desirable, possibly increasing the occupancy rate at an early date and thereby reducing the payback period. The newer equipment is also likely to mean lower HVAC maintenance and repair costs, which could reduce the payback period further. In addition, the owner's tax liability on the income from the property will be reduced by the cost recovery (depreciation) deduction for the improvement. On the other hand, if the cost of the improvement is financed, the debt service on the loan would reduce the owner's cash flow (debt service is deducted from NOI) and return on investment. It would also increase the payback period and lessen the increase in property value.

and their respective costs defines the scope of the project and allows for a decision to defer some items rather than do all the work at once if the needed funds cannot be obtained.

The manager will also explore the specific impact on both income and expenses for the period of construction and after its completion, making a comparison to the expected income and expenses if the building remains as is (i.e., no changes are made). In the real world, rent increases would likely be implemented as leases are renewed (e.g., on a staggered schedule) or as

Typical Components of a Management Plan

- Executive Summary
- Regional analysis
- Neighborhood analysis
- Property analysis
- Market analysis
- Analysis of alternatives
- Cost-benefit analysis
- Conclusion and recommendations

Specific data that formed the basis of the various analyses along with other background information will usually be presented in a series of appendices at the back of the plan.

provided in specific escalation clauses, in which case calculations of increased rental revenue would be more complex. Specific allowance may also have to be made for increased vacancies or lost rental income as well as increased debt service payments if the construction is financed. (Because changes in income, expenses, and debt service affect cash flow as well as NOI, these comparisons are likely to be demonstrated using the cash flow chart.) The value of the property as is and after completion of the rehabilitation will also be compared, and it may be appropriate to apply different capitalization rates to the before and after NOI figures to more accurately anticipate changes in the market over the construction period.

The Completed Management Plan

When a manager assembles a management plan, the various component analyses should be presented in a logical order. The final product will usually consist of the following:

- Regional analysis—Evaluation of the demographic, geographic, and economic conditions of the region (metropolitan statistical area or other defined broad area surrounding the property) and identification of trends that are likely to affect the property.
- Neighborhood analysis—A more narrowly focused evaluation of demographic, economic, and other conditions in the area immediately surrounding the property, including observed trends that appear to affect the property.
- Property analysis—An evaluation of the locational, physical, and financial conditions of the property itself and identification of problems that diminish the property's ability to be successful.

- Market analysis—Specific evaluation of the competition and the property's position in the marketplace based on comparison to similar properties.
- Analysis of alternatives—Description of potential solutions to the property's physical, operational, or financial problems.
- Cost-benefit analysis—Evaluation of the costs of implementing the proposed alternatives and the benefits that will accrue from making the changes. Feasibility depends on benefits outweighing the costs.
- Conclusions and recommendations—Results of the various analyses and the conclusions the manager draws from them and why the manager recommends making certain changes and not others.

The last component, conclusions and recommendations, should recapitulate the major conditions affecting the property, summarize the recommended changes outlined in the plan, and provide a rationale for making specific changes (i.e., expected results), relating the recommendations to the owner's investment goals. This section should also identify other alternatives that were considered and explain why they were not recommended. In addition, it is important to explain the long-term financial impact of recommended changes and their anticipated effect on the bottom line. This will help the owner understand the rationale for the chosen recommendations.

The key elements of the plan—specific problems that were identified, possible alternative solutions, and the recommendations resulting from the analyses—are usually also highlighted at the beginning of the document in an *executive summary*. This summary can provide valuable insights to help guide the property owner through the various components of the plan rather than having this important information appear only once at the end of the document.

A management plan that is part of a proposal to manage a property may be a very detailed, comprehensive document. This is particularly true if there are major structural problems that require early attention. A rehabilitation or modernization program may require two or more years to be fully implemented, and related construction work may have an impact on tenants' business operations. Some tenants may have to be relocated in the building for a short time. On the other hand, a tenant whose lease is about to expire may choose to relocate to another building rather than accommodate the extended disruption that accompanies rehabilitation construction. Both of these situations are likely to affect rental income during the period of change—the first may require a rent *abatement;* the second will incur costs of finding a replacement tenant.

When a rehabilitation is done over a period of years, the manager will likely perform additional financial analyses related to payback period, return on investment, and expected increase in property value. These types of situations warrant use of the discounted cash flow (DCF) method to determine the *net present value (NPV)* of the property and the *internal rate of return (IRR)* on the owner's investment. These calculations rely on the assumption that a dollar today is worth more than a dollar at some future date, a concept known as the *time value of money*. (Note: The concepts and calculations of NPV and IRR are beyond the scope of this book.)

Once a management arrangement is established, and especially after a major rehabilitation, the management plan prepared annually (or more frequently) may be fairly simple. In some instances, the annual operating budget may be the annual management plan. However, it is prudent for office building managers to continually update the property analysis and market analysis (regional and neighborhood analyses, analysis of supply and demand, and absorption data) components of the plan. These types of information are vital for continued successful—profitable—operation of an office building because they ensure that building conditions and rental rates remain competitive. They also help the manager identify trends in the economy at large and the local marketplace that can impact property operations and profits.

Additional Resources

Following is a list of selected professional and trade organizations, publishers, and publications, some of which have been cited in the text. More detailed information about these and other trade associations and professional organizations can be found in the *Encyclopedia of Associations* published annually by Gale Research, Inc. Additional related books can be found in *Books in Print* published by R. R. Bowker. Both of these resources are available on line; libraries usually maintain subscriptions to the on-line services. Several of the books listed have older copyright dates, and some of them may be out of print. These may be accessible at libraries, or they may be available for purchase from bookstores that specialize in used and out-of-print books.

Organizations

American Industrial Real Estate Association (AIR), 700 South Flower Street, Suite 600, Los Angeles, CA 90017 (phone: 213-687-8777; fax: 213-687-8616; web page: www.airea.com).

Organization of real estate professionals specializing in commercial and industrial properties; publishes standard industrial and commercial lease forms as well as other contract forms related to commercial and industrial property operations and management.

American Institute of Architects (AIA), 1735 New York Avenue, N.W., Washington, DC 20006 (phone: 202-626-7300; fax: 202-626-7587; web page: www.aia.org).

Organization of professional licensed architects; publishes standard forms used in contracting for architectural, construction, and related services.

American Institute of Certified Public Accountants (AICPA), 1211 Avenue of the Americas, New York, NY 10036 (phone: 212-596-6200; fax: 212-596-6213; web page: www.aicpa.org).

National professional organization of certified public accountants; resource on accounting practices and standards.

American Insurance Association (AIA), 1130 Connecticut Avenue, N.W., Suite 1000, Washington, DC 20036 (phone: 202-828-7100; fax: 202-293-1219; web page: www.aiadc.org).

Trade organization formed by merger of National Board of Fire Underwriters, Association of Casualty and Surety Companies, and American Insurance Association; publishes information related to property/casualty and workers' compensation insurance.

American Society of Heating, Refrigerating and Air-Conditioning Engineers (ASHRAE), 1791 Tullie Circle, N.E., Atlanta, GA 30329 (phone: 404-636-8400; fax: 404-321-5478; web page: www.ashrae.org).

Technical society of HVAC and refrigerating engineers that conducts research and publishes reference materials on HVAC systems, equipment, and applications, including engineering standards.

American Society of Interior Designers (ASID), 608 Massachusetts Avenue, N.E., Washington, DC 20002 (phone: 202-546-3480; fax: 202-546-3240; web page: www.asid.org).

Professional society of interior designers; provides referrals to designers.

American Society of Mechanical Engineers (ASME International), Three Park Avenue, New York, NY 10016 (phone: 212-591-7722; fax: 212-591-7674; web page: www.asme.org).

Develops boiler, pressure vessel, and power test codes as well as safety codes and standards for elevators, escalators, and other mechanical equipment.

American Society of Plumbing Engineers (ASPE), 8614 West Catalpa Avenue, Suite 1007, Chicago, IL 60656 (phone: 773-693-2773; fax: 773-695-9007; web page: www.aspe.org).

Organization of consulting engineers involved in design and specification of plumbing systems; publishes information related to plumbing engineering.

Appraisal Institute (AI), 550 West Van Buren Street, Suite 1000, Chicago, IL 60607 (phone: 312-335-4100; fax: 312-335-4400; web page: www.appraisalinstitute.org).

Formed by merger of American Institute of Real Estate Appraisers and Society of Real Estate Appraisers; educates appraisers and confers the professional designation Member Appraisal Institute (MAI).

Asphalt Roofing Manufacturers Association (ARMA), 1156 - 15th Street, N.W., Suite 900, Washington, DC 20005 (phone: 202-207-0917; fax: 202-223-9741; web page: www.asphaltroofing.org).

Organization of manufacturers of asphalt shingles and built-up roofing (BUR) and modified bitumen roofing systems.

Building Officials and Code Administrators International (BOCA), 4051 West Flossmoor Road, Country Club Hills, IL 60478 (phone: 708-799-2300; fax: 708-799-4981; web page: www.bocai.org)

Organization of entities concerned with building, fire, mechanical, plumbing, zoning, and housing regulations; publishes *BOCA® National Building Code* (every 3 years), one of several model building codes recognized in the United

States and Canada; also publishes mechanical, plumbing, and maintenance codes.

Building Owners and Managers Association (BOMA) International, 1201 New York Avenue, N.W., Suite 300, Washington, DC 20005 (phone: 202-408-2662; fax: 202-371-0181; web page: www.boma.org).

Organization of building owners, managers, developers, leasing professionals, facility managers, and others representing all facets of the commercial real estate industry; publishes *Standard Method for Measuring Floor Area in Office Buildings* (ANSI/BOMA Z65.1-1996), *Are your Tenants Safe? BOMA's Guide to Security and Emergency Planning,* and *Experience Exchange Report for Downtown and Suburban Office Buildings* (annual).

Building Owners and Managers Institute (BOMI Institute), 1521 Ritchie Highway, Arnold, MD 21012 (phone: 410-974-1410; fax: 410-974-1935; www.bomi-edu.org).

Offers classroom and home study courses leading to the Real Property Administrator (RPA), Facilities Management Administrator (FMA), Systems Maintenance Technician (SMT), and Systems Maintenance Administrator (SMA) designations.

Construction Metrication Council, National Institute of Building Sciences, 1090 Vermont Avenue, N.W., Suite 700, Washington, DC 20005 (phone: 202-289-7800; fax: 202-289-1092; web page: www.nibs.org/cmchome.htm).

Supports metrication of federal construction and promotes use of the metric system of measurement in the U.S. construction industry.

Illuminating Engineering Society of North America (IESNA), 120 Wall Street, 17th floor, New York, NY 10005 (phone: 212-248-5000; fax: 212-248-5017; web page: www.iesna.org).

Organization of engineers, architects, designers, contractors, and others who deal with illumination; publishes lighting standards.

Institute of Electrical and Electronics Engineers (IEEE), 3 Park Avenue, 17th Floor, New York, NY 10016 (phone: 212-419-7900; fax: 212-752-4929; web page: www.ieee.org).

Organization of engineers and scientists in electrical engineering, electronics, and allied fields; publishes standards related to these fields.

Institute of Real Estate Management (IREM), 430 North Michigan Avenue, Chicago, IL 60611 (phone: 312-329-6000; fax: 312-329-6039; web page: www.irem.org).

Offers classroom, home study, and on-line courses leading to the CERTIFIED PROPERTY MANAGER® (CPM®) designation and the ACCREDITED MANAGEMENT ORGANIZATION® (AMO®) accreditation; publishes the annual *Income/Expense Analysis®: Office Buildings* and *Income/Expense Analysis®: Shopping Centers.*

International Conference of Building Officials (ICBO), 5360 Workman Mill Road, Whittier, CA 90601 (phone: 562-699-0541; fax: 562-692-3853; web page: www.icbo.org).

Publishes *The Uniform Building Code* (every 3 years), one of several model building codes recognized in the United States and Canada.

International Council of Shopping Centers (ICSC), 1221 Avenue of the Americas, 41st floor, New York, NY 10020 (phone: 646-728-3800; fax: 212-589-5555; web page: www.icsc.org).

Membership organization of individuals and companies involved in development, management, leasing, and marketing of shopping centers, including retailers; compiles and publishes shopping center operating data; resource on leasing retail space.

International Facility Management Association (IFMA), 1 East Greenway Plaza, Suite 1100, Houston, TX 77046 (phone: 713-623-4362; fax: 713-623-6124; web page: www.ifma.org).

Organization of persons involved with planning, designing, and managing workplaces; provides education leading to the Certified Facility Manager (CFM) certification.

NAIOP—The National Association of Industrial and Office Properties, 2201 Cooperative Way, Third Floor, Herndon, VA 20171 (phone: 703-904-7100; fax: 703-904-7942; web page: www.naiop.org).

Trade association of owners and developers of office and industrial properties; publishes *Industrial Income and Expense Report* every other year.

National Board of Boiler and Pressure Vessel Inspectors, 1055 Crupper Avenue, Columbus, OH 43229 (phone; 614-888-8320; web page: www.nationalboard.org).

Organization that oversees adherence to codes regarding construction and repair of boilers and pressure vessels; publishes *National Board Inspection Code.*

National Climatic Data Center, Federal Building, 151 Patton Avenue, Customer Services Branch, Asheville, NC 28802 (phone: 828-271-4800; fax: 828-271-4876; web page: http://nndc.noaa.gov).

Offers subscription access to local climatological data from the National Oceanic and Atmospheric Administration (NOAA) of the U.S. Department of Commerce.

National Conference of States on Building Codes and Standards (NCSBCS), 505 Huntmar Park Drive, Suite 210, Herndon, VA 20170 (phone: 703-437-0100; fax: 703-481-3596; web page: www.ncsbcs.org).

Organization of state building code officials and other entities interested in building code administration; publishes annual *Directory of Building Codes and Regulations* and offers a variety of publications related to construction.

National Electrical Manufacturers Association (NEMA), 1300 North 17th Street, Suite 1847, Rosslyn, VA 22209 (phone: 703-841-3200; fax: 703-841-5900; web page: www.nema.org).

Develops standards for the manufacture of electrical equipment; participates in developing the National Electrical Code and National Electrical Safety Codes.

National Fire Protection Association (NFPA), 1 Batterymarch Park, Quincy, MA 02269 (phone: 617-770-3000; fax: 617-770-0700; web page: www.nfpa.org).

Develops and publishes fire protection standards—the *Fire Protection Handbook* and *The Life Safety Code® Handbook;* publishes annual compilation of *National Fire Codes.*

National Lighting Bureau, 8811 Colesville Road, Suite G106, Silver Spring, MD 20910 (phone: 301-587-9572; fax: 301-589-2017; web page: www.nlb.org).

Organization of companies involved in lighting; develops guidelines for interior and exterior lighting requirements; provides comparison data on types of lights, illumination they provide, and related costs.

Society of Industrial and Office REALTORS®, 700 - 11th Street, N.W., Suite 510, Washington, DC 20001 (phone: 202-737-1150; fax: 202-737-8796; web page: www.sior.com).

Organization of commercial real estate brokerage specialists; a professional affiliate of the National Association of REALTORS®.

Southern Building Code Congress, International (SBCCI), 900 Montclair Road, Birmingham, AL 35213 (phone: 205-591-1853; fax: 205-591-0775; web page: www.sbcci.org).

Publishes *Standard Building Code* (every 3 years), one of several model building codes recognized in the United States and Canada.

ULI—the Urban Land Institute, 1025 Thomas Jefferson Street, N.W., Suite 500 West, Washington, DC 20007 (phone: 202-624-7000; fax: 202-624-7140; web page: www.uli.org).

Membership organization of developers, architects, and others interested in land use; publishes shopping center operating statistics in periodic reports, including *Dollars and Cents of Shopping Centers* and similarly titled publications covering specific types of retail outlets.

Underwriters Laboratories (UL), Inc., 333 Pfingsten Road, Northbrook, IL 60062 (phone: 847–272-8800; fax: 847-272-8129; web page: www.ul.com).

Establishes product safety specifications for electrical, fire protection, and other equipment and devices and conducts tests to verify that those specifications are met.

U.S. Metric Association (USMA), 10245 Andasol Avenue, Northridge, CA 91325 (phone/fax: 818-363-5606; web page: www.metric.org).

Promotes greater use of the metric system of measurement; publishes bimonthly newsletter *Metric today*.

Publishers

R. S. Means Company, Inc., Construction Plaza, 63 Smiths Lane, Kingston, MA 02364 (phone: 800-334-3509; fax: 800-632-6732; web page: www.rsmeans.com).

Publishes construction cost information and reference books, including *Means Graphic Construction Standards* (1986) and the annual *Means Building Construction Cost Data; Means Interior Cost Data; Means Repair and Remodeling Cost Data;* and *Means Labor Rates for the Construction Industry*.

Government Institutes, Inc., 4 Research Place, Suite 200, Rockville, MD 20850 (phone: 301-921-2300; fax: 301-921-0373; web page: www.govinst.com).

Publishes information on government regulatory topics in environmental, health and safety, and telecommunications fields,

JOB Publications, P.O. Box 20121, Tallahassee, FL 32316 (phone: 850-531-7459; web page: www.littleredbook.com).

Publishes *Handbook of Formulae, Equations, and Conversion Factors for the Energy Professional;* contents also available on searchable interactive CD.

Publications

Alexander, Alan A., and Muhlebach, Richard F.: *Managing and Leasing Commercial Properties: Practices, Strategies, and Forms* (3d ed.; Frederick, Md.: Panel Publishing, 2000).

Beard, Bodie J., Jr., and Zucker, Cher R.: *Forms for Office Building Management and Operations Manual Guidelines* (Chicago: Institute of Real Estate Management, 1986).

Cushman, Robert F., et al. (eds.): *High Tech Real Estate: Planning, Adapting, and Operating Buildings in the Computer and Telecommunications Age* (Homewood, Ill.: Irwin Professional Publishing, 1985).

Dasso, Jerome, and Ring, Alfred A.: *Real Estate Principles and Practices* (11th ed.; Englewood Cliffs, N.J.: Prentice-Hall, 1989).

Fennelly, Lawrence J., and Lombardi, John H.: *Spotlight on Security for Real Estate Managers* (Chicago: Institute of Real Estate Management, 1997).

Griffin, Thomas J.: *The Real Estate Manager's Technical Glossary* (Chicago: Institute of Real Estate Management, 1999).

Harris, Cyril M. (ed.): *Dictionary of Architecture and Construction* (2d ed.; New York: McGraw-Hill, Inc., 1993).

Leasing Retail Space (Chicago: Institute of Real Estate Management, 1990).

Liska, Roger W.: *Means Facilities Maintenance Standards* (Kingston, Mass.: R. S. Means Company, 1988).

Lundeen, Howard K., et al.: *The Tenant Retention Solution: A Revolutionary Approach to Commercial Property Management* (Chicago: Institute of Real Estate Management, 1995).

Marchetti, John (ed.): *Means Illustrated Construction Dictionary* (3d ed.: Kingston, Mass.: R. S. Means Company, 2000).

Mastering Office Leasing: A Practical Guide (Washington, D.C.: Society of Industrial and Office REALTORS®, 2000).

Parks, David C.: *Environmental Management for Real Estate Professionals* (Chicago: Institute of Real Estate Management, 1992).

Poage, Walter S.: *The Building Professional's Guide to Contract Documents* (3d ed.; Kingston, Mass.: R. S. Means Company, 2000).

Power Shopping: A Guide for Building Owners and Managers to Prepare for the Deregulated Electricity Marketplace (Washington, D.C.: Building Owners and Managers Association International, 1996).

Principles of Real Estate Management (14th ed.; Chicago: Institute of Real Estate Management, 2001).

Ramsey, Charles G., et al.: *Architectural Graphic Standards* (10th ed.; New York: John Wiley & Sons, Inc., 2000).

Randolph, Patrick A., Jr. (ed.): *The Commercial Property Lease: Structuring Agreements, Assessing Expenses, and Preventing Liabilities for Landlords and Tenants* (Chicago: American Bar Association, 1993).

Sack, Thomas F.: *A Complete Guide to Building and Plant Maintenance* (2d ed.; Englewood Cliffs, N.J.: Prentice-Hall, 1971).

San Luis, Ed, et al.: *Office and Office Building Security* (2d ed.; Boston: Butterworth-Heinemann, 1994).

Senn, Mark A.: *Commercial Real Estate Leases: Preparation and Negotiation* (Frederick, Md.: Panel Publishing, 2000).

Shear, Mel A.: *Handbook of Building Maintenance Management* (Englewood Cliffs, N.J.: Prentice-Hall, 1983).

Statistical Abstract of the United States (Washington, D.C.: U.S. Department of Commerce, Bureau of the Census, annual); also available on the Internet at www.census.gov.

White, John R. (ed.): *The Office Building: From Concept to Investment Reality* (Chicago and Washington, D.C.: Counselors of Real Estate, Appraisal Institute, and Society of Industrial and Office REALTORS® Educational Fund, 1993).

Glossary

abate To reduce in value, as a tax or rental rate. To demolish or remove, as asbestos-containing material.

absorption rate The amount of space of a particular property type that is leased compared to the amount of that same type of space available for lease within a certain geographic area over a given period.

accrual-basis accounting The method of accounting that involves entering amounts of income when they are earned and amounts of expense when they are incurred—even though the cash may not be received or paid; compare *cash-basis accounting*.

actual cash value (ACV) Insurance that pays a claim based on the purchase price of the item, usually allowing for depreciation because of age and use; compare *replacement cost coverage*.

adaptive use Conversion of an existing structure to a new use (e.g., a former loft building to office space).

add-on factor See *load factor*.

ad valorem tax A tax levied on the basis of the value of the object taxed. Most often refers to taxes levied by municipalities and counties against real property and personal property.

agent A person who enters a legal, fiduciary, and confidential arrangement with a second party and is authorized to act on behalf of that party.

all-risk insurance Insurance that pays for all losses except those identified in the policy as specific exclusions.

Americans with Disabilities Act (ADA) The federal law that prohibits discrimination in employment on the basis of disability and requires places of public accommodation and commercial facilities to be designed, constructed, and altered in compliance with specified accessibility standards.

amortization Gradual reduction of a debt by periodic payments of interest and principal over the term of the loan.

analysis of alternatives A study of a property to determine its *highest and best use,* including tests of legal permissibility, physical possibility, economic feasibility, and potential profitability.

appraisal An opinion of value at a specific point in time. An appraisal is based on information that includes data about competitive properties, market conditions, the national and local economies, and observed economic trends as well as an in-depth analysis of the property being appraised.

asbestos A fibrous mineral used to impart fireproofing characteristics to building materials and provide insulation. Particles that become airborne (as *friable* asbestos) are a human health hazard.

asbestos-containing material (ACM) Any material (e.g., insulation, flooring) that contains more than one percent asbestos by weight.

assessed value The value of real property established by the local authority as the basis for taxation. The tax rate is applied to the assessed value to determine the amount of real estate tax.

assignment The transfer of one person's interest or right in a property (e.g., a lease) to another.

base rent The minimum rent as set forth in a lease for commercial (e.g., office) space.

base year In an office lease, the stated year that is to be used as a standard in determining rent escalations. In subsequent years, operating costs are compared with the base year, and the difference (higher or lower) determines the tenant's rent adjustment.

breakpoint In retail leases, the point at which the tenant's percentage rent is equal to the base rent and beyond which the tenant will begin to pay overages; also called *natural breakpoint.* Sometimes a tenant and owner will negotiate an *artificial breakpoint* that requires the tenant to begin paying percentage rent either before or after the natural breakpoint is reached.

British thermal unit (Btu) The amount of heat required to raise the temperature of one pound of water one degree Fahrenheit.

building standards Uniform specifications that define the quantity and quality of construction and finish elements a building owner will provide to tenants for build-out of leased office space; see also *tenant improvement allowance.*

capital budget An estimate of costs of major improvements or replacements.

capital improvement A structural addition or betterment to real property that increases its useful life.

capitalization The process employed to estimate the value of a property by the use of a proper investment rate of return and the annual net operating income produced by the property, the formula being expressed as:

$$\text{Net Operating Income} \div \text{Rate} = \text{Value} \quad (I/R = V)$$

capitalization rate A rate of return used to estimate a property's value based on that property's net operating income. This rate is based on the rates of return prevalent in the marketplace for similar properties and intended to reflect the investment risk associated with a particular property.

cash-basis accounting The method of accounting that recognizes income and expenses when money is actually received or paid; compare *accrual-basis accounting*.

cash flow The amount of cash available after all payments have been made for operating expenses, debt service (mortgage principal and interest), and capital reserve funds; also called *pre-tax cash flow* to indicate that income taxes have not been deducted.

CERTIFIED PROPERTY MANAGER® (CPM®) The professional designation conferred by the Institute of Real Estate Management on individuals who distinguish themselves in the areas of education, experience, and ethics in property management.

chart of accounts A classification or arrangement of account items.

chlorofluorocarbons (CFCs) Inert organic compounds containing halogen (chlorine and fluorine) atoms used as refrigerants in air-conditioning systems and other applications. Under the Montreal Protocol, CFC refrigerants are required to be replaced with nonhalogenated compounds.

coinsurance A system of insurance under which the insured is obligated to maintain the level of coverage at a stipulated percentage of the total value. In the event of a loss, the insured shares in losses in proportion to the amount that the insurance coverage was less than the required percentage.

cold calling Calling on prospective tenants with whom the leasing agent has had no previous contact in order to interest them in leasing office space.

collateral Property pledged as security for a loan or debt.

commingle To mix or combine; to combine the money of more than one person or entity into a common fund. A prohibited practice in real estate.

common area Areas of a property that are used by all tenants (e.g., lobbies, public corridors, and service areas of office buildings).

comparison grid analysis A process in which the features of a subject property are compared to similar features in comparable properties in the same market. The rent for each comparable property helps to determine an appropriate market rent for the subject.

concession An economic incentive granted by an owner to encourage the leasing of space or the renewal of a lease.

condemnation See *eminent domain.*

condominium A multiple-unit structure in which the units and pro rata shares of the common areas are owned individually; a unit in a condominium property.

containment A remedial method of isolating an environmental hazard such as non-friable asbestos by enclosure or encapsulation.

cooling degree-day See *degree-day.*

cooperative A form of real estate ownership in which one buys shares of stock in a corporation that holds title to a multiple-unit property and thus is entitled to occupy a unit under a *proprietary lease.*

corporation A legal entity that is chartered by a state and is treated by courts as an individual entity separate and distinct from the persons who own it.

corrective maintenance Ordinary repairs that must be made to a building and its equipment on a day-to-day basis; see also *deferred maintenance; preventive maintenance.*

cosmetic maintenance Work done on a building or property that enhances its appearance but does not contribute materially to its operation or preservation.

cost approach A method of valuation based on the estimated value of the land plus the estimated cost to replace the improvements to the land less depreciation.

cost-benefit analysis A method of measuring the benefits expected from a decision (rehabilitation; a change in operating procedures) by calculating the cost of the change and determining whether the benefits justify the costs.

cost recovery See *depreciation.*

curb appeal General cleanliness, neatness, and attractiveness of a building as exemplified by the appearance of the exterior and grounds and the general level of cleanliness.

debt service Payments of principal and interest on a loan.

deductible In insurance, a specified amount the insured party must pay before the insurer pays on a claim.

default Failure to fulfill an obligation; the nonperformance of a duty.

defendant The person alleged to be at fault; the entity that is sued.

deferred maintenance Ordinary maintenance of a building that, because it has not been performed, negatively affects the use, occupancy, and value of the property; see also *corrective maintenance; preventive maintenance.*

degree-day A unit that represents one degree difference in the mean outdoor temperature for one day. Temperatures above 65°F represent *cooling degree-days;* those below 65°F represent *heating degree-days.*

demised premises That portion of a property covered by a lease agreement, usually defined by the walls and other structures that separate one tenant's space from that of another.

demographics The statistical characteristics of a population (e.g., age, education, occupation, and income) used especially to identify markets.

depreciation Loss of value due to all causes, including physical deterioration (ordinary wear and tear), structural defects, and changing economic and market conditions; see also *obsolescence*. The tax deduction that allocates the cost of an asset over its useful life; also called *cost recovery*.

discounted cash flow (DCF) method A method of valuation that discounts all future fiscal benefits of an investment property over a predetermined holding period.

economic obsolescence is a loss of value due to external causes (e.g., market conditions).

effective gross income The total amount of income actually collected during a reporting period; the gross receipts of a property. Gross potential rental income *less* vacancy and collection losses *plus* miscellaneous or unscheduled income.

effective rent The cumulative rental amount collected over the full term of a lease; also used to refer to the actual rent to be paid after base rent is adjusted for concessions, pass-through charges, and tenant improvements.

emergency maintenance Unscheduled repairs that must be done immediately to prevent further damage or to minimize danger to life or property.

eminent domain The right of a governmental body to acquire private property for public use through a court action called *condemnation*. The owner of the property must be fairly compensated, usually based on an appraisal of the fair market value.

employee handbook A detailed description of the personnel policies and procedures of the employer.

endorsement An attachment to an insurance policy that provides or excludes a specific coverage for a specific portion or element of a property; also called a *rider*.

Environmental Protection Agency (EPA) The agency of the U.S. government established to enforce laws that preserve and protect the environment.

Equal Employment Opportunity Commission (EEOC) A U.S. governmental body created under Title VII of the Civil Rights Act of 1964 to end discrimination in the workplace.

equity The interest or value that an owner has in real estate over and above any outstanding debts (e.g., mortgage loans, liens) against it.

errors and omissions (E&O) insurance See *professional liability insurance*.

escalation A lease provision that allows for increases in rent based on increases in operating costs, sometimes based on a standard index such as the Consumer Price Index (CPI) to account for inflation.

estoppel certificate A document by which the tenant states the terms of the lease and the full amount of rent to be paid for the entire term of the lease; commonly requested as part of refinancing or a transfer of ownership.

eviction A legal process to reclaim real estate, usually from a tenant who has not performed under the agreed-upon terms of the lease.

expense stop In an office lease, a clause obligating the property owner to pay operating costs up to a certain amount per square foot per year; tenants pay their pro rata share of any costs in excess of that amount.

extended coverage (EC) An endorsement to a standard fire insurance policy which adds coverage against financial loss from certain other specified hazards.

facility manager A type of real estate manager who, when employed directly by a corporation that owns real estate incidental to its primary business, may be responsible for acquisition and disposition in addition to physical upkeep of the property, record keeping, and reporting on its management, although acquisition and disposition are likely to be handled separately by a corporate asset manager. More broadly, the responsibilities involve coordinating the physical workplace with the people and purpose of the organization.

Fair Labor Standards Act (FLSA) The federal law that establishes minimum wages per hour and maximum hours of work. It also provides that certain employees who work in excess of forty hours per week are to be paid one and one-half times their regular hourly wage. This act is frequently referred to as the federal *Wage and Hour Law*.

fidelity bond A *surety* issued by a third party (usually an insurance company) that protects one individual against financial loss that might result from dishonest acts of another specific individual.

fiduciary One charged with a relationship of trust and confidence, as between a principal and agent, trustee and beneficiary, or attorney and client, when one party is legally empowered to act on behalf of another.

financing The availability, amount, and terms under which money may be borrowed to assist in the purchase of real property, using the property itself as the security *(collateral)* for such borrowing.

flex space Single-story structures that can be configured to accommodate a single tenant or multiple tenants or with varying proportions of office and warehouse or manufacturing space according to individual tenants' needs.

friable Easily crumbled or reduced to powder.

functional obsolescence A condition of obsolete design or use of a property.

garden office building An office building one to three stories tall, usually located in a suburban area.

general partnership The business activity of two or more persons who agree to pool capital, talents, and other assets according to some agreed-to formula, and similarly to divide profits and losses, and to commit the partnership to certain obligations; compare *limited partnership*. General partners assume unlimited liability.

gross leasable area (GLA) Commonly used term when referring to the size of a retail tenant's space, usually expressed in square feet.

gross lease A lease under the terms of which the landlord pays all operating expenses of the property and the tenant pays a fixed rent; compare *net lease*.

gross potential rental income The sum of the rental rates of all spaces available to be rented in a property, regardless of occupancy; the maximum amount of rent a property can produce.

gross up In commercial leasing, adjustment of variable operating expenses that are passed through to tenants in a new building or one that is not fully occupied to more closely reflect those expenses under full occupancy (usually around 90 percent).

heating degree-day See *degree-day*.

highest and best use That use of real property which will produce the highest property value and develop a site to its fullest economic potential.

home-officing A work strategy in which employees use computers, fax machines, telephones, and the Internet (e-mail) to connect with the central office from their homes; compare *telecommuting*.

income capitalization approach A method of valuation based on the net operating income (NOI) of the property; see also *capitalization; capitalization rate*.

inflation An economic condition occurring when the money supply increases in relation to the amount of goods available, resulting in substantial and continuing increases in prices.

insurable value The value of property for insurance purposes; the replacement cost of a building and other improvements to land.

insurance producer Any of several entities who can sell insurance policies, including an insurance *agent* who represents a specific insurance company, an insurance *broker* who represents the client in obtaining insurance, and an *independent agent* who contracts with selected insurance companies. Usually insurance written by a broker must be countersigned by an agent of the insurer.

internal rate of return (IRR) The true annual earnings of an investment expressed as a percentage; a method used by investors to determine cash returns in relation to cash invested.

janitorial maintenance Day-to-day upkeep and cleaning of the interior and exterior of a building.

joint venture An association of two or more persons or businesses to carry out a single business enterprise for profit.

kilowatt-hour (kwh) A unit of energy equal to 1,000 watts expended for a period of one hour.

landlord One who owns real property that is leased to a tenant; see also *lessor*.

lease A contract, written or oral, for the possession of part or all of a landlord's property for a stipulated period of time in consideration of the payment of rent or other compensation by the tenant.

leasing agent A person who is directly responsible for renting space in assigned properties.

lessee The tenant in a lease.

lessor The landlord in a lease.

liability insurance Insurance protection against claims arising out of injury or death of people or physical or financial damage to property.

lien A claim against property by a creditor under which the property becomes security for the debt owed to the creditor; see also *mechanic's lien.*

lien release A document executed by a provider of contract services (labor and materials) under which the contractor relinquishes the claim imposed against the property where its services are being performed.

lien waiver A voluntary relinquishing of a subcontractors' right to make a claim *(mechanic's lien)* against a property for payment of labor or materials already provided. Such waivers are required for release of construction loan funds from the lender.

limited liability company (LLC) Created by state statute, a business ownership form that functions like a corporation—its members are protected from liability—but for income tax purposes is classified as a partnership. Income and expenses flow through to the individual members. The arrangement offers considerable flexibility in its organization and structure.

limited partnership (LP) A partnership arrangement in which the liability of certain partners is limited to the amount of their investment; compare *general partnership.* Limited partnerships are managed and operated by one or more general partners whose liability is not limited; limited partners have no voice in management.

load factor The percentage of space in a building that is added to its usable area to account for lobbies, corridors, and other common areas; sometimes also called *add-on factor.*

maintenance The upkeep and repair of buildings and equipment.

management agreement A contractual arrangement between the owner(s) of a property and the designated managing agent, describing the duties, stating the compensation, and establishing the authority of the agent; and detailing the responsibilities, rights, and obligations of both agent and owner(s).

management fee The monetary consideration paid monthly or otherwise for the performance of management duties.

management plan An outline of a property's physical and fiscal management that is directed toward achieving the owner's goals.

market analysis An evaluation of supply and demand conditions in a particular area for a particular type of goods or services. In office building management, the process of identifying the specific group of prospective tenants for a particular property and then evaluating the property by that market's standards for rental space.

market approach A method of valuation based on a comparison of data from recent sales of similar properties in the market.

marketing All business activity a producer uses to expose potential consumers to available goods and services, including selling, advertising, and packaging. For rental property, methods used to attempt to lease space.

market price The price a property can actually be sold for at a given time as agreed to by a willing buyer and a willing seller; often, but not always, synonymous with *market value*.

market value The price that a piece of property might be expected to bring if offered for sale in an open market comprised of willing buyers and sellers where the property has been available for sale for a reasonable period of time; compare *market price*.

material safety data sheet (MSDS) Information accompanying hazardous materials which, in addition to physical characteristics, catalogs hazardous properties (e.g., toxicity, flammability, explosion potential), identifies recommended protective devices and clean-up procedures, and lists first aid treatment in the event of exposure.

mechanic's lien A claim against a property to collect payment for materials or labor provided, it restricts clear title to the property until the amount owed is paid in full.

mixed-use development (MXD) A large-scale real estate project having three or more significant revenue-producing uses, incorporating significant physical and functional integration of its components (i.e., intensive use of land), and conforming to a coherent plan.

modernization The process of replacing original or outdated equipment with similar features that are of up-to-date design.

mortgage A conditional transfer or pledge of real property as security for the payment of a debt; see also *collateral*. The document used to create a mortgage loan.

negotiation The process of bargaining that precedes an agreement; in commercial leasing, the bargaining to reach a mutual agreement on rental rates, term of the lease, and other points.

neighborhood analysis A study of a neighborhood and comparison with the broader economic and geographic area of which it is a part to determine why individuals and businesses are attracted to the area.

net lease A lease that requires the tenant to pay a share of specific property operating expenses in addition to base rent; compare *gross lease*. The terms *net-net* and *net-net-net* (or triple net) are also used, depending on the extent of the costs that are passed through to the tenant. Definitions of the terms vary with location and type of property.

net operating income (NOI) Total collections (gross receipts) less operating expenses.

net present value (NPV) The difference between the cost of a real estate or other investment and the discounted present value of all anticipated future fiscal benefits of that investment.

nonrecourse Having no personal liability. In lending, the lender may take the property pledged as collatoral to satisfy a debt but may not take other assets of the borrower.

obsolescence Lessening of value due to being out-of-date (obsolete) as a result of changes in design and use; see also *economic obsolescence; functional obsolescence; physical obsolescence*. An element of *depreciation*.

Occupational Safety and Health Administration (OSHA) An agency of the U.S. Department of Labor established to enforce regulations regarding workplace safety and health.

operating budget A listing of all anticipated income from and expenses of operating a property, usually projected on an annual basis.

operating expenses All expenditures made in connection with operating a property with the exception of debt service, capital reserves (and/or capital expenditures), and income taxes.

operations manual An authoritative collection of information that describes the organization and its goals, explains policies that guide its operations, outlines specific procedures for implementing those policies, assigns responsibility for performing various functions, and contains the various documents (forms) for performing the work; also called *standard operating procedures manual.*

overage See *breakpoint; percentage rent.*

partnership See *general partnership; limited partnership.*

pass-through charges In commercial leasing, operating expenses of a property that are paid by the tenants, usually on a pro rata basis and in addition to base rent.

payback period The amount of time required to recover the cost of a capital investment.

percentage rent In retail leasing, rent that is based on a percentage of a tenant's gross sales (or sometimes net income or profits), often set against a guaranteed minimum or base rent and therefore considered *overage;* see also *breakpoint.*

physical obsolescence A condition of aging (deterioration) or deferred maintenance of a property.

plaintiff The party who files a lawsuit or complaint.

polychlorinated biphenyls (PCBs) Organic compounds produced by replacing hydrogen atoms on a biphenyl with chlorine atoms and used in various industrial applications, including heat transfer agents in electrical transformers.

preventive maintenance A program of regularly scheduled inspection and care designed to detect and resolve potential problems *before* major repairs are needed.

principal In real estate, one who owns property; in real estate management, the property owner who contracts for the services of an agent; in finance, the amount of money that is borrowed in a loan as distinct from the interest on such loan.

professional liability insurance In real estate management, insurance to protect against liabilities resulting from honest mistakes and oversights (no protection is provided in cases of gross negligence); also called *errors and omissions insurance.*

property analysis A study of a property referring to such items as deferred maintenance, functional and economic obsolescence, land location and zoning, exterior construction and condition, plant and equipment, unit mix, facilities, and expected income and expenses.

proprietary lease See *cooperative.*

pro rata Proportionately; in office building leasing, based on the size of individually leased spaces in relation to the whole. Office tenants commonly pay proportionate shares of operating expenses and other costs *(pass-through charges).*

psychographics A market research tool used to determine consumer preferences; in office leasing, used to determine what factors about a property are likely to appeal to particular prospective tenants.

public relations (PR) The promotion of goodwill between one entity and other entities by distribution of information and assessment of public reaction.

radius clause A provision in a retail lease that prevents a retailer from opening and operating a similar—and therefore competitive—business within a certain radius from the shopping center.

real estate Land and all improvements in or on it.

real estate investment trust (REIT) An entity that sells *shares of beneficial interest* to investors and uses the funds to invest in real estate or mortgages. Real estate investment trusts must meet certain requirements such as a minimum number of investors and widely dispersed ownership. No corporate taxes need to be paid as long as a series of complex IRS qualifications are met.

recourse The right to demand payment, as of a loan.

refurbish To freshen up or clean.

regional analysis A detailed study of a region, usually the area surrounding and including one or more neighboring cities, to determine the force of various factors affecting the economic welfare of a section of the region, such as population growth and movement, employment, industrial and business activity, transportation facilities, tax structures, topography, improvements, and trends.

rehabilitation The process of restoring something damaged or deterioriated to a prior good condition.

renovation The process of restoring to a former state of soundness or newness.

rent Payment made for the use of space; periodic payments made under a lease.

rentable area The area in an office building on which rent is based and which generally includes the space available for tenants' exclusive use plus identified common areas less any vertical penetrations (air shafts, stairways, elevators) in the building; compare *usable area*.. The term is applied to the building as a whole, to individual floors, and to portions of floors.

replacement cost coverage Insurance to replace or restore a building or its contents to its pre-existing condition and appearance; compare *actual cash value*.

request for proposal (RFP) Written specifications for services to be provided by the bidder, often including the scope of work and details of design and use and asking for specifics regarding materials, labor, pricing, delivery, and payment.

reserve fund Money set aside to provide funds for anticipated future expenditures.

retainage Money held back from payments to a contractor, usually a percentage of the total cost of the project, until any outstanding work (e.g., punch list items) is completed satisfactorily.

retrofit The replacement of fixtures or facilities in a building with new equipment that is more efficient, usually in terms of energy consumption, fire protection codes, or accommodations for new technology.

return on investment (ROI) A measure of profitability expressed as a percentage and calculated by comparing periodic income to the owner's equity in the property (cash flow ÷ equity = % ROI). It can be calculated either before or after deduction of income tax.

rider See *endorsement*.

security deposit An amount of money advanced by the tenant and held by an owner or manager to ensure the faithful performance of the lease terms by the tenant. Part or all of the deposit may be retained to pay for rent owed, miscellaneous charges owed, unpaid utility bills, and damage to the leased space that exceeds normal wear and tear. Limitations on withholding may be imposed by state and local laws.

shares of beneficial interest Shares sold by *real estate investment trusts (REITs)*; they are traded on the stock markets similar to corporate common stock.

sick building syndrome (SBS) Acute symptoms exhibited by building occupants apparently linked to time they spend in the building but for which no specific cause or illness can be identified.

sole proprietorship A business enterprise carried on by one person.

space planning The process of designing an office configuration for maximum functional efficiency based on a prospective tenant's space utilization needs, aesthetic requirements, and financial limitations.

specifications A written document detailing the types of materials, methods of installation, and operating parameters for a particular contract.

standard operating procedures manual See *operations manual*.

sublease A lease given by a tenant or lessee to another entity to use or occupy part or all of the tenant's leased premises for a term shorter than the tenant's own term. Usually the original tenant retains some rights or obligations under the original lease.

subrogation In insurance, the right of an insurer to attempt to recover an obligation paid to the insured party for damage caused by an at-fault third party; see also *waiver of subrogation.*

surety See *fidelity bond.*

syndicate A type of professionally managed limited partnership formed to invest in different types of real estate.

telecommuting A work strategy in which employees connect to their employers' offices directly via telephone lines; compare *home-officing.*

tenant One who pays rent to occupy real estate; see also *lessee.*

tenant improvement allowance In office leasing, an amount a landlord agrees to spend to improve the leased space for a tenant before move-in or as a condition of lease renewal; see also *building standards.* A *standard tenant improvement allowance* is a fixed dollar amount allowed by the owner for items that may be installed in the leased premises at no charge to the tenant. Payment for tenant improvements is part of the lease negotiations.

tenant manual A compilation of management policies and procedures that relate to tenants and the use of their leased space.

tenant mix The combination of businesses and services that lease space in an office building.

term The duration of a tenant's lease; the duration of a mortgage (e.g., a thirty-year term).

therm An amount of heat equal to 100,000 Btus.

time value of money The assumption that a dollar today is worth more than a dollar at some future date. The basis of compounding to determine future value or discounting to determine present value.

traffic report A record of the number of prospects who visit or make inquiries at a property and the factors that attracted them to it.

umbrella liability insurance Extra liability coverage that exceeds the limits of one's basic liability policy.

usable area The area in an office building that is available for the exclusive use of a tenant; compare *rentable area.*

use clause In a retail lease, a provision that restricts a retail tenant's use of the rented space by specifying what can and cannot be sold.

vacancy rate The ratio of vacant space to total rentable space in an office building, expressed as a percentage.

valuation An estimation or calculation of the worth of an object; the process of determining an object's worth.

Wage and Hour Law See *Fair Labor Standards Act.*

waiver of subrogation In insurance, a relinquishment of the insurer's right of subrogation, usually stated in a specific provision of the insurance policy; see also *subrogation.*

workers' compensation insurance Coverage obtained by an employer to pay compensation and benefits awarded to an employee in the event of employment-related sickness or injury.

workletter An addendum to the tenant improvement clause of a lease that lists in detail all the work to be done for the tenant by the landlord.

zoning A legal mechanism under which local governments regulate the use of privately owned real property to promote orderly development and prevent conflicting land uses. Establishment of independently controlled sections within an HVAC system such that the temperature and other conditions in each zone (space or group of spaces) are regulated by a separate control.

Index

T

Other Publications Available from IREM

Books

Forms for Office Building Management and Operations Manual Guidelines
Principles of Real Estate Management
The Real Estate Manager's Technical Glossary
Spotlight on Security for Real Estate Managers
The Tenant Retention Solution: A Revolutionary Approach to Commercial Real Estate Management

Forms

General Management Agreement
Office Building Exterior Inspection Form
Office Building Interior Inspection Form
Transition: Taking Over a Management Account
Transition 2: Terminating a Management Account

Research Reports

Certified Property Manager® Profile and Compensation Study
Accredited Management Organization® Profile Study
Income/Expense Analysis®: Office Buildings
Lease Escalators and Other Pass-Through Clauses
Minimum Standards for Property Management Accounting Software